W9-BJH-476

THE VOICE AND VOICE THERAPY

fourth edition

Daniel R. Boone, *University of Arizona*

Stephen C. McFarlane, *University of Nevada Medical School*

PRENTICE HALL, ENGLEWOOD CLIFFS, NEW JERSEY 07632

Library of Congress Cataloging-in-Publication Data

Boone, Daniel R.
  The voice and voice therapy.

    Bibliography: p. 263
    Includes index.
    1. Voice—Care and hygiene.   2. Larynx—Diseases.
  3. Speech therapy.   I. McFarlane, Stephen C.   II. Title.
  [DNLM: 1. Speech, Esophageal.   2. Speech Therapy.
  3. Voice.   4. Voice Disorders—therapy.   5. Voice
  Training.   WV 500 B724v]
  RF540.B66   1988   616.85'5   87-35816
  ISBN 0-13-943721-5

To our wives, Mary and Patty

 © **1988, 1983, 1977, 1971 by Prentice-Hall, Inc.**
A Division of Simon & Schuster
Englewood Cliffs, New Jersey 07632

Printed in the United States of America

10   9   8   7   6   5   4

ISBN 0-13-943721-5

PRENTICE-HALL INTERNATIONAL (UK) LIMITED, *London*
PRENTICE-HALL OF AUSTRALIA PTY. LIMITED, *Sydney*
PRENTICE-HALL CANADA INC., *Toronto*
PRENTICE-HALL HISPANOAMERICANA, S.A., *Mexico*
PRENTICE-HALL OF INDIA PRIVATE LIMITED, *New Delhi*
PRENTICE-HALL OF JAPAN, INC., *Tokyo*
SIMON & SCHUSTER ASIA PTE. LTD., *Singapore*
EDITORA PRENTICE-HALL DO BRASIL, LTDA., *Rio de Janeiro*

CONTENTS

4 THE VOICE EVALUATION   76

5 VOICE THERAPY FOR PROBLEMS OF VOCAL HYPERFUNCTION   114

6 VOICE THERAPY FOR SPECIAL PROBLEMS   185

PREFACE

If someone had asked me in the 1950s what would be the best professional job in the field of audiology and speech-language pathology, I would have answered, "Being a professor in a major university where I can teach, see patients, and supervise graduate students in clinical practicum, and do clinical research." Never did I realize then that I was prophesying the very kind of position that I have occupied for the past fifteen years in the Department of Speech and Hearing Sciences at the University of Arizona.

It is probably impossible to do clinical teaching and research without first seeing and continuing to see patients with the disorders that one is teaching and researching. The tremendous advances in instrumentation sophistication in the past twenty years have challenged clinicians to incorporate what is new and relevant to patients with the disorder. As late as the middle 1960s we were still measuring fundamental frequency by counting striations on a phonellograph; in the late 1980s innumerable instrumentation is available that can give us real-time data specific to modal frequency and frequency range of a particular utterance. We can replace the quality rating scales of the 1950s with real-time printouts of spectral aperiodicity and perturbation measures of jitter and shimmer.

Our present challenge is to present instrumental data, primarily as feedback information in therapy, in a context and language that patients can understand. Further, we have to limit patient information so that we do not overwhelm patients with graphs and data printouts that may provide more information than human beings can understand or use. Even though our scientific base in respiration, phonation, and resonance has grown tremendously in the past forty years, the application of that knowledge base in the clinical process is still an art (and I predict *should* and *will* always be).

In the first edition of *The Voice and Voice Therapy* in 1971 I wrote that the book was "an attempt to take some of the magic out of voice therapy." Although we know a lot more now about vocal physiology and have much improved instrumentation for evaluation and use in therapy, the art of application (what I meant by "magic") is still there. Subsequent editions of this book mirror the growth of knowledge about voice and the application of this knowledge to therapy. We have kept in mind that the primary reader of *The Voice and Voice Therapy* is a student learning about voice disorders and what to do about them. What may seem to be redundancies and oversimplifications to the sophisticated reader are, in my opinion, quite appropriate for the new student. We hope, however, that the clinician (speech-language pathologist, voice coach or teacher, otolaryngologist) and voice scientist will find our discussion of voice disorders and their management of some stimulation and value.

For me a great learning experience is participating in the Annual Symposium on Care of the Professional Voice sponsored by The Voice Foundation. These annual meetings, held at Julliard School in New York City, encourage a healthy exchange of knowledge and speculations among speech scientists, otolaryngologists, speech-language pathologists, voice coaches and teachers, actors, and singers. As a group, these specialists attempt to speak in language that others can understand. They borrow (and reject) ideas from one another. Many of the ideas in this fourth edition may well have had their genesis from someone's paper and a discussion of that paper at the Care of the Professional Voice meetings. Such ideas then get refined in subsequent journal studies of similar topics or confirmed as they originally stood or modified by clinical application and clinical research.

In Chapter 1 of this fourth edition, we have restored some of the original emphasis from 1971 on vocal hyperfunction as the primary culprit contributing to many voice disorders. In Chapter 2 we have attempted to integrate new knowledge on vocal physiology, and we have related it to vocal tract structures and functions presented in previous editions. Chapter 3 comprises a critical look at many voice disorders and emphasizes both etiology and management of particular disorders. Chapter 4 has been greatly expanded from previous editions with both photographs and descriptions of new instrumentation that aids the clinician in voice evaluation and diagnosis. From what teachers of voice disorders courses have told us over the years, Chapter 5, with its twenty-five therapy approaches, probably continues to be the most valuable chapter in the text. Special problems such as aphonia, spastic dysphonia, or dysarthria are described in Chapter 6, and differential therapy recommendations are given for each disorder. Various resonance problems related to faulty nasal and oral resonance, as well as specific management strategies for each, are described in Chapter 7. The text concludes with Chapter 8, which considers the problems of voice related to laryngeal cancer and the problems of total rehabilitation faced by the laryngectomee, the patient who has had a total laryngectomy.

You will note that this edition of this text has a coauthor, Stephen C. McFarlane, Ph.D. I first became aware about five years ago of Dr. McFarlane's innovative work with various voice patients. His clinical enthusiasm and use of clinical instrumentation in voice therapy was overwhelming. We became good friends, and we conducted several voice workshops together. Through my interactions with Steve, I became aware that the typical voice patient demonstrated real problems in the supraglottal areas of the vocal tract. Steve's use of video nasoendoscopy gave convincing evidence that there was far more to faulty voice than faulty respiration or problems at the level of the vocal folds. Through nasoendoscopy with my colleague Kim Pershall, M.D., I began to appreciate from a different perspective why voice therapy works. Many of the techniques we used in voice therapy (chanting, open mouth, yawn-sign, and so forth) were successful because of their immediate effects in opening up the supraglottal airway. A normal voice requires a relatively open and relaxed airway.

The reader will recognize a lot of Dr. McFarlane's contributions to this edition of *The Voice and Voice Therapy* and will see pictures of Steve and some of his patients. Dr. McFarlane has been head of the Department of Speech Pathology and Audiology in the School of Medicine at the University of Nevada at Reno for the past twelve years. Before that, he was at Portland State University and at the University of Washington in Seattle. He brings an enthusiasm toward his clinical work that we do not see enough of in our profession. His voice patients get the best evaluation and diagnosis possible, and he is successful with voice patients with whom many of us simply would not succeed. His thoughts and words permeate many of these pages.

We also wish to express our appreciation for the helpful criticism and suggestions from our reviewers: Richard Ham, Florida State University, and Charles L. Wilhelm, Fort Hays State University.

In my opinion, this edition is the best yet. When commenting on this completed manuscript to my greatest supporter, my wife Mary, I heard myself saying, "Maybe this time we got the thing right." With Steve's help, I think we did.

Daniel R. Boone, Ph.D.
Tucson, Arizona

Functional —
related to abuse
or misuse

Organic →
related to disease
or pathology

symptomatic
voice therapy —
use vocal
mechanism in
better way

1

THE VOICE
AND VOICE THERAPY

The majority of voice disorders appear to be related to laryngeal abuse and vocal misuse. Therefore, many such voice disorders are successfully treated by symptomatic voice therapy. If vocal abuse and misuse can be identified and then reduced, the focus of symptomatic voice therapy is a search for the best voice possible with the least amount of patient effort. Organic voice problems often require medical-surgical treatment by a physician and voice therapy by a speech-language pathologist.

When we speak and sing, we use our vocal mechanisms in a very special way. We must quickly make an adequate respiratory *inspiration* (breathe in), and then prolong the *expiration* (breathe out) to match the vocalizations we wish to say or sing. We must coordinate the respiration with the desired pitches and loudness of *phonation* (voice) and with the required articulation and voice resonance. The best speakers and singers are often those who, by natural gift or training or by a studied combination of both, have mastered the art of blending respiration-phonation-articulation-resonance into a beautiful sounding voice. However, a patient with a voice disorder may use these same vocal mechanisms in a faulty manner. Faulty use of voice can often be corrected by helping the patient use the vocal mechanisms in a better way. In this text we call the methods used for modifying voice symptoms *symptomatic voice therapy.*

Although the majority of voice problems in both children and adults does appear to be related to faulty usage of normal vocal mechanisms, many voice problems result from various diseases and pathologies of respiratory, laryngeal, and resonance structures. Voice problems related to abuse and misuse are known as *functional voice disorders;* voice problems related to disease or pathology are known as *organic voice disorders.* A functional voice disorder, such as hoarseness with no laryngeal disease, can often be treated successfully by symptomatic voice therapy alone. An organic voice disorder, such as hoarseness resulting from paralysis of a vocal fold, may require a combination of medical-surgical treatment and voice therapy. In this text, we consider both functional and organic voice disorders, their causes, and their treatment.

A large population of people has voice disorders, although the exact dimensions of this population are difficult to identify. Different criteria are employed for determining what is a voice problem. Andrews (1986), for example, has reported that there are different voice expectations for males and females; what might be considered a normal voice in a male might be considered a problem voice in a female, and vice versa. Special populations of people, such as cheerleaders, may demonstrate a 75 percent prevalence of laryngeal pathology following continuous cheering for several weeks (Case, 1984). We might speculate that the prevalence of voice disorders among the cheerleaders' classmates who are not actively cheering would be quite low.

A recent national incidence study among school-age children found the prevalence of voice disorders to be 3 percent (Hull, Mielke, Willeford, and Timmons, 1976). In a study of 32,500 children in the schools, Senturia and Wilson (1968) found that 1,962 (or about 6 percent) of them had voice deviations (their definition of voice deviation included disorders in both phonation and resonance). The incidence of voice disorders varies according to the criteria used to determine whether the voice is normal or sounds pathological. If prevalence of voice disorders is based solely on phonation (frequency-intensity-quality) impairment, the prevalence will be lower than if resonance deviation is also included. Boone wrote in 1980 that for phonation disorders the "prevalence is probably in the neighborhood of 3 percent. If resonance-based voice disorders are included, then we would expect that a reasonable figure might be a percentage point or two higher" (1980c, p. 313).

Patients with voice disorders may use their vocal mechanisms in a faulty manner, often with too much effort or force. Sometimes, however, the disordered voice is a symptom of a physical disorder. Let us consider separately functional disorders of voice and organic problems that can produce voice disorders.

FUNCTIONAL VOICE DISORDERS

People with functional voice problems produce their faulty voices in different ways. Some do not coordinate their respiratory functions with what they want to say. They may not take big enough breaths for the length of the planned utterances, which could require them to take "catch-up breaths" in the middle of vocal passages. They may also expire too much air before they begin to speak. Such lack of coordination between respiratory control and phonation demand is a typical functional voice problem. Often some therapy in developing a quick and adequate inspiration, followed by some practice in extending the length of the expiration, can correct this problem.

Another functional voice problem is a person speaking at too low or too high a pitch level, having a voice that always appears inappropriately loud or hoarse (despite the normal appearance of the vocal folds). Occasionally, patients with severe voice symptoms seem to shut down the entire airway, not only shutting the vocal folds and the laryngeal structures above them, but retracting the tongue and contracting the muscles of the throat (Pershall and Boone, 1986). Such patients require voice therapy directed at creating an open airway, as observed when they yawn and then sigh. Functional abuse (such as excessive throat clearing) and vocal misuse (such as yelling) can eventually lead to actual tissue changes of the vocal folds (such as nodules or polyps), which contribute further to what sounds like a faulty voice.

The following description of a young boy with vocal nodules illustrates a functional voice disorder that is frequently observed in a young primary school population:

Eli, age 7, was described by his parents as a boy "who was always talking, yelling, and letting the family know that he was around." For the past year Eli often demonstrated a low-pitched, hoarse voice, particularly toward the end of the day, after many hours of noisy play. His hoarseness was noticed by his pediatrician, who subsequently referred him to an ear-nose-throat specialist, an otolaryngologist. Initial attempts by the otolaryngologist at indirect laryngoscopy were not successful because of the boy's intolerance for the laryngeal mirror. After a second visit, however, the physician was able to see Eli's vocal folds, and he found small bilateral vocal nodules. Eli was then referred to the speech-language pathologist in the same hospital, who took a thorough case history from both the parents and the boy. A number of abusive noises the boy produced were heard, and a gross determination was made of how often these abuses occurred. The speech-language pathologist saw Eli for several sessions, during which he provided graphic materials that showed Eli in language he could understand how abusing his voice had produced the "little bumps he now had on his vocal folds." The counseling was coupled with requests that Eli make serious attempts to curb his yelling and funny noises. Each time he found himself making a noise, he was asked to chart it on a time graph the clinician gave him to take home. After several weeks of monitoring his yelling behavior with the help of his parents, Eli returned for another visit with the otolaryngologist. This time laryngoscopy showed that Eli's nodules were much smaller. It appeared that curbing his vocal abuses lessened the laryngeal strain he was experiencing, which reduced the size of his vocal nodules.

The management of Eli's voice problem required a few sessions of counseling specific to his vocal abuses. If he had needed voice therapy over a longer period of time, the focus of his therapy would have been to discover what kind of abuse or misuse was present and then to design a program to reduce that abuse. We would also have searched with him for the best voice he could produce.

The voice clinician must continually search for the patient's best and most appropriate voice production. This searching is necessary because so much vocal behavior is highly automatic, particularly the dimensions of pitch and quality. The patient cannot deliberately break down vocalization into various components and then hope to combine them into some ideal phonation. Voice therapy techniques are primarily vehicles of facilitation—

that is, we try a particular therapy approach to see if it facilitates the production of a better voice. If it does, then we utilize it as therapy practice material. If it does not, we quickly abandon it. As part of every clinical session, we must probe and search for the patient's best voice. When an acceptable production is produced, we use this "best" voice as the patient's voice target. The easiest achieved and/or best-sounding voice is often used as the patient's target in voice therapy.

Functional voice problems range from producing no voice at all (*aphonia*) to producing a tight, strangled-sounding voice (*spastic dysphonia*). In functional aphonia, the vocal folds appear normal on examination. When the patient attempts to produce voice or phonate, the vocal folds separate further. This separation of the vocal folds, which prevents a normal voice from occurring, is not done willfully by the patient; rather, the individual's attempt to produce voice seems to result in a separation (*abduction*) of the folds rather than an approximation or closing (*adduction*). Fortunately, patients with functional aphonia generally have an excellent therapy prognosis, and they usually completely recover their voice after symptomatic voice therapy.

An opposite problem, characterized by the vocal folds adducting too tightly, is observed in spastic dysphonia. When the patient is asked to phonate, the entire larynx seems to close down, and structures above the vocal folds close in a sphincteric movement so that the true vocal folds are approximated tightly together (see Chapter 2). The patient struggles to push out the expiratory air against the tight larynx, which results in the strangled, tight-sounding voice of spastic dysphonia. Although the literature does report successful management and therapy results for spastic dysphonia, the problem is among the most difficult of voice disorders to treat by symptomatic voice therapy.

THE SITES OF VOCAL HYPERFUNCTION

Vocal hyperfunction is defined in this text as the involvement of too much muscle force and physical effort in the systems of respiration, phonation, and resonance. Identification and description of the specific anatomical sites and physiology required for each of these vocal parameters can introduce the reader to the problem of vocal hyperfunction.

Respiration

The larynx in the human and in other mammals functions basically to protect the airway by preventing foreign bodies (mucus, liquids, food) from entering the respiratory tract by aspiration or inhalation. Obviously, beyond counting on this primitive valving function, humans have learned to prolong expiration to produce vocal fold vibration. Such vibration or phonation can be heard in vocal communications, including speech and song. Phonation as part of speaking or singing requires a continuous closing or opening of the vocal folds, with shortening or elongation of the folds as needed for continuous variations in frequency. Variations in intensity require continuous changes in air pressure and volume. The sounds that are produced require continuous changes in the airway above the vocal folds, produced by movements of the larynx, the pharynx, the tongue, the mandible, and the soft palate.

The regulation of this outflow of air and phonation is basically involuntary and highly automatic in everyday speech; however, public speakers or actors or singers learn to take in quick breaths and then extend them over a prolonged period of continuous voicing. Singers, for example, require an additional supply of air in excess of those obtained in normal inhalation and are able to replenish their air supply quickly and efficiently. Singers must be able to sustain prolonged expiration.

Unusual force or muscle tension (hyperfunction) can be observed in various phases of respiration among both normal persons and clinical voice patients. Although normal speakers without vocal pathology can tolerate vocal stresses related to inadequate and inefficient respiration, patients with vocal pathology usually cannot tolerate such respiratory inefficiency. Perhaps the most common problem of respiration observed among voice patients is the attempt to speak on an inadequate expiration. The inspiratory phase may be inadequate for the phonatory task. Untrained singers may elevate their shoulders, using their neck accessory muscles for inhalation. *inadeq.* *expir.*

A useful method for observing the relative muscle contributions during voicing between chest and abdominal muscles has been reported by Hixon (1987). For example, voice patients are observed who literally use chest and abdominal muscles in competition with one another. Rather than contracting or expanding the chest (thorax) in direct coordination with contraction or expansion of the abdomen, these two anatomical sites may be "pulling and pushing" against one another. Lecturers or singers, in their need to get in a "big" breath, to take a maximum inhalation, may display obviously distended abdomens, fixed thoraxes, elevated shoulders with the associated neck accessory muscles in a hypertonic state, and possibly heads thrust forward. Although such "deep breathers" may have increased their air volume, they are in no position to parcel out their exhalations for a controlled sustained phonation. More commonly, perhaps, we see patients who suffer not from too little or too much inhalation, but from improper utilization of their expirations. A speaker may let out so much expiration early in a verbal passage that by the end of the sentence, he or she is short of breath. *improper* *use* *of* *expir.*

Normal speakers generally demonstrate adequate inspiration-expiration for the daily needs of voice. In fact, as pointed out some time ago by Otis and Clark (1968) typical subjects in their respiratory studies appear to match closely prolonged expiration with the amount of verbalization they intend. Professional users of voice demonstrate much more vigorous respiration and show much muscular participation in large, quick inspiration followed by steady expiration that can produce vocal beauty and intensities not possible from untrained speakers or singers. Many voice patients have problems with inspiration-expiration movements as well as poor timing and control of sustained expiration—symptoms of voice that are related to lack of respiratory control.

We discuss normal respiration and its role in supplying expiratory air pressures and volumes needed for normal phonation in Chapter 2; there, we also consider some of the respiration problems of patients with voice disorders. In Chapter 5, we demonstrate several therapy approaches that have been found helpful in improving respiratory function and control for voice.

Phonation

↑ freq of vibration / ↑ vibrations
↑ pitch / ↑ loudness

Voice or *phonation* is produced by vibration of the vocal folds. This phonation is produced by expiratory air flow coming from the lungs, passing between the approximated vocal folds, and setting the vocal folds into vibration. How elastic or tense these folds are, indicated by their elongation and thickness, determines their frequency of vibration; the faster they vibrate (higher frequency) the higher the perceived pitch of the voice. How vigorously the vocal folds vibrate, caused by the air pressure below them and the velocity of air passing between them, determines the intensity of phonation or the perceived loudness of voice. Although respiration problems may obviously contribute to faulty voice, the majority of voice problems seem to result from faulty approximation of the vocal folds.

The space between the vocal folds is known as the *glottis*. Many vocal problems originate at this glottal level, particularly along the inner membraneous border of each vocal fold. The vocal folds are brought together muscularly for phonation; likewise, they are separated by active muscle contraction of a pair of muscles (described in Chapter 2) whose primary function is to abduct the vocal folds. The glottal posture of the vocal folds, their thickness, elasticity, and degree of approximation, has much to do with the quality of the sounds of phonation. Many functional voice disorders are the result of faulty physiology of laryngeal muscles, particularly in the faulty approximation or bringing of the two vocal folds together.

Sometimes the vocal folds are approximated too tightly together. The membranes that cover the vocal folds are placed so firmly together that the larynx acts as a valve, preventing the flow of air that normally sets the vocal folds into vibration. The resulting voice is tight and sounds at times almost like the strained voice of the laryngeal "stutter" or spastic dysphonia. An opposite problem may be observed when the vocal folds are brought together in such a lax manner that far too much breath escapes between them, which produces a whispered or very breathy voice.

Voice authorities disagree about the influence of inappropriate pitch level or fundamental frequency on the development of various vocal pathologies. For some patients it might appear that an inappropriately low or high pitch level is a primary etiological factor in a vocal disorder, but for other patients faulty pitch levels have developed secondarily from the increase of vocal fold mass due to early polypoid or nodule growth. That is, sometimes the inappropriate pitch level produces the dysphonia, and sometimes the prolonged dysphonia produces vocal fold tissue changes and thus alters pitch. It is important for any speaker or singer to use the vocal mechanism optimally with regard to fundamental frequency. Speaking or singing at an inappropriate pitch level requires excessive force and contraction of the intrinsic muscles of the larynx, which leads to vocal fatigue or the hoarseness related to a tired vocal mechanism.

A common pitch deviation may be the inappropriately low pitch of young professional males, such as teachers or clergy members, who speak at the bottom of their pitch ranges in an attempt to convey some extra authority through their voices. Young professional women may also speak at fundamental frequency values well below the normative values of the average adult female. An inappropriate pitch level, whether too low or too high, requires unnecessary muscle energy to maintain the necessary vocal fold adjustments of length and mass to produce the "artificial" voice. Of the many variables we identify as hyperfunctional voice behaviors, inappropriate pitch level is one of the easiest of the disorders to remedy. Sometimes just by raising or lowering the fundamental frequency slightly, patients will experience a lessening of the energy they employ to speak, which will result in a noticeable decrease in their dysphonia.

Initiation of phonation at the beginning of words is known as *glottal attack.* We often hear *easy* or *soft glottal attack* in voicing patterns that are considered typical of a Southern accent, or in what may be called a legato in music—the soft, uninterrupted voicing pattern that seems to flow without break. Words begin softly, and a blend of unvoiced air gradually becomes voiced. In Southern dialect the words not only begin softly, but most of the vowels in the utterance are prolonged as well. Soft glottal attack as a vocal style appears to be easy on the vocal mechanism; however, a politician or performer with such an easy attack may sound a "bit boring and too passive" in overall presentation.

The opposite type of voicing mode is known as the *hard glottal attack.* Phonation is abruptly initiated, so that often each word sounds like an individual entity with its own initial stress, and stresses put on the beginning of words. We often hear hard glottal attack in the voicing patterns of people in such large Eastern cities as New York or Philadelphia. Their overall speaking patterns appear much faster, for example, than what we hear in Southern speech. Speaking with hard glottal attack is often characterized as vocal hyperfunction. Voice therapy may entail a patient's deliberately attempting an easier vocal attack to take the "work" out of voicing.

Vocal abuse and vocal misuse can contribute to voice problems. By vocal abuse we mean that the laryngeal mechanisms are used excessively in various nonverbal abusive ways, such as continuous coughing, throat clearing, laughing, crying, or smoking. Such abusive behaviors can have negative effects on laryngeal function and sometimes on vocal production as well. Vocal misuse may consist of excessive or inappropriate voicing, such as speaking with excessive vocal hard attack, speaking at the wrong voice pitch, speaking too loudly, or speaking too much. The additive nature of the vocal fold edema (swelling) or tissue engorgement that may result from excessive voicing, such as screaming or yelling, enlarges the vocal folds. This vocal fold enlargement changes the sound of the voice. The patient, in turn, reacts to the vocal change and begins to employ other vocal behaviors to compensate for the changed vocal mechanism. These compensatory behaviors further contribute to what is perceived as some kind of voice problem.

Coughing and excessive throat clearing frequently contribute to dysphonia and laryngeal pathology, and sometimes add edema and irritation to an already pathological condition. True infection of the larynx is often the primary etiological factor in dysphonia, and patients experience acute or chronic laryngitis; instead of imposing upon themselves temporary periods of voice rest during the infectious stage of the disease, patients may continue to phonate, which compounds vocal fold irritation. Lecturing or serious singing on top of an existing laryngeal infection can have disastrous aftereffects and perhaps damage the vocal mechanism permanently. External irritants, particularly once laryngeal pathology has been established, may exacerbate certain vocal pathologies; smoking, excessive alcohol consumption, smog, and dust have all been identified as culprits that help maintain various laryngeal disorders. It would appear that once any kind of vocal abuse has been identified, intelligent efforts by the patient to reduce such abusive behavior might noticeably lessen vocal symptoms.

Resonance

Much of the beauty or the quality of the voice is produced by the resonating chambers that begin within the larynx itself, extend into the pharynx, the oral cavity, and the nasal cavity above. Fant (1960) introduced the acoustic theory of voice, often called the *source-filter theory*, which in effect says that the voice we hear emitted from the mouth or nose is composed wholly of the original phonation from the vocal folds that has been modified by successive supralaryngeal structures. Each vowel produced has its own unique vocal tract configuration, as described by Sever (1982):

> Specifically, for voiced sounds, the glottal signal is the input to the vocal tract. Due to the ability of the vocal tract to assume different three-dimensional shapes for the production of different vowels, the resonance characteristics of the vocal tract will change accordingly. It follows that, as the glottal signal is transmitted through the vocal tract, it will be modified in a manner that will be different for each vowel. (p. 26)

The voice, originating by the air stream vibrating the vocal folds, is amplified in the upper airway cavities of the neck and head. This amplification is called *resonance*. In normal voicing, the vocal fold vibrations produce the source of sound that flows into the resonating tubes of the vocal tract (the hypopharynx, the oral pharynx, and the nasal cavities, all described in Chapter 2). The vocal tract is much like an extended tube starting immediately within the larynx and extending up the throat into the oral cavity, which is, in turn, coupled with the nasal cavity. Certain sounds or voice frequencies are amplified selectively, depending on the surface, shape, and restrictions of the resonating cavities. The resonating cavities have particular compatible natural vibrations that respond optimally to certain frequencies of the sound spectrum, known as *resonance frequencies*. If the sound wave frequencies in the upper airway are compatible with the natural resonances, natural amplification and resonance will occur. Many cavity resonators, however, are altered by changes in surface and shape so that natural resonant frequencies are changed. This may alter natural frequency of vibration and result in a dull voice lacking amplification and resonance. Some speakers alter or diminish their natural resonance potential by using various hyperfunctional behaviors. According to Perkins (1981), where the individual places the voice, low or high in the resonating tract, has much to do with ease of phonation and how the voice sounds to the listener.

The first resonating cavity that has immediate influence on the glottal voice is within the larynx itself. Viewing the larynx from above with various viewing procedures, such as through the nasoendoscope (explained in subsequent chapters), we can observe muscle effects within the supraglottal larynx (false folds and aryepiglottic folds) changing the opening within the superior larynx by their contraction and relaxation. The superior laryngeal opening is continually changing shape. From within the larynx, the glottal tone (at this point, a sound wave) travels into the lower pharynx (hypopharynx). The hypopharynx itself is continually changing shape by muscle contraction and relaxation, which, in turn, change the topographic surface (soft-relaxed versus taut-tense) of the hypopharyngeal cavity (Pershall and Boone, 1986). The hypopharynx and the oropharynx continually change shape, both horizontally and vertically, during speaking and singing (Laver, 1980). The pharynx appears to change its shape continually during speech and singing, and these pharyngeal shapings contribute greatly to the resonance of the voice.

In normal speaking and singing, the oral opening within the mouth is continually changing. In fact, the production of each vowel demands a unique positioning of tongue and lips and opening of the mandible. One form of vocal hyperfunction is seen in the patient who speaks with severe mandibular restriction, or "talking through one's teeth," which forces all vowels to be produced primarily by tongue movement alone. The mandible is locked shut, and the molars are clenched tightly together.

For the various adjustments required in producing vowels, the patient changes the dimensions of the oral cavity by flattening or elevating the tongue, with little or no size change contributed by the movement of the mandible. Many patients with mandibular restriction complain of symptoms of vocal fatigue, pain, or fullness in the hyoid area after prolonged speaking or singing. The entire burden of articulation is on the tongue. Mandibular restriction is a common diagnostic entity in many patients with hyperfunctional voice disorders. Recognizing this, Froeschels (1952) developed the chewing approach in voice therapy. Voice clinicans using the chewing approach for selected voice patients generally report that it not only promotes greater mobility of the mandible, but that it also reduces other oral hyperfunctional postures.

The overall positioning of the tongue within the oral cavity influences the resonance of the voice. Laver (1980) describes "neutral lingual settings" where the normal individual carries the overall tongue mass within the oral cavity most of the time. In normal speech, the tongue makes obvious phonetic adjustments, such as moving the tip to touch behind the gum ridge behind the upper, central teeth, but more often the main tongue body remains in a "neutral" position. Occasionally speakers have thin, baby-sounding voices; such individuals generally produce this baby voice by carrying the overall tongue body in a high, forward position. If such an anterior tongue posture is identified (by testing) as a cause of a baby-sounding voice, it can often be changed to a more neutral position by voice therapy. An opposite problem, carrying the tongue excessively posterior, produces the *cul de sac* voice, sometimes heard in deaf patients and in patients with athetoid cerebral palsy. Posterior tongue carriage, as a hyperfunctional tongue position, can often be eliminated using some of the voice therapy techniques we discuss in Chapters 5 and 7.

Some patients display problems in nasal resonance that are related to variations in coupling the oral and nasal cavities together. In normal voice, only the nasal consonants (*m, n, ng*) are given nasal resonance by relaxing the velum and allowing the velopharyngeal port to be open. The sound waves then pass into the nasal cavity for further resonance. Although most patients with excessive nasalization have structural symptoms (cleft palate, short velum, severe head cold, and so on), occasional voice patients keep the velum and pharyngeal wall separated for wholly functional reasons.

Most hyperfunctional behaviors affecting resonance alter the size, shape, and surface of the resonating cavities, as well as their preferential response to certain frequencies. The best-sounding voice is often one with the best resonance because of compatibility between the frequency of vibration of the vocal folds and the resonant frequencies of the supraglottal (above the vocal folds) resonators. Voice therapy is often effective in identifying unnecessary force and tension at the various sites of the upper airway. Once such hyperfunctional behavior is identified, such as speaking through clenched teeth, the patients should be made aware of the forceful behavior and its noticeable effect on the voice. The clinician asks the patient to produce the hyperfunctional behavior and then contrast it with an easy behavior (such as using voice while the teeth are clenched and then voicing with a wide-open mouth). The patient is then asked to hear the difference in the sound of the voice between the two contrasted behaviors, effort versus ease. When natural resonance is uncovered, often by using a more natural or neutral setting of the mouth, the improvement of the voice may be marked.

VOICE DISORDERS RELATED TO ORGANIC PROBLEMS

Not all voice problems are related to vocal hyperfunction. Many people have vocal difficulties and other symptoms of disease of the vocal tract (shortness of breath or hoarseness, to name a few). Various physical conditions, in fact, can alter frequency, intensity, quality, or resonance of the voice. However, a functional component to the voice problem may well exist. For example, patients may have shortness of breath that forces them to say only a few words per utterance, but with some voice training they could learn to extend the number of words per breath. Organic voice problems can be caused by physical changes in respiratory function, changes in the structure and movement of the vocal folds, severe sensory loss (such as deafness), or structural changes within the pharynx, oral, and nasal cavities.

Any voice problem that lasts more than a week should be medically investigated for possible physical causation. Sometimes the required treatment will be medical-surgical, and voice therapy will only help to find and maintain the best possible voice. Some organic voice problems are static, relatively fixed, and not responsive to medical treatment; for these problems, voice therapy becomes the only remediation possible. Although specific disorders of voice related to organic problems and their management will be presented in Chapter 6, let us consider a voice problem related to a physical cause.

Charles, a 58-year-old chef, began to experience a shortness of breath that only allowed him to say about five words per breath. Physical examination indicated that he had severe pulmonary emphysema, probably directly related to his smoking about three packs of cigarettes daily. In fact, he reported to his doctor that in his 20s and 30s, he had smoked four packs a day, but he had cut back because the continuous smoking interfered with his preparing meals in his restaurant. Extensive pulmonary and respiratory testing revealed that Charles had lost most of his lung elasticity, which was confirmed by his inability to empty his lungs quickly on various tests. When asked to count as far as he could on one breath, he could only count to five; he could prolong a vowel for only eight seconds. Endoscopic examination showed that Charles had additive growth along the glottal margin of the vocal folds, a condition diagnosed as leukoplakia. Although no medical treatment was recommended for Charles's pulmonary emphysema, much of the leukoplakia was removed surgically. In voice therapy, Charles practiced extending his expirations. With practice, he could count to fifteen on one breath, extend vowels for over fifteen seconds, and say eight to ten words on one expiration. Functionally, despite the irreversible lung disease, Charles was able to increase his ability to say more words with less shortness of breath. Following the surgery on his vocal folds, he received some voice therapy to help establish a voice pitch level he found acceptable.

The case of Charles illustrates a speech-voice problem caused by two organic diseases, pulmonary emphysema and laryngeal leukoplakia. Voice therapy helped the patient learn to breathe more efficiently for speech; in effect, Charles learned to say more words per expiration. Surgical removal of the laryngeal lesions followed by voice therapy helped reestablish an acceptable voice. As illustrated here, voice therapy can often be effective in helping voice patients with various organic voice problems develop the best voice possible.

Impairment in Respiration

The respiratory system functions as the activator of voice. The expiratory air-flow pressures and volumes passing between the approximated vocal folds set the folds into vibration, which produces voice. Therefore, any compromise of respiratory function can have a direct effect on speech (number of words said) and voice (loudness, pitch, quality). Lung volume may be reduced by space-occupying lesions in the lungs, such as various forms of cancer or fluids in the lung; a reduction in air volume will reduce the amount of air the speaker can use for voice. Diseases of the airway, such as bronchitis or emphysema, can decrease lung elasticity and make it more difficult for the patient to sustain air flow and voicing. Although organic disease of the respiratory system may require medical treatment, voice therapy can often help patients develop the best respiratory control possible for speech and voice. Like Charles, most voice patients can improve their functional respiratory expiration by working on it directly.

Impairment in the Movement of the Folds

There are several physical ways that the movement of the vocal folds may be impaired. The vocal folds normally move toward one another (adduct) for phonation by the active contraction of the intrinsic laryngeal muscles. The folds are held together by active muscle contraction during phonation, working against the tendency to be blown apart by the air flow beneath and between them. The adduction of the folds is sometimes compromised by destruction of the nerves that innervate these laryngeal muscles, as described in Chapter 3. This produces weakness or paralysis of the laryngeal muscles, resulting in vocal fold paralysis.

Other neuromuscular problems may prevent normal vocal fold approximation as a result of some kind of destruction within the cerebrum, perhaps as a result of a stroke or some form of degenerative disease. When phonation is impaired because of a problem in the central nervous system (CNS), the problem is usually part of a *dysarthria* (speech-voice-fluency impairment secondary to CNS involvement). We discuss dysarthria and its voice symptoms in greater detail in Chapter 6. Overall management of voice problems related to neural innervation requires medical care as well as the short-range and long-range participation of a speech-language pathologist.

Sometimes, the movement of the vocal folds may be inhibited by a laryngeal web growing between the glottal margin of each fold. If such a web is identified, it is usually removed surgically, followed by intensive voice therapy which is necessary for reestablishing voice.

Mass-Size Changes in the Vocal Folds

A severe cold accompanied by laryngitis is a good example of a voice problem related to a mass-size change of the vocal folds. In laryngitis, for example, the patient experiences severe swelling and redness of the membrane that covers the vocal folds; this irregular thickening along the total anterior-to-posterior border of the folds contributes to the lowering of pitch and the hoarseness we commonly hear in laryngitis.

A common additive mass to the vocal folds is either vocal nodules or vocal polyps, usually the result of continuous vocal abuse and misuse. Most of the mass-size changes that lead to dysphonia are clearly observable growths, such as the warty-like papilloma seen in the larynges of children or the leukoplakia-type lesion described in the case illustration of Charles. The mass added to the vocal fold will drastically change the vibratory characteristic of that fold, and will usually result in a lowering of fundamental frequency. The added mass is often on the margin of the vocal fold, and so it prevents the two folds from optimally approximating one another.

Occasionally, a patient may demonstrate some kind of endocrine or metabolic disorder that changes the mass of the vocal folds and results in voice changes that are difficult for the patient to tolerate. Most additive lesions to the vocal folds, unilateral or bilateral, can change the sound of the voice by lowering pitch, decreasing loudness, and increasing breathiness.

Resonance Changes

[handwritten: hyponasal / denasal / hypernasal]

The majority of resonance problems are related to excessive nasality (*hypernasality*) or insufficient nasality (*hyponasality* or *denasality*). Although some people are hypernasal for wholly functional reasons (their natural voice is always nasal sounding), the majority of people with hypernasality speak that way for physical reasons. Obvious effects, like an unrepaired cleft palate or a short soft palate, will allow excessive coupling between the oral and nasal cavities, which results in an escape of air and sound waves through the nose. Some patients with hypernasality have difficulty moving the muscles of the throat and soft palate because of weakness or paralysis of the muscles. This form of hypernasality, perhaps the result of a stroke or a symptom of a progressive neurological disease, is classified as a dysarthria. Some speech and voice therapies provided for patients with dysarthria are presented in Chapter 6. Management of patients with excessive nasal resonance is detailed in Chapter 7.

The opposite problem, insufficient nasal resonance or denasality, is usually caused by some kind of obstruction in the nasopharyngeal and nasal cavities. Allergies, enlarged adenoidal tissue, and severe head colds are typical physical problems that may cause denasality. The primary treatment and management of patients with denasality is medical-surgical; voice therapy for denasality is rarely helpful.

SYMPTOMATIC VOICE THERAPY

Patients with vocal complaints often show symptoms related to the improper functioning of respiratory, phonatory, and resonance systems. These symptoms often appear to be related to abuse and/or misuse of the vocal mechanisms, with or without the development of laryngeal pathologies. Some voice problems are created solely by abuse and misuse. Other voice problems may be the result of organic or physical problems. In most cases, however, how the patient uses the vocal mechanisms has much to do with how the patient sounds. The focus of *symptomatic voice therapy* is helping the patient optimally use the systems of respiration, phonation, and resonance for the easiest produced and best-sounding voice possible.

Although the original causes of voice problems may never be identified (identifying laryngeal disease is easier), why vocal problems continue or maintain themselves is often a complex issue. For many voice patients

[handwritten: optimally use; respiration, phonation, resonance]

the original cause of the initial dysphonia may be long past—that is, patients may speak the way they do today because this is the way they spoke yesterday. Respiration, phonation, and resonance are the result of highly automatic motor behaviors. It appears, therefore, that improper vocal production quickly becomes automatic and involuntary, often resisting an individual's attempt to overcome it. Direct modification of the symptoms is not always recommended. For example, if it were determined at the time of a voice evaluation that a patient with functional dysphonia spoke with excessively hard glottal attack, direct work on such sudden-onset vocalization might not be the desired target behavior in voice therapy. Rather, reducing loudness and slowing down the speaking rate might soften glottal attack without ever working directly on it.

Sometimes a voice problem serves a patient well, either consciously or subconsciously, and the patient may resist changing the sound of the voice by symptomatic voice therapy. In his classic work, *Voice of Neurosis* (1954), P. J. Moses argued that to eradicate the vocal symptom is only to encourage the patient to develop another symptom, perhaps more maladaptive than the voice disorder was. For various problems of maladaptive function and neurosis, however, behavioral therapy has been successful in reducing aversive symptoms without observable symptom migration (Stevens, 1968; Wolpe, 1987). In reviewing voice cases over time, it would appear that more often the emotional or psychological problem that may have precipitated the voice problem has disappeared. Much of the continuing dysphonia thus appears to be related to a habit set of faulty phonation. Often, then, a direct attempt at vocal symptom modification is warranted, sometimes supplemented by some counseling and support provided by the voice clinician. In addition to voice therapy some voice patients will require professional counseling by a psychologist or psychiatrist who works closely with the voice clinician.

To be effective, symptomatic voice therapy first requires the identification of any kind of vocal abuse or misuse that may contribute to the voice problem. Once such abuse-misuse is identified—for example, continued throat clearing—the clinician must help the patient develop methods for reducing the behavior. Taking the "work" out of phonation is often a primary task in therapy. In symptomatic therapy, the clinician and the patient attempt various voice-producing tasks (see Chapter 5) that seem to produce optimal respiration, phonation, and resonance. Sometimes, reducing vocal effort will initially result in a poorer-sounding voice; for example, a child with vocal nodules who begins to produce voice with minimal unneeded effort may initially sound more dysphonic. In time, the voice may sound much better. Sometimes, too, the easiest produced voice is often the one that sounds better, such as what we frequently observe in functional dysphonia.

In this text we call the techniques that work in voice therapy *facilitating approaches*. When particular facilitating approaches are identified as helpful in therapy, much of symptomatic voice therapy is devoted to practicing the approach for reestablishing a more optimal method of voice production.

SUMMARY

The thesis of this chapter and the rest of the text is that most voice disorders appear to be related to laryngeal abuse and vocal misuse. Such disorders, whether they are wholly functional or organic in origin, can be successfully treated by symptomatic voice therapy. Thorough evaluation of a voice problem and possible identification of abuse-misuse are important requisites for the successful treatment of people with voice disorders.

2
THE NORMAL VOICE

Voice therapy is often "antagonistic" therapy. We are trying to undo what patients have done to their voice through "overworking" the mechanism. To be effective in voice evaluation and therapy clinicians must have a good working knowledge of the structures involved in phonation. Also, they must have a knowledge of the function of these structures. This chapter presents the structures and functions necessary for respiration, phonation, and resonance with a current view of the clinical physiology of these events.

Although we separate the normal speaking voice into three individual parts (respiration, phonation, and resonance) for purposes of study, we must remember that the three components of voice are highly interdependent on one another. For example, without the expiratory phase of respiration there would be no voice phonation or resonance. Also, these three processes are constantly changing simultaneously. Let us first consider the structures and function of respiration, particularly as they relate to production of voice.

RESPIRATION

Humans have learned to use respiration for speech by sustaining their exhalations for phonation. Both speaking and singing require an outgoing air stream capable of activating vocal fold vibration. When "training" their voice, speakers or singers frequently focus on developing conscious control of the breathing mechanism. This conscious control, however, must always be consistent with the physiological air requirements of the individual. When a problem occurs with respiration, it is often the conflict between the physiological needs and the speaking-singing demands for air that causes faulty usage of the vocal mechanism. Our dependence on the constant renewal of oxygen supply imposes certain limitations on how many words we can say, how many phrases we can sing, or how much emphasis we can use on one expiration.

Nose - nasal cavity - nasopharynx - oropharynx

Mouth - oral cavity - oropharynx

→ hypopharynx - larynx - FVF - TVF - trachea - bronchial tubes - lungs - bronchioles - alveolar sacs

Respiration Structures

Inspired air enters through the nostrils and passes into the nasal cavities into the nasopharynx through the open velopharyngeal port into the oropharynx. For mouth breathers, the air would enter through the open mouth, pass through the oral cavity over the surface of the tongue and into the oropharynx. The air would then flow through the hypopharynx. From the hypopharynx (Figure 2–1), the inspiration would flow into the larynx, pass between the ventricular or false vocal folds, and pass between the true vocal folds down into the trachea or windpipe. At the bottom end of the trachea, the airway divides into the two bronchial tubes shown in the accompanying photograph of the lungs and tracheal bifurcation (Figure 2–2). The bronchial tubes further branch into divisions known as the bronchioles, and they eventually terminate in the lungs in little air sacs known as the alveolar sacs. Some of the bronchioli are visible in Figure 2–2, but most of the bronchioli and all the alveoli are covered by the pleural membrane that covers the lungs.

The ribs connected to the twelve thoracic vertebrae and their connecting muscles play an active role in respiration, as we shall see when we discuss respiratory function. The thorax can move in several ways. For example, the rib cage wall expands for inspiration of air and collapses for expiration. Sometimes the accessory muscles in the neck assist in deep inspiration when they contract because they elevate the shoulders and increase the vertical dimension of the thorax. At the base of the thorax is the important diaphragm, a composite of muscle, tendon, and membrane that separates the thoracic cavity from the abdominal cavity. As the diaphragm contracts, it descends and increases the vertical dimension of the thorax; as the diaphragm relaxes, it ascends back to its higher position. The diaphragm has direct contact with the lungs, and only the pleural space comes between the lungs and the diaphragm; the shape of the diaphragm, its superior contour, can be seen on the lower surface of the cadaver lung. The relaxed diaphragm is high in the chest within the rib cage, and the stomach and liver lie directly below it. As the diaphragm contracts and descends, it pushes from above on the contents of the abdomen below, often displacing the abdominal wall by pushing it outward on inspiration. The abdominal wall is composed primarily of the abdominal muscles that sometimes play

Figure 2–1.
The respiratory tract. Note the resting level of the diaphragm as outlined in the diaphragm contour.

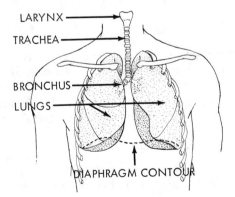

LARYNX

TRACHEA

BRONCHUS

LUNGS

DIAPHRAGM CONTOUR

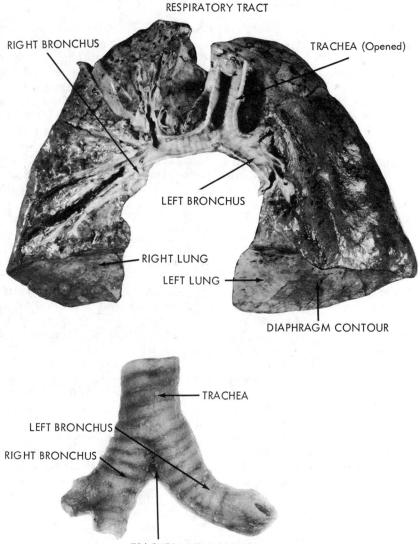

RESPIRATORY TRACT

RIGHT BRONCHUS

TRACHEA (Opened)

LEFT BRONCHUS

RIGHT LUNG

LEFT LUNG

DIAPHRAGM CONTOUR

TRACHEA

LEFT BRONCHUS

RIGHT BRONCHUS

TRACHEAL BIFURCATION

FIGURE 2-2. Lungs and tracheal bifurcation. Photograph illustrates the tracheal bifurcation that introduces air into the lungs by way of the left and right bronchi.

an active role in expiration. We identify those muscles of the thorax and the abdomen that relate to respiration as we discuss respiration.

Respiration Function

The respiratory tract functions much like a bellows. When we move the handles on the bellows apart, the bellows become larger, the air within it becomes less dense than the air outside it, and the outside air rushes in. The inspiration of air into the bellows is achieved by active enlargement of the bellows' body. Similarly, in human respiration, the inspiration of air is achieved by active movement of muscles that enlarge the thoracic cavity. When the thorax enlarges, the lungs within the thorax enlarge. The air within the lungs becomes less dense than atmospheric air, and inspiration of air begins. The air is expired from the bellows by bringing the handles together, decreasing the size of the bellows' cavity, thus compressing the air and forcing it to rush out. In human respiration, however, much of expiration is achieved by passive collapse of thoracic size and not by active muscle contraction. This is an extremely important fact and can be valuable information for voice clinicians.

Much of expiration is passive. Hixon, Mead, and Goldman (1976) have described human respiration as having two types of forces that are always present: passive forces (such as the elastic lungs) and active, volitional forces (such as contraction of muscles of inspiration). The pleural membrane that covers the lungs clings almost adhesively to the inner wall of the thorax. As the thorax expands by muscular contraction, the lungs within it expand. The inherent elastic force of the lungs is always there. Their elastic recoil will be as fast as thoracic collapse allows. In fact, in at-rest expiration (the expiration during the quiet breathing of sleep, for example), the expiratory phase of respiration is wholly accomplished by the elasticity of the inherent or passive forces.

Passive Components   Much of the air pressure or "power" required for normal speech can be supplied by the passive factors of respiration (passive exhalation). This is desirable because no muscle action is required to supply this breath power, and thus, there is no tendency to "overdo" (hyperactivity) the effort. When a long phrase or other speaking task (such as increased loudness) requires more effort or "breath power," we make up the difference between the power provided by passive factors and the needed amount of breath power by using the abdominal musculature.

Active Components   A key problem for many voice-disordered patients is the tendency to "squeeze" the glottis closed in order to produce the needed power, rather than to increase air pressure by contracting the abdominal muscles. We can better understand this "mistake" by a simple analogy. If we are watering flowers in a garden and we want to reach the far row of plants, we can either place a thumb over the end of the hose and squirt the water further (increase the power), or we can increase the water power by turning the faucet further. When we squeeze the glottis closed, we are "putting a thumb over the end of the hose." When we contract the abdominal muscles we are "turning the faucet" and increasing the air flow. Even though squeezing the glottis tends to increase the vocal power, vocal quality is diminished because the voice sounds strained. If this method is habitual, the excessive effort becomes the basis of a hyperfunctional voice disorder. Such effort may lead to vocal nodules, contact ulcers, vocal polyps, recurring laryngitis, or loss of voice.

When we need increased power to speak louder, to stress words, or to

Use abd. muscles ∅
close glottis tight
for ↑ sound, stress,
→ etc.

extend a phrase when singing or speaking, we should use the larger muscles of the abdomen and "turn on the faucet" controlling the source of air. Thus, the pressure at the valve (the larynx) is not excessive, and vocal quality is improved with delicate laryngeal tissue not subjected to stress and strain. Vocal quality is not diminished, and adverse tissue change is avoided. Voice clinicians may use this water analogy and teach patients how to monitor breath control by properly using expiratory reserve volume via the abdominal muscles, rather than excessive glottal valving in the larynx.

Relaxation Pressure   The best (most efficient and most pleasing vocal quality) voice is produced at mid air-pressure levels and mid lung-volume levels of air, as shown in the relaxation curve in Figure 2–3. To demonstrate this, simply take about a half-breath and produce an /i/ vowel for five seconds at a medium loudness level. Then listen to the vocal quality. Now take a very deep breath and produce the same /i/ vowel for five seconds at medium loudness. The vocal quality will generally be poorer with the effort to control the high air pressure, and will contribute to the perception of poor quality. Finally, produce the same /i/ vowel for five seconds at medium loudness immediately after releasing three-fourths of your air supply. Again, the vocal quality will suffer as you try to compensate for the low air pressure and low lung volume.

FIGURE 2-3.   The relaxation pressure curve. The passive forces of exhalation tend to generate force during inhalation that works to restore the lung and rib cage system to the normal resting state or equilibrium. After active inhalation, these passive forces of exhalation rebound to provide some of the expiratory force needed for speech. There is a nearly linear relationship between relaxation pressure and lung volume in the range between 20 and 70 percent of the vital capacity. This curve represents the pressure generated by the passive factors of the respiratory system.

This exercise demonstrates how vocal quality is affected by extremely high or low air pressure at high or low lung volume. It translates into an excellent clinical-stimulation technique. We can often change the vocal quality of our dysphonic patients by instructing them to use the midrange of air pressure and lung volume. Teaching a shortened phrasing pattern may be important to teaching breath-stream management.

We frequently use *glottal fry* to improve vocal quality in hoarse patients. We instruct patients to (1) let out half the air, and (2) produce an "ah" and let it die away in a popping sound. The glottal fry requires a very low amount of air flow and can be sustained with little air pressure. After producing a glottal fry of about 60 to 75 Hz for ten seconds five or six times, the patient is told to repeat the phrase "Easy does it." The quality of the voice is almost always better than the typical voice produced by a patient with nodules, a polyp, or cord thickening. During this procedure, we are ready to record the voice. We immediately ask the patient's name, and we also record the response. Thus, we have a comparison on tape of the voice with vocal improvement ("Easy does it") and the typical voice (the name.) When we ask patients to listen to both samples and tell us which sounds better, they invariably answer the "Easy does it." This procedure is an important step because it demonstrates (1) the ability to improve the voice, and (2) a self-monitoring skill for initiating better breath-stream management while reducing laryngeal effort.

We now need to consider the muscles of respiration that contribute active, volitional force in inspiration, as shown in Figure 2-4. The primary muscle of inspiration is the diaphragm, as already noted. Perhaps the external intercostals play the next most important role in inspiration; because of their oblique angulation, when they contract, they lift the rib below, enlarging the rib cage on a somewhat horizontal plane. Slight elevation of the upper thorax is achieved with contraction of the pectoralis major and minor, the costal elevators, the serratus posterior, and the neck accessory muscles (primarily the sternocleidomastoid). The primary inherent elasticity and recoil of thoracic structures come into play when the active muscles of inspiration cease contracting and relax, but some muscles of expiration can

Figure 2-4.
The thoracic surface muscles of respiration, including the pectoralis major, the external and internal intercostals, the scalene, pectoralis minor, and the sternocleidomastoid muscles. Bones readily identified include the clavical, sternum, scapula, and ribs 1 to 8. (J. M. Palmer, *Anatomy for Speech and Hearing.* New York: Harper & Row, 1972, p. 149. Used with permission.)

[handwritten annotations: expiration: ① 4 abd. m. int. obliques; ext obliques; transverse; rectus ② internal intercostals ③ post. inf. serratus]

assist in expiration. These expiration muscles may contract in some conditions of talking, singing, and forced expiration such as we use in playing wind instruments. The primary muscles of expiration are the four abdominal muscles, the internal oblique abdominal, external oblique abdominal, transverse abdominal, and the rectus abdominal. Some thoracic decrease can also be achieved by active contraction of the internal intercostals (they slant upward in the opposite direction of the external intercostals) and the posterior inferior serratus.

In passive respiration, the kind of breathing we do when sleeping, the active contraction of inspiratory muscles produces the inspiration, and the expiration phase of the respiratory cycle is wholly related to the passive (nonmuscular) collapse properties of the thorax. These passive factors may include lung elasticity, rib untorquing, visceral recoil, and gravity's pulling the ribs down to a resting position. When we add the function of expiratory muscles to the passive expiration, we alter the duration and force of the expiration. For example, while speaking long passages, we may well begin with passive expirations; active contraction of expiratory muscles comes after passive expiration has begun. Any time we prolong the expiration beyond a simple tidal volume (see definitions below), we have added some active muscle contraction of the expiratory muscles.

Figure 2–5, the simple tracings of a pneumotachometer, shows the relative time for inspiration-expiration for a passive, tidal breath, for saying the numbers "1, 2, 3, 4, 5," and for singing the musical passage, "I don't want to walk without you, baby" from the old song by that title. Note that the inspiratory time during normal tidal breathing is much longer than the quick inspiration for speech and singing. This is noted by the rapid rise of the tracing from a resting baseline in an almost vertical move. In the tidal breath the rise from the baseline is gradual and sloped rather than vertical.

In subsequent discussions we use the following terms to describe aspects of respiration. Methods for evaluating respiratory volumes and capacities will be discussed in Chapter 4.

Lung Volumes and Capacities

Tidal volume (TV) is the amount of air inspired and expired during a typical respiratory cycle; it is determined by the oxygen needs (not the speaking or singing needs) of the individual.

Inspiratory reserve volume (IRV), known also as *complemental air* (Comroe, 1956), is the maximum volume of air that can be inspired beyond the end of a tidal expiration.

Expiratory reserve volume (ERV), known also as *supplemental air,* is the maximum volume of air that can be expired beyond the end of a tidal expiration.

Residual volume (RV) is the volume of air that remains in the lungs after a maximum expiration. No matter how forceful the expiration, the residual volume cannot be forced from the lungs.

Vital capacity (VC) is the total amount of air that can be expired from the lungs and air passages from a maximum expiration; it represents the total volumes previously listed, with the exception of residual volume (which cannot be expired).

Figure 2-5.
Pneumotachometer tracings measure air flow over time. Note the relative time for inspiration as opposed to expiration for three conditions: tracing A (three tidal breaths) produces an inspiration-expiration time ratio of about 1 to 2; tracing B (counting from 1 to 5 on eight trials) produces a ratio of about 1 to 3; tracing C (singing twice, "I don't want to walk without you, baby") yielded an inspiration-expiration ratio of approximately 1 to 10.

Total lung capacity (TLC) represents the total volume of air that can be held in the lungs and airways after a maximum inspiration. It can only be measured by special volume displacement tests (not by measuring the total expiratory volume).

In the normal inspiratory-expiratory cycle of tidal volume, the relative timing of inspiration-expiration, as shown in Figure 2–5, is only slightly longer for expiration. Human beings appear to have a slight bias toward longer expirations, which is apparently quite compatible with the need to extend expiration for purposes of communication. The respiratory system supplies the activating part of phonation, as described in the myoelastic theory of phonation later in this chapter.

Influencing types of respiration are the interactions and pragmatics between the speaker and the listener, the type of utterance being produced, the background noise in the setting, the relative arousal level of the autonomic nervous system, the comfort of the speaker, and so forth. Therefore, some of the ensuing descriptions of the physiology of respiration, when lifted out of speaking or singing context, often appear to be deceptively

simple. For example, when an individual begins to speak or sing, the inspiration time unit is often shortened (by employing more vigor to the muscles
of inspiration) and the expiration time is obviously extended. Hixon, Mead,
and Goldman (1976) have studied the dynamics and function of the thorax,
rib cage, diaphragm, and abdomen during speech and have concluded that
there are marked differences in respiratory function according to body position and type of speech task. For example, utterances that required near-
total use of a patient's vital capacity activated different activity zones, depending on whether the patient was in an upright or supine body position;
the inspiratory activity "was governed predominately by the rib cage and
the abdomen in the upright body position and the diaphragm in the supine
position" (Hixon, Mead, and Goldman, 1976, p. 297). It appears that during
the inspiratory phase preceding speech, we shorten our inspiration and
then use the chest wall and the abdomen in different ways for the expiratory
phase (when we are actually speaking). We renew inspiration and "catch
up" on inspiration during conversational passages, tucking in the abdomen
with a slight elevation of the rib cage. Hixon and Abbs have written that
the "importance of this shape is that it forces the diaphragm—our major
inspiratory muscle—into a highly domed position where its action results
in the development of great amounts of inspiratory force very rapidly"
(1980, p. 63).

Bless and Miller (1972) and Otis and Clark (1968) have written that
normal speakers adjust inspiration-expiration to match the linguistic utterances they wish to make. Inspiration during conversation, public speaking,
and even singing happens quickly, and it is usually masked from the view
of all but the searching eye. After a quick inspiration, normal speakers then
begin the passive expiration, quickly using the tidal volume and adding the
sustained expiration of the expiratory reserve. Fluctuations of expiratory
air flow, to meet a speaker's demand for stress and changes in vocal intensity, are apparently made by slight chest wall adjustments. Increases in air
flow and subglottal pressure are made quickly and with little visible effort
to match the linguistic or artistic needs of speakers or singers. Gifted talkers
or singers also learn to take little, quick "catch-up" inhalations sandwiched
within what appears to listeners to be a continuous expiratory flow. When
breath support or perhaps breath control is a problem in a voice disordered
patient, it is often related to failure to take these "catch-up" breaths at appropriate places. At other times, the tendency to push too hard in extending
the expiratory reserve volume produces the strained vocal quality.

PHONATION

The airway requires various protective structures to prevent the infiltration
of liquids, the aspiration of food particles and fluids during *deglutition* (swallowing), and the inhalation of foreign bodies during respiration. In most
higher mammals, particularly humans, the larynx serves as the basic valve-
like entryway to the respiratory tract. All incoming and outgoing pulmonary air must pass through the valving glottal opening of the larynx. Negus
(1957) wrote that the primary biological roles of the larynx are, first, to

prevent foreign bodies from moving into the airway and, second, to fixate the thorax by stopping the air flow at the glottal level, which permits the arms to perform heavy lifting and extensive weight-supporting feats. This primitive, valve-like action appears to be the primary function of the human larynx. Using the laryngeal valving mechanism for phonation has required the development of intricate neural controls that permit humans to use the approximating valve-like vocal folds for the precise phonations required in speaking and singing.

The valving action of the larynx functions because, first, we have a fixed framework (the laryngeal cartilages); second, we are able to open (abduct) and close (adduct) the valve, primarily by using the intrinsic muscles of the larynx; and third, the valving mechanism receives external support from the extrinsic muscles of the larynx.

Laryngeal Structures

Prominent above the trachea is the larynx, with its large, protective thyroid cartilage housing the individual cartilages, muscles, and ligaments that compose the total laryngeal body. In some people, particularly in adult males, the thyroid cartilage (called the "Adam's Apple") is so prominent that it can easily be seen rising high in the neck during swallowing, dropping low during conversational speech, and rising slightly on high notes during singing.

Photographs of the five primary laryngeal cartilages (cricoid, thyroid, paired arytenoids, and epiglottis) are shown in Figures 2–6 through 2–10. Two other small paired cartilages, the corniculates (small cone-shaped bodies that sit on the apex of the arytenoids extending into the aryepiglottic folds) and the cuneiforms (tiny cone or rod-shaped cartilage pieces under the mucous membrane covering the aryepiglottic folds), apparently play only a minimal role in the phonatory functions of the larynx. Read the legends under each of the cartilage photographs thoroughly, observing some of the other structures that are also identified.

The three major cartilages seem to play separate roles, and each one is dependent on the others, primarily by muscle action and ligament attachment. The cricoid appears almost as an enlarged and complete tracheal ring, forming the solid base of the larynx (other tracheal rings are incomplete or three-quarter rings). It is circular in shape, and the two triangular-shaped arytenoids sit on top of its high posterior (signet-shaped) wall. We shall see later, that the arytenoids rock, slide, and rotate on their articular facets on the cricoid by action of the intrinsic laryngeal muscles. Surrounding the cricoid and arytenoids is the U-shaped thyroid cartilage, which has several articulations with the cricoid cartilage below. All the laryngeal cartilages (similar to cartilage throughout the skeletal system) are coated with a tough leathery covering (the perichondrium), which gives the lateral view of the larynx in Figure 2–6 such a waxy look. This perichondrium covering has been removed in the subsequent photographs of the separate cartilages.

There are two main groups of muscles of the larynx: the extrinsic and the intrinsic. The extrinsic muscles have one attachment to the larynx and another attachment to some structure external to the larynx. The extrinsic

FIGURE 2-6. A lateral left view of the larynx, with the left half of the thyroid cartilage removed. The unretouched photograph shows a remarkable view of the ventricle opening between the true folds and the false folds. Structures may be identified by the letters in the line drawing: (A) cut edge at lamina of thyroid cartilage; (B) arch of the thyroid cartilage; (C) superior horn of the thyroid cartilage; (D) arytenoid cartilage, right; (E) articular facet of the cricoid and arytenoid cartilage; (F) inferior horn of the thyroid cartilage; (G) cricoid cartilage; (H) tracheal ring; (I) vocal fold, right; (J) ventricle; (K) ventricular fold or false fold.

muscles give the larynx fixed support and elevate or lower its position in the neck. Functionally, the extrinsic muscles (all but the cricopharyngeus) may be divided into two groups, elevators and depressors:

elevators	depressors
digastrics	omohyoids
geniohyoids	sternohyoids
mylohyoids	sternothyroids
stylohyoids	thyrohyoids

The extrinsic elevators lift the larynx high during swallowing and slightly during production of high singing notes. The depressors lower the larynx after deglutition and after high-note singing; they also lower the larynx a bit for production of low singing notes. Actually, normal speakers should experience only minimal vertical excursion of the larynx. Trained singers keep the height of the larynx nearly constant while singing a range of high and low notes (Sataloff, 1981).

The other extrinsic laryngeal muscle (other than the elevators and depressors) is the cricopharyngeus, which fuses with the lower portion of the inferior pharyngeal constrictor. The sphincter-like fibers of the cricopha-

FIGURE 2-7. Four views of the cricoid cartilage. In all photographs, ligament and muscle attachments and the membraneous covering have been removed, showing the bare cartilage. The line drawing shows the overall superior contour of the cricoid, and the anatomical site of the four cricoid photographs (a) indicates that photograph A was taken from that view. Photograph (A) shows the posterior surface of the cricoid; the difference in texture (smooth and rough) is related to ossification; the smooth portions represent the ossification. Photograph (B) shows an anterior view. (C) shows the right lateral view of the cricoid ring with the cartilage tipped upward, exposing the superior rim of the signet portion of the cartilage; upon this clearly defined rim rotate the two arytenoid cartilages. (D) shows a right lateral view of the cricoid; note the contrast in thickness between the thin anterior portion of the ring and the high signet posterior portion. This difference in size is also shown in Photograph B).

ryngeus, originating from the posterior wall of the cricoid cartilage, help anchor the larynx in the fixed position in which it usually lies. In her fourth edition of *The Voice and Its Disorders,* Greene (1980) writes that "the steadying influence of the cricopharyngeus on the larynx during phonation is of importance" and that the cricopharyngeus "is in fact an antagonist to the cricothyroid muscle" (pp. 36, 38). The distance between the larynx and the

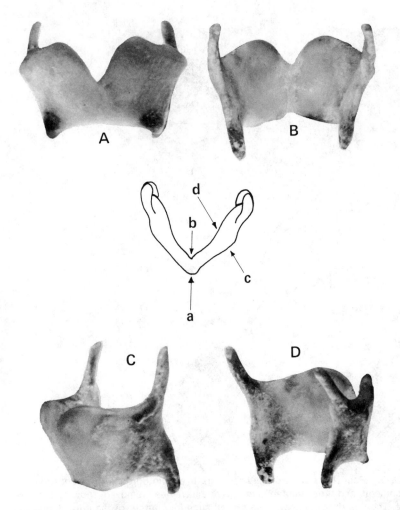

FIGURE 2-8. Four views of the laryngeal thyroid cartilage. The letters in the line draw-ing of the superior view of the thyroid cartilage indicate the side of the cartilage photo-graphed. Photograph (A) shows a direct frontal view of the thyroid. (B) shows a posterior view of the cartilage; note the clear extension of the inferior and superior horns on each side. (C) shows primarily the thyroid cartilage wall. (D) shows the thyroid posteriorly from a three-quarter view. The size and shape of the thyroid cartilage can be extremely vari-able in normal individuals (Dickson and Maue-Dickson, 1982). Asymmetry is often seen in normal individuals (Kahane, 1983).

hyoid bone, as determined by the function of the extrinsic muscles, is often the focus of instruction by singing teachers in the production of a good-singing voice. However, it does not appear that the good speaking voice requires much active muscle movement from either elevators or depressors. The sphincteric action of the larynx and its phonatory capabilities ap-pear to be the function of the intrinsic muscles of the larynx, which we consider in more detail than we did the laryngeal extrinsic muscles. The

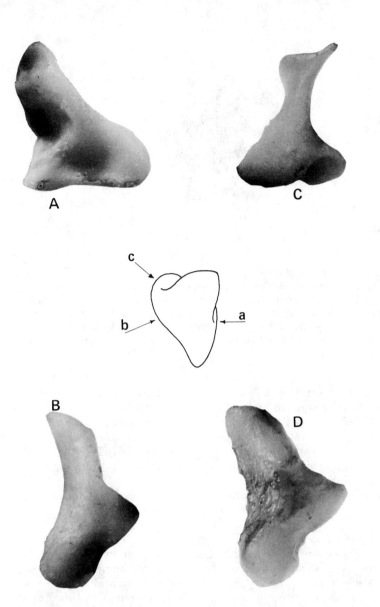

FIGURE 2-9. Four views of an arytenoid cartilage after removal of ligament, muscle, and membrane attachments. Photograph (A) shows a lateral view of the indentation (fovea) toward the base, which receives the attachment of the thyroarytenoid muscles (vocal fold); the higher indentation on the left margin receives the ventricular fold; the muscular process to which the posterior and lateral cricoarytenoids are attached are visible at the right base. (B) shows a medial view of an arytenoid that has been tilted up slightly to the left; the right angular corner is the vocal process. (C) shows a posterior-lateral view of the muscular process at the base; note toward the right base the cricoarytenoid articular facet (point of joint articulation). In (D), a view similar to (B), the camera lens picks up the base of the cartilage as well as its medial wall; the curving base of the arytenoid allows it to rotate, slide, and rock upon the cricoid rim below during adduction and abduction and tensing of the vocal folds.

A   B

FIGURE 2-10. Two views of the epiglottis, which has been removed from its attachment on the lower, internal surface of the anterior portion of the thyroid cartilage. For purposes of photography, the cartilage has been denuded, excising away its ligament and muscle attachments and its membraneous covering. (A) shows the epiglottis from a frontal-lateral view; the rotation of the cartilage permits us to see the concave epiglottal contour. (B) shows the epiglottis in its whole anterior dimension, which represents the lingual surface.

larynx has six intrinsic muscles. Four of them are clearly identifiable in the photographs and drawings in Figure 2–11. One pair of muscles, the posterior cricoarytenoids, is known as the lone vocal fold abductor (these muscles open the glottis by separating the folds at the posterior larynx). The other five intrinsic muscles can be classified as adductors (they close the glottis by bringing the posterior portion of the vocal folds together), although they have other functions.

The following brief descriptions identify each muscle in Figures 2–11 and 2–12.

Posterior Cricoarytenoids This lone abductor muscle (E in Figure 2–11) is the largest laryngeal intrinsic muscle. The fibers originate from a middle depression on the posterior surface of the cricoid and angle up, inserting in the muscular process of the arytenoid on that side (right-sided fibers go to the right muscular process, and so on). This paired muscle is innervated by the recurrent laryngeal nerve. Its primary function is to abduct the folds by rotating laterally the vocal process of the arytenoids.

Lateral Cricoarytenoids This paired muscle (F in Figure 2–11) functions as a direct antagonist to the posterior cricoarytenoid as it plays its adductor role. The lateral cricoarytenoid originates from the upper border of the arch of the cricoid cartilage and inserts into the muscular process of the arytenoid on the same side. Innervation is also the recurrent laryngeal nerve. When this muscle contracts, it rotates the muscular process forward and at the same time causes the vocal process of the arytenoid (and the attached posterior part of the vocal fold) to "toe in" at the midline.

FIGURE 2-11. Intrinsic structures of the larynx. The basic laryngeal cartilage structures are: (A) cutaway of right thyroid wing; (B) left thyroid cartilage wall; (C) left arytenoid cartilage; (D) posterior of cricoid cartilage. The other sketches and photographs identify the following intrinsic muscles: (E) posterior cricoarytenoid; (F) lateral cricoarytenoid; (G) oblique arytenoid; (H) transverse arytenoid; (I) aryepiglottic; (J) thyroarytenoid (vocal fold); (K) ventricular fold; (L) identifies the epiglottis.

ACTION OF
CRICOTHYROID
MUSCLE

ACTION OF VOCALIS AND THYRO–ARYTENOID MUSCLES

FIGURE 2-12. The cricothyroid muscles can be seen in the drawing on the left, obliquing from the inner superior surface of the cricoid cartilage up to the thyroid cartilage. The medial fibers of the vocalis section and the lateral section of the thyroarytenoids are seen in the drawing on the right. (Reprinted with permission from *The CIBA Collection of Medical Illustrations*, illustrated by Frank H. Netter, M.D. All rights reserved. © Copyright 1964, CIBA Pharmaceutical Company, Division of CIBA-Geigy Corporation.)

③ *Transverse Arytenoids*   These muscle fibers (H in Figure 2–11) originate from the lateral margin and posterior surface of one arytenoid and insert on the same sites on the opposite arytenoid. The transverse arytenoids are not paired muscles, per se. They transverse the distance between the two arytenoids. Innervated bilaterally by the recurrent laryngeal nerves, when these muscles contract, they approximate the bodies of the arytenoid cartilages together, functioning as adductor intrinsics as well as fold compressors.

④ *Oblique Arytenoids*   This muscle (G in Figure 2–11) originates from the muscular process of one arytenoid and courses obliquely upward and across to the apex of the opposite cartilage. The fibers actually continue obliquely to the lateral border of the epiglottis and are known as the aryepiglottic muscles after they leave the arytenoid apex. The aryepiglottics become part of the aryepiglottic folds, which also include some cuneiform cartilage and membrane; these folds are active in the swallowing mechanism. The oblique arytenoid muscles are innervated bilaterally by the recurrent nerves and are active in bringing the vocal folds closer together by approximation of the apex of each arytenoid cartilage.

⑤ *Thyroarytenoids*   The paired thyroarytenoids, shown in Figure 2–12, form the bulk of the muscular portion of the vocal folds. The inner section of the thyroarytenoids is known as the vocalis section and the larger, more lateral fibers are known as the thyromuscularis, or external thyroarytenoids (Zemlin, 1981). As Figure 2–12, shows, the fibers originate on the inner surface of the thyroid cartilage and extend posteriorly to where they insert in the vocal process (vocalis fibers) and the lateral surface (external thyroarytenoid) of the arytenoid cartilages. The inner border of the vocal fold contains the vocal ligament that originates at the anterior commissure and extends to the vocal process end of the arytenoids.

In summary, the vocal folds include both sections of the thyroarytenoids, the inner surface of the arytenoid cartilage, and the vocal ligament. The whole apparatus is covered with a tough, white membrane known as the conus elasticus. Figure 2-12 shows the individual components of the vocal folds, and Figure 2-13 shows the white membraneous covering of the vocal folds (as they appear to the eye), with the folds in an open abducted position. The muscular aspect of the folds, the thyroarytenoids, are also innervated by the recurrent laryngeal nerve, and they seem to have a dual function. They shorten themselves as required for producing lower phonation frequencies, and, by their own muscular tension and elasticity, they work as glottal adducting structures.

Cricothyroids Figure 2-12 shows the anteriorly placed paired cricothyroid muscles that lie external to the larynx. This muscle pair is made up of two parts or portions: the obliqua and the recta. The fibers originate from the anterior-lateral arch of the cricoid cartilage and end in two distinctly different insertions. The lower fibers (obliqua portion) insert near the lower horn of the thyroid cartilage, and the more superior fibers (recta portion) course to the lower margin of the lateral thyroid cartilage wall. This pair of muscles is innervated by the superior laryngeal nerve. When they contract, they increase the distance between the thyroid and arytenoid cartilages, thus contributing to pitch elevation by stretching the vocal folds; the tensing of the vocal folds (by elongating them) is an adducting action.

Phonation Function

It is difficult to discuss the cartilages and the muscles of the larynx without some description of laryngeal function. Before we describe function and laryngeal physiology, we should review the various laryngeal struc-

Figure 2-13.
The normal vocal folds photographed using indirect mirror laryngoscopy, showing the open glottis during a normal expiration. The anterior portion of the two folds is at the top of the picture; the mirrored view of the right fold is to the left, the left fold is to the right; the posterior vocal process ends of the folds are at the bottom of the picture. The dark central inverted V area is the open glottis.

Myoelastic Aerodynamic Theory

tures that have been presented. We subscribe to the *myoelastic aerodynamic theory* of phonation (Van den Berg, 1968). It begins basically with an expiration (air volume and air pressure), setting the approximated (closed) vocal folds in vibration as the air flow passes between the folds (transglottal pressure). In the prephonation period, the vocal folds may be abducted in the expiration position (Figure 2–14A). The folds approximate one another for phonation as phonation begins (Figure 2–14B). The five laryngeal adductor muscles contract to bring the vocal folds together.

Two of the adductors—for example, the lateral cricoarytenoid and the thyroarytenoids—have very rapid contraction times, sometimes as fast as fifteen msec, which Martensson (1968) has written is "exceedingly fast and surpassed only by the extrinsic eye muscles" for speed. It would appear that vocal fold adduction is achieved in milliseconds, prior to the onset of voicing. As the folds approximate, they begin to obstruct the air flow passing through the glottal level of the airway. Zemlin (1981) states: "It is extremely important to note that complete obstruction of the air passageway is not necessary to initiate phonation. If the glottal chink is narrowed to about 3 mm, a minimal amount of air flow will set the folds into vibration" (p. 183).

The subglottal pressure builds up when the folds are approximated. The volume of expired air leaving the lungs is impeded at the level of the glottis, resulting in an increased velocity of air flow through the glottis. Subglottal pressure increases (with respect to the supraglottal air pressure), and the vocal folds are blown apart, equalizing supraglottal and subglottal pressure (the opening phase of one cycle of vibration). Because of the mass of the folds (their muscle and ligament covered with a membrane) and the *Bernoulli effect*, they come back together again to their previous approximation line (the closed phase of the phonatory cycle). The Bernoulli effect is the "sucking" attraction of the vocal folds toward one another, caused by

FIGURE 2-14.   Three photographs of the vocal folds. In (A) the vocal folds are open in the expiratory position. In (B) the folds have approximated and are in the phonation position. In (C) the vocal folds are in the typical inverted Y position for whispering, with the muscular portion of the folds approximated laxly and the posterior one-third of the cartilage portion rotated apart. (Photographs A and B appear larger than C because of the false vocal folds overlap the true cords frequently during whispering.)

✱ ~125 times/sec = adult male

the increased velocity of air passing between them. This results in a suction that draws the folds together.

The vibratory cycle of the vocal folds can be summarized as follows: The intrinsic adductors approximate the folds as expiration begins. Subglottal pressure increases. The air flow passes through the glottal opening and blows the folds apart. The static mass of the folds and the Bernoulli suction bring them back together again. The vibratory cycle then repeats itself. This is repeated approximately 125 times per second in the phonation of an adult male.

During normal phonation, the vocal folds approximate one another in their total anterior-posterior dimension. The photographs in Figure 2–14 show the relative approximation contours of the vocal folds during normal phonation and also during normal expiration and whispering. The vocal folds appear slightly shorter during phonation and whispering in the photographs—that is, the vocal folds are always longer in the open abducted position than in the closed adducted one. The configuration of the glottis for whispering is characterized by an open, posterior chink, with the arytenoid cartilages and their vocal processes angled in an open, inverted V position. Although the vocal folds are parallel to one another during whispering, they do not firmly approximate. This lack of adduction, particularly in the posterior chink, produces frictional sounds when the outgoing air stream passes through, producing what we perceive as whispering.

The vocal folds appear to be maximally long during at-rest breathing and shortened somewhat during phonation. In fact, at the lower end of an individual's pitch range, at the level where conversational phonation is generally found, the vocal folds are considerably shortened. When we speak about the length thickness of the folds, we refer to fundamental frequency, or the pitch of the voice that we hear. Fundamental frequency is directly related to how many vibratory closings-openings (cycles) the vocal folds make in one second. The rate of vibration is related to their thickness-length-elasticity. A short, thick, somewhat lax fold vibrates at a much slower rate than a long, thin, tense fold. The length of the vocal folds increases almost in a "stair-step" fashion, corresponding to increases in frequency. By using X-ray laminagraphy, which permits cross-sectional, coronal viewing of the vocal folds, Hollien (1962) found that the mean thickness, or mass, of the folds systematically decreased as voice pitch increased. It appears, then, from the multiple studies conducted on vocal fold length and thickness by the Hollien group, that fundamental frequency, or voice pitch level, is directly related to the length and thickness of the individual's vocal folds.

The relative differences between men and women in vocal fold length (approximately 20mm for men and 15mm for women) and vocal fold thickness appear to be the primary determinants of differences in voice pitch; the typical fundamental frequency for men is around 125 Hz; for women, around 200 Hz. Table 2–1 shows examples of normal pitch values, including pitch range and fundamental frequency. When individuals phonate at increasingly higher pitch levels, they must lengthen the vocal folds to decrease their relative mass and increase their tension. Increases of pitch, therefore, appear to be related to lengthening of the vocal folds, with a corresponding

fundamental frequency = cycles/second

VF length (20 mm ♂; 15 mm ♀)
VF thickness determinants in pitch
$$F_0 = \sim 125 Hz - ♂$$
$$\sim 200 Hz - ♀$$

decrease of tissue mass and an increase of fold elasticity. Lowering the pitch is directly related to shortening the folds.

It would appear that both the cricothyroids and possibly the cricopharyngeus play active roles in elongating the vocal folds, which in turn increases their elasticity. The vocal folds are stretched by the action of the cricothyroids, which increase the distance of the arytenoids from the thyroid cartilage by drawing the cricoid cartilage up toward the thyroid, which in effect lowers the posterior cricoid rim. The cricopharyngeus, when contracted, can pull the cricoid slightly posterior, adding to vocal fold elasticity. For a detailed description with accompanying drawings of the elongation functions of the cricothyroid muscles, see the phonation chapter in *Normal Aspects of Speech, Hearing, and Language* (Broad, 1973). Relaxation of the cricothyroids with the simultaneous contraction of the thyroarytenoids appears to be essential for shortening and thickening the folds, which lowers the pitch of the voice. Greene (1980) has suggested that the cricopharyngeus may play an antagonist (shortening) role to the cricothyroids.

It appears that at the upper end of the natural pitch range, increased elasticity of the vocal folds results in increased glottal resistance, requiring

TABLE 2-1.   Normal Fundamental Frequency (F_0) and Pitch Ranges for Four Voices (Bass, Tenor, Alto, and Soprano)

Note on Piano	Physical Hz	Typical F_0 and Pitch Range			
		(Bass)	(Tenor)	(Alto)	(Soprano)
C6	1,024				1,040
B	960				
A	853				
G5	768				
F	682			700	
E	640				
D	576				
C5	512		550		
B	480				
A	426				
G4	384				
F	341	340			
E	320				
D	288				
C4	256				F_0 256
B	240				
A	213			F_0 200	
G3	192				
F	170				170
E	160				
D	144		F_0 135	140	
C3	128				
B	120				
A	106	F_0 100			
G2	96		95		
F	85	80			

increased air pressure to produce higher-frequency phonations. Increased tension of the vocal folds requires greater air pressure to set the folds into vibration. Van den Berg (1968) has written that the average person must slightly increase subglottal pressure in order to increase voice pitch; however, because increasing subglottal pressure has an abducting effect on the vocal folds, the folds must continue to increase in tension to maintain their approximated position. Although the primary determinant of pitch appears to be the length, mass, and tension of the vocal folds, increases in pitch level are usually characterized by increasing subglottal pressures.

The vocal folds can elongate and stretch only so far. If singers want to extend their pitch range beyond what normal vocal fold stretching can do, they are forced to produce a falsetto voice. We might describe the production of the falsetto voice in this manner: the folds approximate with tight, posterior vocal process adduction. The posterior cartilaginous portion is so tightly adducted that little or no posterior vibration occurs while the anterior portion vibrates rapidly. The lateral portions of the thyroarytenoid do not actively vibrate to produce the falsetto voice. The inner vocalis segment of the muscle is extremely contracted (and thus thinned out) along the vocal ligament. As the membrane wraps the ligament, the membrane itself becomes the primary vibrating structure during falsetto. In falsetto the vocal folds may remain somewhat open, although parallel, which gives falsetto its characteristic "breathy" quality. Judson and Weaver (1965), Rubin and Hirt (1960), and Hollien (1962) have all described the falsetto (called the "loft" register by Hollien) as a production of the vibrating membrane on the anterior two-thirds surface of the glottal margin.

The kind of pitch opposite from the falsetto is the low glottal fry. Greene (1980) described the *fry* as the pulse register, the "lowest range of notes and synonymous with vocal fry, glottal fry, creak and strohbass" (p. 81). The glottal fry sounds something like the sputter of a low-powered outboard motor. Zemlin (1981) wrote that fry is produced when the folds are approximated tightly with a flaccid appearance along the glottal margin. Moore and von Leden (1958) found that during fry a double vibration of the folds is followed by a prolonged period of approximation (almost two-thirds of the vibratory cycle). Vocal fry may well be the normal vibratory cycle we use near the bottom of our normal pitch range. Some speakers may add fry to their phonation, to give, in their minds, an authoritative quality to what they are saying. Although fry does not appear to be a vocal abnormality, some voice patients successfully work to eliminate it by elevating their pitch levels slightly and increasing subglottic air pressure.

Related to the production of voice pitch and the pitch range of any individual is *voice register*. It appears that a particular register characterizes a certain pattern of vocal fold vibration, and the vocal folds are approximated in a similar way throughout a particular pitch range. Once this pitch range reaches its maximum limit, the folds adjust to a new approximation contour, which produces an abrupt change in vocal quality. Van den Berg (1968) describes three primary forms of voice register: chest, midvoice, and falsetto.

The frontal, coronal view of the folds sketched in Figure 2–15 shows the thickened folds of the chest or normal register contrasted with the thin

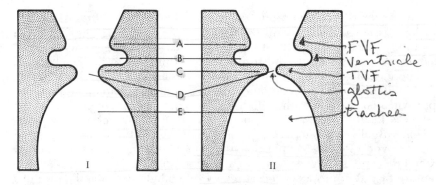

[Handwritten annotations on figure: FVF, Ventricle, TVF, glottis, trachea]

FIGURE 2-15. A line tracing on a tomogram that presents an X-ray frontal view of the vocal folds showing vocal fold approximation contours for (I) chest register, and (II) falsetto register: (A) ventricular fold; (B) open ventricle; (C) vocal fold; (D) glottis, opening between folds; (E) trachea. Note the thicker fold approximation for the chest register, as opposed to the thinner, superior approximation of the two folds during the production of the falsetto register.

folds of the falsetto register. From the perceptual viewpoint, voice register is confined to the similar sound of an individual's voice at various pitches. Although this similar quality is undoubtedly related to the similarity in vocal-fold approximation and vibration characteristics, teachers of voice strive to blend the various registers, so that the difference in quality of voice becomes almost imperceptible as the singer goes from one register to the next. Some singers seem to have only one register; no matter how they change their pitch, their voice always seems to have the same quality, with no discernible break toward the upper part of the pitch range. Such persons' frontal X-rays would probably show a relatively stable contour in the approximations of the vocal folds. An excellent review of the literature and detailed description of voice register may be found in Luchsinger and Arnold (1965).

The intensity of the voice, perceived as loudness of the voice, is directly related to changes in subglottal and transglottal air pressures. Hixon and Abbs (1980) have written, "Sound pressure level, the primary factor contributing to our perception of the *loudness* of the voice, is governed mainly by the pressure supplied to the larynx by the respiratory pump" (p. 68). It appears that the trained voices of actors or singers increase intensity by increasing both subglottal pressure and air flow rate (similar to the water hose analogy mentioned earlier), with only minimal increase of glottal tension (Bouhuys, Proctor, and Mead, 1966). At very loud levels untrained voices often increase in pitch as part of the loudness. It is difficult for untrained voices to produce loud sounds at very low pitch levels.

As voice intensity increases, the vocal folds tend to remain closed for longer periods of time during each vibratory cycle (see Figure 2–16), and the greater intensity of voice is characterized by greater excursion of the vibrating folds. It would appear that, as intensity increases, increased glottal tension impedes the rate of air flow, increasing subglottal pressure. At lower pitch levels this tension during intense phonations is minimal. It causes

closed phase

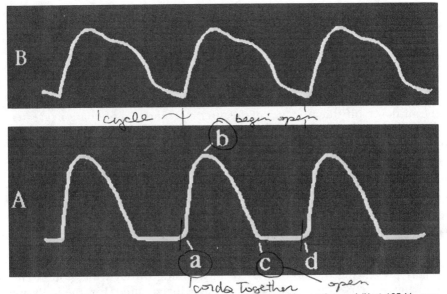

1 cycle — *begin open*

b

a   *c*   *d*

cords Together   *open*

FIGURE 2-16. The two laryngograms represent (A) a prolonged vowel /i/ at 125 Hz normal intensity, and (B) at a louder intensity. The letter *a* represents the beginning of the closing phase as the cords come together; at *b* the cords are completely together and beginning to open; at *c* the cords are open; at *d* the open phase is completed and another cycle begins. The closed phase (*b* to *c*) is much longer in the louder production (B). The open phase (*c* to *d*) is shorter in the louder production (B).

singers, for example, to run out of air sooner when producing varying intensities at low pitches than at high ones. Evidently, speakers or singers who continually require a loud voice could use their vocal mechanisms more optimally by developing their expiratory skills and relying more on increased subglottal air pressure and increased air-flow rates, and less on increased glottal elasticity, to achieve louder intensities.

Besides pitch, loudness, quality, and register as measurable dimensions of voice, Perkins (1983) has added constriction and vertical focus to the production of voice. He describes the feeling of constriction on a continuum of open (the yawn) to closed (the swallow). Imagery or feeling is used to determine the vertical focus of the voice, "the perception associated with the placement of the focal point of the tone in the head" (Perkins, 1983, p. 113). At the low end of the vertical focus, speakers or singers feel their voice is being squeezed out of the throat, whereas at the high end the focus seems to be high in the head. Vocal efficiency seems to occur best at the higher end of the vertical placement. It has been our experience that subjects given these instructions relative to the imagery of constriction and verticality produce voices with greater aperiodicity (hoarseness) at the low end of the vertical scale and greater vocal clarity at the high end. In time, the Perkins' construct of constriction and vertical focus may well have greater measurement potential and utilization.

Vocal quality may well be related primarily to supraglottal resonance, but important components of the spectrum of the laryngeal tone have their origins at the level of the glottis. How the vocal folds are approximated together, laxly or tightly, in part determines the quality of the voice. Many individuals can produce several different voices, all at the same pitch level, by varying the approximation characteristics of the vocal folds. A breathy voice is often produced by adding phonation to the ongoing expiration, with the folds only laxly approximating one another. Spectrographic analysis of the breathy voice shows us that noise and aperiodicity produced by the air flow typify the first part of the utterance, and that phonation (greater periodicity) comes in after some delay.

The three spectrograms in Figure 2–17 contrast the breathy voice (with much aperiodicity and noise) with the harsh voice (with hard glottal attack) and the normal voice. Each of the spectrograms was produced by the same normal speaker prolonging an /i/. In hard glottal attack, the opposite kind of vocal onset is observed. Here the first voicing patterns begin abruptly with the onset of expiration. The glottis seems to be held tightly until a sudden release of air sets the folds into vibration. Faulty positioning of the vocal folds is also characteristic of patients with spastic dysphonia. These patients bring the folds so tightly together that they act like a valve, almost totally preventing the flow of air from traveling through the glottis. The patient's voice is strained and has a strangle-like quality. How the folds are approximated has much to do with how voices sound.

Study of the vocal fold "set" aspect of phonation has been limited to such methods as high-speed film, viewing the larynx through indirect laryngoscopy, or employing spectrograms displaying visually the voices that we hear. Even though we know something about the extreme of breathiness and hard glottal attack, our knowledge of vocal fold physiology for most of the voices we hear is relatively lacking in regard to vocal fold approximation and its effect on quality. The development of flexible videoendoscopy and glottographic instruments has allowed us to study the production of this disorder further. McFarlane and Lavorato (1984) have discussed the use of videoendoscopy in the study of voice disorders. We discuss this topic in detail in Chapter 4, where we present evaluation procedures.

RESONANCE

The fundamental frequency produced by the vocal folds would be a weak-sounding, "reedy" voice without the additional component of resonance. Years ago one of the authors observed a patient who had been cut from ear to ear with a massive wound that opened immediately superior to his thyroid cartilage. Before the wound was sutured, we heard the patient's feeble attempts at phonation. Much of his air flow and sound waves escaped through the wound opening. The result was a voice that was truly unique. Someone even likened it to the thin bleat of a baby lamb. Apparently, what is perceived as the quality, timbre, and loudness of the voice is produced by the supraglottal resonators. Even though the structures of the chest and trachea may play some role in resonance, this role is not as clearly defined as that of the supraglottal resonators of the pharynx, oral cavity, and nasal cavity.

✱ supraglottal resonators: ✱
quality, timbre,
loudness

1
Breathy

2
Normal

3
Harsh

Figure 2–17.
Three spectrograms of the same speaker producing the vowel /i/ under three conditions: breathy, normal, harsh. The relative spacing of the formants stays the same as the signal source changes.

Structures of Resonance

The vocal tract begins, for all practical purposes, at the level of the glottis. The air flow and sound waves probably have some beginning passage in the ventricular space (B in Figure 2–18) between the true folds (A) and the ventricular folds (C). In Figure 2–18 the cavities of the vocal tract have been shaded in black. The epiglottis (D), by its concavity, probably serves as a deflector or sounding-board resonator as sound waves travel between the aryepiglottic folds (E) into the hypopharynx (F). The hypopharynx is the cavity directly above the esophagus (G). Its anterior border comprises the structures and opening of the larynx (G); its sides and back wall are composed of the lower pharyngeal constrictors (G).

The oropharynx (J) is just before the tip of the epiglottis. The small angular space between the front of the epiglottis and the back of the tongue (L) is called the vacula (I). Cutting away the mandible (K) in a lateral view is the great body of the tongue, which occupies most of the oral cavity and forms the constantly changing floor of that cavity. The hard palate is designated (O), with the soft palate or *velum* (N) forming the roof of the oral cavity. The lips, teeth, and cheeks play obvious front and lateral roles in shaping the oral cavity. The middle and superior pharyngeal constrictors form the lateral and posterior muscular wall of the oropharynx (H). The site of the velopharyngeal closure, necessary for the separation of the oral and nasal cavities required for oral resonance, is the Passavant's pad (M) area of the superior pharyngeal constrictor; most subjects do not have much Passavant area enlargement. As shown in Figure 2–18, superior to the velopharyngeal contact point, the posterior pharyngeal wall makes a sharp angulation forward, forming the superior wall of the nasopharynx (P) and continuing on as the superior wall of the nasal cavity. We make no further structural breakdown of the nasal cavities (Q) as a prelude to our discussion of resonance. Note that Figure 2–18 also shows the lateral walls, pillars of fauces, muscles of the palate, pharynx, and tongue. If we look again at the overall lateral view of the vocal tract, we see that the total darkened areas look slightly like a large letter *F*. The vocal tract in the photograph resembles a reversed *F* because the velopharyngeal port is open, connecting the oral and nasal cavities together. If the port were closed at the velopharyngeal contact point (M), the vocal tract opening available for voice resonance would resemble a printed *r*, formed only by the pharynx and the oral cavity opening above the surface of the tongue.

Mechanism of Resonance

A vibrator, such as the string of a violin or the vocal folds, originates a fundamental vibration (or sound waves), which by itself produces weak, barely audible sounds. This vibrating energy is usually amplified by a resonating body of some type. For example, a violin string, when plucked, will set up a fundamental vibration; this vibration becomes resonated by the bridge to which the strings are attached, which then sets into vibration the sounding board below and in turn the main resonating body of the violin (the chest), which provides open cavity resonance. When all the violin parts are working together in harmony, the fundamental tone of the involved

FIGURE 2.18. The F-shaped vocal tract, shown in both the line drawing on the left and the photograph of a cadaver head on the right. The letters A through O identify various structures of the vocal tract.

string becomes louder and fuller in quality. The same string stripped out of its mount on the violin and then plucked (even with the same amount of tension to the string) will sound less intense and thinner in quality.

The violin provides a ready example of the two main types of resonance, the *sounding-board effect* and the *open-cavity effect.* When a particular string of the violin is bowed, the air waves that develop are low in amplitude and barely audible; however, because the vibrating string is stretched tightly over the bridge of the violin, it sets the bridge itself into vibration. The bridge functions as a sounding board. The sounding board then vibrates, setting into vibration the air over a much larger area, increasing the loudness of the tone. The sounding-board vibration also introduces the sound waves into the violin cavity itself. The main body, or chest, of the violin provides cavity resonance to the source sound of the vibrating string. The string vibrating alone, which is similar to laryngeal vibration without supraglottal resonance, produces a barely audible tone. The cavity resonance provided by the body of the violin increases the volume of the vibrating string. The size and overall shape of the resonating cavity has an obvious relationship to the resonance of a vibration.

Every frequency of vibration has an ideal resonating cavity size and shape. The ideal is represented by the cavity that seems to give the loudest tone and the tone with the fullest amount of amplification to its overtones. This may be thought of as *acoustic efficiency.* This observation can be easily tested by placing a tuning fork over a large glass and varying the amounts of water in the glass. At a particular level of water, the glass will provide optimum resonance, heard as increased loudness of sound. The lower the frequency of the vibrating wave, the larger the size of the resonating cavity. The thinner string of the violin requires a much smaller resonating body than the larger string of the bass viola, which requires a resonating body as tall as the person who plays the instrument.

The human vocal tract is continually changing. As Minifie (1973) has written:

> During the production of vowels the vocal tract may be viewed as a tortuously shaped tube open at one end (the opening between the lips) and bounded at the other end by a vibrating valve which has the effect of closing off the tube at the larynx. The three-dimensional geometry of this tube may be altered through the contraction of muscles which regulate the movements of the tongue, velum, pharynx, mandible, lips, epiglottis, and larynx. These structures may be moved individually or in various combinations. The combination of structures which move during the production of a particular speech sound will determine the unique vocal tract configuration, and hence, the unique acoustical filter for that sound. (p. 243)

Some areas of the vocal tract, depending on their configuration, are compatible with the periodic vibration coming from the vocal folds and amplify the fundamental frequency and its harmonics. For example, a fundamental frequency of 125 Hz will resonate harmonic frequencies at 250, 375, 500 (each subsequent harmonic frequency is a whole number multiple of the fundamental), and so on. The continuous vocal tract tube is constantly interrupted at various sites from the intrusion and movement of various structures. Some of the interruptions or constrictions may be severe, such as carrying the tongue high and forward in the oral cavity. Any movement of mandible, tongue, or velum, for example, will greatly alter the opening of the oral cavity. Some of the movements have no effect on the fundamental or sound source; some of them filter or inhibit the fundamental. What finally emits from the mouth or the nasal cavity perceived as voice has become a complex periodic signal with the same fundamental frequency as the vocal fold source, but highly modified in its overall sound characteristics. We can hear several familiar voices all saying the same few words at the same fundamental frequency, and still be able to differentiate each voice and assign it to each familiar person. The vocal characteristics related to the individualization of each person's vocal tract will have given each voice its own unique characteristics (*vocal quality*) as the result of the amplification and filtering unique to each vocal tract.

The *F* configuration of the supraglottal vocal tract is constantly changing. What happens in any one portion of the tract influences both the total flow of air and sound wave through the total tract and the sound that eventually emits from the mouth (or nose). By action of the pharyngeal constrictors and other supraglottal muscles, the overall dimensions of the pharynx are always changing. The membranes of the pharynx and the degree of relaxation or tautness of the pharyngeal constrictors have noticeable acoustic filtering effects. Higher frequency vocalizations seem to receive their best resonating effects under a fairly high degree of pharyngeal wall tension. Lower frequencies appear to be better amplified by a pharynx that is somewhat relaxed. This may be related to the short wave length of high frequency sounds and the long wave length of the low frequency components.

The oral cavity, or mouth, is as essential for resonance as the pharynx. Of all our resonators, the mouth is capable of the most variation in size and shape. It is the constant size/shape adjustment of the mouth that permits us to speak or, more accurately, allows us to be understood. Our vowels and diphthongs, for example, are originated by a laryngeal vibration, but shaped and restricted by size/shape adjustment of the oral cavity. The mouth has fixed structures (teeth, alveolar processes, dental arch, and hard palate) and moving structures. We are most concerned with the moving structures, primarily the tongue, velum, and mandible, in our study of voice resonance.

The tongue is the most mobile articulator, and it possesses both extrinsic and intrinsic muscles to move it. Each of the extrinsic muscles can, upon contraction, elevate or lower the tongue at its anterior, middle, or posterior points and extend it forward or backward. The intrinsic muscles control the shape of the tongue by narrowing, flattening, lengthening, or shortening the overall tongue body and elevating or lowering the tongue tip. The various combinations of intrinsic and extrinsic muscle contractions can produce an unlimited number of tongue positions with resulting size/shape variations of the oral cavity. In addition to the tongue movements, the lowering and closing of the mandible contributes to the formation of specific vowels. The relationships of these cavities to vowel formants have been well described in several references, such as the Peterson and Barney study

(1952), and in chapters by Netsell and by Daniloff in *Normal Aspects of Speech, Hearing, and Language* (1973).

The structural adequacy and normal functioning of the velum are also important for the development of normal voice resonance. The elevation and tensing of the velum, as well as some pharyngeal wall movement, are vital for achieving velopharyngeal closure. A lack of adequate palatal movement, despite adequacy of velar length, can cause serious problems of nasality. Although the velum probably serves as a sounding-board structure in resonance, it plays an obviously important role in separating the oral cavity from the nasal cavity. The movement and positioning of the velum changes the size and shape of three important resonating cavities: the pharynx, the oral cavity, and the nasal cavity. Therefore, any alteration of the velum (such as a soft-palate cleft) may have a profound influence on resonance. Velar movement is only one component contributing to velopharyngeal closure (Zwitman, Gyepes, and Ward, 1976). Closure patterns that separate the oral and nasal cavities from one another may include velar action coupled by posterior pharyngeal wall movement, or velar action with active lateral and posterior pharyngeal wall movement. Regardless of the type of closure pattern (velar-posterior-lateral pharyngeal wall), the site of closure is generally in the Passavant's area (designated as M in Figure 2–18).

The fundamental frequency that comes from the vocal folds is modified throughout the vocal tract. Movements and constrictions within the tract contribute to the overall amplifying or filtering of the voice signal produced by the vibrating vocal folds. Faulty use of the structures of the vocal tract often leads to excesses in quality and resonance.

SUMMARY

In our review of the respiratory aspects of phonation we found that the outgoing air stream is the primary activating force of voice. The efficient user of voice develops good expiratory control. A description of the physiology of phonation reviewed the structures and mechanisms of normal phonation, including frequency and intensity. Supraglottal structures and functions specific to quality and resonance were also reviewed. The entire vocal tract contributes to the amplification and filtering of the fundamental frequency into the final unique voice of any speaker.

3
VOICE DISORDERS

Voice disorders result from faulty structure or function somewhere in the vocal tract: in respiration, in phonation, or in resonance. A traditional way of looking at voice disorders is to divide them into two etiologic (causative) categories: functional or organic. Functional voice disorders are usually caused by faulty use of vocal mechanisms. Organic voice problems are related to some physical change in structure or function at various sites of the vocal tract. As we consider different functional-organic voice disorders in this chapter, we also look at the various sites of the vocal tract to see how they may be contributing to the voice disorders.

Most vocal disorders are characterized by changes in the sound of the voice. Such changes have many different names—*hoarseness, harshness, huskiness, stridency,* to name only a few. Unfortunately, there is little common agreement about what these terms mean among listeners. In this text, we use a more generic term, dysphonia, which means any alteration in phonation. This lack of a common vocabulary for the various parameters of voice production and voice pathology is perhaps related to the number of different kinds of specialists who are concerned with voice—the laryngologist, the singing teacher, the speech-voice scientist, the speech pathologist, and the voice-and-diction teacher. The laryngologist is primarily interested in identifying the etiological and pathological aspects for purposes of treatment; the singing teacher uses imagery in an attempt to get the desired acoustical effect from the student; the speech-voice scientist has the laboratory interest of the physiologist or physicist; the speech pathologist often attempts to use the knowledge and vocabulary of all three of these disciplines; and the voice-and-diction teacher assesses the dynamics of voice production and uses whatever is necessary to "get" the best voice. It is no wonder that interdisciplinary communication among voice specialists breaks down.

The general public tolerance of an indifference to voice problems makes the early identification of voice pathologies difficult. Hoarseness that persists longer than several days is often identified by the laryngologist as a possible symptom of serious laryngeal disease. And it may be. Hoarseness is certainly the acoustic correlate of improper vocal fold functioning, with or without true laryngeal disease. The distinction between organic disease of the larynx and functional misuse has been a prominent dichotomy in the consideration of phonatory disorders. It is important for the laryngologists, in their need to rule out or identify true organic disease, to view the laryngeal mechanism by laryngoscopy in order to make a judgment about organic-structural involvement. In the absence of structural deviation, the laryngologist describes the voice disorder as functional.

Functional aphonia, for example, may be a wholly functional voice problem. The patient may exhibit normal breath flow and an adequate open pharynx and oral cavity for normal resonance, but lack voice. When a functionally aphonic patient attempts to use voice, the vocal folds instead of adducting together abduct further apart. The result is basically a whisper. A patient can also functionally misuse the vocal tract (such as by inadequate breath support or excessive glottal attack or by closing down the supraglottal mechanisms), which, in time, may lead to organic changes of structure, such as bilateral vocal nodules. Such nodules might well have been caused by excessive vocal abuse and misuse. Once the nodules develop, however, they contribute to the poor voice that is often characterized by low pitch, excessive breathiness, and severe hoarseness. Many structural organic alterations of the larynx (such as cancer or granuloma or web) can have profound effects on the larynx and the vocal folds in particular, which can result in serious alterations of voice.

A normal voice requires relatively normal usage of respiratory, phonatory, and resonance mechanisms. Conversely, poor use of these mechanisms can produce faulty voice. Some poor voices result from faulty respiratory timing and control; for example, the patient may "run out of air" in the middle of a verbal passage. Instead of renewing the breath with some kind of catch-up inspiration, the patient continues to attempt to vocalize. The resulting insufficient air flow and subglottal pressure can be heard in the dysphonic voice toward the end of the utterance. Changes in the mass-size-tension of the vocal folds result in changes of frequency, also characterized by fluctuations in voice pitch.

Normal phonation requires that, in addition to proper mass-size adjustments, the two vocal folds approximate one another optimally along their entire length (from the anterior commissure up to, and including, the vocal process). The easy imitation of voices by some actors suggests that individuals are able to vary the strength of fold approximation. Consistent with this observation is the further one that most functionally caused dysphonias are related directly to under- or overadduction of the vocal folds and to alterations in air flow. In underadduction, the folds are too laxly approximated, resulting in a breathy type of phonation. Sometimes, after prolonged hyperfunctional use of the voice, the folds will show an open chink posteriorly; actually, this posterior chink is the incomplete adduction of the vocal processes. Overadduction of the folds results in the tight valving of the glottal mechanism, so much so that the individual may be unable to phonate for speech.

Spastic dysphonia is a severe overadduction problem. The voice sounds strained, like the kind of phonation we hear from someone attempting to talk while lifting a heavy object; the valving action of the larynx (fixed, tight adduction) overrules the individual's desire to phonate, and phonation becomes almost impossible. Often, conditions that increase the mass-size of the vocal folds—that is, thickening, nodules, or polyps—will, by their size, make the optimum adduction of the vocal folds impossible. Glottal growths, such as nodules, and polyps, interfere with the approximating edges of the vocal folds, and they often produce open chinks between the approximating folds on each side of the growth. Any structural interference between the approximating edges of the vocal folds usually results in some degree of dysphonia. Occasionally, unilateral or bilateral paralysis of intrinsic muscles of the larynx results in paralysis of one or both of the vocal folds, producing obvious voice problems related to faulty approximation.

On nasoendoscopy, we often observe resonance being altered by surprisingly large movements of supraglottal structures (false folds, aryepiglottic folds, pharyngeal walls, tongue). For example, the tight voice of spastic dysphonia is not only produced by tight sphincteric closure of the vocal folds, but by pronounced supraglottal shutoff or valving as well. By watching the movements of the oro- and hypopharynx during nasoendoscopy (Pershall and Boone, 1986), we have come to appreciate the dynamic role that these structures have in both vocal quality and resonance. Supraglottal structures play an important role in the production of both normal and abnormal voice.

Table 3.1 lists twenty-six voice disorders, some primarily the result of misuse of vocal mechanisms, and some the direct result of organic changes of vocal mechanisms. The left column lists twelve voice disorders whose etiology appears to be primarily functional; the names of many of these functional voice disorders describe, in effect, the vocal changes they cause. The right column lists fourteen organic conditions of the vocal tract that

TABLE 3–1. **Twenty-six Voice Problems Related to Either Faulty Usage of the Vocal Mechanisms or to Organic Changes of Vocal Mechanisms**

Functional Disorder	Organic Disorder
Contact Ulcers	Cancer
Diplophonia	Dysarthria
Functional aphonia	Endocrine changes
Functional dysphonia	Granuloma
Phonation breaks	Hemangioma
Pitch breaks	Hyperkeratosis
Spastic dysphonia*	Infectious laryngitis
Thickening (vocal fold)	Laryngectomy
Traumatic laryngitis	Laryngofissure
Ventricular dysphonia	Leukoplakia
Vocal nodules	Papilloma
Vocal polyps	Pubertal changes
	Vocal fold paralysis
	Webbing

*The etiology of spastic dysphonia is unknown. It may also be classified as an organic disorder.

may contribute to various vocal pathologies. The organic disorders are more often labeled by etiology than by the acoustic alterations they may produce.

VOICE DISORDERS RELATED TO FAULTY USAGE

In this section, we consider the voice problems listed in the left-hand column of Table 3.1. These voice disorders result from using the vocal mechanisms in a faulty manner. For reader convenience, we consider separately each of these functional voice disorders, including their possible etiology and management, in alphabetical order, as they appear in Table 3.1.

Contact Ulcers

As we mentioned in Chapter 2, the total length of the glottis can be divided into thirds: the anterior two-thirds is muscular (vocalis portion of the thyroarytenoids) and covered by a membrane; the posterior third is cartilaginous (arytenoids) and covered by a membrane. *Contact ulcers,* which form along the posterior third of the glottal margin, seem to result from excessive slamming together of the arytenoid cartilages during production of low-pitched phonation coupled with excessive glottal attack. The speaker is usually a hard-driving person who speaks in a loud, controlling low pitch, often with words punctuated with sudden onset.

The typical symptoms of contact ulcers are deterioration of voice after prolonged vocalization, accompanied by pain in the laryngeal area or sometimes pain that lateralizes out to one ear. Laryngoscopy usually reveals bilateral ulcerations with heavy buildup of granulation tissue along the approximating margins of the posterior glottis. Greene (1980) labeled the toughened membraneous tissue changes on the posterior glottis as "pachydermia," citing the work of Kleinsasser (1979); Greene (1980) wrote that "contact ulcers are not actually ulcers or granulomas but consist of 'craters' with highly thickened squamous epithelium over connective tissue with some inflammation (edema)" (p. 147).

The diffuse irritation of the posterior glottis often associated with contact ulcers may be the result of esophageal reflux, sometimes associated with diaphragmatic or hiatal hernia. The patient experiences esophageal reflux while sleeping, which results in the pooling of acid secretions in the vocal process end of the glottis (Cherry and Margulies, 1968). In studying the sensitivity of the posterior larynx to gastric juices, Delahunty and Cherry (1968) were able to produce experimentally contact ulcers and granulation tissue in dogs by swabbing gastric juices on their vocal folds. It now appears that patients with contact ulcers who also demonstrate marked irritation of laryngeal-pharyngeal tissue are candidates for a thorough examination of the gastrointestinal tract. If a hiatal hernia, for example, is found with contact ulcers, the patient is best treated with antacids and voice therapy. Elevating the head of the bed is also helpful.

The focus of voice therapy for patients with contact ulcers is to take the effort out of phonation. The patients must learn to use a voice pitch level that can be produced with relatively little strain, to speak with greater mouth and jaw relaxation, to speak at lower levels of volume, and to eliminate all traces of excessive glottal attack. Contact ulcers are rare today. Those patients who do have them, however, seem to respond well to voice therapy.

Diplophonia

The term *diplophonia* means double voice. A diplophonic voice is produced with two distinct voice sources, each voicing simultaneously with the other. Occasionally, someone may produce a double voice with one vocal fold in a different mass-size-tension mode than the other fold—that is, one fold vibrates at a different vibratory speed than the other one. For example, a woman with a large unilateral vocal polyp was observed who spoke with a diplophonic voice. Her normal vocal fold vibrated at its normal frequency, while the involved fold (much enlarged with a broad-based polyp) vibrated more slowly and produced the diplophonic voice. Other possible causes of diplophonia that have been reported are laryngeal web, vocal-cord paralysis, ventricular fold vibration simultaneous with true fold vibration, and aryepiglottic vibration added to normal fold vibration. Theoretically, any bodies (folds or structures) that can approximate in the vocal tract, through which outgoing air flow can pass, have the potential for producing a sound (or voice).

The treatment of diplophonia is aimed at eliminating the source of the second voice. Sometimes, surgical removal of a unilateral mass or elimination of a laryngeal web will result in a single voice. More often, diplophonia is corrected by voice therapy (which we discuss in Chapters 5 and 6).

Functional Aphonia

Patients with *functional aphonia* speak with a whisper. In order to rule out some form of laryngeal involvement, such as vocal fold paralysis, these patients must be examined by either laryngoscopy or endoscopy. When functional aphonic patients are requested to say "ah," their vocal folds instead of coming together, abduct further apart.

Functional aphonia has no physical cause. In fact, it is frequently described as a *hysterical* or *conversion* symptom, according to Aronson, Peterson, and Litin (1966), who found these two terms used by various laryngologists for twenty functional dysphonic and aphonic patients they had observed. Although functional aphonia may well be a form of conversion hysteria, Brodnitz (1971, p. 65) recommends that we avoid using the term in the "presence of the patient because of the social stigma attached to it." Usually patients have had several temporary losses of voice before the disorder becomes permanent. Temporarily aphonic patients may derive some reinforcing gains from their loss of voice, such as not having to give speeches or not being able to preside over meetings. Aphonia may even become permanent after moments of acute stress by maintaining itself for various reasons. Aronson, Peterson, and Litin (1966) report that in ten out of twenty-seven patients they studied the onset of functional dysphonia or aphonia was associated with an event of acute stress; in thirteen of the twenty-seven patients it was associated with stress over a longer period of time. The onset of functional aphonia is sometimes related to the patient's having experienced some laryngeal pathology or other disease. For example, Boone (1966b) described the physical origin of functional aphonia in two patients, one who became aphonic after a meningitis attack, and the other after a laryngeal operation, when she could not end the voice rest imposed upon her by the laryngologist. Both these aphonic patients were highly responsive to voice therapy.

Patients with functional aphonia communicate well by gesture and whisper. Typical aphonic patients whisper with clarity and sharpness. Aphonic patients rarely avoid communication situations; conversely, they communicate effectively by using facial expressions, hands, and highly intelligible whispered speech. What they lack in communication is voice. Embarrassed and frustrated by lack of voice, aphonic patients generally self-refer to a physician or speech-language pathologist. Despite Greene's (1980) warning that many patients with functional aphonia may require psychological counseling, most aphonic patients completely recover their normal voice. Aphonic patients as a group, in fact, have an excellent prognosis. It is almost as if for whatever reason the patient has lost the "set" for phonation. The voice clinician's task is to help the patient "find" his or her voice, primarily by helping the patient use vegetative phonations, such as coughing or inhalation phonation. The patient then extends the vegetative phonation into the production of a vowel, then into single words, then phrases, and so on.

By using behavioral modification approaches, such as those suggested by Eysenck (1961), Sloane and MacAulay (1968), and Wolpe (1987), we have had excellent success in directly working on voice. Typical aphonic patients experience restoration of normal voice in very few voice therapy sessions. Wilson (1987) described the "sudden and complete recovery" of several teen-age girls who responded well to symptomatic voice therapy. Suggested methods of symptomatic voice therapy for functional aphonia will be presented in Chapter 6.

Functional Dysphonia

Some of the most disturbed voices we hear may have no organic or physical cause. Patients may approximate the vocal folds in a lax manner, producing breathiness, or in a tight manner, producing symptoms of harshness or tightness. In addition, patients may shut their voice off by bringing the ventricular folds together or by pursing off the larynx by firm, sphincteric-like closure of the aryepiglottic folds. Voice problems that do not result from an organic pathology may be called *functional dysphonia*—a term that conveys very little to the voice clinician other than the important implication that there is no structural pathology present. In fact, the common usage of the term functional dysphonia is confined to those dysphonias where the problem persists independent of any kind of pathology observed on laryngoscopy. After a history of continuing dysphonia, the typical patient is finally examined by laryngoscopy and found not to have any additive lesion, such as nodules or papilloma or granuloma (or whatever). In many cases of functional dysphonia, we can hardly visualize the vocal folds by nasoendoscopy because they are often covered by an almost complete supraglottal shutoff (ventricular and aryepiglottic fold adduction). Functional dysphonia appears to be the product of both laryngeal and supralaryngeal shutdown. In addition, patients complain of many vague disorders—throat "fullness," pain in the laryngeal area, dryness of mouth while talking, neck tightness, and so on—that are usually related to vocal fatigue.

A functionally caused dysphonia does not necessarily sound different from one that is organically caused. Some of the hoarsest voices are produced by people whose larynges demonstrate no pathology whatsoever; on the other hand, serious organic problems, such as beginning cancer, may produce no alteration of the voice. Anyone with persistent dysphonia (no longer than ten days) ought to undergo a laryngeal examination to determine the possible cause of the problem.

Aronson (1980) objects to the term "functional" dysphonia on several grounds, because he thinks that such problems are generally psychogenic in nature:

> A psychogenic voice disorder is broadly synonymous with a functional one but has the advantage of stating positively, based on an exploration of its causes, that the voice disorder is a manifestation of one or more types of psychologic disequilibrium—such as anxiety, depression, conversion reaction, or personality disorder—which interferes with normal volitional control over phonation. (p. 131)

As discussed in Chapter 1, we believe that most functional voice problems may be treated symptomatically, by working on dimensions of voice directly to improve the sounds of the voice. In most cases, however, clinicians should offer patients much psychological support, in an attempt to minimize their anxieties and concern, and should search with the patients for the best voices they can produce. The first dimension of voice to be evaluated and worked on if necessary is fundamental frequency. If a patient has no organic problem contributing to dysphonia but has a faulty pitch, the clinician should use various facilitating approaches (see Chapter 5) to develop an appropriate pitch. The vocal intensity of the voice is also measured; if the patient has a loudness problem, direct attempts to change the volume can be initiated. For the occasional patient whose voice loudness is directly related to shyness and insecurity, working on respiration and loudness per se would be less effective than attempting to improve self-concept and interpersonal relationships. The majority of voice patients with vocal intensity problems, however, are quite responsive to symptomatic therapy designed to increase their voice loudness. Clinicians help these patients change their pitch and loudness and evalute how the patients view the changes. The clinicians should observe how the patients respond to direct modification of pitch and loudness. For patients who resist such direct approaches, counseling or concurrent psychotherapy might be appropriate.

Quality of voice is often the primary problem in functional dysphonia. The vocal folds may approximate one another in a faulty manner and produce alterations in quality; words such as *hoarse, harsh, strident,* and *breathy* are applied to these quality dimensions of functional dysphonia. Harshness is often the product of overapproximation of the folds when they come sharply together, producing what is also perceived as hard glottal attack. Sometimes harshness is accompanied by inappropriate loudness, high pitch, possible tongue retraction, and contraction of the pharyngeal constrictors. Harshness often indicates a voice that requires a lot of effort and force to produce. The opposite problem may be breathiness, produced by folds that may approximate too loosely. Laxity of approximation generally produces an escape of air, perceived as breathiness. Sometimes, as Brodnitz (1971) suggests, the breathy, tired voice appears only after prolonged hyperfunctional voice use. It may emerge late in the day, after a patient has done a lot of phonating, particularly if such phonation has required a good deal of effort and force.

Functional dysphonia often becomes "the" voice of the person—the way that person talks. For such persons, voice therapy is often not successful, and in many cases should not even be initiated, particularly if the patient wants his or her voice "that way." For patients who are motivated to change the quality of their voice and who are diagnosed as having functional dysphonia, voice therapy is remarkably successful.

Phonation Breaks (Abductor Spasms)

A *phonation break* is a temporary loss of voice that may occur for only part of a word, a whole word, a phrase, or a sentence. The individual is phonating with no apparent difficulty when suddenly a complete cessation of voice occurs. Such a fleeting voice loss is usually situational and it usually happens after prolonged hyperfunction. Typical patients with this problem work hard to talk, often speaking with great effort, and suddenly experience a complete voice break. Such patients usually struggle to "find" their voice by coughing, clearing their throat, or taking a drink of water. In most cases, phonation is restored and remains adequte until the next phonation break. Other than continued vocal hyperfunction, no physical condition seems to cause these phonatory interruptions.

Voice patients who experience phonation breaks or abductor spasms rarely show them during voice evaluation sessions. In their histories, however, such patients report the occurrence of phonation breaks, often with much embarrassment when they occur. Occasionally patients have been told by their employers that they must learn to use their voices correctly (without voice breaks) or they would lose their jobs. Fortunately, the treatment of phonation breaks is relatively simple: taking the "work" out of phonation. Some of the voice therapy techniques described in Chapter 5, designed to reduce vocal hyperfunction, are most effective in eliminating the phonation break problem. Specific therapy procedures for phonation breaks or abductor spasms are discussed in Chapter 6.

Pitch Breaks

There are two kinds of *pitch breaks*. One is a developmental phenomenon seen primarily in boys experiencing marked pubertal growth of the larynx, and the other is caused by prolonged vocal hyperfunction, particularly speaking at an inappropriate pitch level.

The rapid changes in the size of the vocal folds and other laryngeal structures produce varying vocal effects during the pubertal years. Boys experience a lowering of their fundamental frequencies of about one octave; girls, a lowering of about two or three notes. This change does not happen in a day or two. For several years, as this laryngeal growth is taking place, boys will experience temporary hoarseness and occasional pitch breaks. Wise parents or voice clinicians witness these vocal changes with little comment or concern. These mass-size increases of puberty tend to thwart any serious attempts at singing or other vocal arts. Luchsinger and Arnold (1965) point out that much of the European literature on singing makes a valid plea that the formal study of singing be deferred until well after puberty. Until a male child experiences some stability of laryngeal growth, the demands of singing might be inappropriate for his rapidly changing mechanism.

The age and rate of pubertal development varies markedly. From the pediatric literature we find that the main thrust of puberty for any one child seems to take place in a total time period of about four years, six months (Marshall and Tanner, 1970); the most rapid and dramatic changes occur toward the last six months of puberty (this is when pitch breaks if they occur, may be observed in some boys).

Younger children and adults might experience a different kind of pitch break, related to the voice breaking an octave (sometimes two octaves) up or an octave down when speaking at an inappropriate pitch level. When individuals speak at an inappropriately low frequency, their voice tends to break one octave higher; if they speak too high in the frequency range their voice may break one octave down.

The tracings in Figure 3–1, recorded on a Visi-Pitch, show the inappropriately low fundamental frequency tracings of a 39-year-old minister, suddenly breaking into abrupt upward shifts. His lower F_o value was 100 cycles and his higher (the pitch break F_o) was 300 cycles. We discuss pitch breaks

FIGURE 3–1.
A Visi-Pitch tracing of the voicing pitch breaks of a 39-year-old minister. The lower tracing is a prolonged /a/ at about 100 Hz, breaking abruptly to the high tracing at 300 Hz. The pitch breaks occur when he sustains phonation at the lowest voice he can produce.

further in the next chapter when we discuss finding a pitch level appropriate for the mass-size of the individual's vocal folds, which can help avoid or eliminate sudden, unwanted shifts in vocal frequency.

Pitch breaks can also result from overall vocal fatigue. Heavy users of voice, such as actors after prolonged rehearsals, may begin to experience pitch breaks after hours of prolonged voicing. Such continued vocal hyperfunction, speaking with too much effort, will sometimes result in either pitch or phonation breaks. Such pitch breaks are usually warnings that the vocal mechanisms are being overworked. With a little temporary voice rest and easy phonation, fatigue-induced pitch breaks usually disappear.

Spastic Dysphonia

Probably the most extreme form of a hyperfunctional voice disorder is *spastic dysphonia.* Patients' voices sound strained, choked off with the attempts to voice, as if they are trying to push the outgoing air stream through a tightly adducted laryngeal opening. Endoscopic examination (Davis, Boone, Carroll, Darveniza, and Harrison, 1987) shows that the tight voice is indeed produced by hyperadduction (severe approximation) of the true folds, often accompanied by tight closure of the false vocal folds (ventricular folds) with supraglottic constriction of the aryepiglottic folds and contraction of the lower pharyngeal constrictors. The total laryngeal and lower pharyngeal airway appears to close down. No wonder we hear a strangle-like voice in such patients.

In addition to the problem of voicing, patients with spastic dysphonia complain about the difficulties they experience trying to force expiratory air out whenever they desire to phonate. Aronson (1985) comments that the tight voice during adductor spastic dysphonia "occurs only during voluntary phonation for communication purposes and not during singing, vowel prolongation, laughing, or crying" (p. 157). The patients soon learn to expect phonation difficulties whenever they attempt to speak. In this sense, spastic dysphonia resembles stuttering. In European writings, in fact, the condition is sometimes called the "laryngeal stutter." However, most patients with spastic dysphonia experience some normal voice in certain situations. Case histories of these patients reveal that such situations as "talking to my cat" or "speaking to others in a pool while I tread water" are times when patients have experienced normal voice.

The most common type of spastic dysphonia appears to be related to tight laryngeal adduction (known as adductor spastic dysphonia). Aronson (1985), however, also describes a second form of the disorder, known as abductor spastic dysphonia. Patients with this disorder exhibit normal or dysphonic voices that are suddenly interrupted by temporary abduction of the vocal folds, resulting in fleeting aphonia. After such momentary aphonia, the patients' voice patterns are restored again (until the next aphonic break). Endoscopy shows that the vocal folds of such patients abduct suddenly, "exposing an extremely wide glottic chink" (Aronson, 1985, p. 187). More often than not, the abductor spasms appear to be triggered by unvoiced consonant sounds. The abductor-type disorder is a much rarer form of spastic dysphonia. For example, Davis et al. (1987) reported that of twenty-five successive cases of spastic dysphonia observed in a Sydney, Australia, hospital, twenty-four were adductor-type and one was an abductor-type. The abductor spasm can often be treated successfully as a phonation break.

The cause of the disorder is still unknown. In fact, the generic name *spastic dysphonia* includes disorders with several different causes or etiologies. In two recent studies (Aminoff, Dedo, and Izdebski, 1978; Davis et al., 1987) spastic dysphonic patients have been examined by voice scientists, speech-language pathologists, neurologists, otolaryngologists, and psychiatrists. Both studies found some patients with no sign of neurological disease and others with some symptoms of neurological disease (with or without essential tremor). Both studies found no evidence of laryngeal pathology or psychiatric involvement in any of the patients studied that could justify the severity of the voice problems. In the Australian study (Davis et al., 1987), spastic dysphonic patients exhibited significantly decreased air-flow rates when speaking, as compared to a normal control group. The decreased air flow would seem to be directly related to laryngeal-pharyngeal constriction (which was also observed on endoscopy). What is the cause of such airway constriction? Although the cause of spastic dysphonia is still unknown, more patients than not do seem to exhibit neurologically based problems. Case (1984) agrees with this view. He writes: "Few professionals today consider spastic dysphonia a psychogenic voice disorder. Rather, it is classified more as having a neurogenic etiology with possible psychogenic byproducts" (p. 180).

Despite the possible neurogenic cause of the disorder, drug therapy has not been an effective method of treatment. Speech-language pathologists tend to treat the disorder behaviorally and also psychologically. In general, however, voice therapy has not been reported in the literature as a particularly successful treatment for spastic dysphonia. Voice therapy attempts for spastic dysphonia are described further in Chapters 5 and 6 in this text. A surgical approach (described in Chapter 6), cutting the recurrent laryngeal nerve on one side, creating a unilateral vocal fold paralysis, has been reported as helpful (Dedo and Izdebski, 1983a). These authors report beneficial long-term results on 306 patients, as determined by voice analysis and patient self-reports.

Thickening (Vocal Fold)

Various inflammatory conditions of the larynx, such as infectious and traumatic laryngitis, may produce irritation and swelling (*edema*) of the vocal folds. Another form of enlargement along the glottal margin of the vocal folds is known as *vocal fold thickening*. Whereas vocal nodules and polyps are more focal lesions (occupying less space) on the vocal folds, thickening is a broader-based lesion that often covers the anterior two-thirds of the glottal margin or the membrane covering the muscular portion of the vocal fold. There are basically two types of thickening. One represents early tissue reaction to vocal fold trauma, often a precursor to vocal nodules or polyps; the second is the result of prolonged irritation that often results in extensive polypoid degeneration and more advanced changes of the vocal folds. Let us consider each of these thickening changes separately.

In most cases, vocal fold thickening results from continuous vocal abuse. Continuous use of loud voice, screaming and yelling, in time may result in some tissue changes along the glottal margin. We have only to observe vocal fold vibration on videoendoscopy to appreciate the vigorous adduction of the folds and participation of supraglottal structures (ventricular and aryepiglottic folds) that accompany coughing, yelling, or screaming at higher pitches. As a volunteer subject with videoendoscopy, one of the authors witnessed bilateral tissue changes on the glottal margin (beginning of redness) of his own folds after only five minutes of continuous staccato yelling of the word "peach." Such yelling is a benign vocal experience compared to the continuous screaming of some young children at play.

The cause of early vocal fold thickening thus seems to be the same as the cause of vocal nodules, primarily vocal abuse and misuse. However, other reported causes of thickening and vocal nodules have been summarized by Andrews (1986):

1. Constitutional tendency
2. Chronic upper respiratory problems
3. Psychological living environment—for example, size of family
4. Physical living environment—for example, air pollution
5. Personality and adjustment
6. Endocrine imbalance, especially thyroid
7. Vocal abuse, sudden straining of the voice; continuous use of abusive practices
8. Vocal misuse: incorrect pitch and loudness (p. 107)

Certain children and adults are very sensitive to vocally irritating events. For example, some people can use vocal folds excessively and never develop any tissue changes that result in vocal symptoms. Others, with the slightest allergy, cold, or vocal abuse-misuse, develop aversive glottal margin problems. The emotional and physical environment undoubtedly negatively affects many people. In the case of children or adults with vocal fold thickening, such environmental influences cannot be allowed to continue without some attempt at modification. The overwhelming cause of vocal fold thickening, however, is vocal abuse and misuse. Until such vocal excesses are identified and reduced in frequency (they can rarely be totally eliminated), vocal thickening, nodules, and polyps cannot be successfully treated.

Vocal fold thickening can usually be reduced by a voice therapy program that promotes easy and proper use of the vocal mechanisms, with heavy emphasis on curbing vocal abuse-misuse. This example of a 6-year-old with vocal fold thickening is, unfortunately, typical:

Edith was referred for a voice evaluation because of chronic hoarseness. Indirect laryngoscopy found that she had bilateral cord thickening with no demonstrable history of allergy or infection. Her parents were counseled to do what they could to help Edith eliminate unnecessary crying and yelling, and Edith was sent home. On a subsequent visit to the laryngologist, no change in cords was observed by laryngoscopy. It was thus decided to "strip" the thickenings surgically. This was done with excellent results. Three weeks after surgery the child demonstrated clear cords bilaterally, free of thickening. After a postoperative period of approximately three months, the family returned to the laryngologist, complaining of the child's recurring hoarseness. Laryngoscopy found that Edith once again had bilateral cord thickening, with the early formation of a vocal nodule on one fold. It was then decided to begin voice therapy. Special efforts were made to identify particular vocal abuses by the child, and a school playground situation was isolated as the cause of continuous vocal strain. Eliminating this and other adverse vocal behavior gradually eliminated the vocal nodule and nearly eliminated the bilateral thickening, as well.

The preceding case illustrates that surgical treatment of cord thickening, without removing the abusive cause of the problem, will not always be a permanent solution to the vocal problem. Reducing the source of the irritation (such as eliminating an allergy, reducing smoking, or curbing vocal abuse) is probably the best management of the problem.

A second form of vocal fold thickening is often more diffuse, because it frequently indicates a more advanced tissue reaction to prolonged laryngeal abuse and misuse. The vocal fold swelling is broader than the anterior-middle third site that is the typical location of nodules or polyps. Rather, the swelling may extend along the glottis from the anterior commissure to the beginning of the vocal process of the arytenoid cartilages. Much swelling, known as *polypoid degeneration,* is characteristic. If, in addition to vocal abuse-misuse, the patient is a heavy smoker or alcohol consumer, the increased mass of the folds can seriously compromise all attempts at vocalization. The primary treatment of extensive polypoid degeneration may be medical-surgical, supplemented by voice therapy. Trial voice therapy at first is warranted. The primary thrust of voice therapy is to identify possible laryngeal abuses (such as throat clearing) and voice abuses (such as speaking with excessive glottal attack), and then to provide the patient with methods for reducing these aversive behaviors. Many of the voice therapy facilitating approaches presented in Chapter 5 have been effective in reducing overall vocal fold thickening.

Traumatic Laryngitis

In *functional laryngitis* or *traumatic laryngitis,* patients experience swelling of the vocal folds as a result of excessive and strained vocalization. The voice sounds hoarse, lacking in volume. Typical functional laryngitis may be heard in the voices of excited spectators after a football or basketball game. In the excitement of the game, with their own voices masked by the noise of the crowd, the fans scream at pitch levels and intensities they normally do not use. The inner glottal edges of the membrane become swollen (edematous) and thickened, an expected consequence of excessive approximation. The increased edema of the folds is accompanied by irritation and increased blood accumulation. The acute stage of functional laryngitis is at its peak during the actual yelling or traumatic vocal behavior, with the vocal folds much increased in size and mass. Brodnitz (1971) wrote that functionally irritated vocal folds appear on laryngoscopic examination to be much like the thickened, reddened folds of acute infectious laryngitis. There is an important difference in treatment, however. For functional or *nonspecific laryngitis*—which is usually the result of continued irritation by such causes as allergy, excessive smoking and alcohol drinking, and vocal abuse—the obvious treatment is to eliminate the vocal irritant whenever possible. In the case of functional laryngitis secondary to yelling or a similar form of vocal abuse, eliminating the abuse usually permits the vocal mechanism to return to its natural state. The temporary laryngitis experienced toward the end of a basketball game is usually relieved by a return to normal vocal activity and most of the edema and irritation vanish after a night's sleep.

Chronic laryngitis may typically produce more serious vocal problems if the speaker attempts to "speak above" the laryngitis. The temporary edema of the vocal folds alters the quality and loudness of the phonation; the speaker increases vocal efforts; this increase in effort only increases the irritation of the folds, thereby compounding the problem; and finally, if such hyperfunctional behavior continues over time, what was once a temporary edema may become a more permanent polypoid thickening, which sometimes develops into vocal polyps or nodules. For this reason, functional laryngitis should be promptly treated by eliminating the causative abuse and, if possible, by enforcing a short period of complete voice rest.

Voice rest in itself is not a "cure" for most voice disorders. This is not true, however, for traumatic laryngitis. Voice rest, which means no phonation or whispering for several days, is usually enough for irritated vocal fold margins to lose their swelling and return to their normal shape. It is important that voice rest designed to promote healing of irritated vocal fold surfaces *not* include whispering; whispering (as most people do it) still causes too much vocal fold movement, and irritation from the rubbing together of the approximating surfaces of each fold is still possible. Recent studies have shown that during whisper the ventricular folds often may be brought into function (Pearl and McCall, 1986).

The events that cause traumatic laryngitis must be identified and curbed. If such hyperfunctional vocal behavior continues over time, such changes as polypoid thickening, vocal nodules, or vocal polyps may occur.

Ventricular Dysphonia

Ventricular dysphonia, sometimes known as *dysphonia plicae ventricularis or false fold phonation,* occurs more often than previously indicated (Boone, 1983). Ventricular dysphonia is produced by the vibration of the approximating ventricular folds. Sometimes the ventricular voice becomes the substitute voice of patients who have severe disease of the true folds (such as severe papilloma or large polyps). The ventricular voice is usually low pitched because of the large mass of vibrating tissue of the ventricular bands (as compared to the smaller mass of vibrating tissue of the true folds). In addition, the voice has little pitch variability and is therefore monotonous. Finally, because the ventricular bands have difficulty in making a good, firm approximation for their entire length, the voice is usually somewhat hoarse. This combination of low pitch, monotony, and hoarseness makes most ventricular voices sound unpleasant. If no persistent true cord pathology continues to force patients to use their ventricular voices, this disorder usually responds well to voice therapy. Sometimes, however, *hypertrophy* (enlargement) of the ventricular bands is present; this makes their normal full retraction somewhat difficult.

Ventricular phonation is difficult to diagnose by the sound of the voice alone. Laryngoscopic examination during phonation shows the ventricular folds coming together, covering from view the true cords that lie below. Some ventricular dysphonias display a special form of *diplophonia* (double voice), whereby the true folds and ventricular bands phonate simultaneously. Identification and confirmation of what vibrating structures the patient is using for phonation can best be made by frontal tomographic X-ray (coronal) of the sites of vibration. Ventricular phonation can also be diagnosed by nasoendoscopy and endoscopic stroboscopy (McFarlane and Lavorato, 1984). In ventricular phonation, the true vocal folds will be slightly abducted, with the ventricular bands above in relative approximation. In normal phonation, the opposite relationship between the true folds and the ventricular bands occurs—that is, the true folds are adducted and the ventricular bands are positioned laterally from the midline position. Once ventricular phonation is confirmed by laryngoscopy or X-ray, any physical problem of the true cords that might make normal phonation impossible should be eliminated. An occasional patient with much true fold pathology or absent true folds will need to be taught ventricular phonation (usually an impossible task). We consider both the elimination of ventricular phonation and its occasional need to be taught when we review voice therapy for special problems in Chapter 6.

Vocal Nodules

Vocal nodules are the most common benign lesions of the vocal folds in both children and adults. They are caused by continuous abuse of the larynx and misuse of the voice. These causative abusives are well described by Case (1984), who places "yelling and screaming, making a hard glottal attack, singing in an abusive manner, speaking in a noisy environment, coughing and excessive throat clearing" at the top of the list of twenty-four vocal abuses-misuses (pp. 104–105). Nodules, as shown in Figure 3–2, are generally bilateral, whitish protuberances on the glottal margin of each vocal fold, located at the anterior-middle third junction. This nodule site is the midpoint of the muscular vocal fold, involving the membrane that covers the vocal ligament and vocalis inner border of the vocal fold. In the early stages of nodule development, the nodular mass is soft and pliable. With continuous abuse-misuse, the lesion becomes more fibrotic and slightly larger.

As the bilateral nodules approximate one another on phonation, there is usually an open glottal chink on each side of the nodule. This open glottal chink of each fold (produced by the nodules coming together in exact opposition of one another) results in a lack of complete vocal fold adduction. This faulty approximation leads to breathiness in the voice. Also, the increased mass of the nodules added to the vocal folds contributes to a

FIGURE 3-2.
Bilateral nodules on the vocal folds of a 23-year-old woman. Note that the vocal fold nodule on the viewer's left is twice as large as the nodule on the opposite fold.

lower voice pitch and increased aperiodicity (usually judged as hoarseness). This leads to a breathy, flat kind of voice that often seems to lack appropriate resonance. Patients complain that they need to clear their throat continually and often that they have excessive mucus or "something" on the vocal folds. Excessive throat clearing often becomes an identified vocal abuse, which may lead to further enlargement of the nodules. Typical patients with vocal nodules complain that their voices seem to deteriorate with continuous voicing; they may start the day with good voices that become increasingly dysphonic with continuous vocal usage. With prolonged speaking and singing, perhaps coupled with vocal abuse and misuse, phonation rapidly deteriorates.

Small nodules and recently acquired ones can be successfully treated with voice therapy. Yamaguchi et al. (1986), reporting on voice therapy success with twenty adult females with vocal nodules, found that vocal nodules "either disappeared or were reduced in size" after three to four months of voice therapy in 65 percent of the cases. Boone (1982) developed a four-point program for adults with vocal nodules that focuses on: identifying abuse-misuse; reducing the occurrence of such abuse-misuse; searching with the patient for various voice therapy facilitating approaches that seem to produce an easy, optimal vocal production; and using the facilitating approach that works best as a practice method.

Although we strongly recommend voice therapy as the primary treatment for nodules, we also acknowledge that larger nodules and long-established ones may be treated by surgery, followed by a brief period of complete voice rest and then voice therapy. It is not unusual clinically for new nodules to appear several weeks after surgical removal of nodules in both children and adults. Unless the underlying hyperfunctional vocal behaviors are identified and reduced, vocal nodules have a stubborn way of reappearing.

Vocal nodules in children before puberty are more common in boys, who are generally aggressive and noisy, busy controlling people with their voices. As boys get older, there is less evidence of nodules, and adolescent females show a higher prevalence of additive lesions related to vocal abuse (Toohill, 1975). The prevalence is also higher in those adult females who, according to Aronson (1985), are "talkative, socially aggressive, and tense, and have acute or chronic interpersonal problems that generate tension, anxiety, anger, or depression" (p. 136). Nodules result from vocal hyperfunction and are therefore often observed in people who in general exhibit "hyperfunctional" personalities. Although symptomatic voice therapy has been effective in reducing or eliminating vocal nodules, patients with vocal nodules often require strong psychological support by the voice clinician, and sometimes psychological counseling and therapy, as well.

Vocal Polyps

Vocal polyps, more often unilateral than bilateral, occur on the same anterior-middle third site on the vocal fold(s) as nodules (See Figure 3–3). Polyps and nodules are both related to vocal hyperfunction, and both have some physical similarities. Stone (1982) labels a polyp as a "morbid excrescence, or protruding growth, from mucous membrane" (p. 94). The lesion is usually soft, often fluid-filled, and occurs in the inner margin of one vocal fold; because of its softness, it does not irritate the membraneous tissue on the opposite fold (as opposed to the bilateral pathology usually observed in vocal nodules). Unlike vocal nodules, which result from continuous vocal fold irritation, polyps are often precipitated by a single vocal event. For example, a patient may have indulged in excessive vocalization, such as screaming for much of an evening, which produced some hemorrhaging on the membrane at the point of maximum glottal contact. A polyp forms out of such hemorrhagic irritation by eventually adding mass that becomes fluid filled. Once a small polyp begins, any continued vocal abuse, or misuse will irritate the area, contributing to its continued growth. A typical polyp lies on the glottal margin, interfering with the approximation of the normal fold.

Polyps, which may be broad-based (sessile-type) or narrow-necked (pedunculated), usually occur in the larynx on the inner margin of the affected fold. An excellent description of polyps, their formation, and their treatment was developed by Kleinsasser (1979), who described the lesions as "gelatinous" and responsive to surgery. Laser surgery has become the surgical treatment of choice for vocal fold polyps (Yates and Dedo, 1984). Unless the causative behaviors are identified and prevented from further

FIGURE 3–3.
A soft, unilateral polyp on the right vocal fold of a 34-year-old woman.

occurrence, however, polyps often recur after surgery. With voice therapy and attempts to use the laryngeal mechanisms more optimally, polyps can be permanently eliminated.

The voices of patients with unilateral polyps are characterized by severe dysphonia. The normal vocal fold vibrates at one frequency while the additive lesion seriously dampens the vibration of the involved fold, resulting in what is perceived as hoarseness and breathiness, often requiring (or so the patient thinks) continuous throat clearing. Voice therapy requires identifying and reducing vocal abuse-misuse and searching with the patient for the best voice that can be produced using various voice-facilitating approaches (see Chapter 5). Voice therapy was successful in eliminating a unilateral polyp from this woman:

Jane was a 29-year-old teacher who was active in competitive sports. She admitted to doing a lot of yelling during her softball season, when she ended up with a hoarse voice that would not go away. Her teaching schedule required her to give six hours of lectures each day, supervise a study hall, and assist in girls' field hockey events. Finally, by noon each day she had no voice. Subsequent laryngoscopy found her to have a broad-based polyp (about 5 mm in width) on one fold. Voice therapy was initiated that focused on reducing loudness, developing a soft glottal attack, and opening her mouth more as she spoke. An immediate consequence of the therapy was that when she spoke easily, without effort, her voice at first sounded "more hoarse." She kidded her students and colleagues that she would sound worse in the beginning as she learned to use her voice with less effort. In about twelve weeks, the unilateral polyp completely disappeared, and Jane's voice became normal. She then made continuing efforts to avoid any kind of vocal abuse and misuse and has maintained a trouble-free larynx and normal voice.

VOICE DISORDERS RELATED TO ORGANIC CHANGES OF VOCAL MECHANISMS

In Table 3-1, fourteen organic disorders of vocal mechanisms that might cause voice problems were listed. In these disorders, the faulty voice is usually related more to a physical condition than to a vocal abuse-misuse per se. We now present each disorder in alphabetical order, first considering the etiology of the disorder, and then following with a brief discussion of its overall management.

Cancer

Cancer or *carcinoma* in the vocal tract is a life-threatening disease that requires serious medical-surgical management. Lip and intraoral cancers rarely contribute to changes in voice, but they may have obvious negative effects on articulation. Extensive oral lesions involving the tongue, perhaps even requiring partial or total surgical removal of the tongue (*glossectomy*), seriously affect articulation and vocal resonance.

15000/yr.
new oral
CA cases.

The American Cancer Society (1980) reported that in the United States about 15,000 new patients annually develop some form of oral cancer. Some of the identified causes of oral cancer include smoking (particularly pipe smoking), chronic infections, herpes, repeated trauma to the irritated site, and leukoplakia (whitish plaque). Often patients first experience chronic lesions in the mouth or on the tongue that do not seem to heal. Usually continuous pain near the lesion site brings the patient to the physician. The majority of these oral lesions are treated successfully with microsurgery (removal of small lesions) and radiation therapy. The primary goal of surgery-radiation therapy is to eradicate the primary lesion so that it does not spread (*metastasize*) to another adjacent or remote body site.

Sometimes carcinoma is detected in the nasal sinuses and at sites within the pharynx, although such lesions are relatively rare. The most serious vocal tract malignancies, however, are those that involve the larynx, which, by their position in the airway, present a serious potential threat to airway adequacy. According to Case (1984), "laryngeal cancer comprises 2 to 5 percent of all malignancies diagnosed annually in the United States" (p. 241).

In general, there are three classifications of laryngeal cancers, depending on the site of the lesion: supraglottal, involving such structures as the ventricular and aryepiglottic folds, the epiglottis, the arytenoid cartilages, and the walls of the hypopharynx; glottal, from the anterior commissure to the vocal process ends of the arytenoids; and subglottal, involving the cricoid cartilage and trachea. The treatment combines radiation therapy and surgery for small to moderate lesions; extensive cancer requires perhaps a hemilaryngectomy or total laryngectomy. We discuss both of these later in this chapter, and we consider laryngeal cancer, rehabilitation after laryngectomy, and the role of the speech-language pathologist in some detail in Chapter 8.

Dysarthria

Many voice disorders are symptoms of some kind of neurological disease or dysfunction. *Dysarthria* is a motor speech problem that is the result of damage somewhere to the central or peripheral nervous systems. "Dysarthria is the generic name for different motor speech problems that may be caused by a number of nervous-system diseases" (Boone, 1987, p. 145.) Lesions to the recurrent or superior laryngeal nerves involve the peripheral nervous system (they usually cut or traumatize the innervating nerve to the larynx), and they may result in unilateral or bilateral vocal fold paralysis. (We discuss vocal fold paralysis separately later in this chapter.) The vocal problems that are symptoms of a dysarthria are usually related to lesions of the central nervous sytem, which might be related to such disorders as cerebral palsy, Parkinson's disease, amyotrophic lateral sclerosis, multiple sclerosis, or multiple strokes.

Previous research (Darley, Aronson, and Brown, 1969) has identified dysarthric symptoms and their associated dysphonias that are related to specific diseases and damage to particular sites of the nervous system. In general, severity of dysarthria is related to the site of the lesion. The lower the lesion in the brain, the greater the severity of the dysarthria; also, bilateral lesions within the hemispheres are more likely to produce dysarthric symptoms than unilateral lesions. Vocal problems may include inability to control respiration, which causes severe problems in vocal prosody and voice loudness. Changes in vocal fold characteristics may lead to changes in pitch, lack of pitch control, and faulty voice quality related to lack of normal vocal fold approximation and supraglottal interference. Resonance defects, such as hypernasality, are often part of the voice symptoms of dysarthria and are frequently related to faulty velar-pharyngeal closure.

Today dysarthria is treated primarily by various medications (such as L-dopa for the patient with Parkinson's disease) and sometimes by surgery (such as relief of spasticity by cutting appropriate muscles in a spastic extremity). We discuss management by the speech-language pathologist of dysarthria as it affects phonation and resonance in Chapters 6 and 7.

Endocrine Changes

Occasionally patients are seen whose voice problems are related to some kind of endocrine dysfunction. Endocrine disorders often have a major impact on developing larynges and cause excesses in fundamental frequency, so that an individual's voice is either too low or too high in pitch. For example, in hypofunction of the pituitary gland, laryngeal growth is retarded. A pubescent child with such a problem will experience a continued high voice pitch. Such a pituitary problem can prevent normal development of progesterone by the ovaries (in girls) and testosterone by the testes (in adolescent males). The resulting lack of secondary sexual characteristics (including a change in voice) is treated by endocrine therapy designed to stimulate normal pituitary function. The opposite problem, caused by some tumors of the pituitary gland, results in a "precocious puberty as well as acromegaly" (Strome, 1982, p. 18). Hypofunctioning of the adrenal glands (Addison's disease) can also contribute to lack of secondary sex characteristics, including a prepubescent voice in males. Sometimes tumors in the adrenal system cause adrenal hormone excesses, causing virilization and a deepening of the voice.

Hypothyroidism, insufficient secretion of thyroxin by the thyroid gland, can produce many physical changes over time, including enlargement of the vocal folds, which, in turn, lowers pitch. Aronson (1985) describes the dysphonia of hypothyroidism as "characteristically *hoarse*, sometimes described as *coarse* or *gravelly*, and of *excessively low pitch*" (p. 65). Such symptoms can usually be well controlled by thyroid hormone therapy. In hyperthyroidism (excessive thyroid), vocal symptoms are less severe, and the patients experience jumpiness and irritability, which result in a breathy voice that may lack sufficient loudness.

Greene (1980) describes the influence of menstruation on the female voice, particularly at premenstruation when estrogen and progesterone levels are at their lowest, resulting in a slight thickening of the vocal folds, which can cause a lowering of pitch and some hoarseness (Frable, 1972). Some female opera singers avoid heavy singing obligations several days before and after menstruation. The climacteric (menopause) is another time when some women may experience vocal changes, particularly a lowering of fundamental frequency. Because of the secretion of excessive androgenic hormones after the menopause, the glottal membrane becomes thicker, increasing the size-mass of the folds, and producing a lowering of voice pitch (Gould, 1975).

It would appear that in any case in which the larynx is under- or overdeveloped for the age and sex of the patient, some endocrine imbalance might be suspected. If some kind of hormonal imbalance is discovered, the primary treatment, if possible, would be hormonal therapy. Voice therapy can be of help to the patient in developing the best vocal performance possible with the changing (because of hormone therapy) mechanism.

Granuloma

There are three kinds of *granulomas*, one resulting from intubation during surgery, another resulting from glottal trauma from abuse-misuse, and a third resulting from gastric reflux. Each of these etiologies suggests a different treatment.

Any patient who is intubated during surgery or for airway preservation risks having a traumatized laryngeal membrane with the subsequent development of granuloma. The risk is particularly greater in children and women, who have smaller airways and are thus more often traumatized by large tubes (Whited, 1979). The physician places a tube down the pharynx into the airway, between the open (it is hoped) vocal folds, and on into the trachea. If the tube is larger than the glottal opening, the patient runs the risk of trauma. Ellis and Bennett (1977) have recommended that in order to prevent intubation granuloma or hemangioma, patients should be intubated with tubes one size smaller than what would be needed "for a snug fit." Some patients, for example, demonstrate sudden changes in voice after general surgery. If the patient who was intubated shows a persistent hoarseness after surgery, indirect laryngoscopy or endoscopy should be performed to confirm or deny the possible presence of an intubation granuloma. If present, such a granuloma may need to be removed surgically. Another form of granuloma may result from vocal fold trauma related to continuous irritation (such as acid reflux) or sudden accident (such as an external injury to the larynx.) Other than intubation granuloma, the most common form is associated with contact ulcers. The literature suggests, in fact, that contact ulcer and related vocal fold granuloma are probably the same disorder, related to continuous trauma.

Patients with granuloma may experience severe dysphonia, characterized by hoarseness, breathiness, and the need to clear the throat frequently. Voice therapy has no primary role in eradication of granulomas. After surgical removal of the offending lesion, voice therapy is usually needed to help the patient regain a normal voice.

Hemangioma

Hemangiomas are very similar to granulomas, differing only in type of lesion. Whereas a granuloma is usually a firm granulated sac, a hemangioma is a soft, pliable, blood-filled sac. Like granulomas, hemangiomas often occur on the posterior glottis, frequently associated with vocal hyperfunction, hyperacidity, or intubation. This blood-filled lesion, when identified, should be removed surgically, As soon as glottal healing permits, a vocal hygiene program and some voice therapy should be initiated.

Hyperkeratosis

Patients often come to their dentist or otolaryngologist because they are concerned about some oral or pharyngeal lesions they have observed. Once professionally identified, these lesions are often biopsied and found to be either malignant (cancerous) or nonmalignant (benign). Laryngeal examination may also locate and subsequently identify, by biopsy, additive lesions in the pharynx or larynx. *Hyperkeratosis,* a pinkish, rough lesion, is often the identified lesion, a non-malignant growth that may be the precursor of malignant tissue change. Hyperkeratotic growths are reactive lesions to continued tissue irritation. Therefore, hyperkeratotic lesions must be watched closely over time for any change in appearance. Favorite sites of hyperkeratosis include under the tongue, on the vocal folds at the anterior commissure, and posteriorly on the arytenoid prominences. Their effect on voice may be negligible or severe, depending on the site and the extent of the lesion.

It is generally believed that chronic irritation of oral and laryngeal membranes over time—for example, as the result of excessive and continued smoking—is the primary etiology of hyperkeratosis. Consequently, the most effective treatment of the problem is eliminating the source of tissue irritation.

Infectious Laryngitis

Some of the same people who experience traumatic laryngitis after only minor abuse-misuse of the voice also experience *infectious laryngitis* when they have a cold. The case histories of such people often contain multiple entries of "loss of voice" or laryngitis. In other individuals, infectious laryngitis is a very rare event that occurs as one of the symptoms of a severe head and chest cold. Infectious laryngitis often develops in a patient who has had a fever, headache, running nose, sore throat, and coughing. Although most problems of infectious laryngitis are viral in origin, the more severe problems (often accompanied by high fever and a very sore throat) may be bacterial infections. Bacterial-caused laryngitis can often be dramatically treated, with relatively quick resolution, through antibiotic therapy. Unfortunately, most laryngitis experienced during a cold (viral in origin) does not respond to antibiotics. The standard treatment is "voice rest, humidification, reduced physical activity, and analgesics" (Strome, 1982, p. 12).

From a voice conservation point of view, absolute voice rest—no attempts at spoken communication, including voice or whisper—should be initiated by the patient with such a laryngeal infection. Whispering should be discouraged, because most people produce a glottal whisper by placing the vocal folds in close approximation to one another, which, in effect, produces a light voice. The irritated, swollen tissues continue to touch and to vibrate. What laryngitis patients need is total voice rest with the vocal folds in the open, inverted-V position.

Laryngectomy

One of the primary functions of the human larynx is to prevent aspiration into the airway. The larynx contains three valve sites (the true folds, the ventricular folds, and the aryepiglottic folds), each of whose valving action allows them to shut off the airway to prevent the inhalation of liquids, foods, saliva, mucus, and any other stray foreign bodies that may be headed through the larynx into the airway. When the larynx is so compromised by disease (such as advanced cancer) or trauma that it cannot safely perform its valving role, the patient becomes a candidate for a *laryngectomy*, the total removal of the larynx. Without the larynx to protect the airway, an opening is created in the trachea (a *tracheostomy*) through which the patient breathes all pulmonary air in and out. The patient must develop a substitute voicing source, such as an artificial larynx or esophageal speech. Recent modifications of the laryngectomy procedure (Singer and Blom, 1980) permit pulmonary air to flow from the trachea through a prosthetic shunt into the esophagus, facilitating the production of esophageal "voice" without extensive special training. We describe the use of and training for other artificial voicing sources in Chapter 8.

The most common reason to perform a laryngectomy is laryngeal cancer. Small, early-detected cancers of the larynx, known as stage I and II cancers, may be treated successfully by radiation therapy and minor surgery (Batsakis, 1979). Larger stage III cancers of the larynx can also be successfully treated by radiation therapy and surgery, and require only the removal of involved structures. In more advanced cancers of the larynx (stages IV and V), the most common treatment is total laryngectomy, preceded and followed by radiation therapy.

Except in cases of traumatic injury to the larynx requiring an emergency laryngectomy, most laryngectomy operations are scheduled only after some counseling has been completed by the surgeon, the speech-language pathologist, and a laryngectomee (a patient who has had the operation). We describe pre- and postoperative counseling, evaluation, and training of the patient with a total laryngectomy in some detail in Chapter 8.

Laryngofissure

With the development of many innovative laryngeal surgeries for type I, II, and III cancerous lesions, the *laryngofissure* surgical approach has become more common. The laryngofissure is used primarily in exploratory procedures in which the surgeon is investigating the extent of malignancy that may be present. An incision of the thyroid cartilage is made vertically, down from the thyroid notch. The split thyroid cartilage is then extended back on each side, permitting good visibility (particularly of subglottal structures) and easy surgical access. Various surgical procedures are then possible through this large anterior opening of the thyroid cartilage (Tucker, Wood, Levine, and Katz, 1979). If extensive carcinoma is found unilaterally (with normal tissue available to still permit laryngeal valving functions), the

Best possible voices c̄ residual structures

patient may then receive a *hemilaryngectomy* (removal of one-half of the larynx). The involved side of the larynx is removed laterally from the midsite where the initial laryngofissure was performed. Structural recovery from a laryngofissure procedure takes about six to eight weeks (Coulthard, 1987).

Patients who receive various surgically reconstructed larynges generally profit from a voice therapy approach that searches with the patient for the best voice possible with those residual structures that are still functional.

Leukoplakia

Leukoplakia are whitish patches that are additive lesions to the surface membrane of mucosal tissue and that often extend beneath the surface into subepithelial space. Athough the lesions are classified as benign tumors, similar to hyperkeratosis, they are considered to be precancerous lesions and must be watched closely. Within the vocal tract, common sites for leukoplakia are under the tongue and on the vocal folds. The primary etiology of these white patches is continuous irritation of membranes. The most common cause is heavy smoking; a heroic effort must be initiated to prevent continued irritation, such as absolute insistence that the patient quit smoking. Continued irritation and subsequent growth of leukoplakia often leads to squamous cell carcinoma.

Although leukoplakia on or under the tongue have only minimal effects on voice, leukoplakia on the vocal folds may dramatically alter voice. The added lesion mass to the vocal folds lowers voice pitch. Because leukoplakia are also random in size and location, they often cause the vocal folds to be asymmetrical, which may result in diplophonia as each fold vibrates at a different rate because of its different size. Leukoplakia that occupy space on the glottal margin may prevent optimal approximation of the folds, contributing to a breathiness and overall dysphonia. The treatment of leukoplakia is medical-surgical, and voice therapy only contributes to developing the best voice possible. In spite of lesion effects, often a functional aspect of the dysphonia can be lessened with therapy.

Papilloma

Papilloma are wart-like growths, viral in origin, that occur in the dark, moist caverns of the airway, frequently in the larynges of young children. They can represent a serious threat to the airway, limiting the needed flow of air through the glottal opening. The majority of papilloma occur in children under the age of 6; for this reason, hoarseness and shortness of breath in preschool children should be evaluated promptly. Although the majority of papilloma stop recurring about the time of puberty, Kleinsasser (1979) wrote that 20 percent persist beyond puberty. Papilloma of the airway in adolescents and young adults must be considered a serious laryngeal disease, primarily because of its recurrence and persistent threat to the airway.

When papilloma occur in the larynx, their additive mass often contributes to dysphonia. For this reason, the voice clinician should be particularly alert to any child who demonstrates dysphonia. Any child with continued hoarseness for more than ten days, independent of a cold or allergy, should have the benefit of indirect laryngoscopy to identify the cause of the hoarseness. If papilloma are identified, the treatment is medical-surgical; treatment includes laser-beam surgery, conventional excision surgery, radiation therapy, and interferon therapy (Lundquist et al. 1984). The papilloma should only be removed when they impinge on the airway. Eventually, when the individual has developed the immunological state needed to resist the viral-inspired papilloma, the papilloma will no longer recur (Kleinsasser, 1979).

The surgical and radiation therapy approach to papilloma is required whenever the papilloma growths begin to interfere with the airway. If the lesion mass does not interfere with respiration or voicing, it is usually tolerated. According to Wetmore, Key, and Suen (1985), there may be complications from continued surgical procedures for papilloma. These authors followed forty patients (twenty-six children; fourteen adults) who collectively had received a total of one-hundred twenty-two laser surgeries for papilloma over six and a half years. Eleven of twelve patients who had undergone more than six operations over this time period experienced anterior glottal webs with persistent vocal fold edema as complications, and their vocalization was seriously affected. Dedo and Jackler (1982) report that laser surgery was clearly the superior procedure for removal of recurring papilloma in 109 patients; with the laser approach, they report that almost half of their patients eventually reached remission and had no recurrence of the lesions. Despite the possible complications from continuous surgery from recurring papilloma, the lesions must be removed when they begin to impinge on the airway. Lundquist et al. (1984) report a medical approach to the treatment of the viral-caused papilloma: injecting the patients intramuscularly with interferon. In following seventeen juvenile patients receiving interferon therapy over a several year period, Lundquist et al. found that "nine were totally cured, four had no more tumor growth but were still being treated, three experienced diminished tumor growth, and one refused further treatment" (p. 386).

The speech-language pathologist is sometimes asked to see a toddler or young child with obstructive papilloma who has had to have an open tracheostomy to permit adequate respiration. Developing functional communication with such a child and fostering normal language growth are the primary concerns of the clinician. Teaching the child to occlude the open stoma with a finger or fitting the child with a one-way valve that covers the stoma (to permit vocalization without finger occlusion) usually permits some voicing. In older children or adults who are being treated surgically for recurring papilloma, helping them to develop the best voice possible with the compromised laryngeal mechanisms is a realistic goal in voice therapy. Some work on respiration control (such as voicing with larger lung volumes of air) or working on loudness and pitch may improve vocal function.

Pubertal Changes

At about age 9, before the onset of puberty, the larynges of boys and girls are anatomically the same size, and they produce about the same voice pitch (265 Hz). Pubertal growth changes in girls begin around 9, with the

[handwritten top margin: For boys: last year of puberty ↑ laryngeal growth + ∆F₀ dramatic.]

onset of puberty, and gradual pubescent changes occur over a four- to five-year period. In boys, puberty begins around 11, and dramatic growth changes occur over the four-to five-year pubertal period. However, notice-able laryngeal growth and the dramatic change in vocal fundamental frequency occur in the last year of puberty; the "average time from onset to completion of adolescent voice change is three to six months, one year at most" (Aronson, 1985, p. 49). By age 17, adolescents of both sexes have usually reached their full child-to-adult development (Offer, 1980). As we discuss elsewhere (see Chapters 2 and 4), the voice pitch levels of males and females drop dramatically after puberty (the male voice drops at least a full octave; the female voice drops almost half an octave).

Laryngeal and airway growth does not happen overnight. Although the changes are gradual, over a four-year period, marked laryngeal growth (particularly in boys) occurs in the last six months of change. During this time of rapid laryngeal growth boys may experience temporary dysphonia and occasional pitch breaks that are not cause for parental or clinical concern. Because these mass changes in puberty tend to thwart any serious attempts at singing or other vocal arts, junior high school is often a poor environment for choral music. A boy who is a soprano in September may well be the choir baritone by June. After reviewing the European literature on vocal pedagogy Luchsinger and Arnold (1965) make a valid plea that the formal study of singing be deferred until well past puberty. Until children experience some stability in laryngeal and airway growth, the demands of singing might well be inappropriate for their rapidly changing mechanisms. Because of such rapid changes, attempting to develop optimum pitch or modal-pitch levels in adolescents should be avoided.

Vocal Fold Paralysis

As presented in Chapter 2, two branches of the vagus cranial nerve, the superior and recurrent laryngeal nerves, have primary motor-sensory functions in the larynx. Laryngeal muscle paralysis can result when either of these two nerves are damaged or severed. The motor component of the superior laryngeal nerve controls the cricothyroid muscles, whose primary role is to change the pitch of the voice by regulating the tension of the vocal folds. The recurrent laryngeal nerve innervates the other intrinsic muscles of the larynx. Its primary function is the abduction (separation) and adduction (closing) of the vocal folds. If these peripheral nerves (or their central nuclei in the brain stem) are damaged or severed, motor function will be compromised, and the affected muscles will be paralyzed.

Although damage to the superior laryngeal nerve is relatively rare, when it is damaged it produces a paralysis (unilateral or bilateral) of the cricothyroid muscles, so that the patient is unable to make elevations or changes in voice pitch. In the case of unilateral damage, one vocal fold would be normal (able to adjust its length and tension) while the fold on the side of the paralyzed cricothyroid could not change its length or tension. This unilateral kind of involvement often results in a diplophonic voice, because one fold vibrates at a different frequency from the other one.

[handwritten bottom margin: Sup. lar. nerve → // → cricothyroid m. ø ↑ or ∆ in pitch. Unilateral - diplophonic. Bilateral - monotone.]

Most freq: Bilateral unilateral c folded in paramedian position

Bilateral paralysis of the cricothyroid muscles results in a startling lack of pitch change, and the voice sounds much like a monotone.

The most frequently observed laryngeal paralysis is a unilateral paralysis with the involved fold paralyzed in the paramedian position. The patient is unable to move the paralyzed fold into the midline for normal vocal fold approximation. This type of paralysis is traditionally called *unilateral adductor paralysis;* the patient is unable to adduct the fold to midline. (The name of the paralysis describes what the involved fold is unable to do.) The cause of unilateral adductor paralysis is usually trauma to the recurrent laryngeal nerve from such causes as neck (particularly thyroid) surgery and accidents. Much rarer is *bilateral adductor paralysis,* whereby both folds are paralyzed in the outer, paramedian position; occasionally, the bilateral positioning is as wide as the glottis can open. Bilateral paralysis is usually caused by a central lesion in the brain stem and is, therefore, a form of dysarthria. The typical voice symptoms of adductor paralysis, particularly the bilateral form, is no voice at all, or *paralytic aphonia.* Unilateral fold paralysis is often temporary because the traumatized nerve can often regenerate. Regeneration is frequently observed within the first nine months after trauma. Surgical correction of vocal fold paralysis is usually deferred until at least nine months after onset, and is accompanied by hope for some nerve regeneration with a subsequent return of vocal function. In the interim period, however, voice therapy can be effective, helping the patient develop some functional voice. Respiration training, the pushing approach, ear training, and promoting hard glottal attack have all been useful in helping the patient with unilateral adductor paralysis to develop some voice.

About 50 percent of patients with peripheral injuries to the recurrent laryngeal nerve experience a return of normal function (Casper, Colton, and Brewer, 1986). If, after nine months, the involved nerve(s) have not regenerated, various medical-surgical approaches are available to develop better laryngeal function, including a useable, functional voice. The most common surgical approach for unilateral adductor paralysis (with the paralyzed fold in the open, paramedian position) is Teflon injection (Weber et al., 1985). Of 111 patients with unilateral paralysis followed by Weber and his group, 85 percent had marked improvement in voice function after injection; two patients developed airway obstruction secondary to edema requiring temporary tracheostomy. Another surgical approach, implanting Silastic in the anterior commissure end of the paralyzed fold, "fattened" the paralyzed fold sufficiently to bring it into approximation with the normal fold and produced satisfactory voice (Koufman, 1986). Another procedure for unilateral paralysis, reported by Crumley and Izdebski (1986), involves reinnervating the paralyzed muscles by nerve grafts from the phrenic nerve, or by grafting a section of the superior laryngeal nerve with a portion of the hypoglossus nerve into the vocal fold adductor muscles. Laser surgery has been successful in decreasing open glottal space (Prasad, 1985) for bilateral adductor fold paralysis, and laser arytenoidectomy for bilateral abductor paralysis has successfully opened the glottis (Lim, 1985). Most surgical attempts at reducing the symptoms of unilateral or bilateral vocal fold paralysis need to be supplemented by voice therapy designed to produce optimum phonation with whatever glottal configuration is found after surgery.

Webbing

A laryngeal *web* growing across the glottis between the two vocal folds (see Figure 3–4) inhibits normal fold vibration, which often produces a high-pitched sound as it vibrates and seriously compromises the open glottis. Webs may be congenital or acquired. A *congenital web*, which is detected at the time of birth, is the result of the glottal membrane failing to separate in embryonic development. Depending on the size of the web, the baby will produce stridor (inhalation noises), shortness of breath, and often a different high-pitched (squeal) cry. Approximately three-fourths of all laryngeal webs cross the glottis (Strome, 1982). The presence of a congenital web requires immediate surgery, often followed by a temporary tracheostomy because an infant larynx will recover over a period of four to six weeks.

Acquired webs result from some kind of bilateral trauma of the inner edges of the vocal folds. Anything that might serve as an irritant to the mucosal surface of the folds may be the initial cause of the webbing. Because the two vocal folds are so close together at the anterior commissure, any surface irritation due to prolonged infection or trauma may cause the inner margins of the two fold surfaces to grow together. To explain further, one principle of plastic surgery is that when approximated together offended tissue surfaces will tend to grow and fuse together. This same principle explains why webbing occurs. The offended surface of the two approximated folds tends to grow together, in this case forming a thin membrane across the glottis. Webbing grows across the glottis in an anterior to posterior fashion, usually ceasing about one-third of the distance from the anterior commissure, where the distance between the two folds becomes too great. Severe laryngeal infections sometimes cause enough glottal irritation to precipitate web formation. Bilateral surgery of the folds, perhaps for papilloma or nodules, can also be followed by a web (Wetmore et al., 1985). External trauma to the folds, such as a direct hit on the thyroid cartilage that causes it to fracture, may damage the folds behind it, thus creating enough glottal irritation for a web to develop. Whatever causes the original bilateral irritation, as a part of healing, both folds grow together anteriorly, forming a glottal web, sometimes called a *synechia.*

FIGURE 3–4.
This congenital laryngeal web was discovered in a 36-year-old woman who complained of a "lifetime with a lousy voice." The web was surgically removed, followed by successful voice therapy.

Laryngeal web may cause severe dysphonia as well as shortness of breath, depending on how extensively the webbing crosses the glottis. The treatment for the formation of a web is surgery. The webbing is cut, freeing the two folds. To prevent the surgically removed web from growing again, a vertical *keel* is placed between the two folds and kept there until complete healing has been achieved. The laryngologist fixates the keel, which is shaped very much like a boat rudder and is about the size of a fingernail, between the folds, preventing them from approximating together. The patient is then on voice rest as long as the keel is in place, because its presence inhibits normal fold vibration. When the keel is removed, often in six to eight weeks, the patient generally requires some voice therapy to restore normal phonation. If there was extensive damage to the larynx from the trauma, it may well be impossible after healing and voice therapy to ever develop the same kind of normal voice the patient had before the accident. The prognosis for voice recovery after webbing and its surgical treatment is highly individualized, depending on the extent of the trauma and the size of the resulting web.

SUMMARY

The majority of voice disorders are related to vocal hyperfunction. Vocal excesses, such as voicing too long and excessive throat clearing, contribute to symptoms of dysphonia or aphonia. Sometimes continued vocal hyperfunction leads to tissue changes of the vocal folds so that such disorders as vocal fold thickening, nodules, polyps, or contact ulcers develop. Organic changes of the vocal folds that may not be directly related to vocal hyperfunction may result from cancer, papilloma, granuloma, and webbing. Various neural problems (such as the cutting of the recurrent laryngeal nerve with a resulting vocal fold paralysis) or neurological diseases produce vocal and resonance changes as part of a dysarthria. In subsequent chapters we examine diagnostic and therapy approaches for these various functional and organic voice disorders.

4

THE VOICE
EVALUATION

Voice evaluation is the first step in the treatment of a voice disorder. Although identification of a deviant voice may come from several sources (parents, teachers, school nurse, employer, or coworker), the voice evaluation must be a carefully and scientifically conducted procedure performed by a competent speech-language pathologist. Voice evaluation may either precede or follow a complete examination of the patient by the laryngologist. However, the laryngological results must be considered with the findings of the voice evaluation in order for the voice clinician to make a tentative voice diagnosis and a treatment plan. It is the province of the voice clinician to make the voice diagnosis (analysis of the acoustic and perceptual factors) and plan voice treatment, just as it is the province of the laryngologist to diagnose laryngeal pathology. These two diagnoses are combined to guide in the best management of the patient's voice disorder.

Successful voice therapy is highly dependent on how well the voice clinician can identify what the patient is doing vocally. The typical voice evaluation is completed after someone else, such as the laryngologist, has already diagnosed the presence or absence of laryngeal pathology that may be contributing to a voice disorder. The speech-language pathologist must make a detailed analysis of what the patient is doing relative to respiration, phonation, and resonance. To do this, he or she makes good use of whatever medical descriptions of the problem may be available, takes a detailed case history, observes the patient closely, uses those testing tools and instrumentations necessary to make an accurate assessment, and introduces to the patient various therapeutic probes (clinical stimulation) to obtain clues about what direction the voice therapy should take.

Although we present the voice evaluation here in a separate chapter, it is important for the reader to appreciate that voice evaluation and voice therapy cannot be separated. Effective voice therapy requires continuous, ongoing assessment. Evaluation and therapy overlap. What is found at the evaluation and given back to the patient as a form of feedback may also have great therapeutic value. Using various therapy approaches as diagnostic probes in an attempt to identify a patient's best possible voice can be an important part of every therapy session. Many of the evaluation procedures and tools described in this evaluation chapter are also used by clinicians in voice therapy.

VOICE SCREENING

Speech-language pathologists in the public schools are in an excellent position to develop voice screening procedures for the early identification of children with voice problems. Most school programs have speech screening programs for new children and for all children in certain grades at specified times of the year. For example, in the fall clinicians may screen all children in kindergarten and third grades. By using some kind of voice screening form, clinicians are able to make better judgments about the parameters of voice. With very little additional testing time per child, a voice screening program can be added to existing speech and language-screening measures.

Different clinicians in various settings have developed various screening forms. The items on the form usually represent the aspects of voice that the clinician considers important for identifying children who may be having voice problems. The screening form helps clinicians focus and organize their listening observations. Wilson (1987) recommends that clinicians use the following tasks in voice screening: counting from one to ten; giving a connected speech sample (one minute); reading a sample (one minute); and prolonging for five seconds each of five selected vowels (high to low). Previous screening forms published by Boone (1973, 1977) have included observations specific to rating the parameters of pitch, loudness, quality, and resonance. These forms have generally been modified as they are field tested and utilized in various settings. We have found, over time, for example, that the rating task must be as focal as possible to be useful. The more parameters to be rated and the more gradations of the rating, the poorer the reliability in using the form. Nonetheless, McFarlane, Holt, and Lavorato (1985) have reported that even lay listeners can be nearly as accurate as speech pathologists or ENT physicians in rating voice disorders if the vocal parameters are well defined and limited in number. These authors used a ten-point scale for each of six vocal parameters (pitch, loudness, hoarseness, breathiness, roughness, and overall vocal quality).

The form in Figure 4–1 offers clinicians the information they need for a screening test (Boone, 1980a). The single criterion for each of the scale judgments (pitch, loudness, quality, nasal resonance, oral resonance) is whether or not the child's voice on that particular parameter sounds like the voices of peers of the same age and sex. If a child's voice appears lower in pitch than that of peers, the (−) is circled on the form; if pitch appears normal, the (N) is circled; if the pitch level is higher than the child's peers, the (+) is circled. This simple three-point scale is especially useful for rating the parameter of pitch because, as McFarlane, et al (1985) point out, all listeners (speech pathologists, lay, and ENT) had the most difficulty making consistent and accurate judgments of the pitch.

Inadequate loudness is specified as (−); normal loudness as (N); and

FIGURE 4-1.
A voice screening form. (*The Boone Voice Program for Children,* Austin, Texas: PRO-ED, 1980)

excessive loudness as (+). Any deviation of quality is represented by (−) or (+); a breathy, hoarse voice is marked as (−), and a tight, harsh voice as (+).

If denasality (insufficient nasal resonance) is noted, the form is checked (−); normal nasal resonance is marked (N); and hypernasality is characterized by (+). Oral resonance deviations do not occur as often as other problems; however, excessive posterior tongue carriage that produces inadequate oral resonance is marked as (−); no problem in oral resonance is (N); and excessive front-of-the-mouth resonance characterized by a baby voice (thin vocal quality) is marked as (+). If the child receives either (−) or (+) on any of the five clinical parameters, he or she should be rechecked. If problem areas are again identified, a complete voice evaluation would be recommended (Boone, 1980a).

The s/z ratio has recently been added as a screening measure (Eckel and Boone, 1981; Tait, Michel, and Carpenter, 1980). The s/z ratio is a measure of how well a child can sustain a prolonged /s/ phoneme as compared with the /z/ phoneme. The /s/ is a measure of expiratory control, and the /z/ sound adds the laryngeal component to the task. Normal speakers yield about the same maximum duration values of both /s/ and /z/; however, there is a slight skewing of longer duration for the /z/ rather than for the /s/. Apparently, when the laryngeal valving contributes to the task, as in voicing, the glottal structure inhibits the air flow, contributing to a longer duration. Individuals with larynges with glottal lesions (such as nodules or polyps)

/s/ - measure : expiratory control.
/z/ - + laryngeal dimension

exhibit significantly shorter /z/ durations than normal subjects, although their maximum /s/ durations appear of normal length (Eckel and Boone, 1981). The s/z ratio is computed by dividing the maximum /z/ time into the maximum /s/ time. Eckel and Boone found that more than 95 percent of their patients with laryngeal pathologies demonstrated s/z ratios in excess of 1.4. The s/z ratio thus seems to provide a quick software measure that might identify those people with dysphonia who have possible laryngeal lesions.

Most screening forms allow a brief space for comments examiners may want to add to the screening data. For example, the notation "she had a bad cold" would be helpful information for a follow up visit with someone previously noted as exhibiting "denasality." At the second visit, screening data are compared with present observations. Arrangements should be made for full voice evaluations for those individuals who on follow-up continue to show some departures in voice from their age-sex peers.

THE VOICE EVALUATION AND MEDICAL INFORMATION

Voice patients evaluated by speech-language pathologists have either been "discovered" in voice screening programs, or referred by teachers and other professionals in the schools, referred by physicians (usually laryngologists), or self-referred. Regardless of the referral source, in early contacts with the patient the speech-language pathologist will arrange for a full voice evaluation. For those patients not referred by laryngologists, part of the evaluation process may include a medical evaluation. Occasional voice patients, such as those who do not talk loud enough or those who use aberrant pitch levels for what appear to be functional reasons, may not require medical evaluation. Patients with voice quality and resonance problems generally require some medical evaluation of the ears, nose, and throat as part of the total voice evaluation.

The most effective voice rehabilitation programs seem to have close team cooperation between the speech-language pathologist and the laryngologist. Unfortunately, some areas of the country have no laryngologists, and it is not uncommon for speech-language pathologists in these areas to report that there are no medical doctors available who can perform *indirect laryngoscopy* (mirror view of the vocal folds). The speech pathologist in such a situation should confer with the patient's local physician, saying, for example, "Tom seems to be hoarse every day. Could you please see that his vocal folds are examined?" Rarely will a physician not appreciate such a request. Physicians who feel that they do not possess the skills required for indirect laryngoscopy will refer the patient to a laryngologist. It is not unusual for patients living in remote areas of the United States to travel several hundred miles for an examination by a laryngologist.

A laryngeal examination must be made before a patient can begin voice therapy for problems related to quality or resonance. As part of the diagnostic process the speech-language pathologist may wish to use therapy approaches as diagnostic probes; for example, asking a patient to turn the head, or receive digital manipulation may provide important diagnostic information about how tighter vocal fold approximation affects voice quality (see Chapter 5). Voice therapy efforts should be deferred until after the medical examination (which would include laryngoscopy) is concluded, because there are occasional laryngeal pathologies, such as papilloma or carcinoma, for which voice therapy would be strongly contraindicated. In such cases, the delay of accurate diagnosis of these pathologies could be life threatening.

The laryngologist's examination includes an assessment of the larynx and related structures. The vocal folds are assessed by indirect mirror, or endoscopic laryngoscopy, and their color, configuration, and position are noted. During the patient's quiet respiration, the laryngologist looks for the normal inverted-V position of the cords. For phonation, the patient is often asked to phonate a relatively high pitch, perhaps by extending an *e-e-e* for several seconds. The higher the pitch, the further the epiglottis and tongue are extended upward, permitting a relatively unobstructed view of the vocal folds. A judgment is made on the adequacy of fold approximation during phonation. Other structures that may be examined include the ventricular folds, laryngeal ventricle, pharynx, tonsils-adenoids, nasal cavities, velopharyngeal mechanism, glands and muscles of the neck, and so on. The laryngologist's examination is directed at finding the cause of the patient's presenting problem and evaluating the overall status of the larynx and related mechanisms. If the laryngologist wants additional information about how the patient uses his or her voice, or if the laryngologist feels voice therapy may be needed, the patient will be referred directly to the speech-language pathologist. Such referral usually requires a written statement by the laryngologist describing the patients' problem. In actual practice, the written referral may be supplemented by a conversation further describing the problem. The laryngologist's referral usually includes an abbreviated statement of the patient's history, a descriptive statement of the presenting problem, what was told to the patient, and a statement indicating treatment direction and probable prognosis.

The following letter of referral from a local laryngologist who placed strong and continued emphasis on voice therapy for most of his patients with hyperfunctional voice problems was taken from a clinic file:

I have asked Pearl to see you for a voice evaluation at the earliest opportunity. This 44-year-old woman works as a secretary to an insurance executive, a position that requires much talking on the telephone. In the past six months she reports continued hoarseness, usually worse at the end of the day, and she complains of occasional pain in the general hyoid region after prolonged speaking. She is married, the mother of three young adult sons. Until six months ago, there was no history of vocal distress.

On mirror laryngoscopy, I found the patient to have small bilateral nodes at the anterior one-third junction. Areas immediately adjacent to the nodes were characterized by increased vascularization, suggesting much irritation at this site. On cord adduction, there is noticeable open chinking on each side of the approximated nodes. Her voice, as you might suspect, is quite breathy with an audible escape of air, probably escaping through the open chinking. Inadequate voice loudness, also, appears to be a problem for her.

I am referring her to you for your ideas on what she may be doing wrong with her voice. If you feel she would benefit from voice therapy, please schedule her. I told her that if you felt voice therapy were indicated, we would begin there. If not, we might attempt surgical removal of the nodules and then instruct her on proper voice usage to prevent their recurrence. She appears strongly motivated to improve her voice and will, I'm sure, gladly accept whatever you recommend.

Physicians develop different methods of describing their findings for the speech-language pathologists. Their descriptions may range from a brief "normal vocal folds" to a multi-page written evaluation. Typically, the speech-language pathologist may receive statements from the laryngologist similar to these:

Large tonsils and adenoids; no need to remove at this time. Larynx normal.

Bilateral thickening runs from the total AP distance on both folds. Could well be related to voice abuse. Could you take her on for voice therapy?

No physical basis for the tight voice. Cords show good mobility and normal function. No cord lesions. Do you think she'd be a good candidate for nerve resection?

A short, relatively immobile velum. Good symmetry. VP distance looks too excessive for normal closure. Recommend a pharyngeal flap. Could you do pressure-flow study and endoscopic photography? We'll staff her next month.

The laryngologist and the speech-language pathologist work together in planning both the evaluative procedures and remediation steps to be followed. Other professionals sometimes included in the evaluation, which we outline in Chapter 7 when we discuss problems of nasal resonance, may include a pediatrician, a neurologist, an orthodontist, a prosthodontist, and a psychologist. Specialization today requires a team of professionals for the effective management of some patients with voice disorders.

We firmly believe in the advantages of a team approach; for example, we very rarely recommend removal of nodules even in adults because voice therapy is generally effective for complete reduction of the nodules. Even in cases of long-standing vocal nodules, we have been able to eliminate the nodules or, in some cases, normalize the voice with some residual nodules left. Note that it is possible to have normal vocal quality with some remaining nodule tissue. In such cases, however, the ENT physician, should be advised not to remove the remaining nodule tissue when the voice is normal in quality. Surgical removal of this small remnant is unnecessary and may actually jeopardize the newly established vocal quality. Such treatment philosophies and observations are best shared when there is a good team relationship between the laryngologist and the voice clinician. McFarlane, Fujiki, and Brinton (1984) have discussed this team relationship:

> The most desired goal is to be regarded by these professional practitioners as peer professionals. This means that we must be able to talk intelligently about their field (be "bilingual," using our jargon and theirs) and their clients, provide a valuable and effective treatment service to their patients, and possess a knowledge and skill base somewhat unique from these other specialties. (pp. 133–134)

Some laryngologists prefer an evaluation form with a glottal figure. This allows them to quickly make their statements and accompany them with a line sketch of the pathology (if present) specific to its site and size. Figure 4–2 shows part of such a form (Boone, 1980a) that would be completed by the examining physician and returned to the speech-language pathologist.

Community health centers and university clinics routinely obtain medical information and some case history data from patients when the initial appointment is made, and, if a voice problem is indicated, schedule the patient first for a medical diagnostic evaluation. Sometimes however, a voice patient will make the initial appointment without identifying the problem as one of voice. If, for whatever reason, a patient arrives to be

VOICE REFERRAL TO PHYSICIAN

To the physician: This child was recently seen for a voice evaluation. Voice therapy has been deferred until a medical diagnosis has been made. Please complete Section 2 of this form and return it with your recommendations.

Name_____Sex M F Birth Date_____Age_____
School_____ Referring Clinician _____ Telephone _____

SECTION 1
Voice Evaluation Summary
(to be completed by Speech-Language Pathologist)

SECTION 2
Summary of Medical Findings
(to be completed by examining Physician)

Indicate site and extent of lesion

Recommendations:
____ Voice therapy recommended
____ Voice therapy not recommended
Comments:

Return this form to:

Physician's Signature

Date

FIGURE 4–2.
A voice referral to physician form such as this provides a systematic way for making referals to the physician. *(The Boone Voice Program for Children,* Austin, Texas: PRO-ED, 1980)

treated for some form of dysphonia but has not had a previous medical examination, the speech-language pathologist must defer final disposition of the patient until the medical information is obtained. The voice evaluation by the speech clinician may begin, however, even in the absence of the medical information. The case history can be taken, and respiration-phonatory-resonance observations and test data can be obtained; only the decision about voice therapy need be deferred.

The ethics and efficacy of speech-language pathologists themselves doing indirect laryngoscopy are worth discussing at this point. Some speech-language pathologists are trained to perform endoscopy or mirror laryngoscopy, procedures that are not difficult to master; these persons use indirect laryngoscopy primarily to teach students laryngeal function and to observe the folds directly to determine any changes during therapy. No speech-language pathologist, however, should use laryngoscopy as a diagnostic device. Primary identification of laryngeal pathology is the clear responsibility of the laryngologist, who is also equipped with the medical techniques required to treat the pathology, once it is identified. For the ethical and legal protection of the speech-language pathologist, the voice patient who comes in for evaluation without prior medical examination should not, at a first visit, be given indirect laryngoscopy by the speech-language pathologist. The diagnostic examination of the vocal cords must be done by the laryngologist. After the laryngologist has made a diagnosis, the speech-language pathologist trained in laryngoscopy may occasionally use mirror laryngoscopy or endoscopy to view the folds; this will facilitate the treatment of the patient by allowing the clinician to make judgments about vocal fold status.

THE VOICE EVALUATION AND THE CASE HISTORY

To understand patients with voice disorders and to understand their problems, it is necessary for clinicians to assemble a case history. Most texts and manuals dealing with diagnosis and appraisal of communicative disorders present general strategies for history taking (Darley, 1965; Dickson and Jann, 1974; Nation and Aram, 1977; and Perkins, 1977b). Recent texts on management of voice disorders that offer suggestions for history taking include Aronson, 1985; Boone, 1980a; Case, 1984; Greene, 1980, and Wilson, 1987.

Many individualized voice evaluation forms are available for clinicians. Most history forms include major headings that include description of problem, cause of problem, consistency or variability of problem, and voice usage. The form shown in Figure 4–3 is typical.

Description of the Problem and Cause

It is valuable for understanding patients to ask directly what they feel are the problems and what might have caused them. It is often effective to ask the same questions of family members or teachers. The different views about what the problem may be and the various guesses about probable causation may offer tips for management. Patients' descriptions often re-

VOICE EVALUATION FORM
The Boone Voice Program for Children
by Daniel R. Boone, Ph. D.

NAME _____ SEX M F   DATE OF BIRTH_____ AGE _____

SCHOOL _____ TEACHER _____ GRADE_____

REFERRAL SOURCE: SCREENING____TEACHER____ PHYSICIAN____ SELF____OTHER ____

EXAMINER _____ DATE OF EVALUATION _____

SECTION 1
History of the Voice Problem

	Child's Report	Parent's Report Informant _____	Teacher's Report
Description of Problem			
Cause of Problem			
Onset of Problem			
Variability Through Day			
Voice Usage			
Abuses:			
Misuses:			
Comments:			

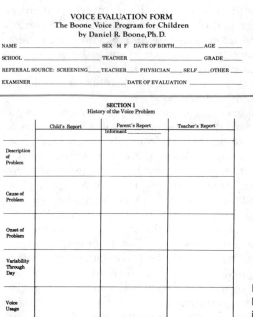

Reports from: child parents teachers

FIGURE 4-3.
History taking for a child is facilitated by obtaining reports from the child, the teacher, and the parents. (*The Boone Voice Program for Children,* Austin, Texas: PRO-ED, 1980)

veal much about their own conceptualization of the problem. What a patient feels the problem is may not be consistent with the opinions of the referring physician or the speech-language pathologist—a discrepancy that may be due to what we call the patient's *reality distance.* This distance may be the result of the patient's lay background and inability to understand adequately what had been explained. Often we hear highly discrepant reports of "what the doctor said" as a patient recounts the diagnoses of previous clinicians. More often this distance is primarily the result of the inability to accept and cope with the real problem. An individual's defenses may force him or her to describe the problem in a way that is not consistent with the perceptions of others. What a patient says about a problem may, however, provide the clinician with insights that no amount of observation or testing can match. This sort of reality distance is well illustrated by the following excerpts from the clinic records of a 28-year-old computer programmer:

Physician's Examination Statement: George was an extremely hard man to examine with indirect laryngoscopy. He was very fearful during our exam and gagged with the slightest touch to the posterior tongue. His vocal folds show broad-based bilateral polyps, about 4 mm wide along the anterior-middle third junction. Trial voice therapy is indicated.

Speech-Language Pathologist's Statement: Patient voices with much audible strain, characterized by diplophonia, hoarseness, and severe glottal attack. Patient participated in all phases of our evaluation with a fixed smile on his face, contrasted with tight, clenched fists. We may well need here a combined voice therapy-counseling approach.

Patient's Statement of the Problem: Now that I have recently found the Lord, I want to serve him. Whenever I go to teach at the church, I seem to lose my voice. My computer work presents no problem, because I don't need the voice much there. It's a problem of going hoarse and even losing the voice when I work with the groups at the church.

Consistently from these descriptions we view a patient who was showing some tension signs when relating to other people. He was hypersensitive during laryngoscopy attempts, his vocal patterns and facial-hand mannerisms suggested tension, and his description of his problem voicing with other people all suggested psychological tension as a possible contributing factor to his dysphonia. Aronson (1980) has written, "If the dysphonia is of greater severity or different in character than warranted by the lesion, a psychogenic component is strongly suspected" (p. 185). The bilateral polyps alone should not have caused the complete voice breakdown the patient experienced while teaching groups at the church. Successful management of this man's problem necessitated a combined voice therapy and psychological counseling approach, similar to what was suggested initially by the speech-language pathologist.

Onset and Duration of the Problem

How long patients believe they have had the voice problem is important. A problem of acute and sudden onset usually poses a severe threat to a patient—that is, it keeps the patient from carrying out his or her customary activities (playing, singing, acting, selling, preaching, or whatever). Sudden onset of aphonia or dysphonia deserves thorough exploration by both the laryngologist and the speech-language pathologist. Some dysphonias develop very gradually. Such gradual, fluctuating dysphonias are often related to varying situations in which patients may find themselves; sometimes they only occur during moments of stress or after fatigue. A history of slow onset sometimes suggest a gradually developing pathology, such as the development of bilateral polypoid degeneration of the vocal folds or dysphonia that is but an early developing symptom of some kind of progressive neurological disease. Long-term chronic dysphonia usually exists for so long because the patient has never been particularly disturbed by the voice problem. Voice therapy, like other forms of remedial therapy, is usually more successful with those patients who are motivated to overcome their problems. Patients with a long history of indifference toward their dysphonia usually present a more unfavorable prognosis than the ones who have recently acquired the disorder, depending, of course, on the kind and relative extent of the pathology involved.

Variability of the Problem

Most voice patients can provide rather accurate timetables of the consistency of their problem. If the severity of a voice problem is variable, a clinician may be able to identify those vocal situations in which the patient experiences the best voice and the worst voice. The typical patient with vocal hyperfunction reports a better voice earlier in the day, with increasing dysphonia as the voice is used more. For example, a high school social studies teacher reported a normal-sounding voice at the beginning of the day; toward the end of a day, after six hours of lecturing, he reported increasing hoarseness and a feeling of "fullness and dryness in the throat." Voice rest and then dinner at the end of the day usually restored his voice to its normal level. Obviously, such fluctuations in the daily quality of the voice enabled the clinician to easily identify the situations contributing to the patient's vocal abuse. Another patient, whose dysphonia was closely related to an allergy and postnasal drip experienced during sleep, presented this kind of variation in hoarseness: severity in the morning upon awakening, decrease in severity with usage of the voice, complete disappearance by late afternoon, and severity again the next morning.

The variation of the voice problem can provide even more specific clues as to what situations most aggravate the disorder. A night-club singer reported that she had no voice problem during the day in conversational situations or while practicing her repertoire. She developed hoarseness only at night and only on those nights she sang. Further investigation of her singing act revealed that the adverse factors were the cigarette smoke around her, to which she was unusually sensitive, and the noise of the crowd, above which she had to increase her volume to be heard. Her singing methods were found to be satisfactory. A change of jobs to a summer tent theater provided her with immediate relief. Variability of situation also affected a housewife allergic to a specific brand of meat tenderizer. This patient lost her voice completely shortly after using the tenderizer during meal preparation. When she discontinued the use of this product, she did not lose her voice; when the product was reintroduced, the aphonia followed.

Description of Vocal Use (Daily Use, Misuse)

Abuse, misuse, and overuse of the voice cause most functional voice problems. It is important for clinicians to determine how voice patients are using their larynges in most life situations. The voice a child or adult exhibits in the speech-language pathologist's office may in no way represent the voice used on the playground, in the classroom, or in other settings. Sometimes patients can recreate some of their aversive laryngeal behaviors as a demonstration for the clinician, but more often a valid search for aversive vocal behaviors requires the clinician to visit the environment where the abuse-misuse occurs. Successful voice clinicians must thus build into their schedules actual visits to playgrounds, theaters, churches, or offices. In reducing one child's vocal abuse (and vocal nodules) a major factor was our visiting the school lunchroom and changing his manner of repeating the phrase "Do you want white or chocolate milk?" three hundred times each day as he passed out the milk during the noisy lunch period. Similarly, we were able to make major vocal gains with a dysphonic attorney only after attending the courtroom trial where we observed his excessively loud and effortful legal objections and jury addresses and modified them first hand. Apparently, only a little voice abuse-misuse in whatever setting is all that may be needed to keep a glottal membrane inflamed or a pair of vocal nodules irritated and fibrotic. Case (1984), for instance, has demonstrated the effects of cheerleading on the larynges of teen-agers, comparing them with laryngoscopy before and after two weeks of attendance at a cheerleading camp. His data strongly suggest that continued cheerleading has a direct aversive effect on the larynges of the majority of the adolescents studied. It is obviously important for the clinician to identify the vocal use pattern of the patient.

Special attention must be given to the identification of playground screaming and yelling in children. One only has to listen to the noise level of the typical primary school playground to realize that yelling at play appears to be a normal childhood behavior. A child with a voice problem, however, often has a history of yelling a little louder and a bit more often than normal-voiced peers. Sometimes public school clinicians must enlist the help of teachers, friends, and the family to determine the everyday vocalization history of the child. Perhaps the most important part of voice therapy for children is identifying vocal abuse and developing strategies to reduce its occurrence.

Additional Case History Information

It is important to determine at the time of the voice evaluation if the patient has ever had previous voice therapy. If so, what type of past therapy would have obvious relevance to present management? When previous voice therapy attempts have failed to improve the vocal quality or have been unsuccessful in reducing a vocal pathology, the knowledge of previous therapy is important. We must, however, make every effort to present the appearance of a *fresh* and *different* approach to the patient who has experienced failure in previous voice therapy (McFarlane and Lavorato, 1983). Even if we use the same goals of therapy as before, we must direct the new approach to voice therapy in a manner that appears to the patient to be headed down a completely different road.

Determining whether other members of the family have similar voice problems is helpful. We have had particular patients present a certain voice problem, only to interview members of the family and find that all or many of them have the same voicing patterns. Deviations in resonance are often the most commonly observed family patterns.

Voice evaluations should also include some kind of health history; an example of a health history taken from a child evaluation form (Boone, 1980a) is shown is Figure 4-4. Certainly for adult patients it is important to determine such conditions as allergies, medication or hormone therapy, excessive smoking, use of alcohol, and use of drugs. Once a patient is com-

SECTION 2
Health History

Informant _____

Birth History

Feeding Problems

Illnesses and Allergies

Accidents

Surgery

Medications

Voice Change

Family Voice Problems

Previous Voice Therapy

FIGURE 4-4. A health history may be organized under topic headings, as shown in this form. (*The Boone Voice Program for Children,* Austin, Texas: PRO-ED, 1980)

fortable with an examiner, or perhaps after voice therapy has begun, a social history should be taken to provide the clinician with useful information about the patient as a person.

THE VOICE EVALUATION
AND OBSERVATION OF THE PATIENT

Observations of our patients often tell us more about them than our histories and our test data. Speech-language pathologists must become critical observers, attempting to describe behavior they see rather than merely labeling it. Writing observations about a patient is one of the few ways clinicians can note what they observe. Even here, however, it is important for clinicians to minimize any subjectivity by describing only what they see and hear, and not adding interpretation to the observation. An example of such a description of what was observed and heard is taken from this case record, which describes a 16-year-old boy, effeminate in appearance, who was being evaluated for an excessively high-pitched voice:

David came into the clinic room with his arms hanging stiffly at his sides, his mouth in a tight contortion producing slight facial tics on the right side, avoiding all eye contact with the examiner. While he would freely volunteer history about himself, he seemed as if he were speaking in a high pitched (probably around E₃) monotone. About five minutes into the interview, he began to tell a long story about himself and his friend, Jamie, and their trip with Jamie's mother to Mexico. Apparently, Jamie's mother had scolded him for having such a high voice, fearing that he might make Jamie talk "that sissy way." David was quick to add, "Jamie was already into gay fun more than I ever was."

The brief preceding paragraph contains much observation and two patient quotes. It describes the patient better than if the clinician had attempted to label the boy's behavior.

Because voice difficulties are often symptomatic of the inability to have satisfactory interpersonal relationships, it is imperative that the clinician consider the patient's degree of adequacy as a social being. The patient who exhibits extremely sweaty palms, who avoids eye contact with the person to whom he is speaking, who uses excessive postural changes or demonstrates facial tics, or sits with a masked, nonaffective facial expression, or who exhibits obvious shortness of breath may be displaying behaviors frequently considered as symptomatic of anxiety. His struggle to maintain a conversational relationship may be accompanied by much struggle to phonate. Such observed behavior in the voice patient may be highly significant to the voice clinician planning a course of voice remediation. The decision about whether to treat a problem symptomatically (that is, by voice therapy) or by improving the patient's potential for interpersonal adjustment (perhaps by psychotherapy) is often aided by a review of the observations of the patient. A patient who demonstrates friendly, normal affect is telling the clinician, at least superficially, that he or she functions well in a two-person relationship; such information may well have clinical relevance. Such observations are extremely valuable to voice clinicians planning treatment approaches. Note, however, that in our experience very few voice patients require referral for psychotherapy.

THE VOICE EVALUATION AND TESTING OF THE PATIENT

[handwritten margin note: 7 parameters: ①pitch, ②loudness, ③quality, ④nasal + ⑤oral resonance, ⑥speaking rate ⑦inflection]

A voice rating scale of some kind aids the clinician in separating the various processes contributing to voice into separate components. A children's voice rating scale is shown in Figure 4–5. This particular scale permits clinicians to observe each of seven parameters: pitch, loudness, quality, nasal resonance, oral resonance, speaking rate, and variability of inflection. Each of the parameters is judged for voice production in three settings: in conversation, in play, and in reading. This particular scale is basically a seven-point rating scale with normal production checked in the middle. To the left of normal are the rating slots for insufficient performance of the parameter to be rated; for example, a voice pitch that appears too low would be rated on the pitch scale to the left of normal. The individual's pitch level is compared with the pitch levels of age peers. The mild, moderate, and severe boxes are checked according to the clinician's judgment.

[handwritten margin note: 3 settings ① in conversation ② in play ③ in reading]

The rating scale is not a test per se but provides clinicians with a structure for systematizing their observations. Actual measurements of frequency, intensity, quality, and resonance are made separately, and these data can often help clinicians make the summary judgments placed on the voice rating scale. Because rating scales force clinicians to focus their measurements and observations into some kind of summary, many voice clinicians have developed scales and found them useful (Perkins, 1971; Wilson and Rice, 1977). Wilson (1987) describes several equal-interval scales having

[handwritten margin note: Rate: ①mild ②mod ③severe]

SECTION 7
Voice Rating Severity Scale

Check (✓) the appropriate boxes

FIGURE 4–5. The voice rating severity scale. This seven-point rating scale enables the clinician to rate seven parameters of voice from observations during conversation, play, and oral reading. (*The Boone Voice Program for Children,* Austin, Texas: PRO-ED, 1980)

ratings from 1 to 7, with interjudge reliability in excess of .90. Let us consider some of the measurement instruments used by speech-language pathologists in voice evaluation.

The Peripheral Oral Evaluation

Careful assessment of the peripheral oral mechanisms is part of the voice evaluation. Although we focus on evaluation of the larynx and respiratory systems, some examination of facial structures, mouth, dentition, tongue, teeth, hard and soft palate, pharynx, and nasal cavities is required. Incorporated into the voice evaluation may be the peripheral mechanism forms offered in such evaluation-diagnosis books as Darley (1965), Dickson and Jann (1974), and Nation and Aram (1977). In our evaluation of the peripheral mechanisms of the voice patient, we must pay particular attention to possible signs of neural innervation problems. Every now and then, when we evaluate a patient with "functional dysphonia," we find some subtle neurological signs of fasciculation and atrophy of the tongue, or asymmetries of the velum related to neural innervation changes, and so on. Subsequent medical-neurological evaluations may find that the early dysphonia is simply the beginning symptomatology of a serious neurological disease. It is important to evaluate the voice patient specific to structural and functional adequacy for all parts of the oral mechanisms.

In Chapter 2 we presented sites of possible hyperfunction where voice patients may experience some difficulty. Let us now review some of these sites of hyperfunction and look at them closely as part of our total peripheral mechanism evaluation. Beyond observing obvious problems in breathing, some attention should be given to the amount of *neck tension*. The accessory neck muscles and the supralaryngeal strap muscles in some patients literally stick out like bands as the patient speaks. Often, *mandibular restriction*, is closely associated with neck tension; affected patients speak with clenched teeth, with little or no mandibular movement. Such restricted jaw movement places most of the burden of speech articulation on the tongue, which, to produce the various vowels and diphthongs in connected speech, must make fantastic adjustments if no cavity-shaping assistance from the mandible is forthcoming. Another externally observable hyperfunction of the vocal tract is unusual *downward* or *upward* excursion of the larynx during the production of various pitches. Any unusual movement upward while phonating higher pitches, or unusual movement downward while phonating lower ones, should be noted. The *angle of the thyroid cartilage* may be felt digitally as the patient sings a number of varying pitches; typically the fingertips will feel little discernible change in thyroid angle as the patient sings up and down the scale. Sometimes, however, the thyroid cartilage can be felt to rock forward slightly in the production of high pitches, as it sweeps upward to a higher position toward the hyoid bone. Any really noticeable amount of lifting or lowering of the larynx, as well as the tipping forward of the thyroid cartilage in the production of high pitches, should be noted as possible hyperfunctional behavior.

The majority of hyperfunctional behaviors associated with voice problems are probably not directly observable from examination of the peripheral mechanism. For example, to determine the extent of the tongue's impinging on the oral/pharyngeal space we would need to rely on oral or nasal endoscopy or videoendoscopy.

Endoscopy

The endoscope may be introduced intraorally or intranasally; the light on the tip of the scope (which comes fiber-optically from an external light source) illuminates the nasal and oral pharynx that is viewed through a window lens on the tip of the endoscope. Of relevance to voice evaluation is that the window lens of the oral endoscope can be directed up at the velopharyngeal closure mechanism or down at the larynx below. A nasal endoscopic voice evaluation is pictured in Figure 4–6. When the oral or

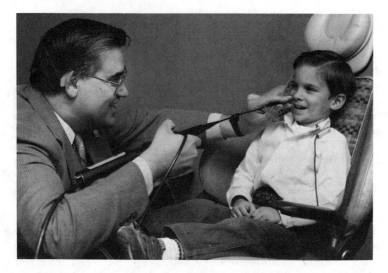

FIGURE 4-6. This 4-year-old boy is examined during the production of connected speech using nasal video endoscopy. Such an examination can be conducted without any topical anesthetic and provides an excellent method for assessing vocal function under typical and therapeutic phonatory conditions. We have been able to perform this examination on children as young as 22 months of age.

nasal endoscope is attached to a small video camera, the examination is termed a videoendoscopic evaluation. It provides a permanent video record of the observations. Using a stop-frame feature of the video recorder and a video printer, we can make a hard copy picture of the observation to include in the patient's file of voice evaluation. When we use a stroboscopic light source instead of a steady-state light source, we can produce a slow motion observation of the vocal physiology (video stroboscopic endoscopy). With such instrumentation we are able to make valuable observations of deviations in both vocal tract anatomy and physiology. With most voice patients, these deviations are subtle, inappropriate vocal adjustments in glottal approximation of the vocal folds, in tongue position, or in pharyngeal constriction, rather than the result of laryngeal lesions. For most observations and measures of intraoral phenomena contributing to normal and faulty voice, we are forced to use various measuring instruments that help quantify aspects of respiratory, phonatory, and resonance function.

Respiration Testing

Because the vocal folds are activated for phonation by the outflowing air stream passing through the closed glottis, some observation and measurement of respiratory adequacy is a necessary part of the voice evaluation. Early phoniatrists placed much emphasis on breathing adequacy, particularly with regard to adequacy of singing; such a view was prominently advocated by Tarneud and frequently cited by Luchsinger and Arnold (1965). Most speech-language pathologists, but certainly not all, continue to show interest in how well voice patients breathe, and particularly in how well patients are able to extend and use their exhalations for phonation. It is commonly recognized, for example, that shortness of breath or speaking after much breath is already expired will noticeably affect phonation. Because lung capacities are generally far greater than the amount of air required for typical speaking situations, patients *use* of air supply is usually more important than their lung volumes. This is true even for patients who present severe breathing disorders such as emphysema or chronic obstructive pulmonary disease, or even with patients who have only one lung. Large lung volumes are more important for singing than for speaking. We shall consider separately those instruments that can be used for measuring various aspects of respiratory movement and, finally, those observations and tests that we can use to assess the patient's use of respiration as it applies to phonation. Specifically, we shall consider separately four types of information: lung volume, air pressure, air-flow, measures and motions of the torso.

Lung volume   It is important to determine how much of the total lung volume a patient uses in phonation. We can easily observe the patient speak or sing, and make a judgment about the overall adequacy of respiration while the patient is performing the task. Does she run out of her air supply before finishing the planned utterance? Is he forced to renew air intake more often than is desirable? Part of evaluating respiratory adequacy is measuring the patient's lung volume.

Specific dimensions of volume that can be measured include *vital capacity* (maximum amount of air that can be expelled from the lungs following a maximum inspiration), *tidal volume* (amount of air inspired and expired in a normal breathing cycle), *inspiratory reserve* (maximum amount of additional air inspired after a tidal inhalation is completed), and *expiratory reserve* (maximum volume of air expired after a tidal expiration). Normal speakers use only a small amount of their total vital capacity when speaking. Hixon, Goldman, and Mead (1973) have written that normal speakers use only about twice the air volume for speech that they use for quiet, easy normal (or tidal) breaths. Does the typical patient use greater or lesser volumes than this?

The capacities and volumes we need to measure are best determined by using wet or dry spirometers. In the wet spirometer, a container floats in water placed in a larger container. As air is introduced to the smaller floating container, it floats higher in proportion to the volume of air introduced. The distance or rise of displacement is measured in terms of cubic centimeters or liters. A 14-year-old boy was recently tested on a wet spirometer and found to have these lung volumes:

Vital capacity	=	3.8 liters
Tidal volume	=	.4 liters (400 cc)
Inspiratory reserve	=	3.3 liters
Expiratory reserve	=	3.4 liters

We see in this example that the normal tidal volume and the maximum amount of air the boy can expire after the tidal breath in several trials approximate his vital capacity or total maximum expiration. Some spirometers are of the dry type. A flexible container enlarges on inspiratory tasks and decreases in volume on expiratory tasks, in both instances measuring the volume of displacement. The wet spirometer appears to have greater clinical usage and also to provide greater volume accuracy. Again, we should point out, however, that volume data do not have the clinical relevance as measures of expiration (pressure and flow) and data specific to neck, thoracic, and abdominal movements.

Air-Flow Pressures   One can hear the effects of air pressure on the perceived loudness of the voice. Greater vocal intensities require higher air-flow pressures passing through the glottis for a shorter time, producing greater excursions of the vibrating vocal folds. In the ensuing section on loudness we further describe the measurement of voice intensities by several methods, such as using a sound-level meter. We often hear symptoms of inadequate air-flow pressure in voice patients who experience varying and inadequate loudness; we may also hear quality disturbances related to inadequate pressure for normal fold vibration.

Relatively inexpensive pressure measuring gauges and manometers are available for the measurement of air-flow pressures. In measuring air-pressure adequacy for voice, we are interested in finding an individual's oral pressures. One way of doing this is to ask the patient to produce a series of *pa* sounds. In the production of *pa* the glottis is open, and the pressure peaks during the production of the /p/ phase of the *pa*. Netsell and Hixon (1978) have found that the oral pressures obtained in the *pa* production or in a blowing task (when the mouthpiece has a small air leak) correspond to the pressures found in the lungs and the glottis. They have concluded that if patients can produce 5 to 10 cm of pressure over a period of five seconds in a sustained blowing task, they probably have sufficient expiratory pressures to produce normal voice.

Pressure measurements are used diagnostically more often when attempts are made to measure velopharyngeal adequacy, described in some detail in Chapter 7. Using some kind of manometric device, the patient is asked to produce a consonant such as /p/ or /k/; oral pressures are taken and nasal pressures (a nasal olive is inserted in the nares attached to the flow tube) are also determined. Sometimes the oral and nasal measurements are taken sequentially back to back, but such measures are perhaps more meaningful when taken simultaneously. For simultaneous oral-nasal pressures, the patient wears a face mask that is divided into oral and nasal sections, which provides separate oral-nasal pressure ratings (Hixon, Saxman, and McQueen, 1967). Oral speech should have little or no nasal pressure flow; as puffs of air escape through an inadequately closed velopharyngeal port, the sensitivity of the pressure gauge would detect such inappropriate escape.

Air-Flow Measures   An important diagnostic measure in voice evaluation is a measurement of air flow, which indicates the volume of air passed through the glottis in a fixed period of time. For example, the normal production of a vowel requires about 100 cc of air passage through the glottis in one second. A patient with large bilateral nodules who cannot effect adequate glottal closure will exhibit much higher air-flow rates and perhaps will use 100 cc in far less than a second. His or her voice would be characterized by much breathiness, and the leakage of air caused by the lack of normal glottal resistance would actually be audible. Poor glottal resistance to the air flow, as would be caused by the formation of nodules on the glottal margin, results in elevated air-flow measures. An opposite kind of problem, where the glottis is highly constricted, such as is observed in spastic dysphonia, results in markedly reduced flow rates.

The rate of flow, particularly when combined with pressure ratings, thus gives much diagnostic information about what is happening to the outgoing air at the level of the glottis. Measurements of air-flow are usually substantiated by critical listening to the voice. If a voice appears to be produced by a relatively lax glottal closure as observed in breathiness, the flow rates are high; if the voice appears harsh and sounds constricted, flow rates are often markedly diminished. Not only is flow rate information of diagnostic importance, it also helps us measure the effects of therapy. For example, as we attempt to move patients into more optimal phonatory behaviors, we see flow rates shift toward normal values (such as 100 cc per second).

An extremely useful instrument is the Phonatory Function Analyzer (see Figure 4–7). This device makes five simultaneous measures of phonation that demonstrate the efficiency of the larynx during phonation. It also demonstrates the interaction of these five measures (phonation time, fre-

FIGURE 4–7. The Phonatory Function Analyzer is used here with a 4-year-old boy to evaluate phonation time (in seconds), fundamental frequency (Hz), vocal intensity (dB SPL), air flow rate (Ml/sec), and total volume of air (Ml) during each phonation attempt. Changes in any of these vocal parameters and simultaneous changes in the other parameters are recorded on the paper at the bottom of the device. The five dials at the top of the device indicate the five parameters to assist the patient and clinician with a real time display.

quency, intensity, air-flow rate, and total volume of expired air) with one another. When one parameter, such as pitch, is altered during clinical stimulation the effect on another parameter, such as air-flow rate, is easily demonstrated. The tracing (see Figure 4–8) from the Phonatory Function Analyzer demonstrates that a slight elevation in pitch during the production of a vowel can reduce the excessive air-flow rate that gives rise to the perception of extreme breathiness in this adult patient with bowed cords. An improved vocal quality, with reduced breathiness, is correlated with the tracing of reduced air flow. The air-flow measurement is made in milliliters per second, which is the practical equivalent of cubic centimeters mentioned earlier.

Another useful device for measuring air flow is the pneumotachometer, shown in Figure 4–9. The patient produces vowel prolongations with air flow captured in the oral mask, and the flow rate is measured by the pneumotachometer. Much data are available for normal flow rates both in children (Leeper, 1976) and adults (Yanagihara and von Leden, 1967), as are many references examining changes in flow for various voice disorder groups (Gordon, Morton, and Simpson, 1978); (Isshiki and von Leden, 1964).

Somewhat related to a measure of flow are the various duration studies that determine how long the individual can sustain a voiced or voiceless expiration (Bless and Saxman, 1970; Eckel and Boone, 1981; Ptacek and Sander, 1963; Tait, Michel, and Carpenter, 1980). One measure of differential duration measures that is used diagnostically in the voice evaluation is the s/z ratio we discussed earlier in this chapter. As mentioned, here the patient is asked first to sustain the /s/ as long as possible, and then to sustain the /z/. The typical s/z ratios of normal subjects approximate 1.0, indicating that the voiceless expiration time (the /s/) closely matches maximum phonation time (the /z/) (Tait et al., 1980). In 95 percent of their patients with glottal margin pathologies (nodules, polyps, thickening), Eckel and Boone (1981) found elevated s/z ratios in excess of 1.4, indicating marked reduction in voiced duration values. The clinical value of the s/z ratio to pressure and flow measures are illustrated by the application of all three measures in this clinical case:

A 19-year-old university singer was self-referred to the University Speech and Hearing Clinic for her continuing "breathiness and hoarseness." Initial voice evaluation techniques included a pneumotachic evaluation, which found air-flow measurements of 240 cc/sec with oral pressure readings of 5.5 cm H_2O; her initial /s/ duration was 18, her /z/ duration was 11, and her s/z ratio was computed at 1.64. Initially, she resisted having a medical evaluation that included indirect laryngoscopy. The clinician, however, knowing that her high s/z value may well have been predictive of laryngeal disease, insisted that she have laryngoscopy. A subsequent examination found her to have bilateral vocal nodules that occupied almost a third of her total anterior-posterior glottal length. Following laryngoscopy, she was enrolled in individual voice therapy. Repeated testing after nine weeks of voice therapy revealed a lower air-flow measure of 219 cc/sec and higher oral pressure readings of 7.3 cm H_2O; her s/z ratios had decreased to 1.28.

FIGURE 4-8.
This tracing from the Phonatory Function Analyzer demonstrates how a change in one vocal parameter (pitch, for example) can make a significant change in another parameter (such as rate of air flow). As the pitch level is raised from 100 Hz to a level of 130 Hz, the air-flow rate is reduced from 260 Ml/sec to a level of 180 Ml/sec. Intensity is also increased from 83 to 88 dB SPL.

FIGURE 4-9. The pneumotachometer provides air-flow data specific to volume. A split mask can be used for picking up flow separately from both the mouth and the nose.

These improved scores all suggested better laryngeal function. Subsequent laryngeal examination confirmed some decrease in the size of the nodules, although small bilateral nodes were still present. Her voice quality had improved. The s/z ratio as used here provided one additional measure and observation for the clinician in conducting the overall voice management of the patient.

A simple but useful clinical maneuver, for the clinician without instrumentation, which can be employed to demonstrate the degree of laryngeal tension, is the application of hand pressure to the patient's abdomen during phonation of the sustained /i/ vowel. The palm of the hand is placed firmly over the middle of the abdomen just above the level of the belt. The hand is pulsed as the phonation is sustained. The more hyperfunction present during the voice production, the less the voice will pulse; conversely, the more relaxed the vocal folds and the larynx are, the more the voice will pulse in response to the hand pressure. When the clinician applies the technique to patients who are producing their typical voice, and then reapplies the technique after using a facilitating approach such as glottal fry, the dramatic difference in vocal pulsing becomes obvious to the patient.

Motions of the Torso   For many years, students of voice have been able to use the *pneumograph* to measure thoracic and abdominal movements during inhalation and exhalation. The pneumograph is usually connected to a recording device, of which there are two main types, the *kymograph* and the

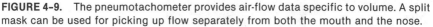

polygraph, both of which provide graphic measurement writeouts. The pneumograph provides straps, which are placed around the thorax or abdomen; at the ends of the straps are rubber tubes. As the tubes are stretched, a partial vacuum is created within them, and the amount of vacuum is communicated to the recording instrument. The pneumographic recordings help speech-language pathologists study the frequency of the respiration cycle, focusing on the regularity of the inhalation-exhalation ratio. How well a patient can sustain an exhalation can be determined very well by using the pneumograph with a kymographic or polygraphic writeout. For the study of differential movements of the thorax in inspiration-expiration, the pneumograph is used less today in favor of newer methodologies.

To study the relative coordination between abdominal movements and thoracic movements, Hixon, Mead, and Goldman (1976) have used *magnetometers* to examine the relative "anteroposterior diameters" of both the abdomen and thorax, particularly as the two areas relate to one another. When using the magnetometers, the clinician can determine the synchrony of movements of the rib cage and the abdomen during speech breathing. Some clinical voice disorders related to such problems as cerebral palsy or other motor-speech disorders produce severe problems in this synchrony between the different parts involved in breathing. Small magnets are placed on the back, on the front chest wall, and on the lower back and abdominal wall; the anterior-posterior distance varies between the magnets in each area (chest or abdomen), and this information can be traced either on an oscilloscope or on some kind of graphic printout.

The experimental use of the *electromyograph* (EMG) in investigating the use of particular muscles in breathing during speech has been explored in several studies reported by Hoshiko (1962), but there has been little regular use of the electromyograph as a clinical tool for respiration assessment. Which muscle is doing what may be determined by the clinical EMG, whereby recordings are made of the variations in electrical potential as detected by needle or surface electrodes inserted into or placed on a muscle. Whenever that muscle becomes active (contracts), its electrical activity is displayed on a graphic writeout.

Movement of the thorax and the downward excursion of the diaphragm can be identified very well by various X-ray techniques. The degree of inflatability, as seen by thoracic expansion and downward movement of the diaphragm, has been evaluated with convenience by *still X-ray.* Still X-rays taken at moments of maximum inhalation and exhalation have been helpful in identifying those sites of respiration (apical versus base of lungs) that show the most deflation or inflation and have provided knowledge about the type of breathing the patient employs: abdominal-diaphragmatic, midthoracic, or clavicular. Similar information can be obtained by viewing the respiratory mechanism in action, assessing actual movement by the use of other X-ray techniques—namely, *fluoroscopy* and *videofluorography.*

Other Aspects of Respiration Testing   The type of breathing the patient uses can often be accurately determined by visual observation. The most inefficient type of breathing, *clavicular,* seems to be the easiest to identify. The patient elevates the shoulders on inhalation, using the neck accessory-muscles as the primary muscles of inhalation. This upper chest breathing, characterized by noticeable elevation of the clavicles, is unsatisfactory for good voice for two reasons: First, the upper, apical ends of the lungs, when expanded, do not alone provide an adequate respiration; and second, the strain in using the neck accessory muscles for respiration is often visually apparent, with individual muscles "standing out" (particularly the sternocleidomastoids, as they contract to elevate the upper thorax). Although little research evidence clearly identifies the negative effects on speech of clavicular breathing, no serious singer would waste time developing such a shallow, upper-lung reservoir of air. Clavicular-type breathing requires too much effort for too little breath.

Diaphragmatic-abdominal breathing may well be the preferred method of respiration, especially if the patient has heavy vocal demands, as in singing or acting-speaking without electronic amplification. If the patient is employing diaphragmatic-abdominal breathing, this should be noted on the voice evaluation form. This use of lower thoracic breathing is usually identifiable by the presence of abdominal and lower thoracic expansion on inspiration, and a gradual decrease in abdominal-lower thoracic prominence on expiration. When asked to take in a deep breath, such a patient will demonstrate, upon inhaling, relatively active expansion of the lower thorax and little noticeable upper-chest movement.

We can perhaps obtain a more accurate assessment of how patients breathe for speech when we ask them to demonstrate various voices, such as a pulpit voice, a calling-the-kids voice, a talking-to-superiors voice, and so on. Most voice patients exhibit breathing patterns that are somewhere in between clavicular and diaphragmatic-abdominal breathing, and for these persons we use the somewhat nondescript term *thoracic* on voice evaluation forms. Thoracic breathers exhibit no noticeable upper thoracic or abdominal expansion on inhalation. The general mode of breathing can often be assessed if the clinician observes the patients closely as they speak.

Measurement of Pitch

Observations of voice pitch tell us whether a voice is low or high for the patient's age and sex, but only when we measure pitch can we determine the exact fundamental frequency of a voice. Of the various aspects of voice, frequency as measured in cycles per second (Hz) is one of the most useful and perhaps the most measurable. As part of a voice evaluation, the patient's total *frequency range* (lowest to highest note) should be determined as a prelude to finding that person's *optimal pitch* (the patient's easiest and most compatible voice pitch). Measurements should be made of the patient's *habitual pitch* (the most frequently occurring or modal pitch level used by the patient). We first discuss the instruments available for measuring these aspects of frequency and pitch.

The Visi-Pitch (Figure 4–10) is an excellent clinical instrument for measuring different aspects of frequency: frequency range, optimal pitch, and habitual pitch. The Visi-Pitch offers both a digital display of frequency and an oscilloscopic display. For determination of range, the patient is asked to say "ah" at a comfortable pitch and loudness level and then repeat

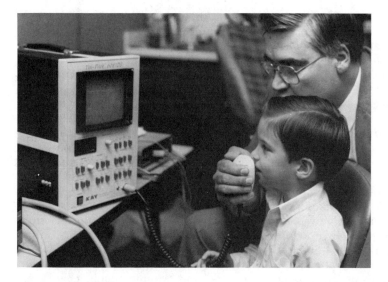

FIGURE 4-10.   A young boy is able to use the visual feedback from the Visi-Pitch screen to modify his pitch and intensity output. Using the split screen (upper/lower) capability, the child and clinician can compare typical performance with performance under clinical stimulation.

the "ah" at decreasing musical steps, down to the lowest "note" the patient can produce. The patient is then asked to produce successively higher notes until reaching the top of his or her range. Even though the clinician will have a digital writeout of fundamental frequency for each separate vocalization, the productions can be stored on the scope and frequency values can be determined after the patient has completed the sequence. A cursor feature on the Visi-Pitch allows the clinician to search the stored tracings on the scope to determine the exact frequency of any particular phonation. The lowest and highest frequencies the patient is able to produce represent the patient's range.

The concept of optimal pitch can be challenged for a number of reasons, but there is some clinical utility in the notion of a pitch level that is best for the patient during the period of initial voice retraining. One level of pitch usually sounds better in vocal quality, and thus the facilitating approach of chant talk takes advantage of this observation (see Chapter 5). Optimal pitch can be determined by using both the frequency and intensity writeouts of the Visi-Pitch at the same time. Optimal pitch is usually the frequency that is slightly louder and clearer in quality; relative changes in both intensity and quality can be determined by the scope tracings (greater vertical excursion indicates greater intensity, and improved sharpness of tracing line indicates better periodicity or improved quality). One way habitual pitch can be determined is by playing a conversational tape jacked into the Visi-Pitch; for every eight seconds of conversation, the most frequently occurring frequency level can be spotted in the scope tracings (which can be stored until they are reviewed) and then measured. The patient can also produce live conversation or oral reading directly into the Visi-Pitch microphone for a time period of eight seconds; the tracings of frequency can be stored on the scope and then measured. The most frequently occurring frequency can be easily identified. The Visi-Pitch has been designed as a clinical instrument that will easily provide frequency data both at the time of the evaluation and as ongoing feedback information during voice therapy.

The Phonatory Function Analyzer, mentioned in our earlier discussion of flow rate and volume, provides an excellent measure of pitch during sustained vowels. If a mask is used, the pitch can be measured in connected speech. Of particular value is the fact that this instrument is capable of five simultaneous measures of voice. The instrument provides a hard copy printout for the patient's chart and also five dials (corresponding to each parameter) that the patient can monitor during voice production.

Another relatively inexpensive clinical instrument for the measurement of pitch is the Fundamental Frequency Indicator. This device is used by holding a microphone to the larynx or under the nose while producing a sustained vowel or /m/. Repeated syllables such as /mimimi/ or /bibibi/ and voiced phrases such a "Miami millionaire" and "Momma made lemon jam" can be produced and measured. The pitch level can be read from the dial, and the red and green light can be set at levels that will indicate a patient's achievement of a certain level of pitch. The device can be useful in establishing a pitch level to begin facilitating techniques such as chant talk, tongue protrusion /i/, or glottal fry (see Chapter 5). The patient's habitual pitch level, pitch range, and optimal pitch level can be determined with this device, as Figure 4–11 shows.

FIGURE 4-11.   This 3-year-old boy is able to make the association between changes in his vocal pitch and the movement of the needle on the Fundamental Frequency Indicator (FFI).

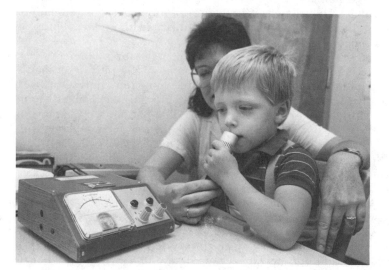

Another useful instrument for extracting fundamental frequency from running speech and for determining pitch range is the Tonar II (Fletcher, 1972). As the patient speaks into the microphone, Tonar II automatically displays at fixed intervals the fundamental frequency of the voice. Although the Tonar II is designed primarily for training in resonance therapy, its digital writeout of frequency is helpful in determining modal pitch or habitual pitch. The Tonar II can also be used to measure fundamental frequency range.

Another instrument for measuring both pitch range and habitual pitch is the Tunemaster III (1975). When the tone switch is on, the instrument is capable of generating pitch levels over a one-octave range; for example, the instrument can generate the twelve semitones from C_3 to B_3, and by switching on the octave switch, one can extend the range up another octave to B_4. When the musical frequency is generated in step-by-step semitones, patients are asked to match the tone with their own voice. For adult male subjects whose fundamental frequencies may be well below C_3 (128 cps), clinicians have to convert the matched pitch of the patients to the instrument pitch level by dropping the machine value by one octave. For example, if the instrument is generating an F_3 and a male patient is "matching" the tone with his lowest pitch production, the patient would be producing an F_2 pitch level. The Tunemaster III is useful for establishing a new pitch level, as described in Chapter 5. With the meter switch on, an internal microphone picks up external sounds. If the sound is within a two-semitone range of a target note that has been predetermined and set in the instrument, a "valid reading" light will go on, and a meter pointer will show how sharp or flat the speaker's pitch is specific to the target pitch.

It is possible to measure frequency range and make other measures of frequency without instrumentation other than a piano or pitch pipe. An initial voice recording made at the time of a patient's first clinic visit is a useful tool for analyzing the patient's habitual pitch level. This analysis can be made after the patient has left the clinic. One method we have used is to stop the recorder at random points and attempt to match the voice pitch level with a *pitch pipe* or a piano. After some experience with a pitch pipe, it is possible to match pitch levels between the pitch-pipe frequency and the patient's voice. This is facilitated by remembering key pitch values for average voices. For example, in cycles per second, the typical adult male voice is somewhere near C_3 (128 cps), and therefore is not very different from the C_3 note on a pitch pipe. Using the pitch pipe, we would start at C_3 and then go by gradations (sharps and flats) until we reached "near" the recorded level of the patient's voice. With an adult female we might select as our beginning pitch A_3 (213 cps) and go up or down to match the patient's voice. A typical starting place for a prepubertal child would be middle C (256 cps). In a two-or three-minute sample from a voice recording, we might select seven or eight voice samples for analysis of pitch level. After we have determined the approximate pitch of the patient's voice samples, we then count the various pitch levels and look for the *modal pitch value* (the pitch level that occurs most often), and record this as the patient's habitual pitch level. Using the modal pitch probably gives us a more valid habitual pitch than averaging the obtained sample values and using the mean.

A patient's pitch range can also be determined by using voice models. This may be done by asking the patient first to match a pitch level provided by the clinician. It is usually easier for patients to match their own voice with another person's voice than to a generated pitch level from some instrument such as a piano, a pitch pipe, and so on. For this reason, it is most useful to have on hand some recordings of normal voices (adult male, adult female, several children's voices), producing vowels, prolonging each vowel for about three seconds. These samples can be recorded on small cassette tapes, discs, or on blank Language Master cards (1979). On playing the sample voice, which should be close to the patients' observed pitch levels, we ask the patients to say "ah" with the sample voice, matching it as closely as possible. This allows us to provide the patients with a model, showing how we want them to sing down to the lowest note they can make, descending by one full note on the musical scale for each production. In our model sample, we prolong each note for about three seconds. Patients' performances should be recorded on tape, whenever possible, and the actual frequency analyses done later in the laboratory. Patients now attempt to sing down to the lowest notes they can produce, then sing up, one full note at a time, until reaching the highest notes they can produce, including the falsetto, and then sing down, one note at a time, until reaching their lowest notes again. Finally, when the lowest notes are reached, they are asked once again to sing up to the highest note of their ranges. This pitch-range task is usually easiest for patients if they are instructed to sing one note at a time, taking a breath between each three-second production. Many voice patients, and perhaps the population in general, have real difficulty matching their own voices to a pitch model and producing a range of their lowest to their highest pitch productions. It may be impossible for some patients with vocal fold pathology, such as nodules or polyps, to vary much the pitch of their voice. By providing various models and encouragement at the right times, the experienced voice clinician can usually obtain some pitch-range information.

Each individual seems to have a voice pitch level that can be produced with an economy of physical effort and energy. This relatively effortless voice production is known as *optimum pitch* and is apparently the pitch level at which the thyroarytenoids and other intrinsic muscles of the larynx can produce vocal fold adduction with only minimal muscular effort. The vibrating frequency emitted from the approximated vocal folds is directly related to the natural length and mass of the thyroarytenoids, without much lengthening or shortening. It is doubtful, however, that optimum pitch represents any exact cycles-per-second value. Optimum pitch is more often found in two or three notes somewhere at the bottom of the individual's pitch range, several notes higher than the lowest possible pitch production. The classic notion of optimum pitch is validated somewhat using the Visi-Pitch, whereby we confirm a note or two toward the bottom of the patient's total range where the periodicity of fold vibration is improved (a sharper line appears on the scope), accompanied by relative increases in intensity.

A traditional way of determining optimum pitch, described by Fairbanks (1960), requires individual patients to phonate their entire vocal ranges, including the falsetto, from their lowest productions to their highest. The total range of full-step musical notes is then counted. For adult males, the optimum pitch level is considered to be the one located one-fourth of the way from the bottom of the total pitch range; for female adults, it might be one or two notes lower than the one-fourth level.

Although the concept of optimum pitch has been questioned (Thurman, 1958), the concept of an "easy, natural" pitch level is useful in voice therapy. Because so many voice patients seem to have problems of vocal hyperfunction, an attempt to have patients produce easy, relatively effortless phonations has obvious diagnostic and therapeutic implications. If a patient can produce a good voice easily, such a voice can become an immediate therapy goal. When an optimum pitch has been determined, the patient should be asked to produce various other vowels and words at that general pitch level. We have used various different vowels to determine which produce the best vocal quality at different pitch levels. Our experience with voice disordered patients has revealed that the /i/, /u/, and /o/ vowels almost always produce the best voices, whereas the /a/ and /ae/ always produce the poorest. A qualitative judgment should be made as to how the voice sounds.

Other validating methods of optimum pitch determination may be used, including these methods described by Murphy (1964):

> (a) the loud-sigh technique: take a deep breath and intone as on expiration; (b) the grunt method: grunt ah or o, gradually prolonging the utterances until a passage is chanted at the original grunt pitch level; (c) the swollen tone technique: stop up the ears, sing ah or hum m up and down the scale until the pitch level at which the tone swells or is loudest is identified; (d) cough sonorously on an ee sound. (p. 95)

We might add to Murphy's list two other brief methods that help determine optimal pitch. Ask the patient to yawn and sigh (the relaxed phonation of a sigh is often the optimum speaking pitch) and also to say "uh-huh" (this somewhat automatically produced, affirmative utterance often approximates the optimum pitch level). The six methods—these two and Murphy's four—usually yield pitch levels that are close to one another, even if not the same. Indications from the Visi-Pitch further help the determination of optimum pitch. Remember, however, that for clinical purposes we are interested in a particular area of the frequency range (usually a note or two, several notes above the bottom of the total range) that seems to produce the "best" voice with the least amount of effort.

Variations in Pitch as a Diagnostic Aid An inappropriate pitch level may at times contribute to the development of a voice disorder. Some vocal fold pathologies, on the other hand, produce changes in voice pitch, often because of the weighting or increased mass-size of the involved fold(s). Some functionally produced low-pitched voices may be called "the voices of profundity." A young professional person may employ an artificially low voice to assert authority and knowledge; a preacher may try to "hit the low ones" in his sermon; a young woman may think a low-pitched voice is more professional sounding. Conversely, a high-pitched voice is often symptomatic of general tension and difficulties in relaxation. In addition, a post-mutational falsetto in a postpubertal male may be the result of serious psychological identity problems, or may serve the patient little or not at all, and persist out of habit or set. If a patient's pitch appears incongruous with his or her chronological age and sex, the clinician should first determine if that patient has the functional ability to speak at a pitch level more compatible with his or her overall organism. If pitch variation is impossible, the condition might be the result of cord paralysis, or of certain virilizing drugs that have permanently changed the vocal folds, or of glandular-metabolic changes.

Variations in Loudness   Some patients are observed to speak too loudly or too softly for particular vocal situations. There is no optimal loudness level for any one individual, as voice loudness will vary according to the situation. In an evaluation session, a clinician can make a judgment about the loudness of the patient's voice. If it appears to be impossible for the patient to speak in a loud enough voice, the dysphonia may be related to vocal fold paralysis, or to increases in the mass of the folds (for example, due to vocal nodules), or to bowed vocal folds worn out from continuous use (myasthenia larynges). Soft voices may also be heard in patients who feel relatively inadequate and inferior, and their softness of phonation is consistent with their overall self-image. There are some neurological disorders, such as Parkinson's disease and bulbar palsy, where the patient characteristically speaks in a voice that may be barely audible. At the other end of the spectrum, are patients who speak with voices that may be perceived as uncomfortably loud. Some dysphonic patients, particularly those who speak with hyperfunction, may have inappropriately loud voices as part of their total problem. Another intensity variation that may be observed at the time of voice evaluation is a patient who speaks with little or no fluctuation in loudness, and perhaps with no variation in pitch.

Because the loudness of the voice frequently varies according to the setting, the interactions of the speaker-listener, background noise levels, and so forth, it is difficult to measure a representative intensity of someone's speaking voice. One of the best ways we have of measuring loudness is to use a sound-pressure level meter that gives the sound-pressure level of the voice for a particular distance (from speaker's mouth to sound-level microphone). To measure voice intensity, patients are seated so that their mouth is about one meter from the microphone. The intensity level of the voice can be read from the sound-level-meter dial in terms of decibels. Remember, however, that this laboratory measure of intensity does not have practical application to the loudness levels the patients may be using in more natural settings.

The Visi-Pitch can provide relative measures of intensities. The Visi-Pitch (1987) "screen is divided into a grid, and each vertical division represents 10 Db of sound pressure level" (p. 2–13). The Visi-Pitch can also provide data for the interaction of frequency and intensity, because the instrument allows the simultaneous plotting of both values. Typically, the speaker, or singer for that matter, uses higher intensity levels for higher frequency levels. With practice it is possible for speakers to hold their pitch level constant and vary the intensity curve without altering frequency. The Visi-Pitch intensity values are relative values that can be inferred from the oscilloscope display rather than from direct measurements of sound-pressure level.

As mentioned earlier in this chapter, the Phonatory Function Analyzer makes careful intensity measurements in dB SPL as intensity interacts with air flow, frequency, total volume of air, and total phonation time in seconds. This makes the instrument helpful both diagnostically and therapeutically with dysphonic patients. Most measures of voice intensity level should be related to other information specific to air flow and air pressure, frequency, relative opening of the mouth, body position, and so on. If intensity measurements are possible, they are usually supplemented by rating scale judgments of loudness, as discussed earlier in this chapter.

Measurement of Vocal Quality

One early diagnostic sign of a voice problem is the emergence of some kind of vocal quality disorder, such as hoarseness or breathiness. Usually some form of *dysphonia* (the term used through this text for all disorders of voice quality) signals to the patient that he or she has a voice problem. At the time of evaluation, the clinician should listen closely to how the patient speaks and attempt to describe what is heard. The verbal description of dysphonia, is extremely difficult, however. Until the state of the art improves, voice clinicians will simply have to grope for terms to describe the voices they hear. Fairbanks (1960) lists three quality conditions, *breathiness, harshness,* and *hoarseness,* that may well be related to difficulties in optimal approximation of the vocal folds on phonation.

In breathiness, we can usually observe an audible escape of air as the approximating edges along the glottis fail to make optimum contact. Breathiness may be related to a patient's functional inability to bring the folds firmly together—the person may have the functional capability of firmer vocal fold approximation, but, for whatever reason, prefers to speak with a breathy voice. Some patients with rheumatoid arthritis take various muscle relaxants that produce excessively breathy voice quality as a side effect. Sometimes breathiness is related to growths on the folds, such as nodules or polyps, which prevent optimum adduction; sometimes it results from cord paralysis, which prevents optimum fold adduction. In a voice signal that is characterized as breathy, the periodicity of vocal tone is reduced and aperiodicity or noise is increased. We frequently observe at the beginning of an utterance marked aperiodicity that decreases as the vocal folds begin to vibrate. The breathy voice is often produced by the vocal folds approximating slowly together after the initiation of the outgoing air stream has already begun.

The spectrograph in Figure 4–12 provides a visual display of what we hear. Figure 2–17 showed that the breathy voice produces noise across the sound spectrum with less definition of a periodic sound wave, as seen in the distinct print of the first three formants in the normal voice spectrogram. Other laboratory measures for quantification of breathiness can be made, such as measuring air flow–air pressure, spectral noise levels (San-

FIGURE 4-12.
A spectrograph used for voice analysis.

sone and Emanuel, 1970), and determining jitter (variations or perturbations in frequency) and shimmer (variations in amplitude) as described by Michel and Wendahl (1971). The perceptual judgments of the clinician and other listeners continue, however, to play an important role in the observation and diagnosis of breathiness.

A harsh voice is usually heard by listeners as unpleasant. Ainsworth (1980) described the difficulty of defining harshness:

> Verbal descriptions of *harshness* are difficult to make without using "impressionistic" terms, i.e., grating, rasping, rough, gutteral, raucous. There often are frequent and "hard" glottal catches, i.e., the initiation of tones with an explosive release of air by the vocal folds, and excessive glottal (vocal) fry which is a low-pitched "popping" sound. (p. 7)

Aperiodicity of laryngeal vibration can be seen in the spectrogram for the harsh voice. Often abrupt initiation of voice is characterized by hard glottal attack. Patients sound as if they are working hard to speak. A harsh voice may be described as strident, metallic, or grating; whatever the description used, the connotation is unpleasant. The Visi-Pitch or any kind of spectrum analyzer like the spectrograph will visualize harshness with increased aperiodicity across the spectrum, a reduction of fundamental frequency, a scatter of resonance across the spectrum, and abrupt glottal attack as observed in sudden initiation of phonation. In our judgments of harshness we often focus on the metallic aspects of resonance, whereby the voice seems to come out of a pharynx and oral cavity that appear to be in a state of hypercontraction. Instead of hearing softness and some absorption of sound waves, we hear a hardness described by Coffin (1981) as a "voice produced by hard, reflective surfaces rather than by soft, absorbing surfaces." It is difficult to verbalize a description of the harsh voices we sometimes hear.

Hoarseness is the most common laryngeal quality disturbance, although the term is often used in a meaningless manner to label any kind of laryngeal problem in phonation. Anything that inteferes with optimum vocal fold adduction can produce hoarseness. Many patients exhibit it on a purely functional basis—that is, because they approximate the vocal folds too tightly or too loosely together, they produce hoarseness. Darley (1965) wrote that "hoarse voice quality combines the acoustic characteristics of harshness and breathiness and usually results from laryngeal pathology" (p. 57). Typical dysphonic patients display the kind of hoarseness we hear in patients with some form of laryngitis. The hoarse voice heard in patients with bilateral vocal nodules includes a breathy escape of air, and is often accompanied by hard glottal attack as patients attempt to compensate for their phonation difficulties. Hoarseness may be related to mucus on the vocal folds, or sometimes to destruction of all or a part of the folds. The spectral printout of the hoarse voice in Figure 2–17 confirms the combination of breathiness and harshness, as we see increased noise across the spectrum with a heavier concentration of acoustic energy in the first formant at the bottom of the spectrogram.

Many patients with hoarseness begin to compensate for their poor voices by driving the mechanism even harder; they may feel, for example, that they must have abrupt initiation of glottal attack to "get their voices started." The Visi-Pitch is easy to use to determine the abruptness of glottal attack combined with hoarseness. Any kind of air-pressure instrument can likewise verify sudden onset of expiration. The visual imprints on the oscilloscope attached to such a monitoring instrument will show sudden and abrupt phonation onsets, characterized by vertical excursions at onset, as opposed to a more gradual sloping rise of the onset curve.

The electroglottograph is an excellent device to demonstrate the abruptness of glottal onset and to depict the ratio of long open phase to closed phase that characterizes the breathy voice. The device also displays aperiodic vocal fold vibration by clearly demonstrating the lack of similarity from wave to wave. The more dissimilar each wave is from the preceding and following waves, the more aperiodicity in the voice. Figure 4–13 shows a glottogram or laryngogram of a prolonged /i/ vowel produced with a very hoarse voice quality. This laryngogram may be contrasted with one of a normal vocal quality and one of a breathy vocal quality during the production of the /i/ vowel.

Clinician judgment of hoarseness must supplement any instrumental measurements we are able to make. The advantage of some kind of instrument quantification of hoarseness at the time of the initial evaluation is that the measurement data can be compared with data taken subsequently during and at the end of therapy. It has also been our experience that the instruments that provide evaluation data can be used to provide feedback to patients in therapy about particular components of voice. For example, for a patient with hoarseness, it may be advantageous to provide visual feedback on the oscilloscope relative to improvement of periodicity as the voice is heard to be "less hoarse." Like most evaluation data, it should be used not only in the diagnostic-decision process in planning therapy, but also given to patients as a continuing feedback and confirmation of their therapy progress. This can be extremely motivational.

Other variations in vocal fold approximation may produce symptoms

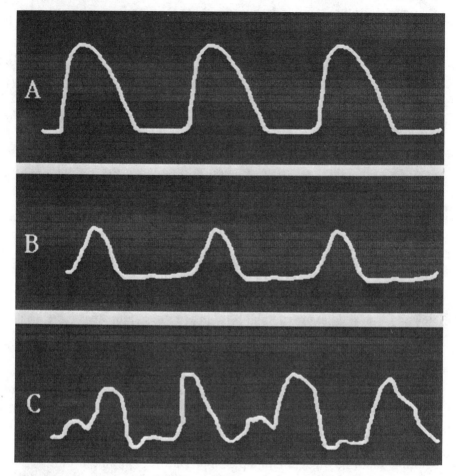

FIGURE 4-13.   These three glottograms are productions of the /i/ vowel with (A) normal vocal quality, (B) breathy quality, and (C) hoarse vocal quality. The normal trace (A) demonstrates a sharp vertical rise, a narrow peak, an even return to baseline, and a substantial open phase. Trace (B), the breathy voice quality, is represented in the sloping voice onset, rather than the sharp vertical rise seen in the normal trace and the long open phase. Trace (C), the hoarse voice, is indicated by the lack of a uniform wave form from one cycle to the next.

of *glottal fry, register variations, pitch breaks,* and *phonation breaks.* Most voice evaluation forms have checkoff lists that would include these terms. *Glottal fry* can be detected using the Visi-Pitch. Instead of a single tracing line representing a single fundamental frequency, the voice is represented by two or more broken lines, indicating that the patient is producing two or three simultaneous fundamental frequencies. The multiple phonation pulses are usually of low frequency and are usually observed at the bottom of the patient's frequency range. The phenomenon of fry is usually observed as a slight hoarseness that comes into the individual's voice toward the bottom of the pitch range. It has been described as sounding like an outboard motor boat, a creaking door, popcorn popping, and so on. Moore and von Leden (1958) termed glottal fry "dicrotic dysphonia." Others have described the vocal folds during the production of fry as thick, with the ventricular bands in close contact with the superior surface of the true vocal folds. It is undoubtedly this thickness of folds that produces the lower fundamental pitch that usually accompanies glottal fry. With some elevation of voice pitch, the fry will often decrease. We consider glottal fry to be a normal vocal register.

Register variations, rarely mentioned in American speech pathology texts, do exist as clinical problems in some voice patients. The concept of vocal register comes from the organ stop, which in German is called "register." Luchsinger and Arnold (1965) wrote:

> In chest voice, the cords vibrate over their entire breadth, whereas the falsetto voice reveals vibration limited to the inner cord margins. When phonating low tones, the cords appear rounded, full, and relaxed, while they are sharp-edged, thin, and taut for falsetto tones. These differences may readily be seen on frontal laryngeal tomograms. (p. 97)

Register variation is related to the relative changes in the cross-section of the vocal folds, produced by differential contraction of the vocalis section of the thyroarytenoid muscle. In his classic article, "The Mechanism of the Larynx," Negus (1957) used the terms *thick* and *thin* to correspond to the cross-sectional differences seen in the production of the chest register and the head register. Sometimes we observe voices that seem incompatible with the resonating bodies of the patient. Certain patients may produce variations by attempting to speak at their lower pitches with vocal folds approximated in the manner typical of high-pitched head register. Conversely, sometimes higher pitches are produced with the folds approximated in their fullest broad dimension, the typical pattern of the low-pitched chest register. Register variation (fold approximation incompatible with the desired pitch level) can best be confirmed by frontal X-ray of the approximating glottal surfaces, as seen in frontal tomograms. Typical tomographic configurations for varying registers were shown in Figure 2–15.

When *pitch break* is observed, it is usually in a voice that is pitched too low. As the patient is phonating, the pitch level suddenly breaks upward to a falsetto level, often one octave above the pitch level the person was using. Pitch breaks may also be observed in a voice pitched too high, and then the break is downward, usually a full octave below the previous pitch level. In an adult patient, voice breaks can be extremely embarrassing. Sometimes pitch breaks are a patient's primary, and perhaps sole, reason for seeking voice therapy. Pitch breaks in children are much more common, but are rarely considered to be clinical problems. Curry (1949) found in his voice studies of adolescents that although voice breaks can occur in males in prepuberty, they are much more common at around the age of 14, when rapid pubertal changes take place. In 18 year olds, Curry found virtually no pitch breaks. Pitch breaks in children, particularly in males at around the time of puberty, are, in fact, fairly common and usually disappear with continuing physical maturation. In adults, pitch breaks are relatively rare and appear most often to be symptomatic of inappropriate habitual pitch levels—too low a pitch with involuntary pitch breaks upward, or too high a pitch with the breaks occurring downward.

The *phonation break* or abductor spasm (see Chapter 6) is a temporary loss of voice that may occur for only part of a word, a whole word, a phrase, or a sentence. An individual may be phonating with no observable difficulty when suddenly a loss of voice or phonation break occurs. Patients who experience voice breaks usually exhibit some degree of voice hyperfunction as they speak. They work to talk. Typical patients with voice breaks may use their voices a lot, such as teachers. After prolonged speaking, they begin to experience vocal fatigue and try to improve the sound of their voice, by raising or lowering the voice pitch or speaking through clenched teeth. The result is increased vocal tension. Finally, while they are phonating, the vocal folds spontaneously abduct and they temporarily lose their voice. By throat clearing, coughing, swallowing water, or whatever, they restore phonation until the next phonation break. Most voice patients, even if they have occasional phonation breaks, will not exhibit such temporary voice loss during evaluation sessions.

The two different types of phonation breaks or abductor spasms result from different causes. First, as we have described, is the cessation of phonation that results from the sudden abduction of the vocal folds, or from the loss of sufficient glottal resistance, such as when two opposing nodules meet and allow too much air to escape. Too little subglottic pressure remains to drive the cords, and phonation is lost momentarily. A second type of phonation break occurs when there is a phonatory arrest, as in spastic dysphonia, hyperkinetic dysphonia, or ventricular phonation. The vocal folds are simply overadducted, which prevents phonation.

Resonance Testing

Our focus in this chapter on evaluation has been on the evaluation of patients with phonation disorders. That is not to say that patients may not have accompanying resonance disorders; phonation and resonance disorders may go hand in hand. Many patients, however, have voice problems that are primarily of voice resonance. We discuss the problems of voice resonance, their evaluation, management, and therapy in Chapter 7.

SUMMARY

The voice evaluation is the time when the clinician first meets the voice patient, providing opportunity for observation and testing. The evaluation continues as part of every therapy session, particularly as the clinician continually searches with the patient for new vocal behaviors. The speech-language pathologist must continue to evaluate and observe the patient's respiratory, phonatory, and resonance functions. Whenever possible, these functions should be quantified with instrumentation. The patient's voice data are used for comparison purposes, to quantify vocal changes between the first visit, subsequent therapy sessions, and the final outcome session. Patient performance, both as observed and as measured, is offered back to the patient as a continuing feedback, helping the patient become aware of voice performance. The evaluation enables the voice clinician to decide on what management steps to take for the patient. If voice therapy is indicated, the evaluation will help the clinician to develop a therapy plan and to pre-dict the patient's outcome prognosis.

Voice Evaluation
Observe / Evaluate
Test
(instrumental
quantification)
Compare: quantify ΔS
1st → final
Performance → feedback
↑ awareness
Management steps
Therapy plan
Outcome prognosis.

5

VOICE THERAPY FOR PROBLEMS OF VOCAL HYPERFUNCTION

The majority of voice disorders are related to vocal hyperfunction; most patients use too much effort and force while speaking or singing. Effective voice therapy for vocal hyperfunction begins with identifying possible vocal abuse and misuse, and then systematically attempting to decrease the occurrence of such aversive behaviors. Next, voice clinicians search with each patient to find the most efficient voice that the patient is able to produce by using various therapy procedures, called facilitating approaches *in this text. Those approaches that facilitate easier, better voice are then used in voice therapy. In this chapter we consider each facilitating approach separately; our discussions stress the procedures and the types of problem for which each particular approach is often found useful.*

As described in Chapter 1, vocal hyperfunction is using the voice with too much effort and force. In voice therapy, patients basically learn to use their vocal mechanisms more optimally. Serious interference to optimal vocalization results from voice abuse and misuse and requires an all-out effort by the clinician to identify such voice abuses-misuses and to establish a program to reduce their occurrence. An example of vocal abuse would be continuous throat clearing. If throat clearing is extensive enough, it alone can produce edematous (swelling) changes of the glottal margin, which causes hoarseness and breathiness. Throat clearing may also result from an additive lesion that serves as a glottal margin irritant, so that the patient clears the throat to change the feeling that "something is there." Such a patient may soon begin to clear the throat out of habit. Continuous throat clearing can add irritation to an already irritated site, and the throat clearing itself may thus become part of the production of the irritation. Efforts must be made, if voice therapy is to be successful, to reduce the occurrence of the throat clearing or any other form of vocal abuse.

Similarly, voice misuse can add irritation to the glottal margin, which can, in turn, contribute to the beginning and the continuation of a voice problem. An example of vocal misuse could be speaking with excessive hard glottal attack. A typical patient speaks with sudden initiation of voice onset, and the voice sounds forceful and strained. To improve the quality of such a voice, the patient should change from speaking in such an abrupt manner to using an easier phonatory style.

There is little difference in the kind of voice therapy given for the different kinds of dysphonia related to vocal hyperfunction. A 10-year-old boy with a husky voice and a normal larynx would require about the same therapy program as his 10-year-old friend with a husky voice and a larynx with bilateral vocal nodules. The type of facilitating approaches might be different, because what helps one person may not help another. Both children would profit, however, from a voice program designed to reduce vocal abuse and misuse, and a voice production program whereby the clinician and the children use various facilitating approaches to find the voice they are able to produce with the least amount of effort. Many adult problems of dysphonia and vocal fatigue demonstrate no structural change of the laryngeal mechanism, either as a cause or as a result. Functional voice problems without pathology usually respond to the same techniques of voice therapy as dysphonias related to cord thickening, vocal nodules, polyps, contact ulcers, and so on. A differential therapy approach—that is, a certain method for nodules, a different one for polyps—is not needed for each voice disorder. Rather, therapy might be more effective and relevant if, after analyzing the voice disorder along the dimensions of pitch, loudness, and quality, clinicians then applied a therapy appropriate to those dimensions.

It would be easy, and very wrong, to identify for patients the various things they are doing wrong vocally and then provide them with a series of specific remedial therapy techniques. Rather, voice therapists must continually search for the patients' best and most appropriate voice production. This searching is necessary because so much of vocal behavior is highly automatic, particularly the dimensions of pitch and quality. Patients cannot volitionally break vocalization down into various components and then hope to combine them into some ideal phonation. Therapy techniques are primarily vehicles of facilitation—that is, a clinician tries a particular therapy approach to see if it facilitates the production of a better voice. If it does, then that approach is utilized as therapy practice material. If it does not, it is quickly abandoned. As part of every clinical session, the clinician must probe and search for the patient's best voice. When an acceptable production is achieved, it becomes the patient's target model in therapy.

Note that the best voice is not necessarily the "best-sounding" one. For example, the voice of someone with vocal nodules may sound "worse" after the individual is instructed to take the "work" out of phonation. Without the excessive loudness or the hard glottal attack, there may not be enough driving air flow and subglottal pressure to produce adequate phonation with the weighted (heavy with vocal nodules) vocal folds. The temporary result may be increased dysphonia; however, the target goal with such a person is to reduce the aversive vocal behaviors. Without the added effort to phonate, the voice may sound increasingly dysphonic. This must be considered a "temporary condition that will exist until the nodules get smaller." Eventually, the voice will also sound better. Meanwhile, the optimal voice is a voicing attempt that is free of unnecessary effort and tension. The patient's own best voice becomes the therapy goal. This requires, of course, the continuous use of feedback to the patient of some aspect of the best voice production. Various kinds of feedback could include the auditory playback of voice productions using a cassette or reel-to-reel audiotape recorder, a looptape recorder, or a videotape recorder, and presenting the patient's production back on a TV monitor, or using various kinds of biofeedback equipment so that the patient might monitor a physiologic aspect of voice production. Biofeedback might include monitoring some aspect of respiration using a manometer or a pair of magnetometers, or letting a patient watch his or her velopharyngeal closure using an endoscope attached to a video unit. Often a patient can progress in voice therapy with only the feedback of his or her own best voice as the target model; sometimes voice patients need additional feedback provided by other devices.

Voice therapy for problems of vocal hyperfunction might well follow this kind of four-point program:

1. Identify abuse-misuse.
2. Reduce occurrence of identified abuse-misuse.
3. Search for the optimum vocalization by using facilitating approaches.
4. Use the approaches that work as practice techniques.

The following description of the vocal management of a 9-year-old boy with vocal nodules utilized this four-point program. Note that his voice actually sounded better when various facilitating approaches were used (this is not always an immediate result of early therapy attempts).

Eric, age 9, had a four-year history of hoarseness and occasional loss of voice. In a third-grade school screening program he was found to have a severe dysphonia by the speech-language pathologist, who referred him to an ENT physician for indirect laryngoscopy. The ENT doctor found that Eric had "large bilateral nodules which occupied about one-third of his total glottal length." A voice therapy program was initiated that put beginning focus on identifying his vocal abuses and misuses. Eric was observed to yell continually at play, clear his throat excessively (sometimes twice a minute), and make funny animal sounds as a way of entertaining his family and friends (and himself). The reduction of abuse-misuse section of the *Boone Voice Program for Children* (1980a) was very successful in providing Eric with the insights he needed to curb his yelling and throat clearing. Various voice therapy approaches were used including chewing, open mouth, and the yawn-sigh. These approaches gave Eric an immediate better-sounding voice, and he subsequently enjoyed using them as therapy techniques. His better-sounding voice was his positive reinforcement. The clinician also found that Eric's intelligence and sensitivity allowed him to profit much from her explanations of his problem. Audio feedback, which confirmed for him the improvement in the way he sounded, was also critical to his progress in voice therapy. The boy saw his public school clinician for individual voice therapy twice weekly for a total of twenty-six weeks. At the end of that time, repeat laryngoscopy found "only a slight thickening on the right fold with the left fold completely normal." His voice began to sound like the voices of other boys his same age. When he entered fourth grade, no further voice therapy was indicated.

Similar to the excellent progress experienced by Eric, voice therapy for problems of vocal hyperfunction often produces spectacular, positive results. Such therapy gains must, however, be followed by a vocal hygiene program (Andrews, 1986; Cooper, 1977; Wilson, 1987) that is designed to prevent further vocal abuse and misuse. Such a vocal hygiene program is presented in Chapter 6.

ESTABLISHING WHERE TO START IN VOICE THERAPY

Voice therapy must begin where the patient is able to perform. We cannot ask patients to do more than they are capable of doing. In addition, the beginning of voice therapy must relate to the final outcome of the therapy. In applying dismissal criteria to seventy-three voice patients (Boone, 1974), we found that at the first therapy session we had to determine the size of laryngeal lesion (if there is one), make a voice recording of the patient, and analyze what kind of physical sensations the patient may experience while voicing. We then compared these initial data to data *after* therapy and used them as part of the decision process in terminating therapy. The effect of subsequent voice therapy could never be fully determined without some preliminary data on the presence or absence of a laryngeal lesion. The site and size of the lesion, if one is present, will greatly determine the beginning steps of voice therapy. For example, large fibrotic vocal nodules might well require a surgical approach, followed by voice rest and then voice therapy. Small, beginning thickenings at the anterior-middle third junction of the folds would offer a prompt and convincing signal for the speech pathologist to initiate a voice program to reduce vocal hyperfunction. Some beginning documentation of the lesion is necessary if we are to compare pretreatment and posttreatment effects.

Voice therapy progress can only be clearly documented if it is built upon thorough beginning diagnostic information. Two important early steps must be taken for voice therapy: an initial voice recording, for both immediate analysis and later comparison, and a determination of the patient's somatic feelings of the disorder (dryness, pain). The initial voice recording should include the patient's name, the date, spontaneous conversation, oral reading, and specific vowel and phrase repetitions that best illustrate the disorder. Subsequent and final recordings should always contain basically the same spoken material. Because many voice problems related to vocal hyperfunction create physical discomfort to the patient, sometimes, in the absence of dysphonia, it is important to determine the patient's self-reports of dryness, pain, fullness, and so forth. Eliminating these symptoms often represents a real improvement to the patient. Initial time in therapy should be spent exploring the speaking conditions and situations that precipitate these self-reports of discomfort.

Voice therapy programs for vocal hyperfunction are highly individualized. A particular approach that works for one patient may not be facilitative for another. Clinicians employ various facilitating approaches to determine whether their application allows patients to produce easier voices (which may or may not sound better). If an approach is successful, it is continued; if it does not seem to help, the clinicians try another approach. Sometimes, some of the steps of an approach are facilitative for good voice while others may not be. We determine both the effects of an overall approach and the steps in that approach by marking a form similar to that shown in Figure 5-1.

VOICE IMPROVEMENT RECORDING FORM
The Boone Voice Program for Children

Name_____ Date Therapy Initiated_____ Date Therapy Terminated_____
Check (✓) if Vocal Abuse Program is in effect_____ .

DATE	FACILITATING APPROACH #	STEP NUMBER		CHECK (✓) APPROPRIATE BOX		
			NEGATIVE CHANGE	NO CHANGE	SLIGHT IMPROVEMENT	GREAT IMPROVEMENT

FIGURE 5-1. The voice probe. The clinician measures the effectiveness of various facilitating approaches with the patient. Each step in administering the approach is measured for the effect. (*The Boone Voice Program for Children,* Austin, Texas: PRO-ED, 1980)

VOICE THERAPY FOR YOUNG CHILDREN

When preschool children are brought to a voice clinic because of some kind of dysphonia, the emphasis is placed on early diagnosis and identification rather than on voice therapy per se. A sudden hoarseness, perhaps accompanied by laryngeal stridor (noise on inhalation), prompts concern that the child may have a serious laryngeal disease, such as papilloma or laryngeal web. Direct laryngoscopy (which often necessitates a general anesthetic in a preschool child) or endoscopy may identify such a lesion. If the problem is papilloma, the management would be primarily medical-surgical. If the problem appears to be related to vocal fold thickening or nodules, or to some other vocal hyperfunction, the family and the speech-language pathologist can together decide what procedures to follow. The management may be confined to counseling with the parents, or it may also involve direct therapy with the child. The child's hyperfunctional vocal behavior may be part of an overall pattern of hyperactivity, which is sometimes a mode of behavior during the preschool years. At the preschool level, voice therapy for hyperfunctional voice problems may not always be warranted.

School-age children often demonstrate hyperfunctional voice problems, most of which are highly remediable with voice therapy. A national speech and hearing survey (Hull et al., 1976) found that about 10 percent of all school-age children (grades one through twelve) did not have acceptable voices; the prevalence was 25 percent at first grade and as low as 3 percent in grades 11 and 12. Most children who have dysphonia exhibit vocal hyperfunction—using too much effort and force as they speak. Most voice programs (Andrews, 1986; Boone, 1980a; Case, 1984; Wilson, 1987) place early emphasis on identifying abuse-misuse and outlining specific steps for reducing the occurrence of such behaviors.

The clinician can probably do nothing more effective than identify those situations in which the child is vocally abusive, such as yelling at a ball game, screaming in the playground, crying, imitating noises below or above his or her speaking pitch range, and so on. Many children maintain their vocal pathologies simply by engaging in abusive vocal behavior for just brief periods each day. It is usually not possible to identify these vocal abuses through interview methods or by observing the child in the therapy room; rather, the child must be observed in various play settings, in the classroom, and at home. This need for extensive observation requires that clinicians solicit the help of the children themselves to determine where they might be yelling or screaming. Teachers can provide some helpful clues about the child's vocal behavior both on the playground and in the classroom. Meeting with parents will often reveal further situations of vocal abuse, and the parents may be asked to listen over a period of time for abusive vocal behavior in the child's play or interactions with various family members. At times, we have had good luck using the siblings or peers to help us determine what a child does vocally in certain situations.

Once the abusive situations are isolated, clinicians should obtain baseline measurements of the number of times a vocal abuse is observed in a particular time unit (an hour, a recess period, a day, and so on). Figure 5-2 shows a vocal-abuse graph, which plots the number of abuses a child had recorded over a period of two weeks.

Notice that the first plot on the abscissa is the first day's baseline measurement, which tells on the ordinate how many times the child caught himself yelling on that particular day—for this child, eighteen separate yells. The overall contour shows a linear decrement in voice yelling, which is a somewhat typical curve for young children. Having to monitor his offensive behavior seems to motivate the child to reduce it. The child may keep a tally card in his pocket on which to mark down each occurrence; at the end of the day, he tallies that day's occurrences and plots the total figure on the graph. The review of the plotting graph is a vital part of the therapy, and the child's pride in his graph (which usually shows a decrement in the behavior) helps him continue to curb the vocal abuse. Some children require assistance in making this kind of plot, and sometimes we ask teachers, parents, or friends to also keep tally cards to record the number of events they observed in a particular time period. If children are given proper orienta-

FIGURE 5-2. At the time of his voice evaluation an 11-year-old boy was found to do a lot of screaming and yelling. He was asked to count the number of times each day he found himself yelling. This graph charts the boy's daily tally of his yelling over a twelve-day period. On the first day he tallied a baseline count of eighteen yells. The general overall contour of the curve shows a marked decrease in the amount of yelling he recorded.

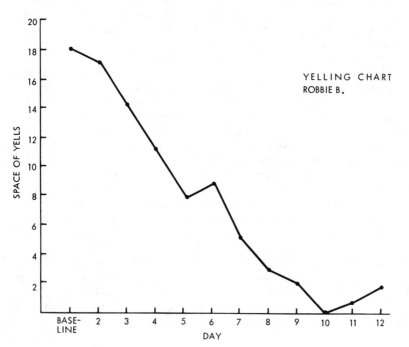

tion to the task and clearly know why they must reduce the number of vocal abuses, their tally counts seem to be higher, and perhaps more valid, than the counts of external observers.

Another method for keeping track of a child's vocal abuses (we have also used the method with a few adults) is to provide the patient with a voice tally card (Boone, 1980a). The card has a series of numbers, each perforated. If, for example, a boy catches himself producing the vocal abuse, he tears off the next tally number. At the end of the day, he can quickly see how many abuses (such as throat clearings) he caught himself doing that day. Actually, the exact number of abuses is not as important as the general task of counting in helping the patient become aware of abusive vocal behavior. The tally method of counting abuses is a prominent part of therapy for children, and its importance in eliminating vocal abuse cannot be overestimated. If it is successful, often no other form of voice therapy is needed. An important prelude to the tally method—indeed to any form of speech therapy, particularly voice therapy—is for the clinician to explain to the child what the problem is, what the child seems to be doing wrong vocally, and what can be done about it. Obviously, a child must first know that there is a voice problem (rarely does a child recognize such a problem independently) before he or she can develop any awareness of it or do anything about it. Such explanations are also especially important because most children with voice problems are not self-referred. Their dysphonias have been discovered by someone else. To the child, there may be no problem.

VOICE THERAPY FOR ADOLESCENTS AND ADULTS

The abusive vocal behaviors of adults are likely to be far more difficult to isolate than those of children. It is the relatively rare adult voice patient whose vocal abuses are bound only to particular situations; preachers or auctioneers whose voice problems appear only on the job may indeed be excellent examples of vocal misuse. Generally, however, dysphonic adolescents or adults have hyperfunctional sets toward phonation. They work to talk in most situations. Sometimes the exaggerated efforts are related to a generalized feeling of tension that becomes more acute in particular settings, such as when they speak to authority figures or when they try to make favorable impressions on listeners. This common observation—that many people with hyperfunctional voice problems exist in a milieu of tension—has fostered the belief among laryngologists and voice clinicians that the symptomatic treatment of voice disorders should be avoided in favor of a more comprehensive psychological approach. Gray, England, and Mahoney (1965) have described an approach that combines some elements of traditional voice therapy with an emphasis on deconditioning patients' anxiety and tensions by using the behavioral approach of reciprocal inhibition. It is this text's point of view that although unresolved tension and anxiety contribute to the voice problems of some voice patients, most patients are fully capable of producing a good, optimum voice, providing someone (the clinician) will only help them "find" it.

Therefore, the primary task of voice clinicians is to explore with patients the various therapy techniques that might produce that "good" voice. We advocate the same approach with adults as we do with children: using facilitating techniques as therapy probes. The approach that works is then used as a therapy practice approach. Once the patients are able to produce a model of their own best voice, this model, and the techniques used to achieve it, become the primary focus of voice therapy.

Voice clinicians also provide patients with needed psychological support, and together they explore various facilitating techniques to be used in particular situations. Hierarchies of stress can often be identified (Boone, 1982, Wolpe, 1987), and behavioral approaches used at these times of stress may minimize symptoms. Patients are taught to isolate those situations in which they experience poor voice and to substitute at those times more optimum forms of behavior—that is, easier voice.

Voice disorders in adolescents and adults often have a negative impact on their lives because they may interfere with life interactions and employment. Some patients become desperate over their vocal problems, and so seek professional help. The family physician is often the first professional who identifies a voice problem as a disorder that needs the expert help of an otolaryngologist or speech-language pathologist. The physician subsequently refers the patient for a voice evaluation that, more often than not, involves the evaluation-diagnostic procedures described in Chapter 4. Voice therapy is often the recommended step after the diagnostic evaluation.

VOICE THERAPY FACILITATING TECHNIQUES

As described in earlier chapters, a *voice therapy facilitating approach is a therapy technique that seems to produce optimum voice.* Using such an approach generally allows an individual to produce voice with less effort and strain, and perhaps even to sound better. This easy voice may be designated the target voice in therapy. Once a particular approach is found helpful in producing the target voice, the approach is used as a practice focus in therapy. Symptomatic voice therapy requires clinicians to probe continually with various facilitating techniques, using the one that seems to produce the target voice, and avoiding those that seem to have negative or little effects. This kind of therapy requires that clinicians search continually for "can do" vocal behaviors. What may work (or facilitate the target voice) for one patient may not work for another patient with the same kind of voice problem. The selection of voice facilitating approaches in therapy is thus highly individualized. Although clinicians should be familiar with the application of all therapy techniques, they should apply such techniques selectively. The selection of a particular approach should not be an arbitrary, trial-and-error decision. Rather, the possible effects on the parameters of pitch, loudness, and quality must be considered.

Table 5–1 lists twenty-five facilitating approaches to be used in voice therapy. Serious students of voice pathology may notice that some approaches listed in previous editions (1971, 1977, 1983) of this text have been omitted in this edition, and that four new approaches have been added. In

TABLE 5-1.   Twenty-Five Facilitating Approaches in Voice Therapy

Facilitating Approach	Pitch	Loudness	Quality
1. Altering Tongue Position			X
2. Change of Loudness	X	X	X
3. Chant Talk		X	X
4. Chewing	X	X	X
5. Digital Manipulation	X		X
6. Ear Training	X	X	X
7. Elimination of Abuses		X	X
8. Elimination of Hard Glottal Attack		X	X
9. Establishing a New Pitch	X		X
10. Explanation of Problem	X	X	X
11. Feedback	X	X	X
12. Glottal Fry		X	X
13. Half-Swallow, Boom		X	X
14. Head Positioning	X		X
15. Hierarchy Analysis	X	X	X
16. Inhalation Phonation	X	X	
17. Masking		X	X
18. Open-Mouth Approach	X	X	X
19. Pitch Inflections	X	X	
20. Place the Voice	X	X	X
21. Pushing Approach		X	X
22. Relaxation	X	X	X
23. Respiration Training		X	X
24. Tongue Protrusion	X		X
25. Yawn-Sigh	X	X	X

The columns above are headed *Parameter of Voice Affected*.

applying various therapy approaches over the years it becomes apparent that certain approaches have only limited utilization; such rarely used techniques have been dropped from this text. Although many new and old approaches have been tried and used in therapy, we have added only four of them to our present list. The current list of twenty-five facilitating approaches is at best arbitrary, but it does represent the most useful approaches for reaching target voice found by these authors. Other voice techniques are described by Andrews (1986), Aronson (1985), Case (1984), Cooper (1977), Filter (1982), Greene (1980), and Wilson (1987).

The facilitating approaches in Table 5-1 are listed alphabetically. After each approach a notation (X) is made to indicate the voice parameters that the particular approach has the potential to influence. For example, approach 1, Altering Tongue Position, in most cases has little influence on the pitch or loudness of the voice; its biggest influence is usually on vocal quality. Consequently, for the three columns in Table 5-1—pitch, loudness, quality—only the quality column is marked with an X. Other techniques, such as 25, Yawn-Sigh, influence all three parameters of pitch, loudness, and quality. Some experienced voice clinicians combine various facilitating approaches in their search with the patient to find the target voice.

Each of the twenty-five facilitating approaches in Table 5-1 is discussed from the following four perspectives:

A. Kinds of problems for which the approach is useful
B. Procedural aspects of the approach
C. Typical case history showing utilization of the approach
D. Evaluation of the approach

1. ALTERING TONGUE POSITION

A. *Kinds of problems for which approach is useful.* The position of the tongue within the oral cavity has a direct influence on both vocal quality and resonance. Laver (1980) describes the lingual "neutral settings" as having the tongue body not too far forward or too far backward within the oral cavity. The distinguishing characteristics of vowels and consonants are produced by tongue positioning, and any group of people speaking the same language will make basically the same tongue movements—that is, if one's vowels or consonants are to be intelligible to one's listeners, he or she must make them in the same way the listeners do. In the faulty positioning of tongue that contributes to voice disorders, it is not the individual phoneme placement that is in error, but the overall carriage of the tongue. Some patients carry the tongue backward, almost occluding the pharynx, which contributes to a hollow-sounding cul-de-sac resonance; the focus of the voice appears to be pharyngeal. Boone has pointed out (1966, p. 691) that "deaf boys and girls, regardless of age, have a tendency for a pharyngeal focus in their vocal resonance." Some voice patients retract their tongues into the pharynx during moments of tension, reporting problem voices only at these times. Other patients have the opposite problem, carrying their tongues too far forward, creating what Fisher (1975) describes as a "thin quality." This is the baby-talk voice; lacking the full resonance of back vowels, it sounds immature or pathologically meek and submissive. Both the muffled voice with posterior resonance focus and the weak, thin voice with anterior carriage can sometimes be favorably improved by direct work in modifying tongue position.

B. *Procedural aspects of approach.*
1. For posterior tongue carriage, these activities will help promote a more forward tongue positioning:
   a) Preface any exercises with a discussion and demonstration of pharyngeal tongue positioning and its effect on voice. Check the posture of the patient and be sure that the chin is neither tucked in toward the chest nor excessively extended.
   b) Begin practice with the whispered production of tongue tip—alveolar consonants, such as /t/, /d/, /s/, and /z/. Require that the patient whisper a rapid se-

ries of *ta* sounds, perhaps ten per breath. After several minutes of using *ta,* go on to the next front-of-the-mouth phoneme. Each practice series of several minutes should be followed by some analysis with the patient of what has just been done—for example, "What does the front-of-the-mouth production feel like?" Keep the early practice confined to whispered productions. Other front consonants that lend themselves well to practice are /w/, /wh/, /p/, /b/, /f/, /v/, /θ/, /ɚ/, and /l/. The following vowels have a relatively high oral focus and lend themselves well to joint practice with the above consonants, /i/, /ɪ/, /e/, /ɛ/, and /æ/.

c) After some success with whispered productions, add voice lightly. Select for oral reading those exercises that are heavily loaded with tongue-tip consonants and front vowels. Practice contrasting this new front resonance with the old posterior resonance. On recorded playback, listen to the difference critically; evaluate the difference in the "feeling" of the two productions.

2. For excessive anterior carriage of the tongue, these activities will help develop a more normal tongue position:

a) After explaining the problem, determine whether the patient is using an appropriate pitch level (often he or she is not).

b) Instruct the patient that he or she does not have to shape the tongue in any particular way. By saying the back vowels aloud in as full a voice as he or she can, the patient has usually already brought the tongue back to where it should be. These vowels should be practiced first in isolation, with some effort given to sustain each one for a period of about five seconds: /a/, /ɑ/, /o/, /v/, and /u/.

c) Practice reading materials heavy with the back consonants /k/ and /g/, and heavy also with the back vowels. When the patient has achieved some success in posterior productions, ask him or her to contrast the old method of speaking with the new, perhaps using both methods for each word or phrase read aloud. Spend some time listening to the two and discussing the difference in sound and feeling between them.

C. *Typical case history showing utilization of approach.* F. D., a 27-year-old male teacher, found himself in situations in which his voice would become muffled and almost inaudible. The voice evaluation found him to have a normal larynx and a "tendency to withdraw his tongue posteriorly into the pharynx during moments of stress." By using the facilitating technique called hierarchy analysis, the patient was able to identify those situations that produced the most stress—situations in which he would almost reflexively draw his tongue back in his pharynx. The patient was taught to alter his tongue carriage to a more anterior position by practicing, in whispers, front-of-the-mouth consonants and vowels. He then practiced using this anterior tongue carriage in various situations in the hierarchy of stress, maintaining optimum tongue position with good voice production in increasingly tense situations. The patient maintained this success in most situations; he reported that only occasional situations, such as speaking up at a teacher's union meeting, were characterized by the old voice.

D. *Evaluation of approach.* Many voice patients appear to develop faulty tongue positioning as part of their overall problem of dysphonia. Altering the main carriage of the tongue, whether it be excessively posterior or anterior, can be achieved to some degree by most patients. A slight alteration of position toward a more normal carriage usually has a profound influence in improving the quality and resonance of the voice. Proper positioning of the tongue apparently enables the oral resonance cavities to function more naturally in filtering the laryngeally produced fundamental frequency. The relatively normal positioning of the tongue appears to be an important component of a normal voice.

2. CHANGE OF LOUDNESS

A. *Kinds of problems for which approach is useful.* Some patients have voices that are either too soft or too loud. The prolonged use of inappropriate loudness levels can result in pathologies of the vocal folds, such as nodules or polyps. Many of the vocal pathologies of children are related to such excesses of loudness as screaming and yelling. Weak, soft voices may develop as a consequence of the prolonged hyperfunctional use of the vocal mechanism that results in the eventual breakdown of glottal approximation surfaces—for example, a patient with vocal nodules who loses much air flow around the nodules and is unable to produce an intense enough vocal fold vibration to achieve a sufficiently loud voice. Some speaking environments require a loud voice, and untrained speakers or singers may push for loudness at the level of the larynx rather than adjust their respiration. Inappropriate loudness of voice is most often not the primary causative factor of a voice problem, but rather a secondary, if annoying, symptom. Reducing or increasing the loudness of the voice lends itself well to direct symptom modification through exercise and practice, and often, if other facilitating techniques are being used, does not even require the use of loudness techniques per se.

B. *Procedural aspects of approach.*
    1. For a decrease in loudness:
        a) See that the patient has a thorough audiometric examination to determine adequacy of hearing before any attempt is made to reduce voice loudness. Once it has been established that the patient has normal hearing, the following steps may be taken.
        b) For young children, ages 3 through 10, the change of loudness steps in the *Boone Voice Program for Children*

(1980a) are useful. Ask the child to develop awareness of five different voices:

(1)   Voice number one is presented as a whisper.
(2)   Voice number two is presented as the voice to use when not wanting to awaken a sleeping person, a quiet voice.
(3)   Voice number three is the normal voice to use to talk to family and friends.
(4)   Voice number four is the voice to use to get someone's attention across the room.
(5)   Voice number five is the yelling voice to call someone outside.

c)   With patients over 10 years old, discuss with the patient the observation that he or she has an inappropriately loud voice. The patient may be unaware of the loud voice, and, if this is the case, he or she should listen to tape-recorded samples of his or her speech. The best demonstration tape for loudness variations would include both the patient's voice and the clinician's, to provide contrasting levels of loudness. Then ask the patient, "Do you think your voice is louder than mine?"

d)   Focus on making the patient aware of the problem. Once the patient becomes aware that his or her voice is too loud, ask, "What does a loud voice in another person tell you about that person?" Loud voices are typically interpreted to mean that the speaker feels "overly confident," or "sure of himself," or that the speaker is putting on a confident front when he or she is really scared, or that he or she is mad at the world, impressed with his or her own voice, trying to intimidate listeners, and so on. Some discussion of these negative interpretations is usually sufficient to motivate the average patient, to learn to speak at normal loudness levels.

e)   Practice using a quiet voice, the voice designated as a (2) in the preceding section b. The practice for the quiet voice can be facilitated by using instruments that give feedback specific to intensity, such as the *Vocal Loudness Indicator* (LinguiSystems, 1980) and the Visi-Pitch (Kay Elemetrics, 1986). The Vocal Loudness Indicator, for example, has a series of lights that are illuminated by increases in voice intensity. Keeping the instrument at a fixed distance, the patient can quickly learn to keep his or her voice at a lower intensity level to prevent the light (all or a few) from coming on.

f)   For practice materials, use some of the excellent voice drill books available for controlling loudness of voice, such as Newcombe (1986) and Modisett and Luter (1984).

2.   For an increase in loudness:

a)   Determine first that the inappropriate softness of the voice is not related to hearing loss, general physical weakness, or a severe personality problem; for these cases, a symptomatic approach is not indicated. The steps that follow are for voice patients who are physically and emotionally capable of speaking in a louder voice.

b) Discuss with the patient the soft voice. A tape-recorded playback of the patient's and clinician's voices in conversation will usually illustrate for the patient the inadequacy of the loudness. After the patient indicates some awareness of his or her soft voice, ask, "What does a soft, weak voice tell us about a person?" Inadequately loud voices are typically interpreted to mean that the speaker is afraid to speak louder, is timid and shy, is unduly considerate of others, is scared of people, has no self-confidence, and so on. Some discussion of these negative interpretations is usually helpful.

c) By exploring pitch level and fundamental frequency, try to achieve a pitch level at which the patient is able with some ease to produce a louder voice. If the patient habitually speaks near the bottom of his or her pitch range, a slight elevation of pitch level will usually be accompanied by a slight increase in loudness. The Visi-Pitch has been useful in helping patients associate changes in pitch with relative changes in intensity. Certain frequencies produce greater intensities. When the patient finds the "best" pitch level, he or she should practice sustaining an /a/ at that level for five seconds, concentrating on good voice quality. He or she should then take a deep breath and repeat the same pitch at a maximum loudness level. After some practice at this "home base" pitch level, ask the patient to sing /a/, up the scale for one octave, at one vocal production per breath; then have him or her go back down the scale, one note per breath, until he or she reaches the starting pitch.

d) Explore with the patient his or her best pitch—that is, the one that produces the best loudness and quality. Auditory feedback devices (such as loop tape recorders) should be employed, so that the patient can hear what he or she is doing. Some counseling may be needed about the practice pitch used, because the patient may be resistant to using a new voice pitch level. Note that the practice pitch level may well be only a temporary one, and not necessarily the pitch level the patient will use permanently. It is important that the work be pursued both in and out of therapy. A change in loudness cannot be achieved simply by talking about it. It requires practice.

e) Sometimes respiration training (which we discuss later in the chapter) is necessary for a patient with a loudness problem. Remember, however, that even though loudness is directly related to the rate of air flow through the approximated vocal folds, little evidence indicates that any particular way of breathing is the best for optimum phonation. Any respiration exercise that produces increased subglottal air pressure may be helpful in increasing voice loudness.

f) Particularly effective in functional voice loudness problems is the pushing approach. When pushing is coordinated with phonation, little air is wasted and vocal fold approximation is firm, both of which result in louder phonation. However, if a patient can achieve adequate loudness through initial counseling, "best" pitch practice, and some help in respiration, the pushing approach and other techniques requiring physical effort can be avoided.

g) For the patient who appears to resist increasing the loudness of his or her voice, it might be necessary to introduce loud noise as a competing sound to the feedback of the patient's own voice. The Lombard effect (speaking at louder voice levels during conditions of competing noise) lends itself well therapeutically to the demonstration of greater voice loudness. The clinician may use white noise, a pure tone (such as 125 or 250 Hz), or the patient's own voice amplified on a simultaneous or delayed auditory feedback device. The procedures of the approach are as follows: (1) ask the patient to read aloud a passage of about 100 words; (2) tape record the patient's oral reading; (3) at about word thirty, introduce the loud competing auditory stimulus; the patient's voice will increase in loudness; (4) at about word fifty, shut off the sound stimulus; the patient will immediately use a softer voice; (5) for the balance of the reading, alternately introduce and stop the sound source at about fifteen-word intervals; (6) complete the procedure by having the patient listen to the recorded playback, noticing the Lombard effect on the loudness of his or her voice. An extension of the approach might be to ask the patient to attempt to match his or her own loudness models.

3. A few patients demonstrate little or no loudness variation. To achieve such variation:

a) Have the patient listen to a tape recording of his or her voice. Then, after making appropriate comments, ask the patient how he or she likes his or her voice, and whether he or she thinks it should be changed. People who become aware of the monotony of their voices, and who are concerned about it, can usually develop loudness inflections with practice.

b) Maintaining an unvarying level of loudness seems to require a great deal of energy. Less work is involved in speaking naturally, which means speaking with a mouth well open and with pitch-loudness variations. The rare patient with hyperfunctional voice problems who speaks in a loudness monotone should be encouraged to increase loudness variation. Any good voice and diction book includes useful practice materials for developing such variation.

C. *Typical case history showing utilization of approach.* C. T., a 31-year-old teacher, complained for more than a year of symptoms of vocal fatigue—that is, pain in the throat, loss of voice after teaching, and so on. Laryngoscopy revealed a normal larynx, and the voice evaluation found that the man spoke at "a monotonous pitch and low loudness level, with pronounced mandibular restriction, at times barely opening his mouth." Early efforts at therapy included the chewing approach, with special emphasis given to varying pitch level and increasing voice loudness. The patient was highly motivated to improve the efficiency of his phonation; he requested voice therapy three times a week and supplemented the therapy with long practice periods at home. After nine weeks of therapy, pretherapy and posttherapy recordings were compared, and the patient agreed with the clinician that he sounded "like a new man." Speaking in a louder voice for this patient seemed to have an immediate effect on his overall self-image, resulting in an almost immediate increase in his total communicative effectiveness. Not only did the patient achieve a better-sounding speaking voice, but he reported no further symptoms of vocal fatigue.

D. *Evaluation of approach.* Inappropriate loudness of voice penalizes the patient. Happily, however, many of the facilitating techniques described in this chapter have some influence on voice loudness, and when inadequate loudness constitutes part of the patient's vocal symptomatology, it is often highly modifiable. In fact, more often than not the use of various other facilitating techniques will have an indirect effect on voice loudness, obviating the need for loudness techniques per se.

3. CHANT TALK

A. *Kinds of problems for which approach is useful.* Voice problems related to hyperfunction are often helped by the chant approach. The chant in music is characterized by reciting many syllables on one continuous tone, creating in effect a "singing monotone." We hear chanting in some churches and synagogues, performed by clergy and select groups. The words run continuously together without stress or a change in prosody for the individual word segments. In singing, the *legato* is very similar to the chant we use in voice therapy. A common dictionary definition of legato is "smooth and connected with no break between tones." The chant in therapy is characterized by an elevation of pitch, prolongation of vowels, lack of syllable stress, and an obvious softening of glottal attack. Once a patient can produce the chant in its extreme form (such as in a Gregorian chant), it can usually be modified to resemble conversational phonation. We have often used chanting with other facilitating approaches, such as chewing, open mouth, and yawn-sigh.

B. *Procedural aspects of approach.*

1. The chant talk approach is explained to the patient as a method that reduces the effort in talking. It is important to point out to the patient that the method will only be used temporarily as a practice method and will not become a permanent and different way of talking. Demonstrate chant talk by playing a recording of a religious chant. Then imitate the recording by producing the same voicing style while reading any material aloud.

2. Then urge the patient to imitate the same chant voicing pattern. Most patients are able to do this with some degree of initial success. For those who cannot chant in initial trials, present a chant recording again and then follow it with the patient's own chant production. Some lighthearted kidding is useful to tell the patient that the chant is a different way of talking and will only be used briefly as a voice training device. If the patient cannot chant after several attempts, use another facilitating approach. For those patients who can chant, go on to step 3.

3. The patient should now read aloud, alternating the regular voice and the chant voice. Twenty seconds has been found to be a good time for each reading condition. Ask the patient to read aloud first in the normal voice, then in a chant, then back to normal voice, then in a chant, and so on.

4. Record the patient's oral reading. On playback, contrast the different sound of the normal voice with the chanted voice. Discuss the pitch differences, the phonatory prolongations, and the soft glottal attack.

5. Once the patient is able to produce chant talk with relative ease, he or she should try to reduce the chant quality, approximating normal voice production. Slight prolongation and soft glottal attack should be retained as the patient reads aloud in a voice with only slight chant quality remaining.

C. *Typical history showing utilization of approach.* C. C. was a 28-year-old woman who sold telephone directory advertising. She began to experience increased dysphonia and "dryness of throat," particularly toward the end of a busy day of calling on prospective customers. On endoscopic examination, she was found to have bilateral vocal nodules with unnecessary supraglottal participation during phonation. She spoke at an inappropriately low pitch, with mandibular restriction and noticeable hard glottal attack. She received voice therapy twice weekly with therapy designed to "take the work out of phonation." The chewing approach, coupled with the chant talk approach, dramatically changed her overall voicing style. She was able early in therapy to incorporate the soft glottal attack of the chant into her everyday speaking voice. Other approaches, such as open mouth and yawn-sigh, were added with various self-practice materials she could practice. The patient reported that she practiced throughout the day in her car, driving between appointments. In about twelve weeks, videoendoscopy revealed that the nodules had disappeared and that her supraglottal larynx stayed open during normal voicing. There was no evidence of hard glottal attack at the time of her clinic discharge.

D. *Evaluation of approach.* The chant-talk approach is easy for most patients to use. Initially, it is important to let the patient know that chanting is only a temporary behavior, designed to take the work out of phonation. We have found that the method works well with children who seem to enjoy the "different" way of talking. For those patients who need to reduce hard glottal attack, the chanting approach seems to produce dramatic results for softening voicing onsets.

4. CHEWING

A. *Kinds of problems for which approach is useful.* Like the chant, the chewing approach has been found effective for reducing vocal hyperfunction. The chewing method, developed by Froeschels in 1924, has been applied as a "natural method" for developing good speech and voice for many kinds of disorders (Weiss and Beebe, 1951). It is always difficult in voice therapy to isolate particular behaviors, such as pitch, quality, or resonance, and work on each one separately. The chewing approach works from a gestalt point of view by encouraging optimum performance of most vocal behaviors. Following the procedures as presented here can make the approach a "fun" activity that immediately changes voice production. During simultaneous voicing and chewing, slight shifts in pitch, less strain in the voice, more optimal glottal attack, and improved vocal quality are often audible. All of these voice changes are related to the decrease in tension that accompanies voicing during exaggerated chewing.

B. *Procedural aspects of approach.*

1. First, explain to the patient that he or she is speaking with unnecessary tension. If appropriate, point out that he or she is speaking with an approximated mandible, through clenched teeth, with so little mouth opening that he or she "speaks like a ventriloquist." Use a mirror to show the patient what he or she looks like while talking. Let the patient see his or her relatively restricted mandibular movement. Then explain how relatively relaxed the jaw, throat, tongue, and lips are when one chews, and how chewing and talking simultaneously often result in a more relaxed voice. Instruct the patient that using the chewing method promotes greater oral movement, and produces a more relaxed voice. Emphasize that the chewing method is only a means to an end. That is, make sure the patient understands that chewing in an exaggerated manner is only temporary, to get the feeling of vigorous action, and that one need not worry about speaking permanently with such exag-

gerated, open-mouthed postures. If patients are sufficiently warned that the method is a temporary way of introducing a more relaxed phonation, and that it will eventually be brought down to a more normal way of talking, few will resist learning it.

2. With both the clinician and the patient facing a mirror, ask the patient to pretend to open the mouth wide, about to bite into a handful of four or five stacked crackers, and then to pretend to chew them. (Usually this imagery is sufficient.) Occasionally, however, you have to actually introduce the crackers and ask the patient to chew them in an open-mouthed, exaggerated fashion, observing himself or herself closely. Follow this immediately by having the patient imitate the chewing that was just done. Point out to the patient the degree of mouth opening, and the movement of the jaw. Spend several minutes establishing a natural and exaggerated motion of chewing.

3. Demonstrate the chewing for the patient and add a very soft phonation. Have the patient imitate you. Brodnitz (1971) warns that "at this stage, many patients will go through the motions of opening and closing the jaws but the tongue is left flat and motionless on the floor of the mouth. A monotonous 'yam-yam' will result" (p. 80). It is therefore important to point out early that the tongue must be kept moving so that a variety of sounds will emerge. The patient should stay with this exercise until he or she is able to produce chewing and voicing simultaneously, with an ever-changing number of different sounds. For the method to be effective, the natural movements of the tongue, as experienced when actually chewing food, should be retained.

4. After the patient has performed the chewing-voicing exercise satisfactorily, introduce some special words for the patient to practice a combination chanting-chewing. In the children's voice program (Boone, 1980a), we play with the chewing approach and use funny names coupled with funny pictures that the names are supposed to represent—for example, "goolagonga, ahlameterah, wandapanda, monamoona, tokalama, cucalamonga." With older patients we may use words and phrases like "lampshade, peaches and cherries, and candy chunks." Either stay with such words until the patient demonstrates that he or she can say them well, or explore with other words, starting with those that the patient is able to produce while still maintaining good chewing.

5. When a few nucleus words are established with the chewing method, ask the patient to count from one to ten, using the same technique. Some practice at this is usually necessary. If the numbers reduce the patient's ability to use the method correctly, go back to an earlier level and reestablish more appropriate chewing. If the patient is able to voice well while chewing and saying

numbers, have him or her listen to himself or herself doing it (using some kind of auditory feedback device, such as a loop auditory tape). It is critical that the patient not only experience the relaxed "feel" of the method, but that he or she also receive some immediate auditory feedback showing the effect of the method on the sound of his or her voice.

6. After a patient has demonstrated an ability to chew and say numbers satisfactorily, he or she can usually tackle more extensive, connected speech. Provide the patient with verbal material to say or passages to read aloud. This chewing-connected speech should usually not begin with true conversation, but rather with neutral verbal material, such as a passage from a book.

7. The last practice step is to use the approach during conversational speech. If the patient experiences difficulty at this level, and in the beginning he or she usually will, have him or her go back to the highest successful level and guide him or her forward from there. When the patient has some success using the method conversationally in therapy, have him or her also use it outside of therapy in comfortable verbal settings. Good listeners in the beginning might be parents, a friend, or a spouse.

8. The great advantage of the chewing method, once it is learned, is that the patient can practice it many times, for a minute or so each time, throughout the day. The average patient's phonation will be noticeably more relaxed when using the chewing method, and because it usually facilitates a better voice, the patient will use it extensively outside of therapy. A great deal of daily practice, maybe as often as five times an hour, should be established.

9. Finally, after several weeks of practicing the method, the patient should be taught how to diminish the exaggerated chewing to a more normal jaw movement. It is important, however, as chewing is deemphasized, that the patient retain the same feeling and the same sound in his or her voice. If, when the chewing is minimized, the patient reverts to earlier faulty phonation patterns, have him or her return to the earlier chewing level where optimum performance was achieved, and proceed forward again from there.

10. Ultimately, the patient just "thinks" the method. By this time the patient has developed an awareness of what oral openness and jaw movement feel like and has experienced the vocal relaxation that accompanies the feeling.

C. *Typical case history showing utilization of approach.* David, a 9-year-old boy with a three-year history of dysphonia, was found to have "bilateral fibrotic vocal nodules." He was subsequently scheduled for twice-weekly voice therapy at school. It soon became apparent to his clinician that he was working excessively hard to produce any kind of voice. Probably as a compensation for the large nodes that prevented good vocal fold approximation, when he wanted to produce a voice that could be heard, he used excessive amounts of air flow and pressure in an attempt to speak louder. His phonations were also characterized by hard glottal attack. The chewing approach was introduced as a means of using voice more optimally and with less effort. The immediate effect of chewing combined with phonation was increased hoarseness and breathiness. The clinician counseled David about how to use his temporary increase in hoarseness "as a means to an end" for developing a better voice. The clinician so successfully created a fun atmosphere for the practice of chewing that David used the exaggerated mouth openings and easy onsets of voice in many situations outside of therapy including home self-practice. Although the chewing approach was the primary therapy approach used, emphasis was also given to reducing abuse-misuse, explaining to David the probable genesis of his nodules, and reducing his overall voice loudness. After approximately six months of voice therapy, David's nodules were reduced to "slight thickenings"; his airflow rates went down, which indicates firmer glottal approximation; and his voice sounded very much like the voices of his classmates. In a one-year follow-up with this consultant, all findings were within normal limits.

D. *Evaluation of approach.* A proper orientation to the chewing approach by the clinician, with emphasis on chewing's being a different and *temporary* way of talking, allows most patients to find the method helpful for producing an efficient voice. It is not a panacea for all voice problems. When involved in the somewhat automatic function of chewing, the oral structures seem to become capable of more synergic, relaxed movement. Relaxing the components of the vocal tract in this way also relaxes the phonatory functioning of the larynx. By employing a common action, chewing, the patient is able to achieve some relaxation of the vocal tract from a holistic point of view, without having to fulfill such impossible direction as "relax your throat" or "relax your voice"; because no individual has volitional control over the vegetative functions of the throat and larynx, compliance with such instructions is quite impossible. Often, however, a patient can achieve such relaxation by combining chewing with phonation.

5. DIGITAL MANIPULATION

A. *Kinds of problems for which approach is useful.* There are several ways that voice clinicians can facilitate a target voice by finger manipulation of the patient's larynx. For voice problems related to an inappropriately high pitch level, external digital pressure by the clinician on the patient's thyroid cartilage is often effective in establishing a lower pitch. The external pressure nudges the thyroid cartilage slightly backward and shortens the vocal folds; this increases their mass and produces a lower fundamental frequency. Another form of digital manipulation, described by Case (1984), involves the clinician's or patient's monitoring any vertical movement (often interpreted as symptomatic of too much force while speaking) by placing fingers on the lateral walls of the thyroid cartilage. Perhaps the most active method of laryngeal manipulation is recommended by Aronson (1985) for problems of vocal hyperfunction, where tension is reduced in the laryngeal area by maneuvering the larynx to a lower position by placing the fingers "over the superior borders of the thyroid cartilage" and working "the larynx gently downward, also moving it laterally at times" (p. 341). Phonation produced by the larynx in a lower fixed position with only minimal vertical excursions is often observed in trained, efficient users of voice, such as professional singers.

B. *Procedural aspects of approach.* The three digital procedures used in voice therapy are quite distinct from one another. We list the steps separately for each of the three procedures:

1. Digital pressure for lowering pitch.

    a. With the exception of some men with falsetto voices, patients will respond to digital pressure by producing a lower voice pitch. Ask the patient to prolong a vowel (/a/ or /i/). As the vowel is prolonged, apply slight finger pressure on the thyroid cartilage. The pitch level will drop immediately.

    b. Ask the patient to maintain the lower pitch after the fingers are removed. If the patient can do this, he or she should continue practicing the lower pitch. If the high pitch quickly reverts back, repeat the digital pressure.

    c. If the method is used to provide the patient with experience hearing and feeling a lower pitch, the patient should practice producing the lower pitch with and without digital pressure on the thyroid cartilage.

2. Monitoring the vertical movements of the larynx.

    a. For a patient with excessive pitch variability and tension related to much vertical movement of the larynx, demonstrate how to place the fingers on the thyroid cartilage and monitor laryngeal vertical movement while phonating.

    b. Ask the patient to produce a pitch level that is several full musical notes off the bottom of his or her lowest note. Keeping the fingers on the thyroid cartilage, ask the patient to lower pitch one note at a time, until the lowest note in his or her pitch range is reached. Usually, the larynx will lower its position in the neck at the low end of the pitch range. Then ask the patient to sing one note at a time up to the top of the singing range, exclusive of falsetto. Toward the top of the scale, the patient should feel (through the finger tips) a slight elevation of the larynx. Review both the lowering and rising of the larynx at the extremes of the pitch range.

     c. Once the patient has experienced vertical move-ment in the preceding steps, point out that in pro-duction of a speaking voice that is relatively free of strain, no vertical movement of the larynx should be felt during digital monitoring. Oral reading and speaking should be developed with little or no verti-cal laryngeal movements. Practice in oral reading with encouraged pitch variability can then be moni-tored by slight digital pressure of the thyroid carti-lage with the patient's confirming (hopefully) no ver-tical movement.

3. Maneuvering the larynx to a lower neck position.

     a. Encircle the hyoid bone with the middle finger and thumb.

     b. With light finger pressure, place the fingers within the thyrohyoid space, just above the thyroid notch. With the fingers over the superior border of the thy-roid cartilage, begin gently to "work" the larynx downward, with downward pressure and slight lat-eral movements. The larynx will usually move slightly downward with this gentle pressure (pro-vided the patient does not fight the movement by observable tension and resistance.)

     c. If the technique does not work, repeat steps a and b a few more times. With the larynx in the lower posi-tion, ask the patient to prolong vowels and monitor laryngeal positioning using the procedure described in step 2. If the lower position is achieved and main-tained, use a number of other voice facilitating tech-niques.

C. *Typical case history showing utilization of approach.* J. F. was a 17-year-old male who had been raised exclusively by his mother until her sudden death about a year before. Since that time he had lived with a maternal uncle who was concerned about the boy's effeminate mannerisms and high-pitched voice. La-ryngeal examination revealed a normal adult male larynx. The boy was found to have a habitual pitch level of around 200 cps, well within the adult female range, but below the level of falsetto. The most effective facilitating technique for producing a normal voice pitch was to apply digital pressure on the external thyroid cartilage. The young man was able to prolong the lower pitch levels with good success, but any attempt at conversation would be characterized by an imme-diate return to the higher pitch. After three therapy sessions, he was able to read aloud using the lower pitch, but was un-able to use the lower voice in conversation except with his male clinician. Subsequent psychiatric evaluation and ther-apy were initiated for "identity confusion and schizoidal ten-dencies." Voice therapy was discontinued after two weeks, when it was clearly demonstrated that the patient could pro-duce a good baritone voice (125 cps) whenever he wanted. Unfortunately, follow-up telephone conversations several months after therapy revealed that he was using his high-pitched, pretherapy voice exclusively.

D. *Evaluation of approach.* With some problems of vocal hyperfunction, particularly cord thickening and vocal nodules, it
is sometimes necessary to work toward lowering the child's
or adult's (but not the adolescent's) pitch level as suggested
by Aronson (1985) and Wilson (1987). Digital pressure on
the thyroid cartilage is an excellent facilitator for many patients developing lower voice pitch. If the method does not
produce a lower pitch level, as it may not do for certain cases
of falsetto, the method cannot be used. Even though the
method may produce an immediate change of voice to a
more desired, lower pitch level, as illustrated in the preceding case history, it may not effect a permanent voice change
without some counseling or psychotherapy. Digital pressure,
though effective in lowering pitch level, rarely brings about
permanent success unless other therapeutic approaches are
used as well.

A well-trained singing or speaking voice is produced
with a minimum of physical effort and relatively little up-
ward-downward movement of the larynx. Some patients
demonstrate excessive pitch variability and unnecessary laryngeal excursion as they speak. An excellent method of
pointing this out to a patient, and of helping him or her
establish a more optimum phonation with only minimal vertical laryngeal movement, is to have the patient place his or
her fingers lightly on the laryngeal thyroid cartilage, feeling
the downward movement as the pitch lowers and the upward
movement as it rises. Lowering the larynx by external digital
pressure, as described by Aronson (1985), has also been
found to be an active procedure for reducing laryngeal-neck
tension for the occasional voice patient who appears to carry
the larynx excessively high.

6. EAR TRAINING

A. *Kinds of problems for which approach is useful.* Most voice therapy
involves the identification and elimination of faulty vocal
habits and their replacement by more optimum ones. The
basic input modality in developing appropriate phonation
is the auditory system, particularly the patient's self-hearing.
No individuals have much awareness of what they are doing
laryngeally, whether they are approximating their folds or
shortening or lengthening them, except as they hear their
own voices. The surprise nearly always evoked in people
hearing their own voices on recordings is one indication of
how gross our self-hearing is. This lack of voice feedback has
always presented problems to clinicians, because patients literally do not know what they are doing when they phonate.
Music teachers have historically attempted to circumvent the
problem by using imagery in their training attempts, because
the voice will often respond appropriately to psychological-
anatomical instructions—for example, "put your voice force-
fully down in your chest"—even though the physiology of
the described event is in error. In voice therapy, we are concerned with making patients critical listeners. Patients, how-

ever, may need practice in learning to listen to their own voices. Davis and Boone (1967) reported that some voice patients, like some people in the normal population, demonstrate difficulty in pitch discrimination and tonal memory as measured by subtests of the Seashore Measures of Musical Aptitude (Seashore, Lewis, and Saetviet, 1980). Such patients may have serious problems in voice therapy in making pitch discriminations and in remembering the sounds of their own target voices. Up to a certain point, gross pitch discrimination and tonal memory can be taught by ear-training practice, wherein the patient learns how to listen critically to his or her own "good" and "bad" voices and to the voices of others. Through auditory feedback devices, such as loop tape recorders, the patient learns to hear and monitor auditorily his or her own phonation. For patients who have defective listening skills, voice training may include instruction in making pitch discriminations, improving tonal memory, and learning to hear one's "good" and "bad" voices. But clinicians should first assess patients' listening skills, because many voice patients have no problem in this area; others, just as some people in the normal population, may have surprisingly deficient listening abilities. The latter group may profit from ear training.

B.　*Procedural aspects of approach.*

    1.　Take a baseline measurement of how well the patient can make pitch discriminations. The ear-training cassette from the *Boone Voice Program for Children* (Boone, 1980a) contains twenty pitch-discrimination pairs that were produced with a music synthesizer and twenty singing voice pitch discriminations. The tape provides for easy contrast discrimination. You may also make your own taped or "live" discrimination presentations, or use the Seashore pitch discrimination subtest, a piano, or pitch pipe. Present to the patient a pair of tonal stimuli, asking if the stimuli are the same as one another or different. Follow this by voiced pitch discriminations, either produced by you or prerecorded. If the patient is unable to discriminate between one whole note and its flat or sharp, the indication is that the patient's pitch discrimination is not normal, but not necessarily that pitch discrimination therapy is needed. In gross departures, however, such as the patient's being unable to discriminate between notes that are more than a third apart (say, between a C_4 and an F_4), some discrimination training may be needed if the patient is ever going to match successfully a target model voice.

    2.　Pitch discrimination training should begin at the patient's baseline "can do" performance. When the patient makes correct discriminations at this level, his or her performance should be positively reinforced. Pitch stimuli can come from a piano, a pitch pipe, or the voice itself; it is often better therapy to mix all three types of pitch stimuli into the practice sequence, rather than to use one type only. Continue this activity for as long as necessary, until the patient is able to discriminate between pitches that are one full musical note apart (for example, C_4 and D_4). This pitch-discrimination approach can be effectively practiced alone, without the clinician, if the patient listens to prerecorded practice materials and makes "same-different" choices as he or she listens. To learn the correctness of response, the patient can mark choices down on paper and then check them against a master sheet. Simple programming equipment has also been successfully used; here, the patient indicates the "same-different" choice, and a light goes on when the choice is correct.

3. Tonal memory therapy also begins where the patient is. That is, if the patient can remember a two-note sequence (via piano, pitch pipe, or voice), the therapy should begin by presenting two two-note sequences and asking the patient to identify which note varies between the two presentations. The ear-training cassette (Boone, 1980a) also contains twenty pairs of contrasting melodies for use in tonal memory practice. It is not necessary for the patient to work beyond remembering a four-note series. When the patient can hear a four-note melody, remember it, and successfully compare it with a second four-note melody (with only one note varying between the first and second presentation), tonal memory is probably good enough for recalling various voice model presentations. Tonal memory therapy is also well suited for self-practice; the patient listens and responds to prerecorded sequences.

4. If a target model voice has been produced by the patient, can he or she discriminate between this good production and a faulty one? It is essential in voice therapy that the patient use his or her own "best" voice as a therapy model whenever possible. The patient may need some practice in learning to listen for his or her own "best" and "bad" voices. Capture the patient's voice productions on recordings, and then edit and splice them into contrasting pairs. The patient should listen discriminatively to these pairings to learn to identify quickly and correctly his or her better phonation. Recordings of other people's voices with similar problems, also paired for discrimination listening, make excellent practice materials. When the patient is consistently able to hear his or her "good" voice, whether or not he or she can produce that voice, there is little need to emphasize ear training. For some patients, just a little listening to their own voices helps; for others, even a great deal of practice is useless. For the rare patient who shows no improvement after trial ear training, further training might as well be abandoned.

C. *Typical case history showing utilization of approach.* C. M., a 9-year-old girl with functional hypernasality, was evaluated by a local cleft-palate team and found to have adequate velopharyngeal closure (as demonstrated by cinefluorography), normal manometric pressure ratios, and normal stimulability for producing good oral resonance in isolated words repeated after the examiner. Voice therapy on a twice-weekly basis was recommended. The focus of therapy was on ear training, helping the patient discriminate between her nasal resonance and oral resonance. The first seven weeks of therapy were spent both in this discrimination listening, which in the beginning was very defective, and in producing contrasting oral and nasal resonations. In the early phases of therapy, orality was stressed only in the therapy and practice sessions, and no attempt was made at any outside carry-over. Eventually, carry-over phrases and sentences were practiced in situations outside the clinic setting. As therapy progressed, the girl showed excellent auditory self-monitoring and was able to develop normal oral voice quality in all situations. Voice therapy was judged a success and terminated after eleven weeks.

D. *Evaluation of approach.* In voice therapy, the patient must become a critical listener to his or her own voice. Some voice patients, like some people in the normal population, have real difficulty making pitch discriminations and judgments of tonal memory. Of these patients, some profit from ear training. The patient must learn to hear, if possible, how he or she is phonating. If the patient's listening abilities are poor, ear training should be initiated. If there is no problem in listening, ear training should be avoided.

7. ELIMINATION OF ABUSES

A. *Kinds of problems for which approach is useful.* There are many ways that one can abuse or misuse the voice. *Vocal abuse* comprises various behaviors and events that have some kind of deleterious effect on the larynx and the voice, such as:
   1. Yelling and screaming
   2. Speaking against a background of loud noise
   3. Coughing and excessive throat clearing
   4. Smoking
   5. Excessive talking or singing
   6. Excessive talking or singing while having an allergy or upper respiratory infection
   7. Excessive crying or laughing.

Vocal misuse means improper use of voice, such as:
   1. Speaking with hard glottal attack
   2. Singing excessively at the lower or upper end of one's range
   3. Increasing vocal loudness by squeezing out the voice at the level of the larynx
   4. Speaking at excessive intensity levels
   5. Cheerleading (Case, 1984)
   6. Speaking over time at an inappropriate pitch level
   7. Speaking or singing (such as a prolonged show rehearsal) for excessively long periods of time.

We could obviously add other abuses and misuses to such a list. Identification and reduction of vocal abuse-misuse are primary goals in voice therapy for hyperfunctional disorders such as functional dysphonia with or without such physical changes as vocal nodules, polyps, or contact ulcers. Therapy cannot be successful until contributory vocal abuse-misuse can be drastically reduced. Optimum usage of the voice, such as the vocal hygiene program outlined in Chapter 6, also requires identifying possible abusive voice situations and making deliberate efforts to minimize their occurrence.

B. *Procedural aspects of approach.*

1. Time must be given early in voice therapy to identifying possible vocal abuse. Once a particular vocal abuse is identified, the patient and clinician should develop a baseline of occurrence. This will often require that the clinician hear and observe the patient in and out-of-clinic environment, such as on the playground, at the pulpit, or in a nightclub. The number of times the particular event occurred must be tallied.

2. Children with vocal abuse must become aware of the impact of such abuses on their voices. With children we use the "Vocal Abuse Reduction Program" (Boone, 1980a), which recommends:

    > an explanation of how additive lesions occur, using the story, *A Voice Lost and Found;* a review of the child's abuses; and a systematic reduction of the child's abuses, using the Voice Tally Card and the Voice Counting Chart (p. 5).

    The focus of the reducing abuse program is to make the child cognitively aware of the relationship of vocal abuse-misuse to increasing symptoms of voice. The story in the program is pictorially illustrated with various vocal behaviors related to changes of "the little bumps on the vocal cords."

3. Discuss identified vocal abuses with the patient, emphasizing the need to reduce their daily frequency. Assign to the patient the task of counting the number of times each day he or she engages in a particular abuse. Perhaps a peer or sibling could be brought in, told about the situation, and asked to join in on the daily count. Depending on the age of the patient, a parent or teacher, spouse, or business associate might be asked to keep track of the number of abuses that occur in their presence. At the end of the day, the abuses should be tallied for that day.

4. Ask the patient to plot his or her daily vocal abuses on a graph. Along the vertical axis, the ordinate, the patient should plot the number of times the particular abuse occurred, and, along the base of the graph, the abscissa, the individual days, beginning with the baseline count of the first day. Instruct the patient to bring these graphs to voice therapy sessions. Keeping a graph usually increases the patient's awareness of what he or she has been doing and results in a gradual decrement of the

abusive behavior. The typical vocal abuse has a sloping decremental curve, indicating its gradual disappearance. Greet any decrement in the plots of the people observing the patient, but particularly in those compiled by the patient, with obvious approval.

C. *Typical case history showing utilization of approach.* Joyce was a 27-year-old secretary who complained of a voice that was often hoarse and that tired easily every day. Subsequent indirect laryngoscopy confirmed a slight bilateral thickening at the anterior-middle third junction. A detailed history and observation of the patient found that she constantly cleared her throat. The throat clearing had become a habit. She rarely felt that she was able "to bring up any mucus" but just cleared her throat in attempt to make her voice clearer. A high-speed motion picture depicting throat clearing was shown to the patient. She was counseled to try to reduce its occurrence. The patient subsequently began to tally her throat clearing and coughing as they occurred, plotting them on a graph at the end of the day. Within two weeks, she was able to change her throat clearing habit. Her vocal quality improved immediately and she never needed formal, long-term voice therapy.

D. *Evaluation of approach.* Identifying vocal abuses and attempting to eliminate them by plotting their daily frequency on a graph is a most effective method of helping young children with voice problems. Adolescents are equally guilty of vocal abuses and profit greatly from keeping track of what they are doing. Typical adult abuses, such as throat clearing, are often eliminated after a week or two of graph plotting by motivated patients. The effectiveness of this approach, in fact, is highly related to the skill of the clinician in motivating the patient to eliminate the abusive behavior. The value of the plotting is more in developing awareness of the frequency of the problem than in the actual count per se. Reduction of vocal abuse has become a primary part of most voice therapy programs for children (Andrews, 1986; Boone, 1980a; Wilson, 1987) and for adults (Aronson, 1985; Boone, 1983; Case, 1984).

8. ELIMINATION OF HARD GLOTTAL ATTACK

A. *Kinds of problems for which approach is useful.* In the facilitating approach just described "speaking with hard glottal attack" was first on the list of vocal misuses. Speaking with abrupt vocal onsets is extremely taxing on the laryngeal mechanism. Pershall and Boone (1986) found on videoendoscopy that after continuous staccato phonation (abrupt-onset phonation) a normal subject began to show slight edema and redness on the anterior-middle third site of the glottal margin. Hard glottal attack is often heard in the voices of people with posterior lesions, such as contact ulcers. Hard glottal attack is an excellent example of vocal hyperfunction: using too much unnecessary effort and force for voice.

B. *Procedural aspects of approach.*
  1. Hard glottal attack is a fairly common phenomenon among actors, politicians, and untrained singers. Play recordings of the voices of such people, and of the patient, for the patient, and then demonstrate the contrasting soft, easy glottal attack. The length of the demonstration should depend on the patient's insight.
  2. Demonstrate a child's vocal attack by letting the patient contrast a recording of his or her own voice with the normal voice of a peer. Then practice using words beginning with /h/, taken from various lists, such as those in Fisher (1975), Moncur and Brackett (1974), or Boone (1980a). Select monosyllabic words, beginning with the aspirate /h/ for soft attack practice. When the /h/ words are produced correctly, introduce other words beginning with unvoiced consonants for similar practice. Then use words beginning with vowels.
  3. Use the whisper-phonation technique. Choose a few monosyllabic words, each beginning with a vowel. The patient's task is to whisper very lightly the initial vowel, prolonging it by gradually increasing the loudness of the whisper until phonation is introduced and, finally, the whole word is said. The whisper blends into a soft phonation.
  4. The yawn-sigh approach is particularly effective in eliminating hard glottal attack.
  5. By definition the chant approach eliminates hard glottal attack by its initiating legato into the speaking voice. It can often be successfully combined with the yawn-sigh or the chewing approach.
  6. Simultaneous chewing and chanting make abrupt onset of phonation impossible.
  7. Once the patient is able to produce easy-onset phonation by chanting, chewing, or yawning-sighing, a good therapy procedure is to have the patient contrast the easy-onset phonation with abrupt-onset phonation. The lack of effort between easy onset and the obvious effort of abrupt onset make a convincing contrast between the two modes of voice onset.
  8. Various instruments are useful in providing the patient feedback about the severity of his or her glottal attack or suddenness of initiation of phonation. The display from a spectrograph or the Visi-Pitch can show the relative onset time of phonations; a vertical tracing at the beginning of the word indicates hard, abrupt vocal attack as opposed to a sloping onset tracing that displays a more gradual onset. Using various facilitating approaches, the clinician and the patient can confirm visually the relative suddenness of onset by the slope of the onset curve. The Voice Monitor (1977) has been found useful. The Voice Monitor can be set at various sensitivity levels to alert the patient to sudden initiation of phonation. When the patient initiates a word abruptly, a light goes on. The patient's task is to continue speaking connected

speech without abruptness of attack to avoid the warning light. Using the Voice Monitor has the advantage of critically monitoring the patient's voice practice without having a clinician in the room.

C. *Typical case history showing utilization of approach.* Louis was a 35-year-old assistant professor of hydrology who came to the voice clinic with the sole complaint of "pain in the throat and hoarseness" after lecturing for more than an hour. A subsequent voice evaluation and visitation to his classes found that Louis was lecturing with a "different voice" than the one he used conversationally. His lecture voice appeared to be at the bottom of his vocal pitch range, and he spoke with excessive glottal attack. He felt (perhaps correctly) that his low-pitched voice and his abrupt way of saying things made him sound a bit more authoritative and "in charge of my subject matter." Although some work in voice therapy involved raising his voice pitch two full steps, focus was on eliminating hard glottal attack. Within a few weeks of starting voice therapy, he reported no discomfort after lecturing, and the dysphonia after prolonged lecturing began to disappear.

D. *Evaluation of approach.* Elimination of hard glottal attack is often easily accomplished in voice therapy. When they begin voice therapy, most patients who speak with hard glottal attack are unaware of the amount of unneeded energy they expend by speaking with such abrupt initiation of voice. Once hard attack is pointed out and an easier vocal onset is taught (perhaps by chewing, chanting, or sighing), the typical patient soon prefers the easier way of initiating vocal onsets.

9. ESTABLISHING A NEW PITCH

A. *Kinds of problems for which approach is useful.* Although it is pretty well established (Bless, 1984; Minifie, 1984) that there is no absolute optimum pitch on which a particular person should speak, some people with voice problems may profit from speaking at a different pitch level. A change of pitch will often have positive effects on voice, such as improving vocal quality and loudness. Speaking at the very bottom of one's pitch range requires too much force and effort. Similarly, speaking habitually toward the top of one's range can be vocally fatiguing. Because a number of instruments available today can portray fundamental frequency in real time (while one is phonating), awareness and feedback of one's ongoing pitch level play prominent roles in establishing new pitches through therapy.

B. *Procedural aspects of approach.*
   1. If pitch needs to be raised or lowered, describe where the patient is and where the target pitch is. The methods for determining habitual and optimum pitches described in Chapter 4 can be applied here. Make a tape recording of the patient producing various pitches, including feedback about the old pitch and the projected target pitch. The playback should always be followed by

some discussion comparing the sound and the feeling of the two pitches.

2. Most voice patients can imitate their own pitch models, once they have been produced by the appropriate facilitating technique. Occasional patients cannot initiate a pitch to match a model, as Filter and Urioste (1981) found in testing college women with normal voices. A useful model can be produced by having the patient extend an /i/ at the target pitch level for about five seconds and recording the phonation on a loop tape recorder. If the loop is set for a five-to ten-second playback, the patient will immediately hear the target production. The loop tape playback will provide the patient with a continuous playback of his or her own voice model of the target pitch. There are many advantages to using the patients' own voices as their voice models, in that they already have voicing experience producing the sounds they are now trying to match. Remain with the loop model /i/ for considerable practice before introducing a new stimulus.

3. Several excellent instruments available today can provide real-time display of fundamental frequency, both with a digital writeout and on a display screen on a monitor: PM 100 Pitch Analyzer, Phonatory Function Analyzer, Visi-Pitch, and B & K Real-Time Frequency Analyzer (see References at end of book). Usually, these instruments permit the clinician to display patient voice values specific to frequency and intensity. The PM 100 and Visi-Pitch each offer split-screen capabilities, whereby a voice model can be put on an upper screen and the patient production displayed on a lower screen, permitting comparisons between model and trial productions. Any instrument that can display fundamental frequency information can provide valuable feedback to a patient attempting to establish a new voice pitch.

4. The Tunemaster III, another instrument listed in the References, provides feedback information relative to correctness of patient production. The desired pitch level is set on the Tunemaster III. The display dial can then provide feedback to the patient whether voice production is within thirty cycles (sharp or flat) of the target frequency. Using the four instruments previously described in step 3, the patient can receive exact digital feedback about the frequency he or she is producing. Any deviation below or above the target pitch level can be given immediate feedback. Of great therapeutic benefit is that the patient will know immediately when he or she is producing the target frequency.

5. Establishing a new pitch is facilitated by working first on single words, preferably words that begin with vowels. Each word is repeated in a pitch monotone (using the target pitch). Occasionally a patient has more difficulty using the new pitch with certain words. Any such "trouble" words should be avoided as practice material, be-

cause what is needed at this stage of therapy is practice in rapidly phonating a series of individuals words at the new pitch level.

6. Once the patient does well at the single-word level, introduce phrases and short sentences. It is usually more productive at this stage to avoid practice in actual conversation, because the patient is better able to use the new phonation in such neutral situations as reading single words, phrases, and sentences. When success is achieved at the sentence level, assign the patient reading passages from various voice and diction books. Success in using the new pitch level can be verified by using the instruments described earlier, in step 3.

7. After reading well in a monotone, the patient may try using the new pitch in some real-life conversational situations. In the beginning he or she may have more success talking to strangers, such as store clerks; patients often find it difficult to use the new pitch level with friends and family, because their previous "sets" may prevent them from utilizing their new vocal behavior. Whatever conversational situation works best for the individual should be the one initially used.

8. It is helpful in therapy to tape record the patient's voice as he or she searches to establish a new and different pitch level. When the patient is able to produce a good voice at the proper pitch level, his or her own "best" voice can then become the therapy model.

C. *Typical case history showing utilization of approach.* John, a 10-year-old boy, was referred by his public-school speech clinician for a laryngeal examination because of a six-month history of hoarseness. The findings included a normal larynx and a "low-pitched dysphonic voice." John could readily demonstrate a higher phonation, which was characterized by an immediate clearing of quality. In the discussion that followed the tape-recorded playback of his "good" and "bad" voice, John stated that he thought he had been trying to speak like his older brother. The clinician pointed out to him that his better voice was more like that of other boys his age, and that the low-pitched voice he had been using was difficult for others to listen to. In subsequent voice therapy with his public-school clinician, John focused on elevating his voice pitch to a more natural level. His success was rapid, and therapy was terminated after six weeks.

D. *Evaluation of approach.* The pitch of the voice changes constantly, according to the situation in which the speaker finds himself or herself. In some voice patients, however, the pitch level appears to be too high or too low for the overall capability of the laryngeal mechanism. In other persons, an aberrant pitch level is just one manifestation of the total personality. Patients with additive masses to the folds (nodules, papilloma, polyps, and so on) may have lower pitch levels than normal because the thicker vocal folds vibrate slower, emitting a lower fundamental frequency. As the lesion is reduced or eliminated, the frequency of the voice becomes higher, perhaps approaching normal limits. For patients with additive laryngeal lesions due to vocal hyperfunction, it is often best to work slowly toward increasing pitch level to approximate levels of the patient's age and sex peers. Occasional voice patients use aberrant pitch levels because of personality factors. Counseling such patients and helping them want to change pitch levels might well have to precede actual symptomatic therapy to alter pitch. Typically, however, voice patients who may need to change pitch levels can do so rather quickly, after experiencing marked improvement in overall voice quality because of pitch change.

10. EXPLANATION OF PROBLEM

A. *Kinds of problems for which approach is useful.* Hearing an explanation of one's voice problem and some description of what may be causing it is often a powerful tool in voice therapy. A patient with a hyperfunctional voice disorder, in particular, often profits greatly from the clinician's describing why he or she has the particular problem. Olsen (1972) found that experienced clinicians in voice therapy spend about 20 percent of their therapy time explaining some aspect of the voice or voice problem to the patients. Clinical experience has taught these authors that if they can help individuals know why they have the voice problem, sometimes nothing more is needed to change a phonation style or to curb vocal abuse-misuse. In the case of those dysphonias that are wholly related to functional causes (such as hyperfunction), it is important that clinicians not confront patients with the implication that they "could talk all right if they wanted to." Instead of saying, "You are not using your voice as well as you could," a clinician might say, "Your vocal folds are coming together too tightly." The latter statement absolves the patient of the guilt he or she might experience if the clinician indicated that the patient was doing things "wrong." The patient will be much more receptive to a statement that puts the blame on the vocal folds. For patients with structural changes of the vocal folds, such as nodules or polyps, it may be necessary to explain that the organic pathology may well be the result of prolonged misuse, and that by eliminating the misuse, the patient will eventually experience a reduction of vocal fold pathology.

B. *Procedural aspects of approach.* In voice problems related to vocal hyperfunction, it is important to identify for the patient those behaviors that help maintain the dysphonia. No exact procedure for this can be laid down; each case has its own rules. For problems related to abuse and misuse of the voice, identify the inappropriate behavior and demonstrate to the patient some ways in which it can be eliminated. In the vocal abuse reduction section of our voice program for children (Boone, 1980a), we put much focus on having the child cognitively approach the problem of vocal abuse. By using comic pictures with an accompanying story text, we help the child understand the consequences of continued abuse. We also emphasize what can be expected (a better voice) if he or she reduces or eliminates such abuses.

For truly organic problems, such as unilateral adductor paralysis, the same explanations must be made, but in terms of inadequate and adequate glottal closure. Most voice patients want to understand what their problems are and what they can do about them. Make use of medical and diagnostic information, but formulate explanations to the patient in language the patient can understand. Such imagery as "your vocal cords are coming together too tightly," or "you seem to place your voice back too far in your throat," may lack scientific validity, but may very well help the patient understand the problem. Make explanations brief and to the point, but take care not to put the patient psychologically on the defensive during the first visit. If, after the evaluation, it appears that some psychological or psychiatric consultation is necessary, further diagnostic-therapy sessions may have to be held before the patient can agree to find out more about his or her feelings. An explanation of the problem does not have to be completed before voice therapy begins; in fact, Olsen's (1972) data suggest that an explanation of the problem is an important part of every session of voice therapy as practiced by experienced clinicians.

C. *Typical case history showing utilization of approach.* Dr. M., a 72-year-old retired professor, developed speech and voice symptoms shortly after retiring. He was diagnosed by a neurologist as having a congenital myotonia (family history revealed that several male relatives had myotonia that began at much earlier ages than the patient's). He came to the hospital speech-voice clinic for "my poor speech." Subsequent evaluations found that Dr. M's primary communication problem was a pronounced hypernasality caused by a relatively immobile velum. Because his disease symptoms were relatively static and his overall speech articulation was normal, a palatal lift was recommended. His nasal voice resonance was isolated as his primary symptom; air-pressure flows and a recording playback were provided the patient, as were detailed explanations about voice resonance and his hypernasality problem in particular. Recordings of several other patients who had been fitted with palatal lifts were played, to demonstrate for the patient the before and after vocal resonance. A description of how a palatal lift is constructed and a prediction of the patient's probable outcome were then provided. The explanation of his problem not only suggested what direction the patient should take to improve his voice, but also convinced him that he would experience a good outcome. The patient was subsequently fitted with a palatal lift, attached to his own modified upper denture. Results were excellent, producing normal air-flow data and a pronounced reduction in nasal resonance. After the lift was fitted, only one counseling and therapy demonstration session was required.

D. *Evaluation of approach.* An explanation of the problem is an important part of voice therapy. Wilson (1979) wrote, "During the initial part of the voice therapy program the child should be taught how voice is produced and given the basic facts about his voice problem" (p. 96). Boone (1980a) and Thurman (1977) have written about ways of letting children know about why they are doing what they are asked to do in therapy. Adults need explanations specific to their vocal pathologies and steps to remediate the problem. All patients need these explanations from the clinician, perhaps supplemented by charts and pictures, as a continuing part of voice therapy. Voice patients who understand how the voice functions and what are their own pathologies are much more apt to be motivated to apply the various therapeutic strategies offered to them by their clinicians.

11. FEEDBACK

A. *Kinds of problems for which approach is useful.* Once the patient is able to produce a model voice—his or her own or one that matches some external model—it is important that he or she attempt to study what the voice feels like and how it sounds. Tactual and proprioceptive feedback are common modalities through which we get some information about our voices as we speak, but we primarily use the auditory feedback system to monitor our own phonation. We have little awareness of what our muscles are doing in the larynx, throat, palate, or tongue, which is why voice therapy relies heavily on the auditory feedback mechanism.

With modern instrumentation, we can provide needed feedback specific to the physiology of respiration, phonation, and resonance. Much of the evaluation instrumentation described in Chapter 4 can be used as effective feedback devices, because they permit the patient to view various ongoing speaking-voicing events as they are occurring. It is sometimes helpful to provide the voice patient with information specific to what he or she may be doing in respiration while producing voice. The physiology of respiration can be studied by placing a pair of magnetometers on the chest wall and another pair on the abdomen; Hixon and his associates have studied relative chest wall-abdominal movements during singing (Watson and Hixon, 1985) and in dramatic performances (Hixon, Watson, and Maher, 1987). This use of magnetometers can provide valuable feedback to the patient attempting to develop more optimal breathing patterns.

Nasoendoscopy, as described in Chapter 4, permits direct observation of the actual physiology of various oral, pharyngeal, and laryngeal events while phonating. Supraglottal participation in vocal quality and resonance can be directly observed; the patient can watch himself or herself using various therapy techniques that produce changes in voice (Pershall and Boone, 1986). Patients who have marginal velopharyngeal (VP) closure can watch the closure of the VP mechanism on a television monitor and use the experience as direct feedback in therapy (Shelton, Paesani, McClelland, and Bradfield, 1975). For patients with problems of nasal resonance, the Kay Nasometer (1987) is a useful feedback device that provides an ongoing ratio of the relative oral-nasal resonance in the patient's voice. By applying a particular therapeutic technique or attempting to match a particular resonance model, the patient and the clinician can get immediate feedback on the patient's production.

Feedback specific to voice frequency and quality can be provided by many electronic instruments, some of which we present later, when we describe some of the procedures using feedback. As the patient is presented various target vocal behaviors to produce or match, instrumentation can provide real-time or delayed feedback specific to the correctness of the response. If the patient is off target in production, he or she can alter the vocalization to more closely match the target model.

Biofeedback specific to the patient's relaxation state can be helpful in voice therapy. The patient is introduced to some kind of biofeedback instrumentation that quantifies physiologic changes, such as galvanic response or blood pressure, which are believed to be correlates of anxiety or systemic tension. As the patient becomes more relaxed, the physiologic tension data go down; increased tension is characterized by increased data values. The patient in effect learns what it feels like to be more relaxed, and the relaxed state is confirmed by lower tension scores as portrayed on biofeedback instrumentation. Once relaxation behaviors are learned (Stroebel, 1983), the biofeedback confirmation of the relaxed state is often no longer needed.

B. *Procedural aspects of approach.*

1. Discuss with the patient the general concept of feedback. Tactual feedback might be illustrated by moving the fingertips lightly over the surface of a coin. Proprioception can be demonstrated by having the patient close the eyes, extend an arm, and slowly raise the arm, bending it at the elbow joint. Muscle and joint proprioceptors tell us where our arm is in space and that it is moving. In the larynx, however, such proprioceptive feedback is essentially lacking; we must rely on hearing our voices as we phonate to monitor what we are doing laryngeally.

2. The conventional tape recorder has never been particularly useful as a training device for auditory feedback. All it can do, essentially, is serve as an amplifying system. By the time you rewind the tape and find the precise recording segment, the patient has already lost his or her focus on that particular stimulus. Many auditory tape devices are available—Language Master, Phonic Mirror, Echorder, Artik (see References at end of text). You can make your own loop tapes for either reel-to-reel recorders or cassettes by following simple procedures (Boone, 1982). The loop playback provides valuable auditory feedback. A loop recording device, for example, set on a three-second delay, will give the patient an im-

mediate playback of what he or she has just said. By using such a device, patients can immediately match what they thought they sounded like with the actual playback of what they sounded like externally. Vowel prolongations, single words, and phrases are used as the stimuli in this delayed-feedback practice. Remember that such practice in self-listening is much more effective if coupled with commentary and questions about what was heard, and what was different between the old voice and the new.

3. Introduce the patient to the feedback instruments that will provide the needed feedback. In respiration, any of the measuring devices for air volume and pressures described in Chapter 4 may be useful. Duration measurements, such as how long one can prolong an /s/, can be used for feedback. The magnetometers can provide ongoing information about respiratory physiology. Videoendoscopy can provide excellent feedback for the physiology of VP closure, pharyngeal and supraglottal laryngeal participation in voicing, and vocal fold movements. Information about pitch and quality—for example, digital and graphic data about the patient's ongoing phonation—can be provided by the PM 100 Pitch Analyzer, the Kay Visi-Pitch, and B & K Frequency Analyzers (see References).

4. Once the patient develops an awareness of what he or she is doing with the help of feedback devices, remove the feedback and see if the patient can then maintain the target production. For example, when the patient no longer can see on a scope the normal coordination of abdomen and thorax in breathing for speech, can the optimum pattern be maintained? Both biofeedback of some physiological system and ongoing auditory feedback eventually need to be phased out of the therapy session to facilitate generalization of improved production outside the therapy.

C. *Typical case history showing utilization of approach.* Cheryl was a 22-year-old university student with vocal nodules and a severe dysphonia. Her voice evaluation showed that she spoke at the very bottom of her limited pitch range. When she spoke one or two full musical notes higher than the bottom of her pitch range, her voice sounded near normal. We spent much time in therapy giving her auditory feedback of her new voice at a higher pitch level, utilizing a four-second tape loop cartridge. This provided Cheryl with immediate feedback about how she sounded. We then coupled the auditory feedback with the visual feedback of a Visi-Pitch scope, where she could witness the increased periodicity of her voice, indicated by a sharper tracing line on the scope. Not only did she sound better to herself, but she could also see that voicing one or two notes higher than she had been produced a smoother, better sounding voice. The voice therapy used the auditory and visual feedback, coupled with some practice reducing excessive glottal attack, opening her mouth more, and so forth. At the end of fifteen weeks of twice-weekly voice therapy, Cheryl's nodules were gone and we all (including the patient) judged her voice as normal.

D. *Evaluation of approach.* As instrumentation is developed that can portray various aspects (respiration-phonation-resonance) of voice, it can play an important role in providing feedback to patients. Once a target behavior has been isolated for a patient, such instrumentation can provide ongoing feedback on the appropriateness of patient production. Feedback presents various visual portrayals (values of frequency, jitter, shimmer, and so forth) of what the patient is hearing. Various facilitating efforts in therapy often produce changes in the sound of voice that are confirmed by different feedback devices. Once an optimal voicing pattern has been established, the use of feedback devices is no longer necessary.

12. GLOTTAL FRY

A. *Kinds of problems for which approach is useful.* True glottal fry is produced in a relaxed manner with very little air flow and very little subglottic air pressure (Zemlin, 1981). Glottal fry, considered a normal voice register, is valuable for patients with vocal nodules as well as for patients with other hyperfunctional problems such as polyps, cord thickening, functional dysphonia, and even spastic dysphonia and ventricular phonation. Although glottal fry can be an extremely powerful facilitating technique to improve voice in the dysphonic patient and is a useful diagnostic vocal probe, it has a second use, as well: It can be an index of vocal fold relaxation. In order to produce a glottal fry of 65 to 75 Hz, which is desirable, the vocal folds must be relaxed. A patient may not always be able to achieve this fry in the first session but the accomplishment of a "good fry" of about 70 or 75 Hz is an index that the larynx has been relaxed. The glottal fry can be produced on either inhalation or exhalation. After producing glottal fry phonation for five to ten seconds and then being asked to say a phrase such as "easy does it," a patient with nodules often experiences normal or near-normal vocal quality for the first time in months.

B. *Procedural aspects of approach.*

1. A common pencil eraser or very dry hard raisin can represent a vocal nodule. When placed between the pages of a hardback book, the eraser keeps the pages apart with a gap on either side of eraser; likewise, nodules produce a gap between the vocal cords, as was shown in Figure 3–2. If the eraser is placed between two marshmallows instead of between the pages of a book, the marshmallows "wrap around" the mass of the eraser. In glottal fry, the compliant vocal cords can "wrap around" the nodules and improve approximation. A clinician can see this with stroboscopic videoendoscopy and demonstrate it to the patient.

2. Ask the patient to let out half of his or her breath and then say /i/ softly holding it until it dies away slowly. Encourage the patient to stretch the /i/ as long as possible.

3. Once the patient has a well-sustained /i/ in the glottal fry mode, have him or her open the mouth medium wide and protrude the tongue. Then have the patient make the tone "larger" by "opening the throat." The desired tone is a deep, resonant, slow series of individual pops, which we describe as sounding "like dragging a stick along a picket fence."

4. Have the patient attempt to produce the same tone on inhalation as on exhalation. Some people are better able to produce the glottal fry on inhalation. Also have the patient alternately reverse the tone—first on exhalation, then on inhalation. Next, have the patient say words such as "on and off" and "in and out" in the glottal fry mode. Suggest that the patient slightly prolong these words and say them on both inhalation ("on," "in") and exhalation ("off," "out"), alternately back and forth between ingressive and egressive air flow. Tape record the glottal fry so the patient has a model or target.

5. When the patient is able to produce these words well and can produce the sustained /i/ or /a/ in glottal fry, ask him or her to say "easy does it," "squeeze the peach," or "see the eagle." These are almost always produced with greatly improved or normal vocal quality. The patient will generally be able to say only a few words with the improved quality and will then need to go back to the glottal fry mode. Tape record these phrases and contrast them with the patient's typical voice. Also ask the patient to judge the two.

6. When the correct glottal fry is learned, instruct the patient to practice for a minute or two several (ten or more) times each day. To assist the patient in practice, suggest that he or she tie practice to the environment—for example, by producing the fry each time he or she sees a school bus or a red car, or during the last two minutes of each hour. The patient must be producing the fry appropriately before you should allow practice.

C. *Typical case history showing utilization of approach.* Mark, a 10-year-old boy, and Brian, an 11-year-old boy, were referred for voice evaluation by an otolaryngologist who had diagnosed bilateral vocal nodules. Both boys had low-pitched, hoarse voices with frequent phonation breaks during connected speech. They had had these voices for nearly one year. After teaching glottal fry as just described, we had "contests" to see who could fry the longest and at the slowest rate. We had the boys say words in the fry mode back and forth to each other. We saw each boy twice a week, once together and once individually, for forty-five minute sessions. In three months, their voices were normal, and the nodules were completely gone. We should note that with one boy, we reduced vocal abuses during his soccer activity, as well.

D. *Evaluating the approach.* The approach appears to work because very little subglottic pressure and very little air flow
are required to produce the glottal fry. Therefore, there is
little stress on the folds. The compliant folds seem to reduce
the amount of friction as they meet during phonation. This
allows the nodules to be reduced or reabsorbed even though
the patient continues to talk. The new talking is done with
little fold tension.

13. HALF-SWALLOW, BOOM

A. *Kinds of problems for which approach is useful.* This technique
is most useful with patients who have unilateral vocal fold
paralysis, severe bowing of the cords, or falsetto voice. All of
these patients have low loudness levels and air wastage.
B. *Procedural aspects of approach.*
1. The instruction to swallow and to *immediately* say a loud
"boom" right "on top of the swallow" is critical. We use
the term "half-swallow" to stress that the patient is not
to swallow and then say "boom" but to say "boom" *during*
the swallow. We also ask the patient to say "boom" with
a low pitch, which we model first.
2. Frequently, after only two or three attempts, the "boom"
is said in a louder and less breathy (often nearly normal)
voice. Record these attempts and play them back to demonstrate the dramatic improvement. Ask the patient to
contrast this "boom" with his or her typical voice.
3. We often use this approach with the head turned to one
side and then the other. Also, we try it with the chin lowered and "tucked" in as well. When the best "boom" is
produced, ask the patient to say "boom /i/", "boom one,"
and "boom /i/ boom" right "on top of the swallow."
4. Gradually increase the length of the phrase after the
"boom" and finally phase out the "boom." Next, phase
out the swallow; by this time, move the head back to the
midline, and raise the chin to the normal position.
C. *Typical case history showing utilization of approach.* Tom, a 64-
year-old retired lecturer for the United States government,
was referred by an otolaryngologist who had diagnosed right
unilateral adductor vocal cord paralysis. He had a weak,
breathy, high-pitched voice (185 Hz) that often failed him in
a noisy environment and at the end of the day. Tom experienced frequent phonation breaks and complained of being
perceived as a woman when talking over the phone. The
half-swallow, boom technique, used exclusively with Tom
when the pushing/pulling technique produced a louder but
very hoarse voice, and produced a normal voice on "boom"
after the fourth or fifth attempt. After twenty-five sessions,
the voice was essentially normal and no longer failed him.
After dismissal from therapy, Tom was able to resume speaking assignments to groups. His voice was no longer perceived as that of a female, and his pitch was 135 to 140 Hz.
This patient, like many others, developed normal or near-

normal voice in the presence of a continuing unilateral adductor paralysis.

D. *Evaluating the approach.* The swallow produces as much closure of the larynx as is physiologically possible. "Boom" is a brief word composed of voiced sounds that can all be produced as the air is released from the physiologically constricted larynx and the oral opening is minimal, which produces some "back pressure on the larynx." The head turning likely also assists, in a mechanical sense, with laryngeal closure.

14. HEAD POSITIONING

A. *Kinds of problems for which approach is useful.* The production of easy, normal voice is sometimes facilitated by changing the position of the head. Head positioning has been found most useful for facilitating both chewing and swallowing in patients with various neurological disorders. For such patients, better oral-pharyngeal competence may result with the head in certain positions. The symptoms of dysarthria, such as in articulation and voice problems, may also be minimized by the relative position of the head during speaking attempts. Occasionally, patients with hyperfunctional voice disorders can experience a marked improvement in voice quality by placing the head in a different position. Several distinct head positions can be tried in therapy in an attempt to find one that facilitates better voice:

1. Normal straight ahead
2. Neck extended forward with head tilted down, face looking up
3. Neck flexed downward with head tilted down, face looking down
4. Neck flexed unilaterally with head tilted to either the left or right, with tilted face looking forward
5. Head upright and rotated toward left or right, face looking in either direction.

Any one head position may change pharyngeal-oral resonating structures in such a way that a change in vocal quality (either better or worse) may occur.

B. *Procedural aspects of approach.*
1. First introduce the approach by demonstrating various head positions, either by photograph, video, or live demonstration. A simple explanation of the technique should accompany the demonstration: "Sometimes changing the positions of our heads can improve the sound of our voices. The head can either be tilted down or back, or to the left or right. Sometimes we can improve the sound of our voices simply by turning our heads to one side or the other. No one head position seems to help everyone. Let us try a few and listen to any changes in voice we hear."

2. The best voicing task to use to search for head position influence is the prolongation of vowels, such as /i/, /ɪ/, /ɛ/, /æ/, /o/, or /u/. Once a position is discovered that is helpful, any kind of voice practice material can be used.
3. Many gradations in positioning are possible between the normal head position and one of the extreme head positions described previously. For example, flexing the neck and bringing the head down in a gradual movement, perhaps at the beginning of the movement, a voice change can be noted. As soon as change can be noted, if it is to occur, the head should be kept at that position without going to the full range of the movement.
4. Neurologically impaired patients may experience some oral-pharyngeal asymmetry from their disease—that is, one side of the neck or oral cavity may function better than the other side. A particular lateral movement of the head may make a sudden and noticeable improvement in voice in such patients. If so, then ask the patient to practice voice material with the head in the lateral position.
5. Patients with vocal hyperfunction—that is, patients who use too much effort to talk—often profit most from neck flexion with the chin tucked down toward the chest. Such downward carriage of the head seems to promote greater vocal tract relaxation. If an easy, target voice is achieved with neck flexion, this head-down position should be held during voice practice attempts.

C. *Typical case history showing utilization of approach.* Mary was a 55-year-old housewife who had vocal difficulties for the past five years. A subsequent voice evaluation found that she had a moderately severe functional dysphonia accompanied by neck tension with severe mandibular restriction, hard glottal attack, and an inappropriately high voice pitch. Voice therapy was scheduled twice weekly with therapy focus on increasing her mouth opening, developing an easy glottal attack with "a legato phonatory style." The chewing and open-mouth approaches were unsuccessful until changing head position was added to the therapy. Mary was instructed to "tuck in her chin," flexing the anterior neck muscles with her face looking downward. Keeping her chin down, she was able to reduce neck tensions; she experienced immediate improvement in vocal quality. In subsequent therapy sessions, she developed an awareness that much of her past vocal strain was related to her tendency to hyperextend her neck; by using the opposite head position with anterior neck flexion, she was able to produce voice with relatively little strain. This change of head position, coupled with other therapy techniques designed to promote greater oral openness and ease of vocal production, helped Mary reestablish a normal voice.

D. *Evaluation of approach.* Using another head position by flexing or extending the neck can have an immediate effect on voice quality. Such an approach is seldom used alone but, rather, in combination with other voice therapy facilitating approaches. Whereas patients with severe functional tensions often profit from anterior neck flexion—as did Mary, as just described—patients with neurogenic voice problems often profit from using some of the other head positions described earlier, in A. Changing head positions to facilitate better voice requires much trial and error. If a particular head position works, use it; if not, try another position.

15. HIERARCHY ANALYSIS

A. *Kinds of problems for which approach is useful.* In hierarchy analysis, the patient lists various situations in his or her life that ordinarily produce some anxiety and arranges those situations in a sequential order from the least to the most anxiety provoking. Individual patients may instead prepare a hierarchy of situations, ranging from those in which they find their voices best to those in which they find them worst. This technique is borrowed from Wolpe's method of reciprocal inhibition (1987), which teaches the patient relaxed responses to anxiety-evoking situations. After identifying a hierarchy of anxiety-evoking situations, the patient begins by employing the relaxed responses in the least anxious of them, and, in therapy, works his or her way up the hierarchy, thereby eventually deconditioning his or her previously established anxious responses. The identification of hierarchical situations (less anxiety-more anxiety; worst voice-best voice) is a useful therapeutic device for most patients with hyperfunctional voice problems, which by definition imply excessive overreacting. Patients with functional dysphonia, or with dysphonias accompanied by nodules, polyps, and vocal fold thickening, frequently report that their degrees of dysphonia vary with the situation. Such patients may profit from hierarchy analysis.

B. *Procedural aspects of approach.*

1. Begin by developing in the patient a general awareness of the hierarchical behavior to be studied. If, for example, the patient is to be asked to identify those situations in which he or she feels most uncomfortable, discuss with the patient the symptoms of being uncomfortable. Or, if the patient is going to develop a hierarchy of situations in which he or she experiences variation of voice, discuss and give examples of what is a good voice or a bad voice. Explain that the patient must develop a relative ordering of situations, sequencing them from "good" to "bad." Some patients are initially resistant to this sort of ordering, perhaps because they never realized that there are relative gradations to their feelings of anxiety or relative changes in their quality of voice. They may not be aware that the degree of their anxiety or hoarseness is not constant.

2. Although the majority of voice patients are soon able to arrange situations into a hierarchy, a few require practice sequencing some neutral stimuli. On one occasion,

a woman was taught the idea of sequential order by arranging five shades of red tiles from left to right, in the order of the lightest pink to the darkest red. Having done this, she was then able to sequence her voice situations, proceeding gradually from those in which her voice was normal to those in which it was extremely dysphonic.

3. As a home assignment, have the patient develop several hierarchies with regard to his or her voice. One hierarchy might center on how the patient's voice holds up with the family, another on how it is related to the work situation, and a third on what happens to it in varying situations with friends. An excellent example of hierarchical situations developed by a woman with vocal nodules is discussed in an article by Gray, England, and Mahoney (1965). After these hierarchies have been developed by the patient at home, review them in therapy.

4. In therapy, use the "good" end of the hierarchical sequence first. That is, begin by asking the patient to recapture, if he or she can, the good situation. The goal of therapy is to duplicate the feeling of well-being or the good voice that the patient experienced in the situation he or she rated as best. Efforts should be made in therapy to recall the good factors surrounding the more optimum phonation. If the patient is successful in recreating the optimum situation, his or her phonation will sound relaxed and appropriate. The recreated optimum situation thus serves as an excellent facilitator for producing good voice. After some success in recreating the first situation on the hierarchy, capturing completely his or her optimum response (whether this is relaxation or phonation or both), the patient will then be able to move on to the second situation. Again the goal is to maintain optimum response. The rate of movement up the hierarchy will depend entirely on how successfully the patient can recreate the situations and maintain optimum response. By using the relaxed response in increasingly more tense situations, the patient is conditioning himself or herself to a more favorable, optimum behavior.

5. Although some patients can recreate situations outside the clinic with relative ease, some cannot. As soon as possible, have the patient practice the optimum response outside the clinic under good conditions, so that he or she will eventually be able to use it in the real world in more adverse situations. The patient must not lose sight of the goal of maintaining the good response in varying situations outside clinic.

6. Some patients succeed in going just so far up the hierarchy, only to reach a situation in which they continuously have a maladaptive response. When this occurs, the patient should drop back to a lower hierarchical level and attempt once more to capture the optimum re-

sponse under more favorable conditions. When a good response is again maintained, efforts at the next level should be resumed.

C. *Typical case history showing utilization of approach.* Laurie was a 24-year-old forest conservationist who worked in an office with ten male conservationists. For six months she had experienced recurring dysphonia, particularly when on the telephone at work. Laryngoscopic examination found that she had an "early nodule formation on her left vocal cord"; during the voice evaluation she demonstrated a relatively normal voice. The patient's dysphonia appeared to fluctuate, and it became particularly severe, she reported, in certain anxiety-provoking situations. As part of her three months of voice therapy, Laurie was asked to develop several hierarchical scales, listing the situations in order, from those in which she experienced a normal voice to those in which she became all but aphonic. Following is the hierarchy Laurie developed for her vocal responses at the office:

Best Voice
1. Calling mother on the phone every day from the office.
2. The female secretary at the office is easy to talk with, particularly when the older men in the office are not around.
3. Dictating on the dictaphone and talking to the secretary are about the same.
4. Bill W. talks to me a lot at the office and on dates.
5. The younger men kid me about going out with them on field trips.
6. The older conservationists at the office keep reminding me that I have only school and no field experience, which always makes me clear my throat.
7. Talking about forestry projects on the phone is hard.
8. I lose my voice entirely when talking to our regional manager, and if I can't get over this, I will lose my job.
Worst Voice

By rank ordering the situations in which she experienced *best* voice and *worst* voice, Laurie developed insight about the role of interpersonal relationships and their direct impact on her voice. Symptomatic therapy coupled with hierarchy analysis in her case did not improve the sound of her voice or reduce the additive lesion on the left vocal fold. Voice therapy was terminated after three months in favor of psychotherapy.

D. *Evaluation of approach.* Most voice patients report great variability in voice quality, depending on how much they have been using the voice, the time of day, and the psychodynamics of the speaking situations. Hierarchy analysis is often helpful for dealing with vocal inconsistencies experienced while talking with different people in various situations. By analyzing the hierarchical situations in which voice deteriorates or improves, the patient develops an awareness of those situational cues that are causing voice changes. Perhaps for the first time, the patient realizes that voice quality is not a constant; typical of the normal speaker, vocal quality fluctuations are somewhat dependent on how relaxed one feels, how comfortable one is with his or her listeners. Therapy then focuses on using the best voice found low on the hierarchy. The patient attempts to use that optimum voice in those situations in which he or she has previously experienced difficulty. Hierarchy analysis is consistently useful in voice therapy.

16. INHALATION PHONATION

A. *Kinds of problems for which approach is useful.* The high-pitched vocalization produced on inhalation is always produced by true vocal fold vibration (Lehmann, 1965). The technique is useful, therefore, for helping patients who are aphonic or who have developed an odd form of phonation, such as ventricular phonation, find true fold vibration. Williams, Farquharson, and Anthony (1975) have written that reverse phonation viewed by fiberoptic endoscopy shows the vibrating folds well. Inhalation phonation is also an excellent method of eliciting true phonation in patients who are experiencing functional aphonia. Greene (1980) writes that inhalation phonation can be effectively used as a therapy approach with the occasional patient who exclusively uses "the ventricular band voice." The method is also useful with the occasional patient who is experiencing a functional *puberphonia*—that is, maintaining an inappropriately high-pitched voice despite a vocal mechanism that has matured beyond puberty. The ease with which most patients produce the high-pitched inhalation voice makes the method useful in establishing or reestablishing true vocal fold vibration.

B. *Procedural aspects of approach.*

1. This particular approach, which is similar to masking, is perhaps better demonstrated than explained. Demonstrate inhalation phonation by phonating a high-pitched hum while elevating the shoulders. It is important to time the initiation of the inhalation with shoulder elevation. Elevate the shoulder so you can mark and stress for the patient the contrast between inhalation (shoulders raised) and exhalation (shoulders lowered).

2. After demonstrating several separate inhalations with simultaneous shoulder elevation and phonation, say "Now, I'll match the high-pitched inhalation voice with an expiration voice." Inhale raising the shoulders and simultaneously humming in a high pitch, then dropping the shoulders on exhalation and producing the same sound of voice. Repeat the inhalation-exhalation matched phonations several times.

3. Then ask the patient to make an inhalation phonation. He or she should repeat the inhalation phonation several times. Now again repeat the inhalation-exhalation

matched phonation, taking care to make the associated shoulder movements. Then tell the patient, "Now drop your shoulders on expiration, making the same high-pitched voice as you do it." With a little trial practice, most patients are able to do it.

4.   After the patient has produced the matching hum, say, "Now, let us extend the expiration like this." Demonstrate a continuation of the high pitch, sweeping down from your falsetto register to your regular chest register on one long, continuous expiration. Repeat this several times. Then say to the patient, "Once I've brought my vocal cords together at the high pitch, I then sweep down, keeping them together, down to the pitch level of my regular speaking voice."

5.   If the patient is unable to produce this shift from high to low, repeat the first four steps. If the patients can make the shift down to the regular speaking register, say, "Now you're getting your vocal cords together for a good-sounding voice." Take care at this point not to rush the patient into using the "new" voice functionally. Rather, have the patient practice some similar hum phonations. After some practice just phonating the hum, give the patient a word list containing simple monosyllabic words for "true" voice practice.

6.   Once the patient is able to produce inspiration-expiration without difficulty, he or she should be instructed to no longer use the pronounced shoulder movements. Elevating and dropping the shoulders are only necessary to mark the difference between inspiration and expiration.

7.   Stay at the single-word practice level until normal voicing is well established. We often spend several therapy periods practicing the new phonation as a motor practice drill without attempting to make the voice conversationally functional. You might say, "Now we're getting the vocal folds together the way we want them." This places the previous aphonia or ventricular phonation "blame" on the mechanism rather than on the patient per se. Counseling with the patient at this time is important. The motor practice gives the patient time to adjust to the more optimum way of phonating.

C. *Typical case history showing utilization of approach.* Derek, a 5-year-old boy, was found to have small bilateral vocal nodules. His speech clinician placed him on complete voice rest, which unfortunately was enforced for five continuous months. At the end of five months, the nodules had disappeared, and Derek was instructed by both the physician and the speech pathologist to resume normal phonation. Despite all his efforts, Derek could only whisper. He became completely aphonic, but whispered easily to all people with much animation and relative comfort. This functional aphonia remained for two months after he was instructed, "Go back and talk the normal way." Derek gestured that he wanted to use his voice but he could not "find it." Therapy efforts for restoring phonation were begun about seven months after Derek's phonations had ceased. Inhalation phonation was initiated, and at the first therapy session Derek was able to produce a high-pitched inhalation sound and to follow his clinician well by matching the inhalation with an expiration sound. He was able to use an expiration phonation, appropriate in both quality and pitch, by the end of the first therapy session. He was scheduled for two other appointments within a twenty-four-hour period, during which he practiced producing his regained normal voice. He was counseled that his "voice is working now and you'll never have to lose it again." The boy has had normal phonation since his voice was restored using the inhalation phonation technique. Counseling to curb yelling and other vocal abuses appeared to be successful, as Derek has experienced no return of the bilateral vocal nodules.

D. *Evaluation of approach.* Some patients who experience either aphonia or ventricular phonation for any length of time lose their ability to initiate normal true fold phonation. The longer the aphonia or dysphonia persists, the harder it might be to use normal voice. Inhalation phonation is a simple way to produce true cord approximation and voicing. The high-pitched voice on inhalation probably results from the vocal folds being longer in their inhalation posture, and even though they may adduct on command, they remain in their longer configuration. This elongated posture thins them, resulting in the higher-pitched phonation. The patient is able to match the inspiration sound with an expiration sound.

17. MASKING

A. *Kinds of problems for which approach is useful.* Patients with functional aphonia are often able to produce normal phonation under conditions of auditory masking. Some patients with functional dysphonia produce faulty voices because of poor auditory monitoring of what they are doing. The masking facilitating approach uses a voicing-reflex test, used by audiologists as the Lombard Test (Newby, 1972). In fact, the Lombard test was first introduced as a method of finding voice in patients with functional aphonia. When asked to phonate in a loud-noise background, patients with functional aphonia sometimes used light voice. In the voice-reflex situation, the patient wears earphones and is asked to read a passage aloud. As the patient is reading, a masking noise is fed into the earphones. The louder the masking, the louder the patient's voice. At loud masking levels the patient cannot monitor well either the loudness or the clearness of his or her voice. Some patients with functional dysphonias actually experience clearer voices when they cannot monitor their productions because of loud masking. The clinician may make a tape recording of all the patient's oral reading, with and without masking, and then play back the results to the patient. The patient may well experience the "proper" set for more optimal phonation during the masking conditions and be able to maintain this improved production without continued masking.

B. *Procedural aspects of approach.*

1. The masking approach is best used without any prior explanation. Because increased voice loudness comes about with increased intensities of masking on a reflexive, nonvolitional basis, there is no need to discuss the method in advance. In fact, there is evidence that some patients can override the voice reflex and maintain constancy of voice loudness despite fluctuations in masking intensity.

2. The patient is seated next to an audiometer. He or she then puts on headphones and listens to a bilateral presentation of masking at a low level, roughly 40 dB SPL. Once the patient acknowledges hearing the masking, the masking stimulus is discontinued. The patient is then instructed to read aloud and to keep reading, no matter what kind of interruption he or she may hear in the headphones. Typically, the patient is asked to read aloud for a total period of about two minutes, with the masking fluctuating off and on throughout the reading. On playback variations in loudness of the patient's voice usually signal when the masking noise was introduced and when it ceased.

3. An audiocassette recording should be made as the patient reads aloud. An aphonic patient's whisper may change to voice under conditions of masking. It is important to have recorded the emergence of voice, which the patient can use in step 5. The dysphonic patient (functional, ventricular, or puberphonic) should also be recorded while using the masking approach. Marked differences in voice quality between the absence or presence of masking conditions will probably be evident.

4. Five-or ten-second exposures to masking are introduced to the patient bilaterally. The intensity levels should be in excess of 90 dB SPL, which is sufficiently loud to mask out the patient's own voicing attempts. Whenever an aphonic patient hears the loud masking, he or she may attempt some feeble vocalization. Under masking a dysphonic patient will produce a louder voice and often a voice with more normal vocal quality, as well.

5. Do not use the masking method beyond the trial stage with those few voice patients who do not demonstrate the voice-reflex effect. If it works well, and produces voice improvement, the method may be used as part of every therapy period. You might then experiment by having the patient listen to tapes of himself or herself, to see whether the patient can match volitionally his or her voice under masking conditions. Recordings can then be made contrasting the voice without masking (attempting to recreate the same voice as heard under masking) and the voice with masking. Try to have the voices sound alike.

6. A patient may profit from reading aloud under masking conditions, and then having the masking abruptly ended to see if he or she can maintain the better voice. Many other variations using the masking noise can be initiated by inventive clinicians.

C. *Typical case history showing utilization of approach.* Lillian was a 9-year-old girl who had a history of vocal nodules that had been previously treated successfully with voice therapy. Several months after therapy had been terminated as successful (no nodules, normal voice), Lillian developed a severe influenza that left her with no voice. She was completely aphonic, and could communicate only by whispering and using good facial expressions and gestures. The aphonia continued for one month (over the December holiday break) before she returned to the voice clinic. The masking approach was used with Lillian after attempts at modeling and request for voice failed. Lillian was asked to read aloud under conditions of 90 dB masking. Her reading attempts were recorded on a twenty-second loop tape. As soon as masking was introduced, light phonation was heard and recorded on the loop cassette. The masking and oral reading were stopped, and Lillian was asked to hear her good voice on the tape. The child clapped her hands in joy that she now had a returned voice. Further masking followed by ear training was used as her voice became stronger. After two follow-up therapy sessions, Lillian was discharged with a normal voice. The pushing approach—producing the word "patch" with sudden extension of arms—was then demonstrated for Lillian to use "if you ever lose your voice again." Hopefully, her "believing" in pushing as a protection against future voice loss will function as a placebo effect and prevent any recurrence of aphonia. Lillian has had no voice problem in the two years since the one month of aphonia.

D. *Evaluation of approach.* The masking approach is most helpful with aphonic patients. It is also helpful for patients with some form of functional dysphonia or young men with puberphonia. If the masking noise is loud enough, in excess of 90 dB SPL, patients cannot hear their voices to monitor phonation. If required to continue speaking by reading aloud under conditions of masking, patients will often produce relatively normal voices under the masking condition. Clinicians should use some care in confronting the patients on audiotape playback with their "good" voices. Improved voices under conditions of masking should be used as the patients' models for their own imitation phonations. Clinicians should use the masking approach with some degree of eclecticism—that is, if the approach works, use it; if it does not, quickly abandon it.

18. OPEN-MOUTH APPROACH

A. *Kinds of problems for which approach is useful.* Encouraging the patient to develop more oral openness often reduces generalized vocal hyperfunction. Opening the mouth more while speaking and learning to listen with a slightly open mouth allow the patient to use his or her vocal mechanisms more optimally. The open-mouth approach promotes more natural size-mass adjustments and more optimum approximation of the vocal folds, and this helps correct problems of loudness, pitch, and quality. Opening the mouth more is also recommended to increase oral resonance and to improve overall voice quality. The voice also sounds louder. Developing greater openness should be part of any voice therapy program wherein the patient is attempting to use the vocal mechanisms with less effort and strain.

B. *Procedural aspects of approach.*

1. Have the patient view himself or herself in a mirror (or on a videotape playback, if possible) to observe the presence and absence of open-mouth behavior. Identify any lip tightness, mandibular restriction, or excessive neck muscle movement for the patient.

2. Children seem to understand quickly the benefits of opening the mouth more to produce better-sounding voices. In our voice program for children (Boone, 1980a), we use a brief story that illustrates two boys, one who talks with his mouth closed and one who speaks with his mouth open. We then introduce a hand puppet and ask the child if he or she has ever been a ventriloquist. The ventriloquist is described as someone who does not open the mouth, in contrast to the puppet, who makes exaggerated, wide-mouth openings.

3. The ventriloquist-puppet analogy also works well with adults. Let the patient observe the marked contrast between talking with a closed mouth and talking with an open one. Ask the patient to watch himself or herself speak the two different ways in a mirror. Instruct the patient that what he or she is attempting will at first feel foreign and inappropriate. The initial stages of letting the jaw relax are frequently anything but relaxed.

4. To establish further this oral openness, ask the patient to drop the head toward the chest and let the lips part and the jaw drop open. Once the patient can do this, have him or her practice some relaxed /a/s. When the head is tilted down and the jaw is slightly open, a more relaxed phonation can often be achieved.

5. In order for patients to develop a feeling of openness when listening, and as a preset to speaking, they must first develop a conscious awareness of how often they find themselves with tight, closed mouths. One way to develop this awareness is to have patients mark down, on cards they carry with them, each time they become aware that their mouths are closed unnecessarily. The marking task itself is often enough to increase a patient's awareness, and over a period of a week the number of mouth closings will decrease notably. Another way of developing an awareness of greater orality is to have patients place in their living environments (on a dressing table, desk, or car dashboard) a little sign that says

"OPEN," or perhaps has a double arrow ($\updownarrow$), or any other code that might serve as a reminder.

6. A patient who wants to achieve greater oral openness must practice a lot. Steps 3 and 4, just described, facilitate greater mouth opening and are thus useful practice tasks. In addition, many voice and diction texts have useful oral openness tasks; see, for example, Modisett and Luter (1984) and Newcombe (1986). Practice procedures for developing greater oral opening may also be found in voice therapy practice kits (Boone, 1980a, 1982) and in voice therapy texts, such as Andrews (1986) or Wilson (1987).

C. *Typical case history showing utilization of approach.* J. J., a 17-year-old high-school girl, was examined by a laryngologist about one year after an automobile accident in which she had suffered some injuries to the head and neck. Laryngoscopic examination found all visible laryngeal structures normal in appearance and function, despite the fact that since the accident the girl's voice had been only barely audible. The speech pathologist was impressed "with her relatively closed mouth while speaking, which seemed to result in extremely poor voice resonance." Voice therapy combined both the chewing and the open-mouth facilitating approaches. It was discovered in therapy that for three months after the automobile accident the girl had worn an orthopedic collar that seemed to inhibit her head and jaw movements. It appeared that much of her closed-mouth, mandibularly-restricted speech was related to the constraints imposed upon her by the orthopedic collar. When using the open-mouth approach with her head tilted down toward her chest, she was immediately able to produce a louder, more resonant voice. The open-mouth approach was initiated before beginning chewing exercises, and both achieved excellent results. Therapy was terminated after six weeks, with much voice improvement in both loudness and quality.

D. *Evaluation of approach.* The voice, both normal and dysphonic, improves in quality with greater mouth opening. Upon opening the mouth a bit more, the voice usually improves immediately. Besides opening the mouth more while speaking, the approach also encourages slight mouth opening while listening. In a previous description of a vocal hygiene approach, Boone (1980b) wrote, "A gentle opening of less than one finger wide between the central incisors keeps the teeth apart and generally fosters a relaxed oral posture" (p. 40). The open-mouth approach has been particularly effective with performers, who often open their mouths well during performance (acting, singing) but may forget the importance of opening their mouths during conversation.

19. PITCH INFLECTIONS

A. *Kinds of problems for which approach is useful.* The prosodic and stress patterns of the normal speaking voice are characterized by changes in pitch, loudness, and duration. In some individuals, the lack of pitch variation is noticeable, because the resulting voice is monotonous and boring to listeners. Speaking on the same pitch level with little variation, which for the average speaker is impossible to maintain, requires the inhibition of natural inflection. It is usually observed in overcontrolled persons who display very little overt affect. Fairbanks (1960), who describes pitch variation as a vital part of normal phonation, defines inflection and shift, "An *inflection* is a modulation of pitch during phonation. A *shift* is a change of pitch from the end of one phonation to the beginning of the next" (p. 132). Voice therapy for patients with monotonic pitch seeks not only to establish more optimum pitch levels, but also to increase the amount of pitch variability. Any voice patient with a dull, monotonous pitch level will profit from attempting to increase pitch inflections.

B. *Procedural aspects of approach.*

1. The patient must first become of aware of his or her monotonous voice by listening to playback samples of voices. Play the patient's voice first, and follow it with samples of voices with excellent pitch variability. Follow the listening with evaluative comments. Have the patient self-evaluate, as well.

2. Begin working on downward and upward inflectional shifts of the same word, exaggerating, in the beginning, the extent of pitch change. Voice and articulation books, such as Fairbanks (1960), Modisett and Luter (1984), or Newcombe (1986), contain good practice materials for improving pitch variability.

3. Using the same practice materials, have the patient practice introducing inflectional shifts within specific words.

4. Pitch inflections can be graphically displayed on many instruments, such as the Visi-Pitch or PM 100 Pitch Analyzer. Set target inflections for the patient, to see if the patient can make his or her pitch level reach the same excursions or movement on the scope as the target model.

5. Record and playback for the patient various oral reading and conversational samples, critically analyzing the productions for degree of pitch variability.

C. *Typical case history showing utilization of approach.* Dr. T., a 51-year-old economics professor, received severe course evaluations from his students, who complained of his "monotonous" voice. On a subsequent voice evaluation, during both conversation and oral reading, he used "the same fundamental frequency with only minimal excursion of frequency." His voice was indeed monotonous, not only in pitch, but in loudness, as well. He also used the same duration characteristics for most vowels. Dr. T. was highly motivated to improve his speaking voice and manner of speaking. Subsequent therapy focus was on increasing pitch inflections and improving loudness variations. He was provided with audiocassette tapes, which he practiced daily, matching the target model productions with his own voicing attempts. After six weeks of voice therapy and intensive self-practice, Dr. T. demonstrated marked improvement in both his conversational and lecture voices. Unfortunately, despite his successful efforts to improve his voice, his course evaluations improved only slightly.

D. *Evaluation of approach.* The quality of one's voice is often improved if effort related to speaking is reduced. It takes some effort to speak in a monotone voice that has only minimal pitch variability. Therefore, increasing pitch variability in a monotonic voice usually contributes to increasing vocal relaxation. Because patients can usually be taught with some ease to increase pitch inflections, such an approach should be used in voice therapy whenever pitch variability appears to be lacking.

20. PLACE THE VOICE

A. *Kinds of problems for which approach is useful.* Many patients with voice problems have long histories of concern about their problems. Many focus on their throats as the anatomical site of their problems. Such patients may profit from this approach, place the voice, because it shifts the focus from the throat to the upper vocal tract. Perkins (1981) has written that "voice that feels focused high in the head" is a more efficient voice, and it can survive extensive vocalization. The clinician helps the patient focus on the area of his or her face under the cheeks and across the bridge of the nose. Most patients with chronic dysphonia experience both difficulty finding their voices and continued expectancy of vocal failure. They clear their throats continually, they make phonation rehearsals, and they worry about the poor vocal quality they are likely to have the next time they attempt to speak. For these patients successful voice clinicians often employ two techniques, respiration training and placing the voice in the facial mask, for two reasons: (1) to improve respiratory control and resonance; (2) to transfer the patient's mental focus away from the larynx and place it with the activator (respiration) and the resonator (supraglottal vocal tract).

B. *Procedural aspects of approach.*

1. In working with children, we use the pictures shown in the facial mask in Figure 5–3. As described in the Boone Voice Program for Children (1980a), we follow these steps: "Give the following explanation to the child, pointing to the appropriate places on the picture. (Point to the shaded area on the boy in the picture.) 'A good sounding voice is made right here. We'll do some things today that will put your voice right here.' (Point to the bridge of the nose in the picture, then touch the child in the same place.) 'Then we'll put some voice right here.' (Point to the cheeks in the picture, then touch the child in the same place.)" (p. 111)

2. With adults we use a similar procedure, but perhaps without the pictures (although this writer uses this same picture with voice patients of any age).

FIGURE 5-3. The imagery of "placing" the voice in the middle of the face is helped by using these two pictures. (*The Boone Voice Program for Children,* Austin, Texas: PRO-ED, 1980)

3. Demonstrate the method by saying "me" and "one" in an exaggerated manner, which will create sufficient nasal resonance to produce some vibration on the bridge of the nose and above the maxillary sinuses.

4. Request that the patient produce the "me" and the "one" in the same manner. Ask the patient if he or she can feel the vibration on his or her nose and high cheeks.

5. If the patient confirms feeling the vibration produced by the nasal consonant, add a few more words that permit the exaggeration of the nasal consonant. Words like "man," "mean," "many," "went" lend themselves well to this beginning work. If this is done correctly, improvement in vocal quality should be audible. The nasal consonants are used not to increase nasal resonance, but to focus the voice higher in the vocal tract than the patient had been previously.

6. If there is an audible improvement in the sound of the voice using the words with nasal consonants, then introduce other words, such a "baby," "beach," "take," and so on, emphasizing the resonance in the facial mask area. Any words may be used at this point.

7. After the patient has had some success in placing the voice "higher," discuss with the patient the imagery of what you are doing. Discuss how this is similar to the singing teacher's using such imagery (we cannot really "place" our voices anywhere), knowing that a singer who has the imagery of "putting his or her voice somewhere" often shows audible, measurable improvement. This is a good place to use some kind of feedback device, such as a spectrograph or the Visi-Pitch, to confirm any changes in voice quality using the approach.

8. Oral reading and conversation in the voice clinic setting, focusing on the feeling and the "set" for using place the

voice are important requisites for generalization of this approach outside the clinic.

C. *Typical case history showing utilization of approach.* Richard was a 44-year-old lawyer who developed a functional dysphonia while still maintaining "a normal larynx." At times, he experienced a normal voice, but at meetings or on the telephone, he often experienced severe hoarseness, pain in the laryngeal area, and the feeling talking at all required much effort. The place-the-voice technique worked better for him than all the other facilitating approaches we used. He found that the imagery of placing his voice "in his face" seemed to free the tightness he experienced in his throat. Increased periodicity of laryngeal vibration and improvement in overall laryngeal function appeared directly related to shifting his voice concern away from his larynx. From our explanation of phonation, he began to understand that the vocal folds come together "slightly," that the real activator of voice is the outgoing air flow, and that the real sound and quality of the voice are formed in the vocal tract above the larynx. The explanations and the practice placing the voice in the facial mask had lasting effects. Place the voice, used with respiration training and explanations of the vocal physiology, appeared to restore normal voice in this professional man. A one-year follow up quickly confirmed that he had maintained his normal voice.

D. *Evaluation of approach.* The goal in using this approach is to transfer the patient's focus from the larynx to the upper vocal tract. The approach is not used to increase nasal resonance; the heavy utilization of nasal resonance in the beginning steps of the approach are used only to develop focus on the area of the nose and face. Singing teachers have successfully used such imagery approaches (Coffin, 1981) for a long time. The method is similar to Cooper's (1977) *um-hum* technique, in which the patient experiences a "tingle or buzz" near the lips or the bridge of the nose. Improvement in vocal quality, using nasal consonants as a method of focusing the voice out of the throat, is part of therapy procedures developed by Wilson (1979, p. 150) and McClosky (1977, p. 143). Once the patient experiences the nasal vibration of production, the clinician shifts to oral productions, keeping, however, focus on the same somatic site. Our experience has been that the approach is helpful to most voice patients except those whose problems have a hypernasality component.

21. PUSHING APPROACH

A. *Kinds of problems for which approach is useful.* The pushing approach is not for use with voice problems related to excessive force and effort. Rather, the approach is useful for patients who have difficulty approximating the vocal folds, from such causes as generalized fatigue, myasthenia, unilateral cord paralysis, or traumatic injury to the vocal folds. Froeschels (1952), who is generally credited with introducing the pushing approach, developed the method initially to in-crease the strength of a weakened soft palate. He later adapted it as a method for increasing the strength of vocal fold adduction. Froeschels also recommended pushing as a temporary technique for people with bowed vocal folds or vocal *hypofunction,* produced by a tired vocal mechanism after continuous vocal hyperfunction.

B. *Procedural aspects of approach.*

1. First demonstrate the pushing method by raising the pa-tient's fists to about shoulder height, and then pushing the arms down suddenly in a rapid, uninterrupted mo-tion until the hands, fully extended, reach to just below the hips. Then instruct the patient to do the same thing by himself or herself. Occasionally, a patient may require some active assistance to ensure that he or she achieves the rapid, downward movement required.

2. After the patient can perform the pushing well, ask him or her to push and phonate simultaneously. Usually only short practice is required for the patient to synchronize the two actions. Phonations produced while pushing are usually louder and have better resonance.

3. Another variation of the pushing approach is to ask the patient to grasp the seat of a chair, and, while gripping the chair, to push down firmly with the arms. Next, ask the patient to add phonation while pushing in this way. Short successive bursts of pushing-phonation should then be practiced.

4. Another variation of the pushing approach using a chair is to ask the patient to sit down on a chair, grip under-neath the chair, and attempt to lift himself or herself up from the floor while seated on the chair. While lifting up, the patient should simultaneously phonate. While the lifting task cannot be completed, the strain of at-tempting to do it while phonating improves voice quality and *loudness.*

5. Once better phonation has been produced through pushing, have the patient listen to it on some kind of auditory feedback loop system. Although the pushing may be the primary facilitator in producing the better voice, the patient should soon attempt to match the same loudness and quality of phonation without pushing. A useful approach would be to have the patient listen dis-criminatively to his or her two phonations, one with pushing and one without, and see how closely he or she can match them in subsequent imitative attempts.

6. Once the patient is able to extend the good voice into a series of practice phrases, the pushing should be stopped. It is generally advisable to terminate pushing as soon as the same voice loudness and quality can be achieved without using it. The primary benefit of push-ing is its initial facilitating role.

C. *Typical case history showing utilization of approach.* Marvin, a 52-year-old attorney, had a two-year history of a "tired" voice that could not be heard during his courtroom appearances.

Laryngoscopic examination showed that Marvin had "severe posterior bowing of the cords, with the vocal processes in a fixed state of slight abduction." Voice therapy focused on slightly lowering pitch level on the pushing approach. On the first day of evaluation therapy, Marvin was able to produce a louder, more resonant voice by combining arm-extension pushing with the lowered phonation. In four therapy sessions, he was able to combine pushing with the more vigorous phonation of practice phrases. Marvin continued in voice therapy for a total of eight weeks, seeing the clinician for thirty-minute practice sessions twice a week. He was soon able to produce good matching phonations without pushing. As for carry-over to the courtroom, the setting where his difficulty had been most penalizing to him, Marvin was able to achieve appropriate phonation by occasionally pushing down hard on his chair while speaking. Laryngeal examination at the end of therapy found "normal vocal fold approximation, with no evidence of vocal process abduction." Voice loudness and quality were highly adequate at the time that therapy was discontinued, but no follow-up evaluation could be made to determine the permanence of these gains.

D. *Evaluation of approach.* For pushing to be effective, the push must be perfectly synchronized with the onset of voice. One of the primitive functions of the larynx is its valve closing during particular physiologic states of the organism, such as during heavy physical effort. The pushing approach, which requires the person to use the upper extremities in a forceful pushing manner, is usually accompanied by glottal closing. This glottal closure is observed in heavy lifting efforts, which are frequently accompanied by primitive vocalizations, indicating relatively firm approximation of the vocal folds. Once the patient is able to match his or her "pushing" voice without pushing, the exercises should be progressively minimized. The pushing method is useful for the occasional patient with a hypofunctional, "worn-out" voice. The method provides such a patient with an immediate increase in both loudness and quality. Remember, however, that most hypofunctional voices have developed that way after prolonged periods of vocal hyperfunction. Therefore, once the stronger voice has been elicited with pushing, the clinician should seek to maintain the same vocal quality and loudness without the pushing, employing other therapy approaches.

22. RELAXATION

A. *Kinds of problems for which approach is useful.* Most dysphonias and laryngeal pathologies are related to prolonged and continued vocal hyperfunction whose reduction is frequently a goal in voice therapy. Using such methods as the chewing approach or the yawn-sigh approach achieves vocal tract relaxation without working on it systemically. It is usually futile to imply to tense patients in therapy that if they would "just relax," all would be well. If patients could relax, they would;

if their tension did not, in fact, serve them in some way, they would get rid of it. A certain amount of psychic tension and muscle tonus is normal and healthy, of course, but some individuals do overreact to their environmental stresses; instead of "running at a slow idle," they are like "fast idle engines," expending far more energy and effort than a situation requires. By relaxation, therefore, we mean a realistic responsiveness to the environment with a minimum of needless energy expended. Some, but certainly not all, voice patients profit from a therapy program designed to reduce unnecessary tension by using relaxation techniques. Relaxation programs (Jacobson, 1957; Wolpe, 1987) and various stress-reducing programs (Staats, 1968; Stroebel, 1983) have been effective in developing greater relaxation and reducing stress in patients with dysphonia. Such relaxation measures might well be combined, however, with voice relaxation techniques such as described by Aronson (1985), Case (1984), or Wilson (1987).

B. *Procedural aspects of approach.*

1. The classical method of differential relaxation might be explained to the patient and applied. Under differential relaxation, the patient concentrates on a particular site of the body, deliberately relaxing and tensing certain muscles, discriminating between muscle contraction and relaxation. The typical procedure here is to have the patient begin distally, away from the body, with the fingers or the toes. Once the patient feels the tightness of contraction and the heaviness of relaxation at the beginning site, he or she moves "up" the limb (on to the feet or hands, and thence to the legs or arms), repeating at each site the tightness-heaviness discrimination. Once the torso is reached, the voice patient should include the chest, neck, "voice box," throat, and on through the mouth and parts of the face. With some patients, we start the distal analysis with the head, beginning with the scalp and then going to the forehead, eyes, facial muscles, lips, jaw, tongue, palate, throat, larynx, neck, and so on. Some practice in this progressive relaxation technique can produce remarkably relaxed states in very tense patients.

2. Various biofeedback devices can help the patient develop a feeling of relaxation. Such feedback as galvanic skin response, pulse rate, blood pressure, or muscle responsiveness through electromyographic tracings all seem to correlate well with patients' feelings of anxiety and tension. By performing a particular relaxed behavior, such as yawning, a patient can confirm his or her particular arousal state by the biofeedback data. Using such biofeedback devices, the patient can soon learn what it "feels" like to be relaxed or free of tension.

3. Wolpe (1987) combines relaxation with hierarchy analysis. The patient responds to particular tension-producing cues with a relaxed response, such as feeling a heaviness or warmth at a particular body site, and maintains

a relaxed response in the tension situation. The patient may instead develop a situational hierarchy specific to tension and voice by attempting to use a relaxed voice at increasingly tense levels of the hierarchy, as outlined in the adult voice program by Boone (1982).

4. Head rotation might be introduced as a technique for relaxing components of the vocal tract. The approach is used in this way: The patient sits in a backless chair, dropping the head forward to the chest; the patient then "flops" his or her head across to the right shoulder, then lifts it, then again flops it (the neck is here extended) along the back and across to the left shoulder; he or she then returns to the anterior head-down-on-chest position and repeats the cycle, rolling the head in a circular fashion. A few patients will not find head rotation relaxing, but most will feel the heaviness of the movement and experience definite relaxation in the neck. Once a patient in this latter group, reports neck relaxation, he or she should be asked to phonate an "ah" as the head is rolled. The relaxed phonation might be recorded and then analyzed in terms of how it sounds in comparison to the patient's other phonations.

5. Open-throat relaxation can also be used. Have the patient lower the head slightly toward the chest and make an easy, open, prolonged yawn, concentrating on what the yawn feels like in the throat. The yawn should yield conscious sensations of an open throat during the prolonged inhalation. If the patient reports that he or she can feel this open-throat sensation, ask him or her to prolong an "ah," capturing and maintaining the same feeling experienced during the yawn. Any relaxed phonations produced under these conditions should be recorded and used as target voice models for the patient. Encourage the patient to comment on and think about the relaxed throat sensations experienced during the yawn.

6. D. K. Wilson's *Voice Problems of Children* (1987) includes an excellent presentation on various relaxation procedures for use with children, developed by Wilson and other authors, which seem to have equal applicability to adults. Most of the procedures described can immediately increase relaxation and reduce tension associated with speaking.

7. Ask the patient to think of a setting he or she has experienced, or perhaps imagined as the ultimate in relaxation. Different patients use different kinds of imagery here. For example, one patient thought of lying in a hammock, but another person reacted to even lying in a hammock with a set of anxious responses. Settings typically considered relaxing are lying on a rug at night in front of a blazing fire, floating on a lake, fishing while lying in a rowboat, lying down in bed, and so on. The setting the patient thinks of should be studied and analyzed; eventually, the patient should try to capture the

relaxed feelings he or she imagines might result from, or may actually have been experienced in, such a setting. With some practice—and some tolerance for initial failure in recapturing the relaxed mood—the average patient can find a setting or two that he or she can recreate in his or her imagination to use in future tense situations.

C. *Typical case history showing utilization of approach.* M. Y., a 34-year-old missile engineer, developed transient periods of severe dysphonia when talking to certain people. At other times, particularly in his professional work, he experienced normal voice. Mirror laryngoscopy revealed a normal larynx. During the voice interview, the speech pathologist was impressed by the man's general nervousness and apparently poor self-concept. In exploring the area of interpersonal relationships, the patient confided that in the last year he had seen two psychiatrists periodically, but had experienced no relief from his tension. Further exploration of the settings in which his voice was most dysphonic revealed that his biggest problem was talking to store clerks, garage mechanics, and persons who did physical labor; some of his more relaxed experiences included giving speeches and giving work instructions to his colleagues. Subsequent voice therapy included progressive relaxation. Once relaxed behavior was achieved, the patient developed a hierarchy of situations, beginning with those in which he felt most relaxed (giving instructions to colleagues) and proceeding to those in which he experienced the most tension (talking with car mechanics). After some practice, the patient was able to recognize various cues that signaled increasing tension. Once such a cue occurred, he employed a relaxation response, which more often than not enabled him to maintain normal phonation in situations that had previously induced dysphonia. As this consciously induced response continued to be successful, the patient reported greater confidence in approaching the previously tense situations, knowing he would experience little or no voice difficulty. Voice therapy was terminated after eleven weeks, when the patient reported only occasional difficulty phonating in isolated situations and increased self-confidence in all situations.

D. *Evaluation of approach.* The popularity of many relaxation and stress-reduction programs today is probably due in part to their offering people with excessive tensions some relief from their agonies. Symptomatic voice therapy focuses on faulty voices and sometimes the tensions associated with (if not the cause of) the vocal problems. A growing number of voice clinicians feel that direct symptom modification, such as teaching relaxed responses to replace previously tense responses, breaks up the circular kind of response that often keeps maladaptive vocal behaviors "alive." In effect, we talk the same way today that we talked yesterday until we learn a better way to respond. Using the voice in a more relaxed manner with less competitive tension is a "better way to respond." Relaxation can take the effort and needless strain out of vocalization.

23. RESPIRATION TRAINING

A. *Kinds of problems for which approach is useful.* In the first part of the twentieth century, some of the earliest articles about voice therapy supported the view that most voice disorders were related to poor breathing patterns—and, indeed, singing teachers and dramatic coaches to this day include breathing exercises and breathing technique as part of their instruction. The modern-day voice clinician, whether a laryngologist or a speech pathologist, places far less emphasis on faulty respiration than his or her predecessors did. Nonetheless, some voice patients, described in earlier chapters, do profit from improving their control of respiration, especially their control of the expiratory phase of the breathing cycle. Although general improvement in total respiration, such as an improvement in vital capacity, has little effect on the voice, any marked departure in the inspiratory-expiratory cycle may produce noticeable voice alterations. As Greene (1980) wrote:

> I am quite unable to envisage how to teach control of expiration and adjustment of glottal resistance without recourse to, first, obtaining an adequate intake of air and, secondly, by training of expiration in production of short and long vowels of varying pitch, volume and resonance, thus reinforcing the patient's awareness of how he is producing voice (pp. 182–183).

B. *Procedural aspects of approach.*
   1. Most voice patients profit from a simple explanation of phonatory physiology—a description of the transglottal pressure and flow of outgoing air that sets the approximated vocal folds in vibration. If the patient demonstrates a problem in this area (and work on respiration should be avoided if no problem exists), describe the problem and what can be done about it.
   2. Demonstrate a slightly exaggerated breath, as used in sighing. The sigh is characterized by a slightly larger-than-usual inhalation followed by a prolonged open-mouth exhalation. Describe the type of breath used to produce the sigh as the "breath of well-being," the kind of easy breath one might take when comfortable or happy—the sigh of contentment.
   3. Demonstrate the quick inhalation and prolonged exhalation needed for a normal speaking task. Take a normal breath and count slowly from one to five on one exhalation. See if the patient can do this; if he or she can, extend the count by one number each time, at the rate of approximately one number per half-second. This activity can be continued until the patient is able to use his or

her "best" phonation during the number counts. Any sacrifice of vocal quality should be avoided, and the number count should never extend beyond the point at which good quality can be maintained.

4. Various duration tasks, such as prolonging vowels, provide excellent practice in expiratory control. Prolonging an /s/, /z/, /a/, /a/, /æ/, or /i/ for as long as possible provides an expiratory measure that can be used for comparison. Take a baseline measurement in the beginning, such as number of seconds a particular phonation can be maintained, and see whether this can be extended with practice. Avoid asking the patient to "take in a big breath"; rather, ask him or her to take in a normal breath of well-being, initiating a lightly phonated sigh on exhalation. See if the patient can extend this for five seconds. If so, progressively increase the extension, to eight, twelve, fifteen, and finally twenty seconds. The voice patient who can hold on to an extended phonation of a vowel for twenty seconds has certainly exhibited good breath control for purposes of voice. Such a patient would not have to work on breath control per se, but he or she might want to combine work on exhalation control with such approaches as hierarchy analysis (to see if he or she can maintain such good breath control under varying moments of stress).

5. Select from various voice and articulation books reading materials designed to help develop breath control. Give special attention to the patient's beginning phonation as soon after inhalation as possible, so as not to waste a lot of the outgoing air stream before phonating. Encourage the patient to practice quick inhalations between phrases and sentences, taking care not to take "a big breath."

6. With young children who need breathing work, begin with nonverbal exhalations. One way to work on breathing exhalation with little children is to use a pinwheel, which lends itself naturally to the game, "How long can you keep the pinwheel spinning?" With practice, a child will be able to extend the length of his or her exhalations (the length of time the pinwheel spins). Another method of enhancing exhalation control is to place a piece of tissue paper against a wall, begin blowing on it to keep it in place when the fingers are removed, and keep blowing on it to see how long it can be kept in place. Both the pinwheel and tissue-paper exercises lend themselves to timing measurements; these measurements should be made and plotted graphically for the child; when a certain target length of time is reached, the activity can be stopped.

7. When working with a singer, actor, or lecturer who needs some formal respiration training, you might take the following steps:

    a) Discuss the importance of good posture, because normal posture is one of the best facilitators of normal breathing. Any real departure from good posture, such as leaning forward with the head (kyphosis), may contribute to faulty breathing.

b) Demonstrate abdominal-diaphragmatic breathing. First, have the subject lie supine, with his or her hands on the abdomen, directly under the rib cage. In this position, distention of the abdomen upon inspiration will be observable. The downward excursion of the diaphragm, which increases the vertical dimension of the chest, cannot be viewed directly (because the diaphragm attachments are behind and inside the ribs); its effect can only be viewed by the outward displacement of the abdomen. On expiration, as the diaphragm ascends, the abdominal distention lessens. In this form of breathing, then, the patient should deliberately try to relax the abdominal muscles during inspiration and contract them during exhalation. If this can be done successfully in the supine position, the patient should try to duplicate the procedure while standing with the back flat against a wall. Continuing to clasp his or her hands on the abdomen will help the patient develop some initial awareness of the difference between abdominal relaxation-distention and abdominal contraction-flattening. As soon as the subject learns to breathe by this relaxation—contraction of the abdominal muscles—introduce some phonation activities to be done on expiration. The voice patient who has been speaking "from the level of his or her throat," without adequate breath support, will often "feel" the difference that a bigger breath makes only when phonation is added. The voice patient who needed respiration training in the first place must have respiration and phonation combined into practice activities as soon as possible.

8. For serious problems in respiration, which are often related to such illnesses as emphysema or bronchial asthma, as a clinician you should enlist the help of other specialists to help the patient improve respiratory efficiency. Physical therapists, inhalation therapists, and pulmonary medical specialists may have the expertise required to assist the patient. The voice clinician can often offer the patient ways of phrasing and using expiratory control to better match what the patient is trying to say and thus supplement the respiration therapy of these other specialists. For example, we have coordinated a breathing-for-speech program for quadriplegic patients, in which the speech pathologist and the physical therapist work closely with the patient to improve both general respiration and expiratory control for speech phrasing and better voice.

C. *Typical case history showing utilization of approach.* Libby was a 45-year-old special-education teacher who complained of vocal fatigue as a regular part of her teaching day. She felt that when she was not working, her voice was not a problem. Observation of Libby during her voice evaluation revealed that conversationally she often began to speak without an adequate inspiration. After five or six consecutive spoken words, her voice would become dysphonic and strained. Her voice problems seemed to occur when her air volumes were low and she was experiencing inadequate transglottal air flow. Subsequent voice therapy, designed to reduce the amount of work she was putting into vocalization, gave some priority to increasing her inspiratory volumes, reducing the number of words she attempted to speak on one breath, and teaching her to take "catch-up" breaths when she needed them. Loop tape recordings were used in therapy to monitor her breath support; she would read a ten-word sentence aloud and then immediately listen to a loop playback of the utterance, judging it for respiratory adequacy and lack of strain. After five weeks of twice-weekly voice therapy working on better respiratory control, Libby developed an easy phonatory style and a voice that served her well in her various life situations, including her teaching.

D.   *Evaluation of approach.* A number of voice patients may profit from some kind of respiration training. At the time of the initial voice evaluation, such patients may have done poorly on air-volume and pressure tests, or exhibited poor expiratory control. Vocal attempts, by such patients are often strained and involve too much effort; symptoms of vocal hyperfunction are common. A slight increase of inspiratory volume may produce an immediate effect of reducing vocal strain and improving overall vocal quality.

24.   TONGUE PROTRUSION

A.   *Kinds of problems for which approach is useful.* Many hyperfunctional voice problems are improved by the tongue-protrusion approach. This approach is especially helpful for patients with ventricular phonation (dysphonia plica ventricularis) or "tightness" in the voice, such as when the laryngeal aditus (laryngeal collar) is held in a somewhat closed position. When the tongue is held in a posterior position or the pharyngeal constrictor muscles are contracted to constrict the pharynx, the voice will sound strained or "tight." A patient with such symptoms is asked to produce /i/ with the tongue extended outside of the mouth (but not far enough to cause discomfort). This works to offset the squeezing of the pharynx. The tongue must not protrude so far outside of the mouth that it causes muscle strain in the area under the chin. The /i/ is produced in a high pitch either at the upper end of the patient's normal pitch range or at the lower end of the falsetto register. This approach can be used simultaneously with the glottal fry or the yawn-sigh.

B.   *Procedural aspects of approach.*

1.   Demonstrate to the patient what is expected by opening the mouth and protruding the tongue while producing a high-pitched, sustained /i/. Stress that the jaw is to "drop

open" comfortably and that the tongue is to be extended comfortably. Many patients are reluctant, at first, to stick out the tongue in the presence of a stranger, so demonstrate and reassure them that this is just what you want. You may touch the patient's chin with the index finger to encourage a little wider jaw opening and say, "Roll the tongue out a little farther."

2. With the mouth open and the tongue out, have the patient go up and down in pitch while sustaining the /i/ vowel. Constantly listen for improved vocal quality. When this is achieved, ask the patient to sustain the tone.

3. Have the patient chant /mimimimi/ at this level with the tongue still out of the mouth. Then instruct the patient to slowly "slip" the tongue back into the mouth while continuing to produce the /mimimimi/.

4. At this point, the pitch is usually still high. Demonstrate a sustained /i/ that is lowered by three steps from the pitch that the patient was producing. This often produces a good quality on the first step or the first two steps, but a return to the poor voice may occur on the third step. Repeat the procedure, but only go down two steps. Sustain the second step. Repeat until the tone is established. You may need to return to the original open mouth and tongue protrusion if the target tone is lost.

5. When the new tone is established, gradually add words to the sustained /i/—for example, "be, pea, me," "see the peach," and "easy does it."

C. *Typical case history showing utilization of approach.* Tammy, a 15-year-old girl, was referred with ventricular phonation of more than eighteen months duration. Her voice, which was consistently hoarse, rough, and low in pitch, was effortful to produce and made her sound like an older male speaker. Tammy had undergone a prolonged bout of flu prior to the onset of the ventricular voice, and she frequently coughed and cleared her throat violently. Strong glottal valving could be heard at times during connected speech. After seven sessions of individual voice therapy using the tongue-protrusion approach just described, Tammy's voice was normal in all situations at home, in school, and at work for the first time in more than eighteen months.

D. *Evaluation of the approach.* This approach appears to work because the tongue, when protruded, pulls its root out of the pharynx and opens the laryngeal aditus. Also, the high pitch is made with a light, breathy approximation of only the true vocal cords. The production of voice with the tongue outside of the mouth is sufficiently novel so as not to trigger the typical pattern of phonation that had become habituated.

25. YAWN-SIGH

A. *Kinds of problems for which approach is useful.* The inspiratory yawn is characterized by maximum dilation of the airway, produced by relaxation of the pharyngeal constrictors and contraction of several suprahyoid muscles. The expiratory sigh that follows the yawn is similarly characterized by extreme airway dilation, as shown in Figure 5–4. Under the sigh conditions, the pharynx appears maximally dilated, and the mucosal surface is somewhat dimpled and irregular (Pershall and Boone, 1986). For problems of vocal hyperfunction (functional dysphonia, nodules, polyps, contact ulcers), the yawn-sigh helps the patient appreciate what an "easy" phonation is, both in terms of feeling its production and in hearing the relaxed sound it produces. The yawn-sigh approach is often combined with other facilitating approaches in therapy. Sometimes the approach is used as a symptomatic relaxed behavior whenever a patient is beginning to experience excessive vocal tract tensions.

B. *Procedural aspects of approach.*

    1. With children explain this approach using the pictures and narrative from the voice program for children in

FIGURE 5-4.   A CT-scan depicting the dilated pharynx of a normal subject producing a prolonged /i/ vowel on an expiratory sigh. This CT-scan was taken near the apex of the arytenoids, showing the horizontal cross-section of the neck and mandible. Vertebral bone is shown in white; the open airway (with a slice of epiglottis across it) is represented in black (absence of tissue).

Boone (1980a). Showing a child the appropriate pictures, we read:

> This girl usually has a tight mouth. She uses too much effort when she speaks. Her voice does not sound good. (Demonstrate) This girl is opening her mouth wide and yawning. She is very relaxed. When she sighs at the end of the yawn, it will be her best voice (p. 127).

2. With teen-agers and adults explain generally the physiology of a yawn—that is, that a yawn represents a prolonged inspiration with maximum widening of the supraglottal airways (characterized by a wide, stretching, opening of the mouth). You may show the photograph in Figure 5–4 and contrast it with other CT-scans of the pharynx taken while subjects were doing other vocal tasks, as displayed by Pershall and Boone (1986). Then demonstrate a yawn and talk about what the yawn feels like.

3. After the patient has yawned, following your example, ask the patient to yawn again and then to exhale gently with a light phonation. In doing this, many patients are able to feel an easy phonation, often for the first time.

4. Once the yawn-phonation is easily achieved, instruct the patient to say words beginning with /h/ or with open-mouthed vowels, one word per yawn in the beginning, and eventually four or five words on one exhalation.

5. Demonstrate for the patient the sigh phase of the exercise—that is, the prolonged, easy, open-mouthed exhalation after the yawn. Then, omitting the yawn entirely, demonstrate a quick, normal, open-mouthed inhalation followed by the prolonged open-mouthed sigh.

6. As soon as the patient can produce a relaxed sigh, have him or her say the word "hah" after beginning the sigh. Follow this with a series of words beginning with the glottal /h/. Additional words for practice after the sigh should begin with middle and low vowels. Take care to blend in, toward the middle of the sigh, an easy, relaxed, relatively soft phonation. This blending of the phonation into the sigh is often difficult for the patient initially, but it is the most vital part of the approach for the elimination of hard glottal contacts.

7. Finally, once the yawn-sigh approach is well developed, have the patient think of the relaxed oral feeling it provides. Eventually, he or she will be able to maintain a relaxed phonation simply by imagining the approach.

C. *Typical case history showing utilization of approach.* Jerry, a 47-year-old manufacturer's representative, had a two-year history of vocal fatigue. He often lost his voice toward the end of the work day. After a two-week period of increasing dysphonia and slight pain on the left side of the neck, a consulting laryngologist found that Jerry had "slight redness and edema on both vocal processes." The subsequent voice evaluation also found that he spoke with pronounced hard glottal attack in an attempt to "force out his voice over his dysphonia." Using the yawn-sigh approach, Jerry was able to demonstrate a clear phonation with relatively good resonance. His yawn-sigh phonations were recorded on loop tape and fed back to him as the voice model he should imitate. Because Jerry reported some stress in certain work situations, the hierarchy analysis approach was used to isolate those situations in which he felt relaxed and those in which he experienced tension. Thereafter, whenever he was aware of tense situational cues, he employed the yawn-sigh method to maintain relaxed phonation. Combining yawn-sigh with hiearchy analysis proved to be an excellent symptomatic approach for this patient, because his voice cleared markedly, and no recurrence of the periodic aphonia was evident. Twice-weekly therapy was terminated after twenty-two weeks, and the patient demonstrated a normal voice and a normal laryngeal mechanism.

D. *Evaluation of approach.* The yawn-sigh is a powerful voice therapy technique for patients with vocal hyperfunction. During the yawn-sigh, the pharynx is dilated and relaxed. When the patient is asked to sigh an /i/ or an /a/, the voice comes out with little effort and sounds relaxed. For some patients with continued vocal hyperfunction, the voice produced on the sigh will feel relaxed, in dramatic contrast to the patient's normally tense voice.

SUMMARY

Successful voice therapy requires that the clinician identify the patient's aversive vocal behaviors and subsequently reduce the occurrence of such abuses-misuses. Voice therapy for most voice problems requires continuous assessment of what the patient is able to do vocally. By using various therapy approaches as diagnostic probes, the clinician searches for the best voice the patient is able to produce. Twenty-five facilitating approaches have been presented; each has detailed specific procedures of application and an illustrative case history showing its particular effects.

6
VOICE THERAPY FOR SPECIAL PROBLEMS

*In Chapter 5, we reviewed twenty-five facilitating approaches that
can be broadly used in voice therapy with various disorders.
Many of these techniques are helpful for voice problems related to
vocal hyperfunction. We now consider therapy approaches for
different voice problems—specifically, functional aphonia,
paralytic aphonia and dysphonia, ventricular phonation, spastic
dysphonia, abductor spasms, dysarthria, severe hard-of-hearing
(deaf), the aging voice, puberphonia, diplophonia, and pitch
breaks. We conclude this chapter with a vocal hygiene program
that is beneficial not only to voice patients but to professional
users of voice as well.*

FUNCTIONAL APHONIA

The diagnosis of functional aphonia is made when a patient is examined by
endoscopy or laryngoscopy while asked to produce and prolong an "eeh"
(/i/). Instead of the folds adducting into the midline position when the patient phonates, they usually abduct further apart. The patients' laryngeal
muscle function is normal, unlike that of paralytic aphonics, whose folds
(one or both) are paralyzed in a fixed position. In aphonia, patients lose
their voice completely and speak in a whisper. Despite the inability to use
voice, most patients with functional aphonia maintain excellent communicative pragmatics—for example, looking at the other person, using appropriate social affect and gestures, and, in general, seeking out communication rather than retreating from it.

   Our use of the term *functional aphonia* to describe vocal mutism is at
variance with two other authors (Aronson, 1985; Case, 1984), who use the
term *conversion aphonia* to highlight the psychological origins of lack of voice
in patients with normal larynges. Aronson distinguishes between muteness
(no articulatory movements, no whisper) and aphonia (an articulated,
whispered air stream), although he does not offer a distinct and differential
treatment regimen for each voiceless condition. Case views conversion
aphonia as "a somatoform" disorder whose symptoms have no organic or
physiologic basis, so that the patient often presents evidence of a "strong
presumption to psychological disturbance or conflict" (1984, p. 205). De-

spite the psychiatric focus given by the label "conversion aphonia," both Aronson and Case describe good success in treating the disorder symptomatically.

We recommend using the term *functional aphonia*, which implies that there is no physical cause for the voicelessness, and, more often than not, that the patient is ready to "release" the symptom and experience an immediate return of normal voice. In fact, functional aphonic patients as a group present excellent prognoses. A typical functional aphonic patient experiences complete return of voice within one to three therapy sessions. As stated in Chapter 3, functional aphonic patients are easily conditioned to continue to speak without voice. Whatever the original cause, the behavior is maintained by the reactions of the people around the patient. Such patients soon develop a *no voice* set toward speaking, and they establish habitual responses; they speak this way today because they spoke this way yesterday. Most patients with functional aphonia express a strong desire to regain their normal voice. (A few patients are served well by their aphonia, and they resist all therapeutic attempts at voice restoration.) The bias of the writers, developed from following aphonic patients over time, is that symptomatic voice therapy is usually effective in restoring normal voices in these patients. Once phonation is reestablished, it remains, and the patient does not develop substitute symptoms to take the place of the previous aphonia.

Successful voice therapy for functional aphonia must begin with the clinician's explaining and discussing the problem with the patient. In the physiological description of the aphonia, the clinician must avoid implying that the patient could phonate normally if he or she wanted. Rather, a description of what the patient is doing ("keeping the vocal cords apart") will make it clear that the clinician knows what the problem is. Following the physiological description, the clinician should say something like, "We will do things in therapy that will bring the cords together again to produce normal voice." The clinician should not (at the first session, at least) ask or show interest in *why* the patient is not phonating. After the explanation and discussion of the problem, the clinician should evaluate whatever nonverbal phonations the patient may have in his or her coughing, grunting, laughing, and crying repertoire, and then describe them to the patient as normal phonatory activities "in which the vocal cords are getting together well to produce these sounds." These nonverbal phonations should then gradually be shaped into use for speech, at first confining any speech attempts to nonsense syllables, and then moving on to single words, but with no early attempts at phonating during real communication. Attempts at phonating in conversational situations (that is, in the real world of talking) should be deferred until good, consistent phonation has been reestablished under laboratory, practice conditions.

Steps to be followed in a symptomatic voice therapy program for functional aphonia might include:

1. *Explanation of problem.* Point out to the patient that even though the vocal folds are normal, the problem appears to be an inability to "get them started producing voice." Focus the explanation *on* the vocal folds and *not on* the patient. Perhaps show a brief videotape depicting normal phonation.

2. *Coughing.* Ask the patient to cough. By definition, patients with functional aphonia are able to use the laryngeal mechanism for coughing. Take care to ask the patient to cough, not to ask, "Are you able to cough?" Most aphonic patients can cough. If the patient coughs, then ask him or her to prolong the cough with an extended vowel. If this phonatory prolongation can be done, then ask the patient to make a series of cough-initiated phonations, using the vowel /i/. If the patient cannot immediately extend the phonation, go to step 3 after the cough.

3. *Inhalation phonation.* This facilitating approach (see Chapter 5) uses true vocal fold phonation. The high-pitched phonation is always produced by true folds. If a patient can match the high-pitched inhalation with the same sound on expiration, ask him or her to prolong the phonation, as in step 2. Once the expiratory high-pitched phonation is established, introduce monosyllabic words beginning with vowels and /h/ for voice practice.

4. *Masking.* This approach is designed to reestablish phonation in patients with functional aphonia. Ask the patient to read a passage aloud in his or her whispered aphonic voice while wearing headphones attached to some kind of noise generator (such as white noise on an audiometer). As the patient reads, introduce loud masking at selected intervals. The patient will often reflexively use voice under the masking conditions. Then play back a recording of the patient's reading attempts, which can often reveal true phonation for the patient. (See procedural details of the masking approach in Chapter 5.)

5. Patients with aphonia should not be pushed too fast. Once normal voice is achieved, often by following one or more of the preceding steps, practice should stay at a single-word (using word lists) level. Making such statements as "Your vocal folds are coming together now" is helpful, because they put the "blame" on the folds rather than the patient (Boone, 1966b).

6. Once voice is established by using single words beginning with vowels or /h/, single word lists using any consonants or vowels can be used. Then progress to polysyllabic words, phrases, and sentences, but defer interactive conversation with the patient until voicing appears consistently.

In functional aphonia, voice can often be reestablished in one therapy session, perhaps followed by several sessions that permit more time for supervised voice practice and counseling. In the last session Case (1984) recommends that the clinician "continue the conversation mode until convinced of vocal stability, then make an appointment for a checkup in a few days" (p. 213). Once voice is reestablished after aphonia, patients rarely experience future recurrences of the same symptom.

If the voice clinician has any doubt about the patient's general emotional stability, as indicated perhaps by the patient's continued inability to produce some phonation, he or she should refer the patient for psychological or psychiatric consultation. Sometimes the aphonic patient profits most from symptomatic voice therapy concurrent with psychotherapy. If psychotherapy is needed, however, the typical case involves a fairly rapid recovery of voice with relatively brief voice therapy and a much longer period of psychotherapy.

PARALYTIC APHONIA AND DYSPHONIA

Most paralyses of the vocal folds happen suddenly because most vocal fold paralyses, particularly unilateral paralysis, are related to trauma or cutting of the recurrent laryngeal nerve. In such unilateral paralysis, the paralyzed fold is fixed in the abducted, paramedian position, unable to adduct to the glottal midline. Because the patient cannot bring the vocal folds together for normal voicing, he or she speaks in an aphonic or dysphonic voice. Looking at the etiology of various forms of vocal fold paralyses, Tucker (1980) found that over 350 of 390 patients studied had unilateral paralysis related to recurrent nerve cut or trauma. Other causes of vocal fold paralysis include bilateral neck trauma and unilateral or bilateral lesions of the vagus nerve nuclei in the brainstem. In his description of neurologic voice disorders in children and adults, Aronson (1985) includes vocal fold paralyses among the possible components of dysarthria, and he gives detailed emphasis to a number of etiologies that may produce changes of voice. Case (1984) elaborates on other forms of voice symptoms from vagus nerve lesions, including some management techniques for producing voice with unilateral adductor paralysis (by far the most common form of vocal fold paralysis).

Unilateral Adductor Paralysis

In this condition, which is usually caused by unilateral involvement of the recurrent laryngeal nerve, the paralyzed fold is fixed in the open paramedian position. Usually aphonia or pronounced dysphonia characterized by severe breathiness results; their severity depends on the degree of possible glottal closure. Because many such unilateral paralyses spontaneously recover within the first six months, conservative intervention measures are used. The surgeon, for example, would hold off doing any kind of surgical reconstruction until it was evident that the paralyzed side of the larynx would not recover spontaneously. Likewise, the speech pathologist would offer the aphonic or dysphonic patient with unilateral paralysis voice therapy that might help establish a temporary voice (until possible nerve regeneration takes place).

During the interim period from onset to possible nerve regeneration, some techniques are useful for establishing some voice, particularly for aphonic patients. First of all, in most cases, the superior laryngeal nerve is still functional. The superior laryngeal nerve innervates the cricothyroid muscles, which help in vocal fold adduction and produce variation of pitch. If the patient can speak in a slightly higher voice pitch, he or she often experiences a firmer voice with less breathiness. Such a patient can then use the pushing approach (see Chapter 5). In unilateral adductor paralysis, the involved cord, despite its paralysis and lack of movement to the midline, still vibrates somewhat due to the force of the passing air stream. Under conditions of pushing, the air-flow rate is accelerated and thus produces a greater vibration of the involved cord; the result is a better-sounding voice.

Other helpful facilitating approaches (described in Chapter 5) include digital manipulation, half-swallow, boom, and head positioning. Patients are also encouraged to speak with increased glottal attack, coupling the pushing approach with deliberate attempts at sudden voicing onsets. Some attention is also given to increasing the efficiency of respiration by encouraging the patient to speak on a larger percentage of air volume, perhaps by saying few words per expiration and by renewing inspirations more often. Remember that these voice therapy techniques are designed to regain temporarily the best voice possible under conditions of a unilateral adductor paralysis. The continued hope is that nerve regeneration and restoration of normal vocal fold function will follow, at which time these techniques of increasing vocal effort for substitute normal voice can be abandoned.

Another method of providing voice for the aphonic patient with unilateral paralysis is to use the artificial electronic larynx (described in some detail in Chapter 8). The artificial larynx provides a substitute voice that may enable the patient to be better heard and understood during the months he or she is waiting for nerve regeneration and the return of normal voice. Our clinical experience has been, however, that patients with sudden onset of aphonia as the result of vocal fold paralysis are resistant to using the artificial larynx. Usually, such patients are quite convinced that the "power" will go on again, and they prefer not to bother with the temporary embarrassment and inconvenience of using an artificial larynx. More often than not, patients are correct that function will return, although the time of regeneration may be anywhere from one to six months after the recurrent nerve was cut or damaged.

If, after nine months, which is about three months after spontaneous recovery of laryngeal function could be expected, no such recovery is evident, several surgical options are open to the patient. The most common surgical approach is injecting Teflon mixed with glycerine into the paralyzed fold (Dedo and Dedo, 1980; Woodson and Miller, 1981). The use of Teflon increases the girth of the paralyzed fold, which usually permits some contact between the normal and paralyzed fold for at least one-third of the anterior glottis (Weber, Neumayer, Alford, and Weber, 1984). Reich and Lerman (1978) found that after Teflon injection a patient with unilateral adductor paralysis experienced a general reduction of perceived hoarseness and an enhancement of perceived pleasantness of phonation.

Several innovative surgical approaches have also had positive impact on voice. Isshiki, Tanade, and Sawade (1978) wrote that Teflon often does not guarantee good results, particularly for patients with a wide glottal opening; they, therefore, surgically pull the muscular processes of the arytenoids with sutures, simulating the action of the lateral cricoarytenoids, rotating the arytenoids so that the paralyzed fold is closer to a midline position. Tucker (1977) reported success in six out of nine patients with unilateral adductor paralysis after taking the nerve-muscle pedicle from the omohyoid muscle on one side and inserting it into the paralyzed thyroarytenoid. Note that no surgical approach should be attempted for at least nine months after onset, with hope in the interim for some nerve regeneration. Many patients experience a return of nerve function, with a restoration of vocal fold function because of nerve regeneration.

It is difficult to assess the effects of various treatments for unilateral vocal fold paralysis, as reported by McFarlane, Holt, and Lavorato (1985), who studied vocal quality after Teflon injection for nine patients, surgical reinnervation for nine patients, and voice therapy for nine patients. Although reduction of breathiness was greater for the surgical reinnervation group, all patients showed demonstrable vocal improvement after some form of surgical or voice therapy intervention. However, the Teflon group was rated the poorest on all vocal parameters. In addition, if a surgical approach is eventually required to produce better voice, voice therapy directed at improving respiratory control of vocal intensity is usually required after surgery.

Bilateral Adductor Paralysis

With both cords fixed in an open, abducted position, the patient will be aphonic. Bilateral adductor paralysis is more often than not the result of central brainstem impairment rather than bilateral destruction of the recurrent laryngeal nerves. The patient's primary problem—more important than the aphonia—is the inability to close the airway. The aphonia resulting from bilateral cord paralysis is frequently accompanied by other symptoms of cerebral dysfunction, such as weakness or paralysis of the tongue, pharynx, or palate. Medical therapy might well include a tracheostomy to improve the efficiency of the airway as a temporary measure, because many cases of bilateral adductor paralysis eventually improve spontaneously.

A permanent bilateral adductor paralysis is sometimes treated surgically. The surgical approach may include rotation of the arytenoids to a fixed, more adducted position, taking care to still preserve the opening of the airway. The surgical reinnervation therapy of Crumley and Izdebski (1986) has been used with some success with patients with bilateral adductor paralysis. Unless some return of vocal fold function is evident, voice therapy for the patient with bilateral adductor paralysis is not too helpful. Rather than receive voice therapy, such patients are often instructed on using the artificial larynx or introduced to some form of electronic speech output system, such as the Vocaid (1986) or Phonic Ear Vois (1987).

Abductor Paralyses

Both unilateral and bilateral abductor paralyses are relatively rare events among patients with vocal fold paralyses (Tucker, 1980). In unilateral abductor paralysis the paralyzed fold remains fixed in the midline position. Phonation is rarely affected because the two folds approximate one another quite well. Quiet, at-rest breathing is usually normal. Only when the patient becomes physically active is he or she likely to experience some shortness of breath because of the narrowing of the airway. Half of the airway is occluded by the fixed midline cord, so that marked abduction of the normal cord is required to achieve an adequate glottal opening for normal breathing. The primary concern of the laryngologist is that the airway be open sufficiently to permit normal breathing; rarely is surgery necessary in cases of unilateral abductor paralysis.

Often, a patient with unilateral abductor paralysis will initially experience a midline paralysis (abductor) that begins to lessen over time, such that the paralyzed fold eventually becomes fixed in the open paramedian position. The injured or severed recurrent laryngeal nerve may also regenerate, returning function to the involved fold. Some patients experience voice symptoms with unilateral abductor paralysis, temporarily or permanently. For example, singers, actors, or professional users of voice may suffer from loss of pitch range, double voice (diplophonia), and problems in pitch register. Effective voice therapy for these patients would be probing with various facilitating approaches to find the one that works best. We have often found ear training, establishing a new pitch, relaxation, and respiration training to be the most effective approaches for developing the best voice possible with a unilateral abductor paralysis (see Chapter 5).

Bilateral paralysis of both vocal folds in the midline position requires immediate medical intervention to help the patient breathe. Emergency medical management of bilateral abductor paralysis includes a tracheostomy. If the symptoms of closure persist for more than a week or so, a medical decision must be made as to whether to construct surgically a new airway within the larynx. Bull and Cook (1976) have described some success for these patients with immediate surgery followed by some voice therapy. "Success" in the surgical treatment of bilateral abductor paralysis means that the patient is able to breathe once again through the larynx, but not necessarily that he or she regains a normal voice; the dysphonia is a small price to pay for the ability to breathe adequately again. However, voice therapy is often useful for those patients who, after surgery, experience varying degrees of dysphonia due to the surgically opened glottis.

Because having an open airway is the primary need of these patients, voice therapy plays a secondary role. However, after some kind of surgical reconstruction is completed, a patient might well profit from ear training, pushing, respiration training, and the trial-and-error use of other facilitating approaches that may help produce a better-sounding voice (see Chapter 5).

VENTRICULAR PHONATION

Ventricular phonation, sometimes called *dysphonia plicae ventricularis*, occurs in its pure form when a patient uses the ventricular or false folds for phonation. Such substitute phonation is characterized by a low-pitched voice related to the relative thickness of the ventricular folds as compared to the true folds. Because of this relatively large tissue mass, there is little chance for subtle changes in mass and thickness (certainly as compared to the normal vocal folds); the result is a monotonous pitch level with minimal frequency variation. A patient who, on laryngoscopy, appears to have a structurally normal larynx and yet speaks with an inappropriately low-pitched, monotonous voice might well be using ventricular phonation.

Nasoendoscopy of patients with harsh functional dsyphonia often shows the ventricular folds coming together as part of a total laryngeal shutdown; the overall laryngeal aditus is closed by spincteric closure of the aryepiglottic folds, which pull the cuneiform prominences seemingly together (Pershall and Boone, 1986). As this total laryngeal closure begins, first the true folds adduct and then the false folds come together. The aryepiglottic folds then cover over the open larynx and neither true nor false folds are visible. Ventricular phonation may be part of such a strained phonation, although it is difficult to single out a particular closure site.

The clinical management of such total-laryngeal closure is facilitated by using the yawn-sigh approach (described in Chapter 5). Under conditions of the sigh, using a prolonged /i/ vowel, supraglottal structures open up, revealing on endoscopy the approximation of the true folds. From the sigh-produced /i/, the clinician can extend the number of sounds and words that the patient can say with the open larynx. Glottal fry and tongue protrusion, also described in Chapter 5, are also helpful techniques for eliminating ventricular phonation.

An occasional patient will develop a ventricular voice as a substitute voice, often because of extensive disease or involvement of the true folds. Some patients have such hypertrophied ventricular folds, often as part of a disease process, that their ventricular folds approximate during attempts at normal phonation and produce either a ventricular or a diplophonic voice.

Usually, a patient with a ventricular voice wants to eliminate the low-pitched, monotonous (often lacking sufficient intensity) voice. In the absence of true cord pathology, voice therapy is often effective in "finding" true cord phonation, which usually provides the patient with a much more satisfactory voice than the false folds can.

Successful therapy for ventricular phonation, as for most other voice disorders, should begin with a frank explanation to the patient of what the problem is. Frontal tomogram X-rays are helpful to demonstrate normal abduction-adduction of both true and false vocal folds. Even with this explanation, however, the patient may not be able to produce true cord phonation volitionally. If that is the case, the best therapy approach is to have the patient practice making prolonged inhalations with an open mouth, followed by sustained exhalations, with no attempt at phonation (see inhalation phonation in Chapter 5). This is followed by having the patient make an effort to phonate on inhalation. With some practice, most patients can produce some inhalation phonation. Inhalation phonation is usually true cord phonation, according to the radiographic observations of Lehmann (1965), who found true fold adduction and marked retraction of the ventricular bands on inhalation phonation. After inhalation phonation is achieved by the patient, efforts can be made to produce a matching exhalation phonation, usually a high-pitched squeaky sound. This is the difficult part of the therapy. Patients will be able to make the inhalation voice with relative ease, but they will have a great deal of difficulty in producing the matched exhalation. This seems to be easier, however, if the patient attempts inhalation-phonation-exhalation-phonation on the same breath cycle. Perseverance in this task is usually the key to eliminating the ventricular dysphonia; several of our therapy failures with ventricular dysphonia seem to have been related to our not sticking with the matched inhalation-exhalation phonations long enough.

The frontal X-ray tomogram is the only sure way to confirm true cord phonation (or ventricular voice, for that matter). However, once the patient is able to produce an exhaled phonation, he or she should be asked to produce varying pitches. True cord phonation has the capability of pitch variation; false cord phonation usually does not. Once true cord phonation is established, the patient must abandon the inhalation-exhalation squeak and blend it down to a more acceptable pitch level.

Occasionally, a patient with laryngeal disease—for example, extensive true cord involvement with papilloma, or unilateral adductor paralysis—needs to develop a vicarious phonatory mechanism. One such mechanism would be the ventricular folds adducting for ventricular production. It is difficult to *teach* someone to use ventricular voice. Rather, for patients who want to develop ventricular phonation, all we can usually do is encourage them to produce various voices, if they can. If true cord adduction is not possible, the phonations produced after such urging will usually be ventricular in origin. If a better ventricular voice can be produced, it will usually be possible to improve it by working on optimal control of exhalation, keeping the mandible open and relaxed, and so on. Increasing both loudness and pitch variability are the usual therapy goals in improving the sound of ventricular voice, but the clinician must realize that both these goals with ventricular voice can be only minimally achieved.

SPASTIC DYSPHONIA

In Chapter 3, we discussed spastic dysphonia as perhaps the most extreme example of vocal hyperfunction. The patient's voice sounds strangled tight, and he or she usually expends much physical effort trying to push the outgoing airstream through the tightly closed larynx. Davis et al. (1987), in studying twenty-four spastic dysphonics of the adductor type in Sydney, Australia, found on endoscopic examination that the tight voice was produced by firm approximation of the true folds that was often accompanied by false fold and aryepiglottic closure, which, in effect, produced a total laryngeal shutdown. Some patients with spastic dysphonia also exhibit additional symptoms of neurological origin, such as tremor, whereas other patients show no other physical symptoms. Aminoff, Dedo, and Izdebski (1978) had twelve patients with spastic dysphonia examined by psychiatrists, neurologists, and otolaryngologists (the Davis study involved similar examinations and findings) and found no evidence of psychiatric or laryngological involvement sufficient enough to cause the severe voice symptoms. The causes of spastic dysphonia of the adductor type may be as varied as the treatments used for the disorder.

Before the procedure reported by Dedo (which we describe shortly), our voice therapy attempts searched with the patients for those situations in which they might enjoy normal voice. Like stutterers reporting on their fluency, patients with spastic dysphonia may demonstrate normal voice when talking to a pet animal, or to a baby, or aloud to themselves. When listeners are introduced, particularly those the patients think are evaluative, their voices tighten and phonation will be difficult.

With some self-study and inquiry from the clinician, such patients can develop a hierarchy of situations, ranging from those in which the voice is normal to those few in which they can barely phonate. The patient must analyze normal vocal behavior and the situations that surround it. The clinician can use the therapy periods to help the patient recreate those environments in which relaxed phonation is best achieved. For example, if the patient has a normal voice when talking to a dog, efforts must be made in therapy to create a situation in which a dog seems actually to be there. This recreating of optimum situations requires much practice if the patient is going to be able to employ normal phonation (as if he or she were actually talking to a dog). If the hierarchy analysis, as discussed in Chapter 5, is going to be effective, a great deal of time must be spent attempting to capture the environmental factors that permit the patient to phonate normally. Without a normal, relaxed phonation to produce at will, a patient will not have an optimum response to use at various levels of the hierarchy.

Although most speech pathologists report generally poor results with therapy for spastic dysphonia, Cooper (1977) reports "direct vocal rehabilitation" as being helpful. His rehabilitation includes working on pitch, quality, breath support, volume rate, and "vocal psychotherapy." Our symptomatic therapy, employing such facilitating approaches as chanting, chewing, glottal fry, place the voice, and yawn-sigh, coupled with hierarchy analysis, to help the patient produce easy phonations, has been less successful. Our attempts for generalization using desensitization approaches have only had sporadic results. One patient was observed to say, "I just cannot understand why I can talk to you and my husband with normal voice, but I cannot talk to the next-door neighbor." The inconsistencies of such patients' voices, influenced by the setting, the listener, the focus of the response, are similar in many ways to what the speech pathologist experiences in working with stutterers. Normal phonation, like normal fluency, may be easier to demonstrate in the clinical laboratory than in the outside, *real* world of talking.

If trial symptomatic voice therapy is unsuccessful for the patient with spastic dysphonia, referral may be made to the laryngologist for consideration of unilateral recurrent laryngeal nerve (RLN) resection. A thorough diagnostic evaluation by both the surgeon and the speech pathologist is followed by injection of Xylocaine into the RLN, which produces a temporary unilateral adductor paralysis. The patient's air flow, relative ease of phonation, and change of voice quality are assessed. If there is marked improvement in air flow (greater flow rates with less glottal resistance) and in both ease and quality of phonation, the decision may be made to cut the RLN permanently. Postoperatively then, the patient usually has an easily produced but breathy voice, similar in sound to the patient with unilateral adductor paralysis. Voice therapy focusing on a slight elevation of pitch, some ear training, increasing glottal attack, and pushing have all been effective in developing a better-sounding voice.

The long-term results of RLN resection have been mixed. Wilson, Oldring, and Mueller (1980) reported a woman who had received a RLN cut thirteen months previously who then experienced a regeneration of the severed RLN and a return of spastic dysphonia; a second RLN resection again produced immediate relief from her phonatory struggle. Over three years Aronson and DeSanto (1983) followed thirty-three patients with spastic dysphonia who had each received RLN cut. Although 100 percent experienced improved voice and ease of air flow immediately after surgery, three years later twenty-one of them, or 64 percent, had failed to maintain their gains and were considered failures. Much different results were reported by Dedo and Izdebski (1983a) on over 306 patients who had received RLN cut for spastic dysphonia; they reported that 92 percent of the patients maintained voice improvement and required less effort to phonate. Those few patients who did not maintain "easier" voices after RLN cut were treated with laser surgery designed to thin the vocal folds, which produced greater lateralization of the folds and an immediate reduction in vocal tightness (Dedo and Izdebski, 1983b).

Some of the confusion in outcome results from either voice therapy or surgical attempts (or both) in the treatment of spastic dysphonia may be related to considering the cause of the strangled voice only at the true vocal fold level. Obviously, tight vocal fold adduction is a primary cause of the problem. However, endoscopy of such patients quickly reveals much supraglottal and pharyngeal participation in the airway shutdown. Voice therapy directed at opening the total laryngeal-pharyngeal airway, such as described previously in treating ventricular phonation using the yawn-sigh approach, seems to produce good voice change at the syllable or single-word level. Beyond the single word, it is difficult for a patient with adductor spastic dysphonia to develop easy, relaxed phonation in true interactive conversation. A voice therapy approach for abductor spasms or phonation breaks is usually much more successful.

ABDUCTOR SPASMS

Abductor spasms of the vocal folds produce temporary phonation breaks. A patient may be speaking with a normal voice (or a dysphonic one) when the vocal folds suddenly separate, and produce a fleeting aphonia. In previous editions of this text, the term *phonation breaks* has aptly labeled these annoying and continuing aphonic breaks. Shipp, Mueller, and Zwitman (1980) introduced the term *intermittent abductory dysphonia* to label these sudden phonatory breaks, which seems to indicate that the patient experiences a sudden change of voice, rather than a sudden loss of voice. Aronson (1985) continues to use the term *abductor spastic dysphonia* to describe these "brief moments of breathy or whispered (unphonated) segments" (p. 187). Davis et al. (1987) questioned the wisdom of including a patient labeled as having "abductor spastic dysphonia" in their study of twenty-five patients with spastic dysphonia, because air flow, otolaryngologic, and neurologic data demonstrated clear differences between "adductory" and "abductory" spastic dysphonia.

Patients and physicians, in fact, often confuse the two terms, adductor and abductor, in describing spastic dysphonia, even though the voice symptoms of the two voice disorders are quite different. Aronson (1985) describes a patient with phonation breaks who demonstrated such confusion. Case (1984) also describes abductor spastic dysphonia, like Aronson's but he does not offer any suggestions for remediation of the problem. For clinical purposes, the term "phonation breaks" seems to describe the behavior of fleeting aphonia, but it does not have the neurological implications that the term "abductor spastic dysphonia" seems to have.

The majority of abductor spasms are related to continuous vocal hyperfunction. If hyperfunctional behaviors can be identified and reduced, the phonation breaks are usually minimized. For example, a local hard-rock disc jockey suffered from phonation breaks when he was attempting to give the news "straight" for five minutes on the hour. It was soon discovered that his broadcasting style away from the news was extremely "hyper" and false and thus produced obvious strain on his vocal mechanism. Voice therapy was directed toward producing a disc-jockey style that was less aversive. The happy result was that he was able to read the news copy free of phonation breaks. Such intermittent losses of voice during voicing are usually the result of prolonged vocal hyperfunction. Once the hyperfunction can be reduced, the phonation breaks usually disappear.

DYSARTHRIA

Problems in respiration, pitch control, vocal quality, and resonance are common symptoms in dysarthria. Dysarthria is observed in patients with various kinds of central nervous system (CNS) and peripheral nervous system (PNS) disorders. The degree and type of dysarthric symptoms depend on where the particular nervous system disease or disorder is located. The most common cause of dysarthria comes from cerebral vascular accidents (CVAs), such as a patient's experiencing a stroke (thrombosis, embolus, or hemorrhage) that results in weakness or paralysis of muscles essential for normal speech. Other causes of dysarthria include trauma to the nervous system, tumors, and degenerative diseases, like muscular dystrophy (MD) or amyotrophic lateral sclerosis (ALS). Aronson (1980) classified types of dysarthria as follows:

Flaccid. "Flaccid (meaning flabby) label implies weakness, lack of normal muscle tone, and reduced or absent type reflexes" (p. 415). We usually see this kind of lesion when the injury is to the brainstem and the cranial nuclei or in the peripheral nerve itself, causing a lower motor neuron-type lesion.

Spastic. The lesion is in the pyramidal or extrapyramidal systems (cortical or subcortical) causing "muscular weakness, greater than normal muscular tone, slow movements, limited range of motion, and hyperactive reflexes" (p. 421). This is the most common type of dysarthria we see in a patient who has had a CVA.

Ataxic. This is a relatively rare dysarthria. The damage is confined to the cerebellum, causing "difficulties in regulating force, speed, range, timing, and direction of volitional movements" (p. 422).

Hypokinetic. Parkinson's disease is the most prevalent kind of disease that produces this kind of dysarthria, which is the result of insufficient dopamine in the basal ganglia. The symptoms include loss of automatic movements, at rest (nonintention) tremor, alterations in movement of muscles of respiration and speech, and increased muscle tone.

Patients in time may demonstrate problems initiating movements (such as oral imitations, walking through doorways, and so on).

Hyperkinetic. Lesions at various sites of the extrapyramidal system from the cortex, down through the tracts, and in the basal ganglia may produce symptoms of acceleration and myoclonus of movements. The patient's speech is jerky, accompanied by severe alterations of voice and resonance. Huntington's chorea is among the more common hyperkinetic diseases, although patients with this disease show a slowing or hypokinetic muscle patterning (McDowell and Lee, 1973).

Mixed. A mixture of flaccid or spastic dysarthria may be evident in the same patient, particularly one with diffuse CNS disease. Such diseases as amyotrophic lateral sclerosis and multiple sclerosis often produce speech and voice symptoms that are the result of both flaccidity and spasticity of various muscles.

If we group all of the speech and voice symptoms under general headings, as Darley, Aronson and Brown (1969) did, we see that dysarthria can manifest itself in symptoms of pitch, loudness, vocal quality, respiration, prosody, articulation, and a general impression of intelligibility and bizarreness. We sometimes see patients for voice evaluation whose problems at the time of the evaluation are the beginning of a serious neurological disease. For example, several times a year in our large hospital with many outpatients, we see a patient who comes in with a "functional voice problem" who is actually showing the early symptoms of a degenerative disease, such as muscular dystrophy or amyotrophic lateral sclerosis. The man described in the following case represents a typical patient with the beginning of a serious CNS disease that was first masked as a functional voice disorder:

John, a 46-year-old college biology professor, began to experience increased hoarseness after lecturing. At times, he would lose his voice completely after a busy, vocally demanding day. Indirect laryngoscopy found that John had "normal vocal folds with good motility, free of lesions." During the peripheral oral evaluation it was noted that John "seemed to have some tongue atrophy with surface fasciculations whenever the tongue was extended." He was subsequently referred for a neurological evaluation where testing, including muscle biopsy of thigh muscles, confirmed that the patient had "lower motor neuron disease or amyotrophic lateral sclerosis." Over a twenty-four-month period, John exerienced an increasingly severe dysarthria accompanied by marked involvement of all four extremities. Although the patient is still alive, his progressive disease continues.

The preceding case illustrates how some alteration of voice, either in phonation, or resonance, or both, may be the early symptom of a neurological disease or disorder. Patients with neurological disorders frequently voice alterations of pitch, quality, loudness, or resonance as part of their symptoms of dysfunction.

The symptoms of dysarthria are sometimes lessened by medical-surgical intervention. Some dysarthrias related to disease can be treated with medication. For example, many patients with Parkinson's disease experience a remarkable lessening of symptoms with the administration of L-

Dopa, which provides them with the dopamine they are lacking, and thus reduces the hypokinetic symptoms and improves the clarity of speech. Symptoms of spasticity that may seriously interfere with speech may also be lessened with muscle-relaxant medications. Patients whose dysarthrias are related to tumors are sometimes helped by neurosurgical intervention—by the removal of the tumor.

Many dysarthric patients experience severe hypernasality, which requires the combined therapies of the prosthodontist and the speech pathologist, who focus on improving velopharyngeal closure (see Chapter 7). The typical dysarthric with hypernasality has a weak or paralyzed soft palate, which may require a palatal-lift prosthesis to make contact with the pharyngeal wall. Those patients with degenerative diseases, even severe ones like ALS, can maintain function and life itself with help from such habilitative therapies as physical therapy and inhalation therapy (McGuirt and Blalock, 1980). Speech pathology services with heavy emphasis on voice therapy can often improve the intelligibility of dysarthric patients, both for those with static and fixed conditions (like CVA) and those with degenerative diseases (like ALS).

For some dysarthric patients, speech and voice can be markedly helped by determining whether either volitional or involitional behaviors are facilitative. Some dysarthrias are related to diseases that produce greater symptoms during nonintention or automatic function (like Parkinson's), whereas others are exacerbated by intention (like multiple sclerosis). We see the effects of nonintention and intention clearly when we ask the patient to count from one to fifteen forward and then backward. The Parkinson patient with nonintention symptoms counts forward with a light voice, rapidly, with poor articulation; however, when the patient counts backward (which requires more intention), the dysarthric symptoms may be markedly less. The opposite situation is seen in the multiple sclerosis patient with intention pathologies; the patient's count forward sounds clearer than the attempts to count backward. The voice clinician should probe with the patient to see if the type of verbal stimulus—nonintention (counting, days of week, and so on), or intention (speaking with an accent, or speaking inappropriately loud)—facilitates improvement in voice. If there is a difference between nonintention and intention, the voice clinician should use this information to help the patient minimize his or her dysarthria. The patient needs much practice using the best intention mode. If there is no improvement of speech function with one intention mode or the other, the clinician must work on the various parameters of voice, using, in many cases, the same voice facilitating approaches recommended for the various voice disorders described in this text.

Altering tongue position, particularly bringing the tongue forward, is often useful (see Chapter 5). We have found that rapid production and forward carriage of the tongue is often facilitated when the patient replaces voice with whisper. Some patients have better intelligibility with whisper or light voice than with full voice. Many feedback devices, such as the endoscope showing velopharyngeal closure on a TV monitor or the Visi-Pitch showing fluctuations in vocal frequency, are useful with dysarthric patients.

Sometimes modeling, providing the patient with the prosody or pitch inflection needed to sound "more normal," can produce change; the procedures outlined in Chapter 5 under ear training are useful to follow. Sometimes hierarchy analysis, coupled with relaxation and easy phonation, enables the dysarthric patient to minimize voice symptoms. Much of what we do in voice therapy with dysarthric patients is to teach them speaking tricks, ways of using the speech and vocal mechanism in an easy, efficient way. Examples of "tricks" to facilitate better speech include speaking with less intensity, making deliberate efforts to employ more nonintention or intention vocal responses, speaking with greater (or less) oral opening, and so forth. Besides focusing on voice and resonance, the speech pathologist gives obvious attention to improving the patient's articulation and developing a more normal rate of speech, which, in turn, improves overall speech-voice prosodic patterns.

HARD-OF-HEARING AND DEAF

Voice problems generally accompany severe hearing loss and deafness. The greater the hearing loss, the greater the likelihood of voice problems related to pitch elevation and pitch variability, faulty resonance, and variations in loudness. Ling (1976) writes that most voice problems among hearing-impaired children can be minimized in "all except totally deaf children if hearing aids are worn" (p. 217). In young children who are born with profound hearing loss that prevents them from ever hearing normal, voicing prosodic patterns of aural-oral language, voice symptoms can be severe. Most such children profit from the early fitting of hearing aids and the use of other amplification devices. Voice symptoms can be modified in such children even if they have profound hearing loss. Older children or adults who acquire a hearing loss greater than 70 dB in the speech range (500, 1K, 2K Hz) after normal voice-articulation-language has been established, may gradually experience some deterioration of voice and articulation; in adults, some time may pass after the severe hearing loss before voice and articulation changes are noted.

Pitch

Elevated pitch and excessive pitch variability are two vocal symptoms often observed in the deaf (Boone, 1966a; Monsen, Engebretson, and Vernula, 1979; Wilson, 1987). Wilson presents useful procedures for both changing pitch levels and for working on the changing pitch levels of intonation. Apparently, the lowering of voice pitch as one moves from childhood through adolescence and then to adulthood requires some acoustic monitoring to match one's normal peer group. The deaf child, or adult, who lacks this auditory feedback appears to need some external guidance to use the acceptable pitch levels of age peers. How can a teacher of the deaf or a voice clinician help a deaf child develop a normally pitched voice as he or she grows older?

Any attempt to change a deaf child's pitch level must begin with a discussion about the need for such a change. This discussion should focus on the child's tested fundamental frequency as compared to normative values for the child's age and sex. The inventive clinician might prepare a chart or graph demonstrating for the child where his or her pitch is and where it ought to be. Lacking an adequate auditory model for his or her pitch target, the deaf child must rely on various visual devices to signal whether his or her voice pitch is too high or too low. Instruments such as the PM 100 Pitch Analyzer (1987), the Phonatory Function Analyzer (1986), and the Visi-Pitch (1987), which are capable of making real-time measurements of frequency as the deaf child or adult speaks, are excellent feedback instruments for therapy. Oscillographic display panels or displays on computer screens can isolate the fundamental frequency for the patient and provide a locked-in display pattern of a frequency he or she has just produced. Most such display units provide a "hold" pattern on the screen that can be used as a target model for subsequent therapy trials.

Innovative clinicians have found several effective ways of making the child or adult aware of pitch level and possible pitch variability. One useful device for altering a deaf person's pitch level is to provide "cue arrows" pointing in the desired direction of pitch change. For example, for a typical deaf child attempting to lower the voice pitch, cards should be printed with an arrow pointing down. These cards should be placed wherever possible in the child's environment—in the wallet, on the bureau or desk, and so on. Also, the classroom teacher and voice clinician can give the child finger cues by pointing toward the floor. Another method for developing an altered pitch level is to have the child place his or her fingers lightly on the larynx and feel the downward excursion of the larynx during lower pitch productions and the upward excursion during higher ones. The ideal or optimum pitch is produced by minimal vertical movement of the larynx. Any noticeable upward excursion of the larynx, except during swallowing, will immediately signal that the child may be speaking at an inappropriately high pitch level. Once an appropriate pitch level has been established, the child may read aloud for a specified time period, placing the fingers lightly on the thyroid cartilage to monitor any unnecessary vertical laryngeal movement.

Improving an inappropriate pitch level is one task that can be achieved by the average deaf child or adult. When the need to change (usually lower) the voice pitch is pointed out to such patients, they are able to do a great deal by themselves by using a pitch meter or some form of visual feedback system that can signal the inappropriateness of a pitch production. Because the average pitch level of most voices is under 250 cps, as much low-frequency amplification should be provided as possible. If deaf children or adults have any residual hearing available to them, it is usually the lower frequency range, below 250 cps, and amplification here might well permit them to achieve some auditory monitoring of their own fundamental frequencies. The clinician should make use of any self-hearing available, because this will prove most helpful in the deaf individual's struggle to alter pitch level.

Resonance

The typical voice of a deaf child who has had no training in developing a good voice is characterized by alterations in nasal resonance, often accompanied by excessive pharyngeal resonance, which produce a cul-de-sac voice. The major contributing factor to these resonance alterations is the excessive posterior posturing of the tongue in the hypopharynx, which markedly lowers the second formant (Boone, 1966a; Monsen, 1976). The tongue is drawn back into the hypopharynx and creates the peculiar resonance heard in deaf speakers; this back resonance sounds similar to the resonance sometimes heard in speakers with athetoid cerebral palsy, or oral verbal apraxia. The cul-de-sac voice has a back focus to it. In addition, the hard-of-hearing or deaf child or adult may demonstrate marked variations in nasal resonance—too much nasal focus (hypernasality) or insufficient nasal resonance (denasality); such nasal resonance variations may be due in part to the posterior carriage of the tongue, as well as to the inability to monitor acoustically the nasalization characteristic of the normal speaker.

Altering the tongue position to a more forward carriage and tongue protrusion (see Chapter 5) can contribute greatly to establishing more normal oral resonance in the voice of a deaf speaker. In addition to the procedures outlined in Chapter 5 for altering tongue position, more detailed procedures and therapy materials for both children and adults are available in *The Boone Voice Program for Children* (1980a) and *The Boone Voice Program for Adults* (1982). Once the tongue has been placed in a more "neutral setting" (Laver, 1980), the deaf patient needs to practice making vocal contrasts between back-pharyngeal resonance and normal oral resonance. The deaf patient needs to develop an awareness of what it feels like to use the lips, the tongue against the alveolar processes, the tongue on the hard palate, and other front-of-the-mouth postures. Such front focus seems to develop only after intensive practice doing tasks that encourage anterior tongue carriage.

The deaf speaker must also work to eliminate hypernasality, if it is present. The patient first needs to become aware of excessive nasal resonance by reviewing feedback from various instruments that measure air flow in acoustic output simultaneously from both the oral and nasal cavities. A two-channel manometer or an air-pressure transducer, equipped with both oral and nasal channels (with a separate mouthpiece and a nasal olive) can provide information about the relative air pressures between the patient's mouth and nose. For example, a patient asked to read a passage with all oral consonants, would only record minimal pressure from the nasal channel. Such a two-channel pressure device could serve as a valuable feedback instrument to eliminate nasal escape of air in voice therapy. How much of the perceived voice is oral and how much is nasal can be determined by the Nasometer. The Nasometer (see Figure 6–1) is a microcomputer-based system that can make an acoustic analysis of the relative amount of nasality in a voice signal. The patient produces voice that is directed into two microphones that are separated by a nasal-oral separator. The computer screen provides real-time feedback about the relative acoustic output between the two channels. The Nasometer provides the same

FIGURE 6-1. The Nasometer produces visual feedback for the patient of his oral/nasal resonance ratio, thus providing a measurement of nasalence. The clinician can set a target level, and the patient's continuous performance can be monitored in relationship to that target level. The peak or highest level of nasal performance is also recorded.

kind of nasal resonance feedback in therapy as the Tonar II (Fletcher and Daly, 1976); both instruments provide valuable visual feedback about vocal resonance for the deaf speaker.

Respiratory Problems

Because of their inability to monitor voice as normal speakers do, deaf individuals may demonstrate problems of respiration associated with voicing. Respiratory function for nonspeech tasks is essentially normal. In their study of respiratory kinematics in ten deaf young adult males ranging from 19 to 24 years old, Forner and Hixon (1977) found, that although the deaf men demonstrated normal tidal volumes, they exhibited marked variation in expiratory control. They often began speaking late in the tidal expirations and seldom matched their linguistic messages with sustained and controlled expirations. The deaf males often took breath refills or exhibited breath holding while attempting to produce connected speech on one expiratory utterance.

Some deaf speakers cannot monitor the loudness of their voices, and they speak with excessive vocal intensity or with great variability in intensity. In comparing forty-four deaf children with forty-four normal children, Boone (1966a) found excessive loudness prominent among the deaf speakers. In therapy attention to loudness can be achieved by using VU meters, as feedback monitoring devices, or a sound level meter, like the B & K Sound Level Meter Type 2225 (1987), to provide real-time feedback about voice intensity variations. Ling (1976) stated that teachers and normal-hearing people in the child's environment should give the child information about the appropriateness of voice intensity. Appropriate loudness of voice and minimal intensity fluctuations can be achieved in voice therapy by using such facilitating approaches as change of loudness and respiration training, designed to develop easy duration control (see Chapter 5). Any kind of oscillograph or monitor displaying vocal productions can provide invaluable feedback for the deaf or hard-of-hearing speaker attempting to develop better respiratory and loudness control.

THE AGING VOICE

After following a number of normal, older subjects at the University of Arizona over a ten-year period (as part of a control group in a dementia study), we have found it difficult to say there are "typical" voice characteristics of an aging population. There appears, instead, to be large intersubject variability. Studying vocal perturbation (jitter, shimmer), Ramig and Ringel (1983), found that their population of forty-eight subjects could be divided into two groups: the physiologically "fit" and those in poorer condition. The group of older subjects (62 to 75 years old) who were tested and demonstrated good to excellent physiologic signs did not show any voice differences from younger, healthy subjects; only the middle-age and old-age subjects who were less physiologically fit demonstrated hoarseness with increased vocal jitter and shimmer.

A number of studies have examined the vocal characteristics of an older population, focusing on both fundamental frequency changes and increased vocal perturbation (jitter). Mysak (1959) found that fundamental frequency began to elevate slightly with increasing age from 50 to 85. A later study by Hollien and Shipp (1972) confirmed that fundamental frequency of male speakers at different ages is characterized by a saucer-type curve, with decreasing fundamentals for each decade in life until after age 50, when a slight increase of fundamentals occurs for each decade. Several studies of aged women (Charlip, 1968; McGlone and Hollien, 1963) found the opposite—that is, as women get older, they seem to demonstrate increasingly lower fundamental frequencies. Some of the confusion from the studies of voice pitch in aging was clarified by a study by Honjo and Isshiki (1980), who studied twenty men and twenty women with a mean age of 75 years and found that the men had "vocal fold atrophy and/or edema" with higher fundamental frequency than younger men whereas the women had "fold edema and slight hoarseness with a lower fundamental frequency" than younger women. If a patient exhibits a marked departure in pitch level from his or her age peers, symptomatic voice therapy using such facilitating approaches as change of loudness, establish new pitch, respiration training may be helpful (see Chapter 5).

As people pass the age of 70, hoarseness or dysphonia may increase.

The atrophy in the folds of men and the edema in the folds of women may well contribute to observed dysphonia (Honjo and Isshiki, 1980). In studying jitter (perturbations in fundamental frequency) in the voices of twenty young adults and twenty older adults, Wilcox and Horii (1980) found significantly greater jitter in the older adults. Measures of jitter provide one measurement of dysphonia. It is not unusual for an aged person to have some hoarseness of voice. Diagnostically, it may be important for the speech-language pathologist to rule out possible causes of the hoarseness other than normal aging, such as related to possible lesions (leukoplakia, carcinoma), to weakness or paralysis (part of a dysarthria), or to endocrinal problems perhaps caused by side effects from excessive hormones, vitamins, or medications. If there appears to be no cause of hoarseness other than the tissue changes of the vocal folds observed in normal aging, voice therapy might be warranted for the patients. The quality of the voice may be improved by such methods as ear training, establish new pitch, feedback, and relaxation (see Chapter 5).

PUBERPHONIA

The high-pitched voice in a young man who has already completed puberty is known as *puberphonia*. The voice may be either at the end of the normal, chest register or in the falsetto register. It is thus sometimes called *"mutational falsetto."* The fundamental frequency of the voice is often in excess of 260 Hz (or at middle C in the singing range). The social penalties for men who speak at such high-pitched levels are obvious; an individual who does so is often judged to be effeminate and perhaps inadequate. It is difficult to find the original physical or psychological factors that may have caused puberphonia. The large majority of young men with inappropriately high voices have excellent voice therapy prognosis; many achieve normal pitch levels and vocal quality after only brief exposure to voice therapy (Aronson, 1985; Case, 1984; Wilson, 1987).

In most cases, laryngeal examination reveals a normal, adult male larynx and an adult vocal tract. Physical examination usually reveals normal secondary characteristics, as well (beard, pubic hair, adult genitalia), indicating that the young man has passed through puberty. If secondary physical growth has not occurred, the problem cannot be labeled puberphonia. By definition, the diagnosis of puberphonia is made by the presence of a high-pitched voice in an individual with normal, secondary sexual characteristics. In the rare case of delayed physical development, the patient should undergo a medical evaluation, which may lead to some kind of endocrinologic treatment (which is usually successful in stimulating pubertal changes). Symptomatic voice therapy, using such techniques as glottal fry and half-swallow, boom, is highly successful in treating puberphonia. As Aronson (1980) has written, "It is one of the easiest and most rewarding disorders to treat" (pp. 147–148). In her treatment of puberphonia, Greene (1980) continues to give the disorder more of a psychological emphasis than most current writers. She describes puberphonias, in fact, as part of discussions of the Oedipus complex, narcissus complex, hero worship, homosexuality, and transsexualism. Greene then develops specific exercises for the clinician to use to help young men with puberphonia develop lower pitch. Similar approaches are outlined by Wilson (1987) and Aronson (1985).

One possible way of helping a patient produce a lower pitch level is to place your fingers externally on his thyroid cartilage and then ask him to phonate an extended "ah." When the "ah" begins, press lightly on the thyroid cartilage (decreasing the length and increasing the mass of the vocal folds) to produce an immediate lowering of pitch; when the finger pressure is released, the pitch may revert back. Repeat the procedure and ask the patient if he can maintain the lower pitch level. This finger pressure, as mentioned under digital manipulation in Chapter 5, is not always effective with falsetto voices. But it is worth trying—and if it works, use it. Most puberphonic patients can also demonstrate normal male pitch levels when they produce such nonverbal phonations as throat clearing, coughing, grunting, and so on. If the patient can produce a normal-pitched, nonverbal phonation, he should then be instructed to prolong the sound, extending it as an "ah" for several seconds. Early attempts to phonate should not involve actual words, but only the nonverbal sounds. Depending on the patient's success in producing nonverbal phonation and his attitude toward doing this, gradually have him phonate words with the lower voice. One successful way of doing this is to blend a prolonged nonverbal phonation into the production of a word that begins with a similar-sounding vowel. Most patients make the transition from nonverbal phonation to production of a few practice words without too much resistance. In the beginning, it is wise to stay on the practice level, using only a few words, before having the patient try to use the lower voice in conversational situations. When the patient is able to produce a few practice words with normal voice, record the new voice and let the patient hear it. It does very little good to record both the falsetto and normal voices, using them for contrast discrimination, because hearing the falsetto as contrasted perhaps with a normal baritone often puts the patient on the defensive. Rather, listen critically with the patient to the lower voice pitch, ignoring the falsetto when analyzing the new production. When the patient listens to the new voice, determine what pitch level it is and then show the patient how this fits into the normal adult male range. If the lower pitch level is in that normal range, make sure the patient realizes this. The typical patient with puberphonia is "hungry" to develop a more normal-sounding voice. With this excellent motivation, a direct symptom-modification approach produces very rapid changes, requiring only brief voice therapy (two or three sessions).

DIPLOPHONIA

The diplophonic voice is usually produced by two distinct voicing sources, each phonating simultaneously with the other. Occasionally, diplophonia is produced by the true folds—if one of the folds has a different mass and tension than the other one. For example, in persistent paralytic dysphonia, the patient's voice may sound diplophonic as the paralyzed fold vibrates faster because of its thinner mass (as a result of lower motor neuron atrophy). Laryngeal webs sometimes phonate in the airstream, producing a high-pitched squeal that joins the vocal fold vibration (altered because of the shorter segments posteriorly beyond the edge of the web) and thus a double voice. The epiglottis may also produce a sound that, when added to the true fold vibration, produces a diplophonic voice.

The first step in treating a diplophonia is to identify the double-voice source. Video nasoendoscopy has been an excellent tool for examining the vocal tract, attempting to identify an extra phonation source. Occasionally, vigorous aryepiglottic muscle activity produces a tight pursing of the superior larynx, which may prevent the viewer from looking underneath. The aryepiglottic muscles can be the second sound source with the true folds vibrating underneath. The ventricular folds sometimes occlude from view the true folds underneath; perhaps, in fact, the most common diplophonic voice sources identified are the ventricular folds, vibrating above the true folds. Any additive lesion to the vocal folds, particularly a unilateral lesion, can change the vibratory characteristics of the folds and produce a diplophonia.

The first consideration in the treatment of diplophonia is whether or not the second sound source can be reduced or eliminated. Surgical eradication of a unilateral additive lesion, for example, might bring the two vocal folds into size compatibility so that their vibratory characteristics were basically the same, eliminating the double voice. Symptomatic voice therapy can often be effective in reducing diplophonia. For example, inhalation phonation (see Chapter 5) is produced by true fold vibration. The voice on inhalation is usually a high-pitched, single voice. Once the single voice is established on expiration, the clinician can usually expand the single phonation into other voicing tasks. The yawn-sigh approach (see Chapter 5) is an excellent way to develop an open, supraglottal airway. As the patient produces a phonated sigh, the supraglottal larynx and pharynx are maximally dilated, which might well eliminate any supraglottal structure, such as the aryepiglottic folds, from vibrating and producing the double voice. Other facilitating approaches from Chapter 5 that might be helpful in searching for a clear, single voice include ear training, glottal fry, half-swallow, boom, and place the voice. Use various approaches as probes to find one that might eliminate the second voice. If a particular technique is effective, then design practice materials incorporating it as the therapy practice mode.

PITCH BREAKS

As we discussed in Chapter 3, there are two kinds of pitch breaks. First, the upward pitch break experienced by some adolescent boys must be considered as a temporary developmental vocal inconvenience and not a voice problem per se. During the last months of puberty some boys experience a one-octave pitch break (the voice breaks upward) as they are using conversational voice. There is no need for voice therapy because this kind of pitch break is temporary. As the laryngeal mechanism reaches full development, the pitch breaks disappear as suddenly as they first appeared. An occasional boy (or his parents) may need brief counseling about the temporary nature of the problem. This counseling is about the only role required of the speech-language pathologist to deal with such adolescent pitch breaks.

The second kind of pitch break is related to continuous vocal hyperfunction, particularly prolonged speaking at an inappropriate pitch level. The voice breaks either one octave upward or one octave downward. Occasionally, patients experience two-octave breaks. The voice breaks in the direction (down or up) where it "would like to be." Although we have well established in previous chapters that there is no such thing as an absolute optimum voice pitch, speaking at the very bottom or top of one's range for extended periods of time may contribute to vocal strain. Pitch breaks are a symptom of that strain. The primary focus of voice therapy for pitch breaks is establishing a new pitch, raising or lowering the fundamental frequency one or two notes. Upward pitch breaks, the most common form of pitch break, is usually related to speaking at the very bottom of one's pitch range. Elevating pitch one or two notes usually eliminates the problem. With the new pitch level, the patient might profit from developing a voice legato with chant talk, using a relaxed voice with chewing, practicing yawn-sigh, eliminating hard glottal attack, and attempting the open-mouth approach (see Chapter 5). A downward pitch break, observed more often in adult women, can usually be corrected by developing a lower voice pitch and using the other facilitating approaches recommended for lowering the pitch level. The final step in eliminating pitch breaks is developing an overall easy, open vocal style as the result of ear training, matching one's voice with target voice models previously tape recorded by the patient and the clinician.

A VOCAL HYGIENE APPROACH FOR OPTIMUM USE OF THE VOICE

Professional users of voice, such as actors, singers, or teachers, must often use the mechanisms of the vocal tract as optimally as possible. Froeschels (1943) first used the phrase "hygiene of the voice" and developed a list of behaviors that could be followed by the serious user of voice to maximize vocal performance. We have found that the voice patient in particular requires guidelines to prevent voice abuse-misuse and to minimize vocal strain. A number of vocal hygiene programs in the literature (Boone, 1980b; Cooper, 1977; Wilson, 1987) offer good rules for using the voice with greater ease, avoiding laryngeal strain and excessive effort while vocalizing. Any serious user of voice, whether a voice patient or not, may profit from attempting to follow some of the twelve voice preserving steps listed in this vocal hygiene program:

1. Identify vocal abuses-misuses (shouting, throat clearing, and so on) and attempt to reduce their occurrence.
2. Develop an easy glottal attack or a legato-type speaking voice.
3. Use a pitch level where you should be. Avoid speaking or singing too low or too high.

4. Keep your speaking voice at the lower end of your loudness range.
5. Take an easy, relaxed breath when speaking.
6. Reduce voice usage by speaking or singing less.
7. Keep a vertical focus in the voice.
8. Avoid tightening your jaw and grinding your teeth. Develop a greater mouth opening.
9. Avoid talking in loud settings (discos, airplanes, and so on).
10. Become aware of humidity and hydration effects on your voice.
11. Avoid making odd sounds with your voice (environmental noises, different voices, and so on).
12. Avoid smoking and excessive use of alcohol.

The vocal hygiene program just listed is a common-sense application for preserving good vocal function. Speech pathologists must take a pragmatic approach in applying the twelve steps to individual patients. Although some patients may obviously profit from following all twelve suggestions, only a few of the guidelines may apply to the typical patient. For any user of voice, however, who experiences some voice symptoms after much voice usage, the vocal hygiene program provides a ready list of possible situations that may cause voice strain. Many of the program steps are natural extensions of the philosophy and therapy-facilitating approaches presented in Chapters 1 and 5. Let us further consider some of the steps of the program.

Identifying vocal abuse and misuse and reducing its occurrence are the most important steps of this vocal hygiene program. As developed in Chapters 1 and 5, vocal hyperfunction with vocal abuse-misuse cannot be tolerated by a serious user of voice or a patient with a voice problem. Identified abuse-misuse can be reduced and, often, totally eliminated. For the individual who has spoken with abrupt, hard glottal attack, developing a legato voice (flowing phonation without breaks between words) can become a much preferred way of speaking and producing a voice free of strain (Lawrence, 1983).

Occasionally speakers voice at too high or low a pitch. Although an "absolute optimum speaking pitch" does not exist, we can get the most "mileage" out of our voices while speaking only a few notes above the bottom of our pitch ranges. Also, it is important to sing within one's range (for example, baritones should avoid singing tenor) and to avoid singing at the bottom or top of one's range for prolonged periods of time (such as throughout a rehearsal). Speaking or singing too loud over time can also have aversive effects on the voice; controlling the intensity of one's voice and speaking at softer levels can often eliminate or reduce vocal strain.

Many speakers and singers work too hard to breathe. In normal speaking and easy singing, the timed or temporal aspects of respiration and the actual number of words spoken or sung correspond amazingly well. By taking a slightly larger breath than normal tidal breathing, we can say or sing a passage before us. We do not have to make a lot of effortful, muscular maneuvers to breathe adequately for most speaking and singing. Some of the practice materials, such as increasing expiratory control, in Chapter 5 are important to use to improve the efficiency of one's breathing for various phonatory tasks.

Reducing voice use can often do wonders for a tired voice. Many voices are destroyed from overwork, perhaps as the result of continuous lecturing by a teacher, or prolonged rehearsals by an actor, or continuous conversation by someone who likes to talk and seldom listens. Reducing vocal output, maybe just a few hours daily, is sometimes a helpful strategy for the patient who is experiencing vocal strain. Perkins (1983) has written that the person who must use voice excessively because of some kind of job demand can experience a more lasting voice by using "vertical focus" as he or she speaks. This view has been translated into the therapy approach in Chapter 5 called place the voice, which seems to give the voice patient a more efficient way of using voice. It does appear from patient report and clinical observation that when speaking in either noisy settings or for prolonged periods of time, a patient will experience a more lasting voice by keeping the voice focus "out of the larynx" and more vertically focused "in the facial mask." The imagery involved in doing this (the imagery words are in quotes) seems effective in producing noticeable acoustic effects (less perturbation).

Avoiding a clenched-jaw posture while listening to others, while watching a play or a movie, and while reading can promote greater vocal tract relaxation. Avoiding the extremes of molar crunching (bruxism) is most important. Developing an awareness of oral opening, keeping the teeth apart with or without open lips, is important for developing greater oral relaxation. Avoiding talking or singing in the presence of loud noise is a good vocal hygiene tip. Prolonged talking in a disco, in an automobile, or around a power mower or boat motor can produce vocal strain and should be avoided.

Excessive dryness is hard on the vocal tract. We are often unaware of the effect on our voices of low humidity caused by furnace heating and air conditioning. Certain medications, such as decongestants taken for allergies and colds, can have pronounced drying effects. The serious user of voice and the voice patient must become aware of the effects of humidity, and when severe low-humidity conditions exist, he or she should make deliberate efforts to elevate humidity levels by using room humidifiers and vaporizers. Watching one's body hydration by drinking plenty of fluids each day can also reduce the symptoms of a dry vocal tract (Lawrence, 1983).

Serious users of voice and voice patients working to regain normal voices should avoid making loud and strange vocal noises. A surprising number of people make an occasional strained vocalization imitating the sound of an engine, an animal sound, or a strange voice. Pushing the laryngeal mechanism into strained, hyperfunctional utterances as an occasional "fun" voice is a counter-productive vocal behavior and should be avoided.

Anyone interested in his or her voice should not smoke. The annual publications from the American Cancer Society consistently tell us that tobacco smoke is a vocal tract irritant that leads to various airway and pulmonary diseases. Smoke is also an aversive drying agent that can further dry the mucosa of the airway. For the voice patient, irritated structures in the vocal tract, such as the vocal folds, become increasingly irritated from exposure to smoke. Both authors of this text require their voice patients to quit smoking as a condition for receiving voice therapy; an irritated vocal mechanism cannot respond to therapy attempts. Moderate to excessive alcohol should also be avoided by the serious user of voice, because alcohol is a vasodilator that can cause the vocal folds to become edematous and thickened, altering their voicing characteristics. Mild or occasional use of alcohol appears to have no negative vocal effects.

SUMMARY

Many problems of voice require special management. Each of the disorders reviewed in this chapter requires that the voice clinician be aware of the uniqueness of the disorder. Therapy approaches for each of these conditions or disorders are often highly individualized. For example, the voice therapy approach for functional aphonia is markedly different from the management steps for paralytic aphonia. Voice problems related to aging, or dysarthria, or deafness are extremely different and require totally different therapy approaches. Yet, all of these disorders have some similarities to one another, and they often profit from therapy attempts that utilize the twenty-five facilitating approaches presented in Chapter 5. The chapter concluded with a twelve-point vocal hygiene program that appears useful not only to voice patients but to anyone who is a serious user of voice.

7

THERAPY FOR RESONANCE DISORDERS

Hypernasality is the most common resonance disorder. It can be an early sign of a neurological disease, or it can be the result of a congenital disorder such as cleft palate. It can also result from a surgical treatment. The cause of hypernasality must be determined as a prelude to successful treatment. Hyponasality or denasality can be caused by a number of obstructions, such as nasal polyps, allergies, or hypertrophied adenoids. Another nasalence problem, assimilative nasality, must be distinguished from either hypernasality or denasality. Speech-language pathologists play a primary role in the diagnosis and treatment of various nasality problems.

Resonance is selective amplification and filtering of the complex overtone structure produced by the vibration of the vocal folds. The vocal folds provide the source of vibration that gives rise to the complex sound waves. These periodic vibrations, characteristic of the normal voice, are filtered in the supraglottal space of the pharyngeal, oral, and nasal cavities, or the upper airway. Our discussion of resonance in Chapter 2 showed that the F-shaped upper airway amplifies and filters the sounds coming into it from the larynx, depending on the frequency of the sound waves and the shape of the particular cavity. The pharyngeal cavity constantly changes its horizontal and vertical dimensions by active movement of muscles, which in turn changes its overall configuration (Pershall and Boone, 1986). An open coupling between the pharyngeal cavity and the oral cavity (particularly when the velopharyngeal mechanism is closed) enables the traveling sound wave to be further filtered by the continuous modifications of oral cavity size that occur during speech. What emerges as voice resonance is the fundamental frequency (laryngeal vibration) modified by the natural resonant frequencies occurring at the various supraglottal sites above the vocal folds, within the pharynx, and through the oral cavity. When the velopharyngeal port is open, the pharyngeal-oral coupling with the nasal cavity is then possible so that sound waves are further absorbed and filtered as they pass through the chambers of the nasal cavity, as for the production of /m/, /n/, and /ŋ/ in English. Problems in pharyngeal-oral coupling, structural and functional, cause the most common resonance problems, disorders in nasal resonance. We consider the evaluation, management, and therapy of nasal resonance problems.

NASAL RESONANCE PROBLEMS

Under the broad heading of nasal resonance fall three types of disorders: *hypernasality, denasality,* and *assimilative nasality.* Although individuals listening to speakers with these problems might only be able to say, "the voices all sound nasal," distinct differences among the three types call for differential management and voice therapy approaches. As a prelude to our discussion of separate approaches, let us define the three terms:

> *Hypernasality.* Hypernasality is an excessively undesirable amount of perceived nasal cavity resonance during the phonation of vowels and voiced consonants. Voiced consonants and vowel production in the English language are primarily characterized by oral resonance with only slightly nasalized components. If the oral and nasal cavities are coupled to one another by lack of velopharyngeal closure (for whatever reason), the periodic sound waves carrying laryngeal vibration will receive heavy resonance within the nasal cavity. Only three phonemes of the English language should receive the degree of nasal prominence produced by an open velopharyngeal port: /m/, /n/, and /ŋ/.
>
> *Denasality.* Denasality is the lack of nasal resonance for the three nasalized phonemes /m/, /n/, and /ŋ/. In the strictest sense, therefore, denasality could be categorized as an articulatory substitution disorder. Generally, denasality also affects vowels, in that the normal speaker gives some nasal resonance to vowels. A voice with this inadequate nasal resonance sounds like the voice of a normal speaker suffering from a severe head cold.
>
> *Assimilative Nasality.* In assimilative nasality, the speaker's vowels appear nasal when adjacent to the three nasal consonants. The velopharyngeal port is opened too soon and remains open too long, so that vowel resonance preceding and following nasal consonant resonance is also nasalized.

Normal English consonants are produced with high intraoral pressures (3 to 8 cm H_2O) with essentially no nasal air flow except for the three nasal consonants that have low intraoral pressures (0.5 to 1.5 cm H_2O) and high rates of nasal air flow (100 to 300 cc sec.), as reported by Mason and Warren (1980). Aerodynamic studies of cleft palate and problems of nasality have provided some needed quantification to help differentiate patients with excessive nasal resonance from patients lacking sufficient nasal resonance (Warren, 1979). From his studies of air pressures and air flow patterns, Warren has estimated the size of the velopharyngeal port. Although most normal speakers demonstrate tight velopharyngeal closure with no air leakage (Thompson, 1978), speakers with openings as small as 5 mm or less may still have voice quality that is perceived by listeners as normal (Mason and Warren, 1980). Patients with nasal voices who produce high nasal air-flow rates are perceived as having hypernasality with denasality, accompanied by low nasal air flows.

Probably no area of voice therapy is more neglected or more confusing than therapy for nasal resonance problems. Historically, the implication in the early literature was that most problems of nasality (usually hypernasality) could be successfully treated by voice therapy—that is, by ear training, as described by Bell in 1890, or by blowing exercises (Kantner, 1947), or by the exercises for the velum suggested by Buller (1942), or by the treatment Williamson used for seventy-two cases of hypernasality, which put some emphasis on relaxing the entire vocal tract (1945). Most of these early approaches were developed for functional hypernasality, but were later applied by various clinicians to problems of palatal insufficiency and cleft palate. For most of these structural problems, however, such approaches as blowing and relaxation were ineffective. If the velopharyngeal mechanisms were structurally unable to produce velopharyngeal closure, no amount of relaxation or exercise could have much effect in reducing excessive nasal resonance. Realistic management and therapy for any problem in nasal resonance, therefore, requires that the patient have a thorough differential evaluation, including detailed examination of the mechanism, aerodynamic studies, functional speech-voice testing, a detailed acoustical analysis of voice, and endoscopic studies.

EVALUATION OF NASAL RESONANCE DISORDERS

There are more similarities than differences between patients with resonance disorders and those with phonation disorders. For this reason, the evaluational procedures outlined in Chapter 4 are equally relevant here. In addition to obtaining the necessary medical data, clinicians must pursue case history information (description of the problem and its cause, description of daily voice use, variations of the problem, onset and duration of the problem, and so on). Clinicians must observe closely how well the patients seem to function in the clinic and in out-of-clinic situations. Considering how subjective our judgments of resonance disorders are, it is crucial that clinicians know how their patients perceive their own voices. A mild resonance problem, for example, can be perceived by a patient and/or others as a severe problem, but a severe resonance problem may be ignored. Indeed, some consider the popular Country Western singer Willie Nelson hypernasal, whereas others think that he sings with "authentic regional twang."

Analysis of Voice in Speech

An obvious way to begin the evaluation of a person with a nasal resonance disorder is to listen carefully to his or her voice during spontaneous conversation. This can provide a gross indication of what the problem may be (assimilative nasality, hypernasality, and so on). It is, however, extremely difficult to make a clinical judgment about nasality by listening to someone as he or she speaks; in fact, such a judgment is likely to be wrong. For example, Bradford, Brooks, and Shelton (1964) found that neither a group of four experienced judges nor one of four inexperienced judges could reliably judge the recorded voice samples of children producing /a/ and /i/ with nares open and closed (by digital pressure). The judges were similarly unreliable when judging nasality from conversational speech samples. Although the judgment that "something is nasal about the speech" is usually correct, few examiners can quickly and reliably differentiate the type of nasality (hypernasality, assimilative nasality, denasality) on the basis of such a conversational sample. Voice quality judgments are more accurate if made on the basis of tape-recorded samples of a patient's conversational speech, his or her vowels in isolation, and his or her sentences (some with only oral phonemes and some loaded with nasal phonemes). The taped sample allows the clinician repeated playback. Focusing on a specific parameter (loudness, pitch, quality) on each playback may increase the clinician's objectivity. To counter the "halo" effect, the influence of a speaker's articulation on the judgment of his or her nasality, Sherman (1954) developed a procedure of playing the connected speech sample backward on the tape recorder, thus precluding the identification of any articulation errors. Reverse playback is most helpful in differentiating between hypernasality and denasality. Spriestersbach (1955) found that the reverse playback of speech samples of cleft palate subjects reduced the correlations between articulation proficiency-pitch level and judgments of nasality. We have found that asking patients to repeat or read aloud passages that are totally free of nasal consonants, such as "Betty Takes Bob to the Show" (Boone, 1980a), or passages that are loaded with nasal consonants, such as "Many Men in the Moon" (Boone, 1980a), helps us differentiate hypernasality, denasality, and assimilative nasality from one another.

We have also found that if we use the following simple screening procedures, we get a good, quick clinical classification of the type of resonance disorder present. These quick tests are simple and require no instruments to perform. First, we have the patient say these two sentences while holding the nose: "My name means money." and "Mary may make many messes." If these sound "plugged" when the nose is held and not plugged when the nose is released, the problem is hypernasality. If there is *no difference* between the nose-held and nose-released conditions, the problem is denasality. Next, we have the patient sustain a loud /s/ while the nose is held and quickly released. If a "snap" is heard on releasing the nose, the problem is probably hypernasality. Next, we have the patient say, "This horse eats grass." "I see the teacher at church." If we hear any "snorting" back in the pharynx, we can assume that it is probably due to inadequate closure of the velopharyngeal port and that the problem is hypernasality. We next ask the patient to say, "Maybe baby, maybe baby." If there is no difference between the two words (maybe and baby) and both sound like "maybe" the problem is hypernasality; however, if both words sound like "baby" the problem is denasality. Finally, we ask the patient to sustain the /i/ and the /u/ vowels, while we gently flutter the nose by occluding the nares with the thumb and forefinger. If we hear a pulsing change in the acoustic signal, the problem is hypernasality.

Patients with hypernasality often have laryngeal abnormalities, as well.

For example, children with velopharyngeal closure problems have a high incidence of vocal cord nodules and polyps (McWilliams, Lavorato, and Bluestone, 1973). Therefore, the clinician must not only make judgments about resonance abnormality, he or she must also listen closely to voice quality. The voice sample then should be analyzed for resonance, vocal quality, and articulation. Besides listening to the voice, the clinician must employ stimulability testing and other testing techniques.

Stimulability Testing

Although stimulability testing was designed for use with problems of articulation, it is also effective with problems of voice. The basic purpose of stimulability testing, as first described by Milisen (1957), was to see how well the patient can produce an errored sound when he or she is repeatedly presented with the correct sound through both auditory and visual stimuli. One way of distinguishing between true problems of velopharyngeal structure (the mechanism is wholly incapable of adequate closure) and functional velopharyngeal inadequacy (the mechanism has the capability of closure) is to see if the patient can produce oral resonance under stimulability conditions (Morris and Smith, 1962). Obviously, the patient's success in producing oral resonance would be a strong indication that velopharyngeal closure is possible. Shelton, Hahn, and Morris (1968) wrote:

> If repeated stimulation consistently results in consonant productions which are distorted by nasal emission and vowels which are unpleasantly nasal, the inference can be drawn, at least tentatively, that the individual is not able to change his speaking behavior because of velopharyngeal incompetence (p. 236).

Success in producing oral resonance under conditions of stimulability would be a good indicator for voice therapy. It is also a favorable prognostic sign.

Another, simple stimulability test is to hold the patient's velum up with a tongue depressor while fluttering the nose during the patient's production of a sustained /i/ vowel. Next, remove the tongue depressor and listen for a difference in resonance. If the difference is dramatic the patient will likely not be able to benefit from voice/speech therapy alone but will require a palatal lift, speech obturator, or surgical management.

Articulation Testing

Articulatory proficiency can provide a good index of a patient's velopharyngeal closure. Nasal emission, the escape of air through the nose, is a most common articulation error on plosive and fricative phonemes among subjects with inadequate velopharyngeal closure. Even though a patient may have his or her articulators in the correct position, in relation to their lingual-alveolar-labial contacts, the error occurs because increased oral pressure escapes nasally through the incomplete posterior palatal closure. The presence or absence of nasal emission, therefore, is a most important diagnostic sign of velopharyngeal adequacy. It is important in articulation testing to distinguish between errors that result from faulty articulatory positioning and errors related to inadequacy of the velopharyngeal structure.

An excellent articulation test for assessing competency of velopharyngeal closure is found in the forty-three special test items from the Templin-Darley Tests of Articulation (Templin and Darley, 1980), known as the Iowa Pressure Articulation Test. This test is particularly sensitive for identifying the presence of nasal emission during the production of certain consonants. However, any standardized articulation test is useful for determining those phonemes that are distorted because of inadequate velopharyngeal closure. The clinician must closely assess the identified errors to determine if lingual placements are accurate to make the target phoneme correctly. Many younger children with velopharyngeal problems exhibit sound substitutions and omission errors in addition to the nasal emission and nasal snort distortion they produce because of inadequate velar closure. Older children and adults with nasal emission problems may well have correct articulatory lingual placements, and their distortions are a product of posterior nasal escape of the air stream. Following successful pharyngeal flap surgery or the proper fitting of an appliance, nasal emission sometimes continues until it is modified through speech remediation. The past learning and the muscular "set" for making distorted nasal emission may continue even though the closure mechanism may now be considered normal. It is usually possible, however, to eliminate nasal emission through therapy, once structural adequacy has been achieved.

The sixteen so-called "pressure consonants" provide the best test of the adequacy of the velopharyngeal mechanism. These pressure consonants—/p, b, k, g, t, d, f, v, s, z, sh, ʒ, dʒ, tʃ, θ, ð/—should be included in any testing of the adequacy of the velopharyngeal port mechanism. Denasality in its purest and most overt form would be exhibited on an articulation test with these oral substitutions for the nasal phonemes: b/m, d/n, and g/ŋ. The sentence "My name means money," would be produced, for example, as "By dabe beads buddy."

Assimilative nasality would be observable only for vowels in words containing nasal phonemes. Nasal emission would be most common in patients with palatal insufficiency in affricates (such as tʃ), fricatives (such as s), and plosives (such as p). Hypernasality per se would not be isolated on an articulation test. Clinicians should be alert to the relatively high number of articulation errors often present in the speech of patients with cleft palate. In fact, from a speech therapy point of view, there is often more merit in focusing on articulation errors in cases of cleft palate than on resonance per se; as speech intelligibility improves, the hypernasality of these patients interferes less and less with effective communication. The type of articulation test or tasks used to assess articulatory proficiency is a matter of clinical choice. However, with the increasing availability of diagnostic aids for determining adequacy of velopharyngeal closure, clinicians must not abandon their articulation assessments, which may well be among the most valid tools for diagnosing velopharyngeal inadequacy. In addition to the most obvious articulation errors in the speech of patients with velopharyngeal inadequacy, such as glottal stops and pharyngeal fricatives, errors may include tongue tip sounds made too far back in the mouth, posterior productions of other sounds and weakened plosives, fricatives, and affricates.

The Peripheral Oral Examination

By direct visual examination, the clinician can make a gross observation of the relationship of the velum to the pharynx, note the relative size of tongue, make a judgment of maxillary-mandibular occlusion, view the height of the palatal arch, survey the general condition of dentition, and determine if there are any clefts or open fistulas in the palate. Remember that direct visualization of palatal length and movement provides only a gross indication of velopharyngeal closure, because the anatomic point of closure is superior by some distance to the lower border of the velum. That is, a lack of velar contact with the pharynx at the uvular-tip end of the velum is not an indication of lack of closure further up, where closure usually occurs. A markedly short palate or a palate with obvious pharyngeal contact can be noted on direct inspection of the oral cavity, and such a notation would be diagnostically important. The less obvious problems of borderline closure cannot be determined by direct inspection and probably require videoendoscopic or fluorographic confirmation, which we discuss in the next section.

The degree of velar movement can be determined with some validity by directly viewing the soft palate. It is extremely important to know when crucial management decisions are being made—that is, when it is being decided whether a child should have a pharyngeal flap or an appliance, or speech therapy (which we discuss in the section on the treatment of hypernasality). Direct observation is only possible during vowel productions; however, the degree of closure of the velopharyngeal port is more critical on consonants and consonant clusters than on vowels. A degree of openness is acceptable on vowels that is not acceptable on consonants. Thus, instrumentation needs to be employed to make accurate observations during the critical production of consonants.

Velar movement is sometimes impaired in what might appear to be a normally symmetrical palate; here, the patient has a sluggish palate, sometimes as a symptom following a severe infectious disease (influenza, encephalitis, and so on). Pharyngeal movement is almost impossible to determine by direct oral examination; it is best seen by lateral-view video fluorographic film or with endoscopy (nasal or oral).

In some problems of nasality, particularly those not associated with palatal insufficiency, the relative size and carriage of the tongue may have some diagnostic relevance. For example, some problems of "functional" nasality may be related to inappropriate size of tongue for the size of the oral cavity, or to innervation problems of the tongue.

The clinician should make a thorough search for any openings of the hard or soft palate that might contribute to an articulation distortion or to some problem of nasal resonance. Some patients have small openings (fistulas) or lack of fusion around the border of the premaxilla, particularly in the area of the alveolar ridge. In some individuals such fistulas may produce air stream noises, creating articulatory distortion, but almost never will such isolated openings this far forward on the maxilla produce nasal resonance. The absence or presence of soft-palate and hard-palate clefts should be noted; if such clefts have been previously corrected surgically, the degree of closure should be noted. In the case of a bony-palate defect, for example, sometimes the bony opening has been covered by a thin layer of mucosal tissue, not thick enough to prevent oral cavity sound waves from traveling into the nasal cavity. This same observation applies to the occasional sub-mucosal cleft at the midline of the junction of the hard and soft palates. The major signs of a submucosal cleft are bifid or split uvula, inverted A-shape defect in the velum, lack of a palpable posterior nasal spine, or a thin soft palate in the midline portion. Any other structural deviations—of dentition, occlusion, labial competence, and so on—should be noted and considered with regard to their possible effects on speech production and nasal resonance.

Evaluation Measures

Many instruments available today can help the clinician evaluate various aspects of nasal resonance. These instruments can also be valuable in the process of deciding what to do for a patient with a nasalization problem. We consider separately instruments that provide aerodynamic data, acoustic information, radiographic visualization, and visual probe information:

Aerodynamic instruments. Pressure transducers and pneumotachometers are instruments of choice for measuring the relative air pressures and air flows emitting simultaneously from the nasal and oral cavities during speech (Warren, 1979). Pressure and flow data are measured from the two channels simultaneously, which permits relative comparisons. Normal speakers, except during the production of nasal consonants, exhibit relatively no nasal pressure or flow. Speakers with nasality problems, show deviations in the relative amount of nasal and oral flows, as is well documented in the recent work of Mason and Warren (1980) and Warren (1979). The aerodynamic procedures basically provide the clinician information about possible leakage through the nose when the velopharyngeal mechanism should be closed. Manometers have also been useful for measuring relative nasal-oral air flows. Manometers measure the amount of pressure of the emitted air stream and do not measure resonance per se. Two types of manometers are used clinically, the water-filled U-tube and the mechanical pressure gauge. Both of these measure air flow pressure and not nasality; however, in comparing oral with nasal readings, some indication of velopharyngeal competence is given, which may, of course, have some relevance to the judgment of nasality. The water-filled U-tube works this way: A glass U-tube is partially filled with a colored liquid, and one end of the tube is fitted into a rubber hose. The free end of the hose is fitted with a nasal olive. The olive is emplaced nasally, and any utterance of the patient that is characterized by nasal emission will displace the liquid and thus provide the patient and clinician with some visual evidence of nasal emission. The second type of manometer, a mechanical pressure gauge, is available but it has not proven to be an effective clinical tool for evaluating poor velopharyngeal function.

Acoustic instruments. The Tonar II was designed by Fletcher (1972) to provide relative data of the acoustic signal emitting from both the oral and nasal cavities: how much of the perceived voice signal is "coming" through the nose, how much from the mouth? The Tonar II provides for a running speech sample, a continuous feedback of the oral-nasal acoustic ratio, which is displayed on the instrument display panel. Because the oral-nasal acoustic ratio fluctuates with each utterance, a one-second or ten-second averaging may be set on the instrument by the clinician. The patient is asked to read or repeat a continuous verbal passage, speaking directly into the two separate microphones, one receiving the oral signal and one the nasal signal. The oral signal value is divided into the nasal signal value to yield the actual oral-nasal acoustic ratio, a process that is done automatically at one- or ten-second intervals (depending on the interval set by the clinician) by the Tonar II (Fletcher, 1972). The typical speaker with normal nasal resonance will experience a "top" oral-nasal ratio of under 10 percent. Speakers with severe hypernasality will experience ratios in excess of 80 percent. One advantage of using the Tonar II to analyze relative nasality is that it provides a continuous value specific to relative nasal and oral resonance in running speech.

Spectrographic and acoustic analysis have had increased use in the evaluation of patients with various voice disorders (Murry and Doherty, 1980; Takahashi and Koike, 1975); but have not been particularly useful in differentiating the types of nasal resonance deviations, such as hypernasality from denasality. It has been demonstrated spectrographically that speakers with increased nasalization demonstrate more prominent third formants with an increase in formant band width, accompanied by a rise in fundamental frequency. In his acoustic study of nasality using the spectrograph, Dickson (1962), concluded there was no way to "differentiate nasality in cleft-palate and non-cleft palate individuals either in terms of their acoustic spectra or the variability of the nasality judgments" (p. 111). It is doubtful that the visual writeout provided by the spectrograph can provide the clinician with any more information about the type of nasality he or she hears than does listening carefully to the same samples. The spectrograph can help identify the aperiodic noise of nasal emission, but differentiating between spectrograms of speakers with hypernasality and those with denasality or assimilative nasality is most difficult. As clinicians learn to use what spectral analyses the spectrograph can provide, however, the instrument may well become a most useful tool for studying various parameters of nasality.

A new instrument that we have used is the Nasometer (1987), produced by Kay Electronics. This adaptation of the Tonar II is clinically very useful. It provides visual feedback on a computer screen for the patient which allows the clinician to set a predetermined level of acceptable nasal to oral ratio. The peak of nasal productions is also demonstrated on the screen. (The Nasometer was pictured in Figure 6-1.)

Radiographic instruments. Radiographic studies of the velopharyngeal mechanism during speech provide ready information about structural and physiological limitations of the mechanism in those patients who demonstrate velopharyngeal incompetence. For example, through a lateral-view film we can determine the relative amount of velopharyngeal opening during speech, the length of the velum, relative movements, and so on (Bowman and Shanks, 1978). However, there are limitations to the use of lateral views attempting to view closure, because lateral wall movement of the pharynx, which may contribute heavily to velopharyngeal closure, cannot be visualized. Sometimes the patient is asked to swallow barium and, as the barium passes through the pharynx, measurements are made of the relative pharyngeal opening as it relates to the velopharyngeal closing mechanism (Skolnick, Glaser, and McWilliams, 1980). The most useful radiographic views of velopharyngeal closure require the patient to make some speech utterances, including phrases and sentences that include pressure consonants. The speech-language pathologist needs to work closely with the radiologist, presenting the speech tasks as the films are made and "reading" the films when they are completed. Sometimes a radiographic display can demonstrate a problem in velopharyngeal closure that cannot be detected by any other method.

Visual probe instruments. Shelton and Trier (1976) have written that direct measures of velopharyngeal competence through the use of "endoscopes, nasopharyngoscopes, and ultrasound apparatus" offer some advantages in making treatment decisions. The oral endoscope (Zwitman, Gyepes, and Ward, 1976) has been a useful instrument for determining the degree and type of velopharyngeal closure, as Figure 7–1

FIGURE 7-1. The velopharyngeal closure mechanism of a 4-year-old boy is examined by oral video endoscopy. Children and adults are routinely evaluated in this manner without the use of any topical anesthetic. When care is taken to build rapport, even younger children can be successfully evaluated.

shows. The body of the oral endoscope is extended above the tongue within the oral cavity so that the lighted tip and viewing window lie just below the uvula and within the oropharyngeal opening. By turning the viewing window up toward the velopharyngeal area, the velum, the lateral pharyngeal walls, and the posterior pharynx may be visualized. Two views of varying degrees of velopharyngeal closure in the same subject are shown in Figure 7–2.

Shelton et al. (1975) have used the oral panendoscope to provide subjects visual feedback about their particular closure patterns; by watching their panendoscopically viewed closure patterns on a TV monitor, subjects have been able to modify their closure patterns. Distinct variations in patterns of velopharyngeal closure have been demonstrated by Zwitman, Sonderman, and Ward (1974). Some subjects have only velar movement without associated pharyngeal wall movement, some subjects primarily have lateral and posterior pharyngeal wall constriction, and some subjects achieve closure by a combination of velar and pharyngeal movements. A nasal fiberoptic endoscope has been developed that places a small flexible scope through the nose and down into the pharynx, offering a view of velopharyngeal closure from above the closure site (Miyazaki, Matsuya, and Yamaoka, 1975). The primary advantage of the nasoscope is that it is not invasive to the oral cavity and consequently does not impede tongue or lip movements (a limitation of the oral endoscope). The oral and nasal endoscopic probes are effective instruments for assessing velopharyngeal competence in patients with nasal resonance problems, because they offer direct observation of velar length and movement, degree of lateral and posterior pharyngeal wall movement, and the kind of velopharyngeal closure the patient is using. Perhaps, most importantly, this examination allows the clinician and the patient to see the various types and degrees of velopharyngeal closure during a variety of phonetic contexts.

FIGURE 7-2.   This oral video endoscopic view of velopharyngeal closure demonstrates two degrees of closure in a sequence from (A) an open v-p mechanism, through (B) the bulging of Passavant's pad with posterior and lateral pharyngeal wall movement (bottom) and the velar movement (top).

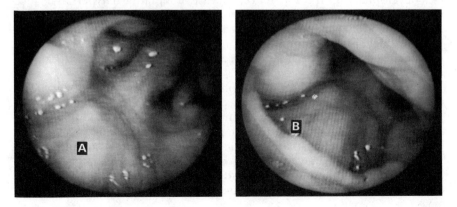

TREATMENT OF NASAL RESONANCE DISORDERS

Hypernasality

The presence of excessive nasal resonance (hypernasality) is relatively dependent on the judgment of the listener. That is, some languages and regional dialects require heavy nasal resonance and therefore consider pronounced nasalization of vowels to be normal. Others, however, such as general American English, tolerate little nasal resonance beyond the three nasal consonants. Thus, a native New Englander with a nasal "twang" exhibits normal voice resonance in Portland, Maine, but when he or she travels to New Knoxville, Ohio, the people there perceive his or her voice as excessively nasal. Variations do exist in the degree of nasality among the voices of the people in Ohio, of course, but a certain amount of resonance variability can exist among any particular population without anyone's being bothered by it. If, however, a particular voice in Ohio (or any other place) stands out as "excessively nasal," then that voice will be considered to have a resonance disorder. The judgment of hypernasality, then, is as dependent on the speech-language milieu of the speaker and his or her listeners as it is on the actual performance of the speaker.

The speaker who is judged to be hypernasal increases the nasalization of his or her vowels by failing to close his or her velopharyngeal port. This failure to close the velopharyngeal opening may be related to structural-organic defects, or it may have a functional etiology. Hypernasality frequently accompanies unrepaired cleft palate or a short palate. Among other organic causes of the disorder are surgical trauma, accidental injury to the soft palate, and impaired innervation of the soft palate as a result of poliomyelitis or some other form of bulbar disease. Sometimes temporary hypernasality may follow tonsillectomy as the patient attempts to minimize the pain by not moving his or her velopharyngeal mechanism. Some people speak with hypernasal resonance for purely functional reasons, perhaps to maintain a lingering internal model of a previously acceptable form of resonance, or perhaps to imitate the voice of someone they consider particularly attractive (such as a famous political figure). Although the majority of persons with hypernasal voices probably have some structural basis for their lack of velopharyngeal competence, the ease of imitating a hypernasal voice tells us that it could be relatively easy to become hypernasal with perfectly adequate and normal velopharyngeal equipment. Hypernasality is one voice problem in which the distinction must be made between organic and functional causes, as the treatment recommended is quite specific to the diagnosis.

If there are any indications of physical inadequacy of velopharyngeal closure, the primary role of the speech pathologist is to refer the patient to a specialist who can provide the needed physical correction—a plastic surgeon, say, or a prosthodontist. The postsurgical result must be evaluated by the speech pathologist after plastic surgery treatment is completed. If a prosthetic form of management is used, then the speech pathologist will be involved in the initial fabrication and fitting of the velar lift or obturator. Subsequent modifications of these devices will be directed by the speech pathologist, based upon the results of his or her speech testing and the patient's response to clinical speech stimulation. There is very little evidence that voice therapy to improve resonance has any positive effect in the presence of physical inadequacy. In fact, there is some indication that voice therapy to improve the oral resonance of patients with palatal insufficiency (those who lack the physical equipment to produce closure) will usually not only fail, but will also be interpreted by the patient as his or her own fault—as a defeat indicating low personal worth—and thus will take an obvious toll on the patient's self-image. An example of the uselessness of speech theapy in the presence of a severe inadequacy of velopharyngeal closure is provided by this case of a teen-aged girl who had received speech therapy for both articulation and resonance for a period of seven years:

Barbara, aged 14, had received seven years of group and individual speech therapy in the public schools and in a community speech and hearing clinic for "a severe articulation defect characterized by sibilant distortion, and for a severely nasal voice." Barbara's mother became upset because of Barbara's continued lack of progress and her tendency to withdraw from social contact with her peers, which, the mother felt, was related to her embarrassment over her continued poor speech. Barbara was evaluated by a comprehensive cleft-palate team, which, after reviewing her history, found that her nasality dated from a severe bout of influenza when she was 6 years old. The influenza had been followed immediately by a deterioration of speech. Subsequent speech therapy records were incomplete, although the mother reported that the therapy had included extensive blowing drills, tongue-palate exercises, and articulation work. Physical examination of the velar mechanism found that Barbara had good tongue and pharyngeal movements, but bilateral paralysis of the soft palate; even on gag reflex stimulation, only a "flicker" of palatal movement was observed. Lateral cinefluorographic films confirmed the relatively complete absence of velar movement. The examining speech pathologist found that Barbara had normal articulation placement of the tongue for all speech sounds, despite severe nasal emission of air flow for fricative and affricate phonemes. Low back vowels were relatively oral in resonance, whereas middle and high vowels became increasingly nasal. It was the consensus of the evaluation team that, with her structural inadequacy, Barbara was (and had been) a poor candidate for speech therapy. It was recommended that she receive a pharyngeal flap and be evaluated again several weeks after the operation. The surgery was successful and had an amazingly positive effect on Barbara's speech. Although hypernasality disappeared, some slight nasal emission remained. Barbara was subsequently enrolled in individual speech therapy, where she experienced total success in developing normal fricative-affricate production.

Such a case dramatically shows the futility of continued speech therapy when real structural inadequacy exists. Without the operation, Barbara could have received speech therapy for the rest of her life, with no effect whatsoever on her speech.

If velopharyngeal insufficiency is found, there are two primary alternatives for treatment, surgical or dental. When structural adequacy is achieved, remediation services of the speech-language pathologist can produce further changes in the patient's speech and resonance.

Surgical Treatment for Hypernasality   The evaluation may reveal the existence of such structural inadequacies as open fistulas, open bony and soft tissue clefts, submucous clefts, and short or relatively immobile soft palates. The plastic surgeon is usually the medical specialist most experienced in making decisions about when and if surgical closure of palatal openings is required. The speech pathologist is best able to assess the adequacy of the velopharyngeal port mechanism during speech. Usually, the major reason for surgical or prosthetic treatment in these patients is to improve speech.

A plastic surgeon wrote, "The surgeon requires the involvement of the speech pathologist in diagnosis as well as therapy" (Grace, 1984, p. 152). This includes preoperative testing, pressure and flow measurements, and mutual evaluation of cineradiographic studies. Paralleling the widespread use of direct endoscopic visual observation in medicine, the development of oral and nasoendoscopy has become an indispensable tool for diagnosing many speech disorders. Although nasoendoscopy is used by some plastic surgeons, it is often used by speech-language pathologists. It should be routinely available in centers managing organically based disorders (Grace, 1984).

When the diagnostic tests have been completed, the speech pathologist and surgeon must arrive at the plan for management. The speech pathologist should be familiar with available options for anatomic correction and should participate in the decision for surgery. "The surgeon must know the alternative treatments and anticipated results of his operations. The timing of surgery can be a mutual decision" (Grace, 1984, p. 152). For those individuals who have cleft palate, the primary surgical procedure usually involves closing the cleft and still maintaining adequate palatal length. Most patients with cleft palate, however, require multiple secondary surgical procedures at later times, such as rebuilding structures or eliminating earlier surgical scars. Many patients with hypernasality have velums that are too short for closure or velums that do not move adequately for closure. Such patients often profit from a surgically constructed pharyngeal flap. Here, the surgeon takes a small piece of mucosal tissue from the pharynx and uses it to bridge the excessive velopharyneal opening, attaching the tissue to the soft palate. This tissue acts as an excellent diverting structure by deflecting both air flow and sound waves into the oral cavity. Bzoch (1964), discussing the physiological and speech results for forty patients who had received pharyngeal flap surgery, reported that the procedure was most effective in reducing both hypernasality and nasal emission (if present) in most of the subjects. Although pharyngeal flap surgery, or any other form of palatal surgery, must not be considered a panacea for all resonance problems, it often helps align oral-nasal structures in such a way that, for the first time, speech and voice therapy can be effective.

Grace, a plastic surgeon, stated:

Postoperative speech testing is mandatory to objectively evaluate the results of surgery and reassess speech goals. The surgeon may profit from observing a postoperative evaluation, much as the speech pathologist would profit from seeing surgery. All too often there is a tendency for the surgeon to divorce the patient when the surgery is completed, with the expectation that the battle will be won or lost by the speech pathologist. (Grace, 1984, p. 154).

When speaking of surgery in cleft-palate patients, Grace (1984) further stated, "In truth, the success of surgery varies widely from patient to patient, and it can not be assumed that anatomy is restored to normal upon completion of the operation" (p. 154).

Dental Treatment of Hypernasality   Both orthodontists and prosthodontists may play important roles in treating individuals with hypernasality, particularly those with cleft palate. The orthodontist may have to expand the dental arches so that the patient can experience more normal palatal growth. The prosthodontist, by constructing various prosthetic speech appliances and obturators, may be able to help the patient preserve his or her facial contour and by filling in various maxillary defects with prostheses, may cover open palatal defects such as fistulas and clefts. The prosthodontist may also be able to build speech-training appliances to provide posterior velopharyngeal closure. In evaluating twenty-one adults with acquired or congenital palate problems, Arndt, Shelton, and Bradford (1965) found that both groups made significant "articulation and voice gains with obturation." Many cleft-palate subjects are fitted by prosthodontists with acrylic bulbs at the ends of their appliances; if the bulbs are well positioned against the posterior and lateral pharyngeal walls, often a noticeable reduction of both nasality and air escape results. Two lateral views of obturators are shown in Figure 7–3. When commenting on the role of the speech pathologist in the prosthodontic management of patients with velopharyngeal inadequacy, Ahlstrom (1984), a prosthodontist, stated, "One of the primary diagnostic services that a speech pathologist can offer is the determination of velopharyngeal competence in patients. This helps the prosthodontist in determination of what type of appliance or procedure may be necessary" (p. 150).

Many patients with dysarthria, which may include a hypernasality component, have immobile velums and thus lack sufficient velar movement to achieve closure. Such patients, who experience weakened or paralyzed soft palates, might well profit from consulting a prosthodontist about being fitted with a lift appliance to hold the immobile palate in a higher position so that some pharyngeal contact will be possible (Mazaheri, 1979). For nasality problems related to velopharyngeal inadequacy, speech pathologists should freely consult both orthodontists and prosthodontists for their ideas on how to achieve adequate functioning of the oral structures.

Voice Therapy for Hypernasality   Any attempts at voice therapy for hypernasality should be deferred until both the evaluation of the problem and attempts at physical correction have been completed. The primary requirement for developing good oral voice quality is the structural adequacy of

FIGURE 7-3.
Two views of speech appliances (obturators). (A) is from an adult with a neurogenic (dysarthria) problem of hypernasality; (B) is from a 5-year-old girl with structural (cleft palate) hypernasality with an extremely short velum following surgical repair. (1) is the palatal part, and (2) is the pharyngeal part. Note that the size of the pharyngeal part of the adult appliance is smaller than the corresponding part of the child's prosthesis.

the velopharyngeal closing mechanism. Without adequate closure, voice therapy will be futile. However, for individuals who speak with hypernasality for functional reasons, voice therapy can help develop more oral resonance. Added to this group are occasional patients who have had surgical or dental treatment that has left them with only a marginal velopharyngeal closing mechanism; in voice therapy, this mechanism may be trained to work more optimally.

Fletcher (1972) has described the Tonar II as a useful instrument for helping patients reduce hypernasality. The instrument was designed to provide patients with ongoing feedback information about their oral-nasal ratio. Fletcher recommends that clinicians set for each patient a ratio "goal." A reinforcement panel can then be connected to the Tonar panel so that the patient can be "systematically and instantaneously notified of success each time he meets the specified goal ratio and criterion of performance" (Fletcher, 1972, p. 331). If the patient is capable of developing greater oral resonance, he or she works incrementally, using the Tonar feedback system, toward the goal of acceptable oral resonance. The nasometer mentioned earlier (see also Figure 6–1) is a less expensive and more practical adaptation or outgrowth of the Tonar. The computer display gives the patient instant feedback information about the peak nasalence level, the target level of oral/nasal ratio, and the moment to moment level of nasalence.

The following facilitating techniques (described in Chapter 5) may be used successfully with the Nasometer or with a tape recorder, nasal listening tube, U-tube manometer, See Scape, nasal mirror, or stethoscope. They can even be used with the unaided ear.

1. *Altering Tongue Position.* A high, forward carriage of the tongue sometimes contributes to nasal resonance. Efforts to develop a lower, more posterior carriage may decrease the perceived nasality.

2. *Change of Loudness.* A voice that has been perceived as hypernasal will sometimes be perceived as more normal if some other change in vocalization is made. One change that often accomplishes this is an increase in loudness; by speaking in a louder voice, the patient frequently sounds less hypernasal.

3. *Ear Training.* If the patient is motivated to reduce his or her hypernasality, a great deal of therapy time should be spent learning to hear the differences between his or her nasal and oral resonances.

4. *Establishing New Pitch.* Some patients with hypernasality speak at inappropriately high pitch levels, which contribute to the listener's perception of nasality. Speaking at the lower end of one's pitch range seems to contribute to greater oral resonance.

5. *Explanation of Problem.* No voice therapy should ever be started without first explaining to the patient what the problem seems to be.

6. *Feedback.* Developing an aural awareness of hypernasality and some oral-pharyngeal awareness of what hypernasality "feels" like is a most helpful therapeutic device.

7. *Open Mouth.* Hypernasality is sometimes produced by an overall restriction of the oral opening. In such cases, efforts to develop greater oral openness may reduce the listener's perception of excessive nasality.

8. *Place the Voice.* Although for some patients, focusing on the facial mask area seems to increase nasality, for other patients, particularly those whose hypernasality is of functional origin, doing so noticeably improves resonance.

9. *Respiration Training.* Increased loudness is often achieved by respiration training.

These techniques achieve their results by altering the speech production—for example, by pitch modification, increased or decreased air flow, reduced air pressure on the velopharyngeal port, or enhanced feedback to the patient by using mirror fogging, acoustic changes, or changes in the location of vibratory pattens. We find these methods very successful with patients who have resonance disorders or whose velopharyngeal ports are "borderline adequate" or better. When the velopharyngeal mechanism is less adequate, surgical or prosthetic management is in order prior to initiating voice therapy techniques. When the degree of velopharyngeal mechanism adequacy is seriously in question, a period of intensive trial voice and articulation therapy may determine the need for other management approaches. This trial therapy should be intensive (three sessions per week minimum) but of short duration, (six weeks), and it should be conducted with the understanding that it is a trial to determine if further therapy is indicated or if some other management approach is required.

Denasality

Except for the nasal resonance required for /m/, /n/, and /ŋ/, vowels in American English require slight nasal resonance. In severe cases lack of nasal resonance produces actual articulatory substitutions for the three nasal phonemes as well as slight alterations of vowels. Denasality (hyponasality) is characterized by the diversion of sound waves and air flow out through the oral cavity, which permits little or no nasal resonance. More often than not, this problem is related to some kind of nasopharyngeal obstruction, such as excessive adenoidal growth, severe nasopharyngeal infection as in head colds, large polyps in the nasal cavity, and so on. Some patients who are hypernasal before surgical or dental treatment emerge from such treatment with complete or highly excessive velopharyngeal obstruction. Perhaps the pharyngeal flap is too broad and permits little or no ventilation of the nasopharynx, or perhaps an obturator bulb fits too tightly and results in no nasal air flow or nasal resonance. Such obstruction is the usual reason for a denasality problem, and the search for it must precede any attempt at voice therapy. We have seen a few cases, however, whose denasality was caused by psychological or other functional factors.

Nasal air-flow competence can be tested simply as part of an overall resonance evaluation: Ask the patient to take a big breath, close his or her mouth, and exhale through the nose. Then test the air flow through each nostril separately, compressing the nares of one nostril at a time with a finger. If there is any observable decrement in air flow, the nasal passages should be investigated medically. Appropriate medical therapy should precede any voice therapy.

Only rarely do patients have markedly denasal voices for wholly functional reasons. Even though their denasal resonance may originally have had a physical cause, that cause is no longer present, and the denasality may remain as a habit, a "set." Occasionally a patient has chosen a denasal voice as a model, for whatever reason, and has learned to match its denasality with some consistency. Voice therapy for increasing nasal resonance might include:

1. *Ear Training.* Considerable effort must be expended in contrasting for the patient the difference between the nasal and oral production of /m/, /n/, and /ŋ/. Oral and nasal resonance of vowels can also be presented for listening contrast.

2. *Explanation of Problem.* The resonance requirements for normal English must be explained to the patient, and his or her own lack of nasal resonance, particularly for /m/, /n/, and /ŋ/, pointed out. If the patient's problem is wholly functional, this explanation is of primary importance.

3. *Feedback.* Emphasis must be given to contrasting what it sounds like and "feels" like to produce oral and nasal resonance. The patient should be encouraged to make exaggerated humming sounds both orally and nasally, concentrating on the "feel" of the two types of productions.

Assimilative Nasality

The nasalization of vowels immediately before and after nasal consonants is known as *assimilative nasality.* Performance on stimulability testing will provide a good clue whether such nasal resonance is related to poor velar functioning or is functionally induced. A few neurological disorders, such as bulbar palsy or multiple sclerosis, prevent the patient from moving the velum quickly enough to facilitate the movements required for normal resonance. The velar openings begin too soon and are maintained too long, lagging behind the rapid requirements of normal speech and nasalizing vowels that occur next to nasal phonemes. Most cases of assimilative nasality, however, are of functional origin, and the patient shows good oral resonance under special conditions of stimulability.

Remember that in connected speech, all sounds are interdependent; as one sound is being produced, articulators are positioning for the next sound. This phonemic interdependence allows for a certain amount of assimilation, even in normal speech. Assimilative nasality, therefore, is another perceptual problem—that is, whether the speaker's nasalization of vowels adjacent to nasal phonemes is excessive or not depends on the perception of the listener. The perception of assimilative nasality is, of course, related to the perception of excessive nasality; a normal, minor amount of nasality in the vowels following nasal phonemes would not be perceived, and increased amounts of nasal resonance would be judged quite differently by different listeners, according to their individual standards and experience. Therapy for assimilative nasality is likewise highly variable. It is, in fact, largely related to the locale (in some areas such resonance is a normal voice pattern), the standards of the speaker or clinician, their motivations, and so on.

The Nasometer is a useful therapy instrument for the patient who wants to reduce his or her assimilative nasality. The clinician and the patient can set oral-nasal ratio goals that favor orality and then work incrementally toward eliminating the assimilative nasal resonance. Voice therapy for assimilative nasality is best attempted only by those patients who are strongly motivated to develop more oral resonance. Faciliting approaches (see Chapter 5) might include:

1. *Ear Training.* Ear training should help patients discriminate between their nasalized vowels and their oral vowels. Patients should listen to recordings of their own oral-consonant/vowel/oral-consonant words as contrasted with their nasal-consonant/vowel/nasal-consonant words, such as these pairs: bad-man, bed-men, bead-mean, bub-mum, and so on. Voice and diction books often contain word pairs matching monosyllabic words using /b/, /d/, and /g/ with those using /m/, /n/, and /ŋ/. Once the patient can hear the differences between oral and nasal cognates, see if he or she can produce them.

2. *Explanation of Problem.* Because nasal assimilations are difficult to explain verbally, any attempt at explanation should be accompanied by demonstration. The best demonstration is to present the contrast between oral and nasal resonance of vowels that follow or precede the three nasal phonemes.

3. *Feedback.* Although feedback can certainly be attempted with the problem of assimilative nasality, experience has found that few patients can monitor well what they are doing during conditions of ongoing feedback. Learning to listen to oneself critically with delayed feedback provided by some kind of auditory loop tape device has been helpful.

THERAPY FOR ORAL-PHARYNGEAL
RESONANCE PROBLEMS

Although during speech both the oral and pharyngeal cavities are con-stantly changing in size and shape, the oral cavity is the most changeable resonance cavity. Speech is possible only because of the capability for vari-ation of such oral structures as the lips, mandible, tongue, and velum. The most dramatic oral movements in speech are those of the tongue, which makes various constrictive-restrictive contacts at different sites within the oral cavity to produce consonant articulation. Vowel and diphthong pro-duction are possible only because of size-shape adjustments of the oral cav-ity that require a delicate blend of muscle adjustment of all oral muscle structures. Although many individuals display faulty positioning of oral structures for articulation, and thus articulate "badly," fewer individuals are recognized to have problems positioning their oral structures for reso-nance. Slight departures in articulatory proficiency are much more easily recognized than are minor problems in voice resonance. Even though an articulation error may be viewed consistently as a problem, faulty oral-pha-ryngeal resonance is usually accepted as "the way he or she talks." Nasality problems are more likely to be recognized by lay and professional listeners as requiring correction than are oral-pharyngeal resonance departures. Any judgment of resonance is heavily influenced by the appropriateness of pitch, the degree of glottal competence as heard in the periodic quality of phonation, and the degree of accuracy of articulation. Because quality of resonance, then, appears basically to be a subjective experience, the goal in resonance therapy must be to achieve whatever voice "sounds best."

Singing teachers have long been aware of the vital role the tongue plays in influencing the quality of the voice, and they devote considerable instructional and practice time to helping singing students develop opti-mum carriage of the tongue (Coffin, 1981). Although the postures needed to produce various phonemes will attract the tongue to different anatomic sites within the oral cavity, with noticeable changes of oral resonance, more objective evidence of the role of the tongue in oral resonance may be ob-tained through spectrographic and videofluorographic analysis. In the spec-tral analyses afforded by the spectrograph, we can study the effects of tongue positioning and the distribution of spectral formants. The second formant seems to "travel" the most, changing position up and down the spectrum for various vowel productions. The primary oral shaper for pro-duction of vowels appears to be the tongue. Decisions about quality reso-nance (for example, is the voice hypernasal or denasal) are, however, almost impossible to render from the visual inspection of spectrograms. It is most difficult to quantify formant variations and relate them to variations in voice quality. In describing the difficulty of spectrographic analysis, Moll (1968) has written that "this presumably more 'objective' measure involves human judgments which probably are more difficult than those made in judging nasality from actual speech" (p. 99). Visual inspection of the spec-trogram is a difficult task, particularly when one attempts to relate formant positioning to judgments of voice quality. As for the video fluorograph, its use for studying tongue, velar, mandibular, and pharyngeal movements, when such movements apply to voice quality, becomes far more effective when a voice track is added. The addition of the speaker's voice not only enables the viewer to match the sound of the voice with the analysis of the speaker's movements, but, more important, provides the viewer with the primary vehicle for determining whether a problem of quality exists; quality judgments cannot be made from the visual study of oral movements alone, but depend primarily on hearing the sound of the voice. By using both the pitch and intensity readings at the same time on the Visi-Pitch (1987), we have found that the stored tracings on the Visi-Pitch scope give useful information specific to better resonance. Often the resonance that sounds better to the ear is represented on the scope as less aperiodic (the frequency writeout has less scatter) and more intense (greater amplitude of the intensity curve). The "better-sounding" voice often comes quite unexpectedly as the clinician and the patient use various facilitating approaches in their search for good oral resonance. Once the "good" voice is achieved, the Visi-Pitch offers useful feedback for the patient, often confirming by improvement in the scope tracings the subjective judgments the clinician and patient have made.

REDUCING THE STRIDENT VOICE

One of the most annoying oral-pharyngeal resonance problems is the strident voice. We use the term *stridency*, which means the unpleasant, shrill, metallic-sounding voice that appears to be related to hypertonicity of the pharyngeal constrictors. Fisher (1975) described the strident voice as having brilliance of high overtones sounding "brassy, tinny, blatant." Physiologically, stridency may be produced by the elevation of the larynx and hypertonicity of the pharyngeal constrictors, which decrease both the length and the width of the pharynx. The surface of the pharynx becomes taut because of the tight pharyngeal constriction. The smaller pharyngeal cavity, coupled with its tighter, reflective mucosal surface, produces the ideal resonating structure for accentuating high-frequency resonance. Stridency may be developed deliberately—for example, by a carnival barker or a dimestore demonstrator for its obvious attention-getting effects—or it may emerge when a person becomes overly tense and constricts the pharynx as part of his or her overall response. A person who has this sort of strident voice—and who wants to correct it—can, in voice therapy, often develop some relaxed oral-pharyngeal behaviors that decrease pharyngeal constriction and lessen the amount of stridency. Anything that an individual can do to lower the larynx, decrease pharyngeal constriction, and promote general throat relaxation will usually reduce stridency. The following facilitating techniques (described in Chapter 5) are most helpful in reducing stridency:

1. *Chewing.* It is almost impossible to produce strident resonance under conditions of chewing. The various steps of chewing, detailed in Chapter 5, should be most helpful in reducing stridency.
2. *Ear Training.* Explore various vocal productions with the patient, with the goal of producing a nonstrident voice. When the patient is able to

produce good oral resonance, contrast this production with recorded strident vocalizations using loop tape feedback devices and following the various ear-training procedures.

3. *Establishing New Pitch.* The strident voice is frequently accompanied by an inappropriately high voice pitch. Efforts to lower the pitch level often produce a voice that sounds less strident.

4. *Explanation of Problem.* Although it is difficult to explain problems of resonance to someone else, sometimes such an explanation is essential if the patient is ever to develop any kind of self-awareness about the problem.

5. *Glottal Fry.* The glottal fry produces two beneficial effects. First, the fundamental frequency is somewhat lower following production of the glottal fry; and secondly, the resonating cavity of the laryngeal aditis is enlarged following the production of the glottal fry (especially on ingressive fry). The relaxation of the folds and the opening of the laryngeal aditis effectively reduce strident vocal quality.

6. *Hierarchy Analysis.* For the individual whose voice becomes strident whenever he or she is tense, it is important to try to isolate those situations in which his or her nonstridency is maintained.

7. *Open Mouth.* Because stridency is generally the product of over constriction, oral openness is an excellent way to counteract these tight, constrictive tendencies.

8. *Relaxation.* It is difficult to produce strident resonance under conditions of relaxation and freedom from tension. Either general relaxation or a more specific relaxation of the vocal tract is helpful in reducing oral-pharyngeal tightness.

9. *Yawn-Sigh.* Because the yawn-sigh approach produces an openness and relaxation that is completely the opposite of the tightness of pharyngeal constriction, it is perhaps the most effective approach in this list for reducing stridency.

IMPROVING ORAL RESONANCE

Two problems of oral resonance are related to faulty tongue position, a *thin* type of resonance produced by excessively anterior tongue carriage and a *cul-de-sac* type produced by backward retraction of the tongue. The thin voice lacks adequate oral resonance, and its user sounds immature and unsure of himself or herself. This problem, which is somewhat common among men and women, is characterized by a generalized oral constriction with high, anterior carriage of the tongue and only minimal lip-mandibular opening. The user of such a voice appears to be holding back psychologically, either withdrawing from interpersonal contact by demonstrating all the symptoms of withdrawal, or retreating psychologically to a more infantile level of behavior by demonstrating a baby-like quality. The first type, who withdraws from interpersonal contact, employs his or her thin resonance situationally, particularly when he or she feels most insecure; the second type uses the thin voice, the "baby resonance," more intentionally, in situations in which he or she wants to appear cute, to "get his or her own way," and so on. The following facilitating approaches (described in Chapter 5) have been useful in promoting a more natural, oral resonance:

1. *Altering Tongue Position.* We discussed the problem of the thin voice in Chapter 5. Specific procedures are developed there to promote more posterior tongue carriage.
2. *Change of Loudness.* When the resonance problem is part of a general picture of psychological withdrawal in particular situations, efforts to increase voice loudness are appropriate for overall improvement of resonance.
3. *Chewing.* Chewing promotes more natural carriage of the tongue.
4. *Establishing New Pitch.* The thin voice is perceived by listeners to be drastically lacking in authority. Frequently, the pitch is too high. Efforts to lower the voice pitch often have a positive effect on resonance.
5. *Feedback.* Those patients whose anterior resonance focus is related to situational tensions may use feedback apparatus to become aware of their varying states of tension. Feedback is best used with relaxation and hierarchy analysis.
6. *Hierarchy Analysis.* Symptomatic voice therapy is based on the premise that it is often possible to isolate particular situations in which we function poorly, with maladaptive behavior, and other situations in which we function comparatively well. By isolating the various situations and their modes of behavior, we can often introduce more effective behavior into "bad" situations, to take the place of the maladaptive behavior. For those individuals who use a thin voice in specific situations, particularly during moments of tension, hierarchy analysis may be a necessary preliminary step to eliminate the aberrant vocal quality.
7. *Open Mouth.* The restrictive oral tendencies of a thin-voiced speaker may be effectively reduced by developing greater oral openness.
8. *Relaxation.* If the thin vocal quality is highly situational and the obvious result of tension, relaxation approaches may be helpful, particularly when used in combination with hierarchy analysis.
9. *Respiration Training.* Sometimes direct work on increasing voice loudness requires some work increasing control of the air flow during expiration.
10. *Yawn-Sigh.* The yawn-sigh approach is an excellent way of developing a more relaxed, posterior tongue carriage.

Patients with a thin voice are often judged by listeners to be immature, young, or lacking in authority. We have provided successful voice therapy to several attorneys, managers, and executives who suffered from thin voice quality that were ineffective for their work. We helped one attorney improve his voice and his performance in the courtroom and during client conferences by using the open-mouth and glottal fry technique.

The cul-de-sac voice is found in individuals of various etiologic groups: patients with oral apraxia; cerebral palsied children, particularly the athetoid type, who have a posterior focus to their resonance added to their dysarthria; some patients with bulbar or pseudobulbar-type lesions, who have a pharyngeal focus to their vocal resonance; and deaf children. The cul-de-sac voice, regardless of its physical cause, is produced by the deep retraction of the tongue into the oral cavity and hypopharynx, sometimes touching the pharyngeal wall and sometimes not. The body of the tongue literally obstructs the escaping air flow and the periodic sound waves generated from the larynx below. Although such a voice is often found in individuals with neural lesions who cannot control their muscles, and among deaf children and adults, it is also produced situationally by certain individuals for wholly functional reasons. Such posterior resonance is very difficult to correct in patients who have muscle disorders related to various problems of innervation, particularly dysarthric patients. Resonance deviations in the deaf may be changed somewhat in voice therapy, as described in Chapter 6. For individuals who produce cul-de-sac resonance for purely functional reasons (whatever they are), the following facilitating approaches from Chapter 5 are useful:

1. *Altering Tongue Position.* Speech tasks designed to promote front-of-the-mouth resonance are helpful here. Review the section on resonance changes in the deaf in Chapter 6. The approaches described there for altering tongue position in deaf children apply to anyone working for more forward resonance.

2. *Feedback.* Posterior focus of voice resonance may for some patients be situationally related to tension. Feedback is often useful for helping these patients monitor their varying tension states.

3. *Ear Training.* If, in the search for a better voice, the patient is able to produce a more forward, oral-sounding one, this should be contrasted with his or her cul-de-sac voice.

4. *Hierarchy Analysis.* If cul-de-sac resonance occurs only in particular situations, perhaps at those times when the individual is tense and under stress, the hierarchy approach may be useful. If the individual can produce good oral resonance in low-stress situations, he or she should practice using the same resonance at levels of increasing stress, on up the hierarchy.

5. *Glottal Fry.* The production of the glottal fry opens the pharynx and the laryngeal aditis, thus enlarging the resonance cavity and adding to the openness of the whole vocal tract. The whole pharynx is relaxed, and thus the cul-de-sac resonance is eliminated.

6. *Place the Voice.* The forward focus in resonance required to place the voice in the facial mask makes the approach a useful one for patients with a cul-de-sac focus. High front vowels and front-of-the-mouth consonants are particularly good practice sounds to use with the place-the-voice approach.

7. *Relaxation.* Posterior tongue retraction during moments of stress is often a learned response to tension. The patient who can learn a more relaxed positioning of the overall vocal tract may be able to reduce excessive tongue retraction.

8. *Tongue Protrusion.* Because the tongue is extended outside of the mouth and the pitch is elevated, the base of the tongue is pulled forward and out of the oral pharynx. This eliminates the retracted tongue position that produces the back quality.

SUMMARY

Resonance deviations of the voice are often produced by physical problems of structure or function at various sites within the upper airway. Primary efforts must be given to identifying any structural abnormalities and correcting these problems by dental, medical, or surgical intervention. Speech-language pathologists play an important role in the early evaluation and diagnosis of a resonance problem, as well as in providing needed voice therapy to correct the problem. For both organic and functional resonance problems, specific facilitating approaches are listed to help patients develop better nasal and oral resonance.

8

VOICE THERAPY FOR PATIENTS WITH CANCER OF THE LARYNX

At this time, the total surgical removal of the larynx is still the most common treatment for cancer of the larynx. Total laryngectomy produces complete loss of the voice as well as other physiological and psychological changes in the patient (laryngectomee). Such amputation has a pronounced effect on the patient and the family. In this chapter, we describe the voice treatment options for partial and total laryngectomy patients, including all forms of alaryngeal voice (esophageal speech, artificial device use, and surgical options).

There have been a number of advances in the approach to managing laryngeal cancer in the past few years. Combined with early detection, these advances have helped lessen the trauma of laryngeal cancer for both the patient and the family. Conservation surgeries and better methods of radiation, as well as earlier diagnosis, have improved the final outcome for patients with laryngeal cancer. Early symptoms the patients first present to physicians include hoarseness, fullness in the throat, swallowing difficulty, pain in the neck or ear, or frequent unproductive throat clearing. Using mirror examination (laryngoscopy) or fiberoptic endoscopy, the physician may identify a laryngeal lesion; the tumor is subsequently studied by direct laryngoscopy and a biopsy (taking a sample of the lesion for microscopic examination). If the lesion is found cancerous, an overall medical-surgical management program is initiated by the physician. The earlier or the sooner the diagnosis of laryngeal cancer can be made, the more favorable the outcome prognosis (Johnson, Newman, and Olson, 1980).

A growing body of people are now diagnosed to have laryngeal cancer. For example, in 1975, there were 9,100 new cases of the disease annually in the United States, as compared with an estimated 10,700 new cases in 1980 (American Cancer Society, 1980). These 1980 data suggest a male-to-female ratio for laryngeal cancer of about five males for every female. The importance of early diagnosis is especially evident from the survival rate data (live more than five years) for laryngeal cancer and cancer in several other sites: larynx, 79 percent; breast, 85 percent; lung, 33 percent; oral, 67 percent

(American Cancer Society, 1980). Patients whose lesions were detected early have less chance of the disease spreading (metastasizing) to other sites. Nonetheless, even though 79 percent of the patients with laryngeal cancer survive at least five years after the diagnosis of their disease, some 32 percent of them experience some metastasis to other body sites.

The type of medical treatment for laryngeal cancer depends on the site and extent of the tumor. A small tumor that invades only one vocal fold can be successfully treated by radiation therapy alone, whereas an extensive cancer invasion of the larynx and the cervical lymph nodes may well require radiation therapy and a total laryngectomy. Because of the variety of tumor types at different sites in and adjacent to the larynx, a joint committee of otolaryngologists and other physicians (radiologists, oncologists) developed a staging category system that places the tumor in a particular staging category according to its extent and site (Batsakis, 1979). A lettering-numbering system is used to categorize the tumor. This enables communication among specialists who know where the tumor is and relatively how extensive it is by its classification number—for example, a Stage I "tumor is confined to one vocal cord with motility of cord maintained" (Batsakis, 1980, p. 137). Stage I and Stage II tumors are often successfully treated by radiation therapy alone and require no surgery. Patients might experience temporary voice problems related to their tumor masses and the effects of radiation therapy; however, the management of their voice problems by the speech pathologist would be entirely different from what would be required for the patient with a total laryngectomy. Therefore, our discussion of management by the speech pathologist of the patient with cancer, focuses separately on three types of patients: first, the patient with an altered larynx (but who still has one); second, the patient with a conventional but total laryngectomy; and third, the patient with a total laryngectomy who has undergone some new surgical procedures that permit the injection of pulmonary air into the esophagus to produce a new voice.

VOICE THERAPY FOR THE PATIENT WITH AN ALTERED LARYNX

One of the primary functions of the larynx is to protect the airway. Therefore, any lesion or neoplasm that grows on a portion of the larynx must be evaluated in terms of its possible threat to the airway. Often, small tumors that occupy a portion of the supraglottal structure (such as the epiglottis) can be successfully treated with radiation therapy, with little or no effect on either respiratory function or on voice. A combined radiation-surgery approach is often effective in permanently eradicating a supraglottal tumor. Less extensive glottal carcinomas can often be treated similarly with radiation-surgery without total removal of the larynx (laryngectomy). Any surgical procedure, however, that compromises one of the vocal folds and its function may cause airway difficulties; aspiration is the most common such complaint. That is, the partially or totally excised vocal fold cannot play its normal closure role, which may result in both aspiration and faulty voice. The surgeon evaluates how much laryngeal tissue must be cut away to remove the invading cancer, hopeful that some respiratory valving and voice can remain. Sometimes vocal fold carcinomas are successfully removed but some surgical reconstruction is required to restore the involved fold its functional capabilities (Som and Arnold, 1960). Various procedures have been used to build up the involved fold, including Teflon injection, tissue grafts, and muscle transplants (Ogura and Biller, 1969; Tucker et al., 1979). Some patients require an extended hemilaryngectomy, which involves a vertical cutting away of one-half of most of the soft tissues of the larynx, and requires major surgical reconstruction of the involved portion in order to effect sphincteric closure capability. Tucker et al. (1979) report success with some patients who have had near-total laryngectomy. They reconstruct the larynx by utilizing the epiglottis as the primary tissue source for creating a new glottis that is capable of valving and producing voice.

Patients who have had successful laryngeal surgery for carcinoma, short of having a total laryngectomy, are often referred to speech-language pathologists for voice evaluation and voice therapy. Each patient is unique, and voice problems are primarily related to the particular glottal configuration present after surgery. Upon the referral of their surgeons to speech pathologists for voice improvement, we find patients who have survived serious operations for laryngeal cancer "high" and receptive to what we are able to do. In most cases, we begin by explaining to the patients that the primary function of the larynx, valving, now appears to be present. After conventional voice evaluation testing (case history, peripheral evaluation, respiration measurements, frequency and intensity measurements, and determinations of voice quality), the focus of the evaluation is on searching with the patients using various therapy facilitating approaches (Chapter 5), to determine which seem to produce better-sounding voices. Patients often need some counseling specific to the observation that the goal is to produce "the best voice possible, and not necessarily the same kind of voice they had before." Such patients require the clinician to explain in detail what can be accomplished in voice, using the altered mechanism as optimally as possible.

In addition to explaining the problem, other facilitating approaches are useful:

1. *Feedback.* Using some kind of feedback device, such as viewing one's respiratory cycle on an oscilloscope or looking at voice frequency level using a Visi-Pitch, seems to help the patient establish an awareness of a new compensatory way of producing voice.
2. *Change of Loudness.* Direct work on increasing loudness will often produce a clearer, more acceptable voice. It may take greater transglottal pressures to produce optimal vibration of the altered glottis.
3. *Ear Training.* The patient usually requires ongoing auditory feedback of his or her various voice productions. The best voice he or she is able to produce using any new method should be captured on some kind of audiotape and fed back to the patient. The patient must learn to listen for the best voice he or she is able to produce with the least amount of effort.
4. *Masking.* Some patients volitionally cannot produce a voice loud and strong enough to be heard. The use of masking sometimes facilitates

the production of the stronger voice. Follow the procedures developed in Chapter 5.

5. *Place the Voice.* The patient with laryngeal cancer naturally has much focus on the "throat." Placing the voice in the area of the facial mask, more imaginary than real, does help the patient divert attention away from the laryngeal area, and often permits the larynx to function in a more natural manner.

6. *Pushing Approach.* Many patients who have had various operative procedures on the larynx lack firm vocal fold approximation for phonation. The pushing approach encourages tighter, almost sphincteric glottal closure, and these patients thus have more normal sounding voices. The approach should be abandoned once clear (less aperiodic) phonation can be established.

7. *Respiration Training.* The patient with an altered larynx may have to increase the optimization of his or her respiratory patterns for speech. The lack of an efficient or normal mechanism may require increased air flows and transglottal pressures to produce normal-sounding phonation.

The successful voice clinician with a patient who has an altered larynx is forced to be eclectic—that is, to find what works to produce the best voice and to avoid those approaches that are not facilitative. The voice therapy for such patients is highly individualized.

The following guidelines have been helpful for developing the best possible voice by the patient with a subtotal laryngectomy or partially altered larynx:

1. First, *sustain the tone* that the patient is able to produce. In order to be able to work with a vocal tone the voice must be durable. Often the tone is best sustained by being produced softly.

2. Next, attempt to *vary the pitch* of the tone. Pitch variation, even a very slight one, often improves vocal quality. This variation is best accomplished by head turning, digital manipulation, chin lowering, loudness changes, head and chin extension.

3. *Interruption and reinitiation* of the tone is the next step. It is important from both a production and monitoring standpoint for the patient to be able to interrupt the tone and reinitiate it without loss of quality, pitch, or loudness characteristics.

4. *Ease of production* is an important factor if a patient is to habituate a style of phonation and begin to use a new voice. All excessive muscle tension and unnecessary effort must be identified and eliminated. Careful observation by the patient and clinician using a mirror is useful. Videotape studies are valuable, as well.

VOICE THERAPY FOR THE PATIENT WITH A TOTAL LARYNGECTOMY

In this section we consider patients who have had a total laryngectomy, utilizing conventional surgical procedures with no fistulas or shunts surgically constructed to introduce air into the esophagus. Such patients are told that they will have a total laryngectomy and that, following the surgery, they will be taught to use voice again. We will consider the preoperative and postoperative visits by speech-language pathologists, the patients' postoperative medical care and problems, and types of voice therapy.

The Preoperative and Postoperative Visits

Surgeons have varying views about the advisability of preoperative or postoperative visits for patients about to have a laryngectomy. We encourage laryngectomees to become members of the International Association of Laryngectomees (IAL) as soon as possible. They will receive the *IAL News* and will quickly realize that they are not alone. We are convinced that preoperative speech evaluation and preoperative speech counseling are vitally important, but the final decision to allow such visits must be made by the surgeon and the patient. The same is true of the decision to have a preoperative visit with a well-rehabilitated laryngectomee. Most of our surgical colleagues also encourage such preoperative visits, counseling, and evaluations. As a matter of fact, attending surgeons on occasion ask us to counsel reluctant patients and to help them decide about surgery. In most such cases, the patients finally opt for the surgery, which they strongly resisted or refused prior to the counseling. The most important factors in changing their decision to have surgery, were careful answering of their questions, playing several tapes of successful alaryngeal speakers, demonstrating the use of artificial devices, and having some of them visit carefully selected laryngectomees.

Some patients, because of too much tissue removal or because of intellectual or personality problems, may never learn to use esophageal speech. To expose such patients before surgery to a good esophageal speaker in fact implies to the patients that they, too, will be able to speak again with a little training. After the operation, such patients may interpret their own faulty voice, as compared with the excellent voice of the speaker who came to visit, as a sign of personal failure. As Diedrich and Youngstrom (1966) have written, "When a successfully speaking laryngectomee pre- or postoperatively visits a patient, there is the implication that the patient will learn to speak as the visitor does. Obviously, this is not true" (p. 138). It might be better at the time of the preoperative visit, if such a visit is requested, to include both a speech pathologist and a laryngectomee, the latter to demonstrate overall successful adjustment (he is back in the community at his former job), rather than good speech per se.

A brief preoperative visit by a speech pathologist and a laryngectomee is perhaps the best way to provide the most relevant information about the patient and also to give the patient some psychological support. It is important for the speech pathologist to assess how the patient speaks *before* the operation. Through conversation, the speech pathologist should roughly evaluate the patient's articulatory proficiency and overall speech intelligibility, and, because the long-term goal is to help the patient achieve intelligible speech, he or she should evaluate the patient's performance (independent of obvious voicing problems) in terms of rate of speech, dialect or accent, articulation errors, degree of mouth opening when speaking, eye contact, and so on. In the brief preoperative contact with the patient and his or her family, the speech pathologist should convey confidence that the "patient *will* talk again." In assuring the patient that a method will be found that he or she will be able to use, the speech pathologist should describe several methods of therapy and give a brief demonstration of the artificial larynx. He or she might tell the patient that as soon as the surgeon gives the "go ahead," the patient will be provided temporarily with an artificial larynx, so that he or she will be able to talk to people instead of writing out messages (as many laryngectomees have been instructed to do, as if using the artificial larynx would "contaminate" their chances of learning esophageal speech).

The speech pathologist should then introduce the laryngectomee companion, stressing in the introduction the laryngectomee's employment, social milieu, and so on. The laryngectomee should then discuss how life after the operation has closely paralleled life before it (hopefully, this is the case). He or she may answer a few of the patient's questions about learning to speak again, or about the local laryngectomee club, and so on. The laryngectomee should make it clear to the patient that after the operation he or she will come back and visit a bit longer. The speech pathologist should conclude the preoperative visit by saying that speech instruction will be started as soon as the surgeon gives the word, and that until that time, after the operation, it will probably do little good to carry out any kind of speech practice.

The surgeon usually requests the postoperative visit a few days after surgery. At this time the speech pathologist and/or the laryngectomee visitant often realize that their role in the patient's rehabilitation is far more than teaching the patient to use a new voice. Not until after the operation, when the patient actually begins to experience its many overwhelming effects, does he or she become frightened and depressed, and require realistic and straightforward answers to questions. Diedrich and Youngstrom (1966) vividly describe the laryngectomee's new problems:

> Laryngeal amputation is much more subtle than losing an arm or leg. In fact, just to say the word amputation gives one a different feeling about what is lost than to say the word laryngectomy. The full impact of amputation of the larynx is not ordinarily apparent. A fully clothed laryngectomee walking down the hall does not look much different from anyone else. It is not until he is asked to speak, cough, breathe, eat, smell, bathe, lift, cry, or laugh that his differences become apparent. In other words little is left unaffected in the laryngectomee's physical, psychological, and social behavior. (p. 66).

The first postoperative visit, therefore, should have a certain amount of flexibility, so that the visitors can respond to whatever questions the patient may have about these physical and psychological changes, and perhaps alleviate some of the patient's concerns about talking again. There is some advantage to bringing along some printed material, such as a few of the pamphlets about laryngectomy problems provided by the American Cancer Society. These materials offer the patient and family answers to many problems they may be facing. Selected laryngectomees from local laryngectomy clubs are often effective in relating their firsthand experiences with some of the postoperative problems the patient may have; for example, the physical problem of mucus in the stoma is often an early complaint, and it should be pointed out to the patient that successful control of excessive mucus at the stoma site is usually developed early. Just as with the preoperative visit, the combination team of the speech pathologist and the laryngectomee visitant is most appropriate for the first visit after surgery.

Some patients are bothered by the physical disfigurement they begin to become aware of postoperatively. The open stoma in the neck is often the first anatomic disfigurement of which the patient becomes aware. The patient who has additional radical neck surgery for the removal of cancerous lymph nodes experiences additional disfigurement and large vertical scarring in the lateral neck area in addition to the laryngectomy. In the immediate postoperative period, the patient's surgical sites are well covered with bandages. As dressings are removed during the days that follow surgery, some patients experience violent feelings toward the dramatic alterations in their appearance. Both the patient and the family may need some guidance by the physician and nursing staff to help them accept the physical changes in appearance as well as in function of respiration and phonation.

Before the first visit to the new laryngectomee, the speech pathologist should ask the surgeon when the patient will be able to begin speech-voice training and when he or she will be able to use the artificial larynx. The decision when to begin either speech training or artificial larynx usage is dependent on the overall surgical healing of the patient. Sometimes difficulty in healing or the development of fistulas will be aggravated by speech practice or by using the artificial larynx. Training should begin, whenever possible, as soon as the patient's physical condition permits. Several studies by questionnaire (Diedrich and Youngstrom, 1966; Horn, 1962) have found that the average time lapse between the operation and the beginning of speech training is from two to four months. In this interim, the average patient relies primarily on writing to communicate. Horn further reports that adequate speech proficiency is not acquired until seven months after surgery, and Diedrich and Youngstrom place the time at up to one year. During this protracted time of acquiring adequate speech, usually of the esophageal type, the typical patient relies on writing as an auxiliary aid to communication. Diedrich and Youngstrom make a strong argument for utilizing the artificial larynx as a regular training device before the patient learns esophageal speech. Why have the patient write communications before or during the early learning stages of esophageal speech when the artificial larynx can provide actual speech practice and oral communication right from the beginning? The artificial larynx helps the patient develop an early awareness of the relative independence of voice from articulation (he or she can still articulate), appreciate the need for phrasing, and develop articulatory skill postoperatively (the reduction in articulation proficiency that some patients experience after surgery responds well to practice). The clinician should demonstrate for the patient the use of an electronic larynx, such as the Western Electric artificial larynx or the Cooper-Rand artificial larynx (both shown in Figure 8–1), which most patients can learn to use

FIGURE 8-1.
Two artificial larynges. The Western Electric artificial larynx (top) is held in the hand and the vibrating head is placed firmly against the neck, permitting its sound vibrations to be introduced through the skin into the patient's hypopharynx. The Cooper-Rand artificial larynx (bottom) is carried in the pocket. A connecting wire is attached to the vibrating oscillator, which is held in the hand and is attached to a small plastic tube that introduces the voice sound directly into the patient's mouth. The Western Electric artificial larynx is distributed through any local Bell Telephone office. The Cooper-Rand artificial larynx is distributed through Luminaud, Box 257, 7670 Acacia Avenue, Mentor, Ohio 44060.

with relative ease. However, *learning* to use an instrument is required, because few patients are able to use one well without some formal instruction. Duguay, who has had experience with thousands of laryngectomees, states that he *teaches all esophageal speakers to use an artificial larynx* (Duguay, 1986, p. 14). We discuss artificial larynx instruction later in this chapter.

The postoperative visit should also, whenever possible, include the patient's spouse. If the visit includes both the speech-language pathologist and a good laryngectomee speaker (who usually represents a local laryngectomee club sponsored by the International Association of Laryngectomees), time should be given for the patient and spouse to ask the visiting laryngectomee some questions directly. Many patients report that the postoperative visit by the laryngectomee provided them with the inspiration and motivation they needed to learn esophageal speech. As more than one laryngectomee has said, "When I heard that he could speak so well without a larynx, I knew that I could, too." The postoperative visit usually concludes with some arrangements made for future voice therapy and perhaps the laryngectomee's promise to visit the patient again soon.

Postoperative Medical Care and Problems of the Laryngectomee

As important as voice restoration may be, and as important as the speech pathologist's role may become, the primary consideration during and immediately after surgery is the preservation of life. Control of bleeding, preservation of the airway, prevention of infection, and nourishment of the patient are of primary concern to the medical team caring for the patient. In the typical laryngectomy, the entire laryngeal mechanism is removed, including the hyoid bone (see Figure 8–2). The hypopharyngeal opening into the esophagus and the esophagus itself are usually well preserved, although some of their spincteral functions may be somewhat diminished by the removal of their attachments (hyoid bone, thyroid and cricoid cartilages). The trachea, which loses its connection with the pharynx and mouth, is brought to the skin surface and is attached directly superior to the suprasternal notch at this level. A permanent opening (tracheostomy) is constructed, through which the patient will forever breathe. After surgery an L-shaped plastic tube (cannula) is placed in the stoma (opening) to keep the stoma open and to prevent natural healing. The stoma must be kept open to permit unobstructed breathing. The inverted L-shaped cannula is used in this way: The tube is placed through the opening with the down shaft of the cannula going below the stoma into the trachea and the horizontal shaft remaining within the stoma opening. Some patients wear the cannula tube only for a few weeks after surgery; some laryngectomees prefer to wear the cannula all the time. If there were known or suspected cancerous nodes in the neck, the patient may have had, in addition to the laryngectomy, a radical neck dissection. This procedure involves the removal of the cervical

FIGURE 8–2.
The throat of a laryngectomee, before and after surgery. The broken lines designate normal structures present before the surgical operation. The patient has had removed (A) the hyoid bone; (B) the arytenoid cartilages; (C) the cricoid cartilage; (D) the thyroid cartilage. Note (E), the posterior tracheal-anterior esophageal wall. After the operation, the residual neck and head structures of the laryngectomee are shown by the solid lines; the new tracheal opening, the tracheotomy, is seen at (F).

lymph nodes as well as many of the normal-appearing nodes adjacent to the suspected cancer site. The dissection is usually done initially on one side only, and is sometimes followed later by the same procedure on the other side. Radical neck dissection greatly increases the site of surgical alteration, and the postsurgical medical and nursing care required is usually more intensive.

The new laryngectomee usually requires a day or two of absolute bedrest following surgery. The head of the bed should be slightly elevated so that the patient's head will be slightly flexed toward the chest, thus avoiding any tension on the sutures. Ambulation is started as soon as the patient's condition permits, frequently on the second or third day. The patient's fluid and caloric intake require constant monitoring, and attention must be given to his or her vital cardiac, pulmonary, and urinary functions. The patient will receive various antibiotics and analgesics (pain killers) as required. To prevent the patient from swallowing, and thus give the pharyngeal and esophageal structures time to heal, the patient is fitted with a feeding tube inserted through the nose and going directly through the pharynx into the esophagus and hence into the stomach. The feeding tube is usually removed on the eighth to the tenth postoperative day, if there is no unhealed fistula (small opening) between the esophagus and trachea or between the pharynx and the outer skin. About the time that fistulas are healed the surgeon gives approval to start voice-speech instruction. The referral to the speech pathologist and the beginning of voice instruction should be started, if possible, before the patient leaves the hospital.

Because of the typical delay between the patient's discharge from the hospital and the first postoperative visit by the speech pathologist, we often conduct the first voice therapy session in the hospital room four or five days postoperatively. This early postop visit, which must have the surgeon's approval, helps the patient start using a few selected words as soon as possible, provides encouragement to the patient and spouse, instructs the patient on beginning to use the speech structures again, and sets the tone for speech-voicing instruction. We use the intraoral Cooper-Rand for this first session in order to minimize any pressure on neck tissues. Most important, we keep these first therapy sessions short, usually no longer than fifteen or twenty minutes. We conclude the session by scheduling the day and time of the next visit, assuring the patient of our continued interest and promoting an atmosphere of prognostic optimism. Also, before the patient is discharged, he or she usually receives detailed nursing instructions on the care of the excision sites, maintenance of the airway, and cleansing of the cannula.

Some laryngectomees are more concerned about physical changes and problems after surgery than they are about their inability to voice. The overall health of the patient eventually becomes about the same as it was before surgery. Typical problems that patients report are related to air intake, changes in digestion, diminished taste and smell, and social adjustment.

Air-Intake Problems   Many new laryngectomees are bothered a great deal by the natural increase of mucus in the trachea and at the stoma site. It is physiologically desirable for pulmonary air to be relatively warm and moist, which is the basic reason for the increase of tracheal mucus in the laryngectomee. In low humidity surroundings there needs to be increased mucus. This problem can, however, be reduced somewhat by moistening the air in the home with a humidifier or steam inhalation device. Coughing is a frequent problem for the laryngectomee. Because the cough is more of an aspirate wheeze, a few people often react negatively to it. Most laryngectomees report that they try to avoid coughing in public, excusing themselves, if necessary, to cough and clean their stomas of excessive mucus in private. The collection of mucus in the stoma area requires systematic care by the laryngectomee. He or she is instructed always to wear some protective covering over the stoma, such as a crocheted bib, a gauze bib, or a foam or plastic screen guard, as shown on the right in Figure 8–3. This covering protects the airway from irritants and also provides a site where moisture (mucus, air stream) can collect to help moisten stoma inhalations. The patient develops a regular schedule for cleaning the stoma covering and removing excessive mucus, using a gauze pad or handkerchief (a lint-type paper tissue should be avoided). Care must be taken to avoid the buildup of mucus crustings at the stoma site; applying a water-soluble salve, such as K-Y or Neosporin, to the stoma will often prevent these crusts from occurring. Most laryngectomees also discover that while bathing and showering, they must take special care to protect the stoma from water; the relative ease with which water can enter the neck stoma makes such activities as

FIGURE 8–3. On the left the laryngectomee displays an open tracheostomy; on the right the stoma is covered with a foam self-adhesive covering (manufactured by Radio House, Inc., Nampa, Idaho, 83651). Used by permission of Dean Rosecrans.

swimming, boating, and stream fishing extremely hazardous. For more detailed descriptions of stoma care, such as cleaning the cannula, refer to materials provided by the American Cancer Society, such as articles on the subject in the *IAL News* (published by the International Association of Laryngectomees). Some of the breathing problems and special needs of the laryngectomee are outlined in *First Aid for Laryngectomees* (1986); for example, if artificial respiration is ever necessary for the laryngectomee, these warnings are given: Keep the neck opening clear, avoid twisting the head to one side, apply oxygen only to the stoma, avoid throwing water on the head, and use mouth-to-stoma resuscitation.

Digestive Difficulties The trapping of air in the esophagus for esophageal speech carries with it the possibility that some esophageal air will move down into the stomach and into the intestinal tract. Gardner (1961) reported that among fifty-four laryngectomees with no gastrointestinal symptoms before surgery, forty-one (76 percent) acquired such symptoms chronically after surgery. Gardner believed that one of the negative features of the swallow method is its high frequency of gastric complaint. The patient swallows air into the stomach and subsequently experiences bloating, pain, and flatulence. Diedrich and Youngstrom (1966) found that 71 percent of their questionnaire respondents reported an increase of gastrointestinal symptoms, because they often trapped "more air than they utilize in the phonation of phrases and short sentences" (p. 122). Other findings specific to digestive problems in the same questionnaire were that about one-third of the respondents had difficulty swallowing and sucking, about half had difficulty drinking from a fountain or drinking soup with a spoon, more than one-third permanently took longer to eat, and the majority suffered an increase of heartburn. Another feeding problem that the laryngectomee must learn to accommodate is that simultaneous eating and talking (difficult and undesirable in normal people) is almost impossible for the esophageal speaker. Some patients who have had extensive pharyngeal surgery experience problems swallowing; for many the hypopharynx and the cricopharyngeus opening is too small. These patients often require that the surgeon effect esophageal dilation using esophageal dilators (bogies) placed intraesophageally to stretch the esophagus to a desired diameter. Patients requiring esophageal dilation may well experience temporary setbacks in their mastery of esophageal voice.

Diminished Taste and Smell Related to the problem of feeding is the possibility that after surgery the patient will experience diminished taste. Forty-one percent of the laryngectomees in the Horn report (1962) and 31 percent of those in the Diedrich and Youngstrom sample (1966) indicated that their taste was less accurate after surgery. In elaborating on the taste problem, Diedrich and Youngstrom wrote that only 4 percent of their group had no sense of taste and that many patients could only detect strong sweet or acid tastes. The sense of smell, however, is usually diminished or wholly absent; the inability to smell normally was reported by 79 percent of Horn's respondents and 95 percent of Diedrich's and Youngstrom's. Over time, however, some laryngectomees do report a gradual increase in their ability to smell, although for the majority of patients the sense of smell remains permanently impaired. Such warning smells as smoke or leaking gas may not be recognized by the laryngectomee.

Problems of Social Adjustment.   The emotional trauma of losing one's voice is particularly poignant in the early postoperative period, when the patient is still in the hospital. At this time a visit by a lay laryngectomee is very important. Whitler (1961) described the typical patient's reaction to this visit:

> One of the first persons to come to see me when I had regained a little strength was a man who had a similar operation some years ago. He walked into the room and with a cheery, broad grin, said, "Hello, Mr. Whitler, you have now joined a rather exclusive group!" I was astounded. Here was a man who obviously lived by breathing through a tube in his neck, exactly like myself, did not have a larynx as I did not have one, and yet here he was talking to me . . . I knew then that if he could so could I. (p. 3)

The great value of the laryngectomee club, usually a chapter of the International Association of Laryngectomees, is the early encouragement it gives the new laryngectomee. Eventually, if his or her total rehabilitation is successful, the laryngectomee no longer *takes* from the organization, but belongs to it for what he or she is able to contribute to new laryngectomees in their first few postoperative months.

The Horn study (1962) of 3,366 laryngectomees offers some interesting data on the psychosocial adjustment of laryngectomees: One of the primary problems the patient faces is financial loss. For example, the average laryngectomee who was employed at the time of his or her operation lost 153 work days (five months). The patient's major resources during this recovery period existed in this order of frequency: personal savings, own full salary continuing, spouse's salary, company sick benefits, medical insurance. One out of five laryngectomees who answered Horn's question about borrowing stated that they had to borrow money to cover some of their medical costs. Horn reported that two out of three respondents reported a drop in income following the operation, and that 60 percent of those reporting a drop attributed it to their laryngectomy and their impaired facility for communication. The percentage of those who retired doubled from 12 percent before the operation to 24 percent soon after, and the percentage of those unemployed rose from 2 percent before to 8 percent after. The greatest job and economic changes, usually to lower income levels, occurred in managerial, sales, clerical, skilled-labor, and semiskilled occupations; professional and unskilled-labor occupations reported little change in status.

Many new laryngectomees are embarrassed about using various forms of alaryngeal speech, particularly with strangers. In the study by Diedrich and Youngstrom (1966), 50 percent of the seventy-two patients who responded to the question about embarrassment replied that there were continuing situations in which they experienced acute embarrassment over the way they spoke. Some probably become tense because of awkward, insensitive listeners whose inept responses embarrass the speaker. There is little laryngectomees can do to reconstruct their listening world, but after contin-

ued success they learn to adjust and take in stride the occasional bad situation. Speech pathologists may sometimes have to counsel laryngectomees
to focus on good speech, and effective communication, rather than on the
occasional breakdowns that may come when speaking with inadequate loudness in noisy situations or to persons with less than adequate hearing. The
laryngectomees' sensitivity to how well they are received by others is a
highly individual thing, perhaps a matter of long-established personality.
Diedrich and Youngstrom (1966) reported that the most frequently listed
factors in overcoming self-consciousness were the patient's "determination
to talk," the feeling that "there was no other choice," and his or her convic-
tion that "one had to make the best of it" (p. 75).

We have found that two attitude statements in particular seem to help
patients survive the rehabilitation period and arrive at total rehabilitation:
"I am going to talk regardless of the problems this form of speech may
present to my listener," and "I have to help my listener adjust to my new
speech pattern by being the best alaryngeal speaker possible, or by being
willing to repeat phrases or words, or by restating an idea in different
words."

Some counseling of both patient and family before the operation, as
well as after, seems to promote optimum long-range rehabilitation. The patient should be clearly told by the surgeon what to expect after the operation about such things as breathing through the stoma, feeding by tube,
inability to voice, or postoperative communication aids (writing pad, artificial larynx, gestures). The family, also, must be given a clear picture of what
the patient's postoperative problems will be. Although family members
should be understanding and concerned, they must avoid becoming overly
protective (such as by cleaning the stoma for the patient); they should allow
the patient to become thoroughly independent, taking care of his or her
own nursing needs and making his or her own rehabilitational and voca-
tional plans. The more that can be done to approximate the living patterns
experienced by the patient before the surgery, the greater the likelihood of
successful rehabilitation.

Kalfuss (1969) has reported that a surprising number of physicians
who perform laryngectomies in relatively large numbers and even in large
urban areas are lacking in knowledge about the methods of alaryngeal
speech available to patients. These surgeons have stated that they are not
certain how esophageal speech is produced and that they are uncomfortable listening to alaryngeal speakers. Finally, many of the responding surgeons in the Duguay (1986) study indicated that they were embarrassed to
discuss various aspects of the postsurgical condition with the patient or the
family. Thus, it is often up to the speech pathologist to counsel the patient
and the family on the physiological and psychological changes following
total laryngectomy or to make a referral for such counseling.

VOICE TRAINING OF LARYNGECTOMEES

The primary goal of speech pathologists working with laryngectomees is to
help the patients develop functional speech. The term *alaryngeal speech,* first

introduced by Kallen (1934), refers to any kind of nonlaryngeal phonation—esophageal, buccal, pharyngeal, via an electronic larynx, or whatever.
The focus of early voice therapy is to help the patient develop a phonation
source, and the most difficult task in therapy is usually to teach the patient
to make the first satisfactory sound. Once the patient is able to achieve some
form of phonation, using some type of alaryngeal mechanism, subsequent
therapy consists of refining the method employed. In esophageal speech,
for example, the most difficult task in therapy is to get the patient to take
in air esophageally and then be able to release it for phonation.

Voice training of the laryngectomee usually begins at the time of the
first postoperative visit. Before the actual initiation of voice training, it is
helpful to determine the adequacy of the patient's hearing. If some hearing
loss is indicated, particularly the high-frequency loss often found in older
persons, some use of amplification may be helpful in therapy. We have also
found that testing the hearing of the patient's spouse can provide useful
information; because the patient will be generating a less-than-optimal
voice signal, overall speech intelligibility is going to be impaired. The
spouse may therefore need audiological testing and may require some kind
of amplification and speech-reading training.

As part of our overall voice training for the laryngectomee, we begin
by considering the artificial larynx. We present procedures for using the
artificial larynx and then step-by-step procedures for teaching esophageal
speech to the patient with a conventional laryngectomy. We specify two
methods of instruction: injection and inhalation.

Using the Artificial Larynx

There has yet to be invented a totally satisfactory artificial larynx for
laryngectomees, although many good artificial instruments are available
commercially. After some demonstration and practice, the typical laryngectomee can effectively master an artificial larynx.

One kind of artificial larynx is the pneumatic type, which requires the
passage of air from the stoma through the vibrating body of the instrument
and on into the oral cavity opening. Perhaps one of the best pneumatic-
type artificial larynges is the Tokyo artificial larynx, which Weinberg and
Riekena (1973) consider easy to use with excellent intelligibility. Pneumatic-
type devices are also relatively inexpensive, compared to other artificial larynges.

The second form of artificial larynx is the electronic type, either the
in-the-mouth-type instrument (such as the Cooper-Rand shown in Figure
8–1) or the neck-type instrument (such as the Western Electric, also shown
in Figure 8–1). The electronic larynx is a battery-powered, transistorized
vibrator that is activated by a button switch. Its vibration usually makes a
continuous buzzing sound, not unlike the sound of an electric razor. Some
models have the capability of pitch variation, which is controlled by the
amount of finger pressure applied to the activating switch. The neck-type
instrument has a vibrator at one end, which must be placed snugly against
the skin of the neck at a particular anatomic site; this site varies for each
individual.

New artificial larynges are continually being developed. For example, Zwitman, Knorr, and Sonderman (1978) report the development of a new intraoral electrolarynx housed in a patient's denture and activated by a hand switch. A variation of this device was recently reported to be clinically successful with patients (Beery, 1986).

The biggest problem in using the artificial larynx is the resistance that many laryngectomees, physicians, and speech pathologists offer to the patient who wants to use one. It is frequently stated that if a new laryngectomee uses an artificial larynx before learning esophageal speech, he or she will never develop good esophageal speech. Furthermore, the argument may proceed, not learning esophageal speech is tantamount to a personal defeat. Today, however, there is far less resistance by professionals to patients using the artificial larynx. We have found that the artificial larynx is usually an aid in learning esophageal speech. We thus teach esophageal speech and use of the neck-type (Western Electric) and intraoral-type (Cooper-Rand) devices at the same time. We then let the patient and family determine the method that best fits their needs. We feel that we need to develop each form of alaryngeal speech to the highest level and that the decision (after being given adequate information) of the best type of speech for them is up to the patient and the family. Some patients prefer to use an artificial device rather than esophageal speech. These patients may find some reassurance from the work of Bennett and Weinberg (1973), who reported that judges generally rated the speech intelligibility of speakers who used the artificial larynx to be superior to that of esophageal speakers.

The speech pathologist might introduce the artificial larynx to the new laryngectomee by following these steps:

1. In telling the patient that efforts will now begin to help him or her learn to talk again, point out that he or she faces two problems—first, learning to articulate (pronounce) words again and, second, finding a new source of voice—and that the articulation will be tackled first. Next, demonstrate that the patient has basically the same capability of articulation that he or she had before the operation, but that he or she may have to make some sounds a bit differently, by employing intraoral pressure for some plosive and sibilant sounds instead of the usual pulmonary air stream. If possible, demonstrate the intraoral whisper, articulating to produce a "sound" with no pulmonary air stream. Then ask the patient to imitate these intraoral productions (which are, in fact, easier for a laryngectomee to produce than for the normal person with a larynx). Warn the patient not to try to push the sounds out by using pulmonary air (the use of pulmonary air will be indicated by excessive stoma noises). You must decide the appropriate level of complexity of the discussion and the amount of positive reinforcement to provide each individual patient. Remember, however, that the simpler the explanation and the more focus given to the actual demonstration, the easier the learning task will be.

2. When the patient is able to produce an intraoral whisper, introduce him or her to an orderly presentation of consonants, perhaps having him or her whisper each one five to ten times. The best presentation seems to be along the general order of acquisition of consonants (/p/, /b/, and so on), first practicing the phonemes that are easiest to pro-

duce, and then going on to more difficult ones. For some patients the nasals /m/, /n/, and /ŋ/ may be difficult to produce and may require special attention that deviates from the developmental order. We stress that the patient should produce these sounds with as little effort or as "little work" as possible. The "trick," we say, is to go at this type of speech with an "easy does it" attitude and approach, even though the natural tendency is to work hard at learning to talk again. The patient should work for clarity of articulation. Point out to the patient his or her relative lip, tongue, and palatal competencies, as demonstrated by accurate whispering of the consonants. Then go back to the first point made in the therapy, that learning to talk again is a twofold process: articulation and voice. Tell the patient that success in practicing the whispered productions means that he or she is doing very well in the first area. The whispering practice will vary in length, depending on the intelligibility and motivation of the patient.

3. Now introduce the artificial larynx, either the pneumatic or electronic type. We limit our suggested procedures to the two types of electronic larynx. For the neck type, place the vibrating surface of the instrument tightly on your own neck at a site where you have previously determined your best voice to be. You might well repeat some monosyllabic words that include some of the phonemes the patient has just finished using in articulation practice. To these articulations, you should explain, the artificial larynx will introduce the second phase of speech, voicing. You might also use the artificial larynx to demonstrate some connected speech. For the oral-type larynx, take care to show that the intraoral tube does not interfere with the movement of the tongue. We have found that introducing the tube toward the corner of the mouth with the tube angled high toward the palate and about halfway back in the mouth seems to provide the best placement. The phrase "How are you?" is good because the vocal tract is open and thus the end of the tube is not occluded by the tongue. The success of this production is due largely to resonance (vowels and diphthongs) and has a high probability of working for the patient.

4. Next, in offering the instrument to the patient, take a great deal of care to achieve a good *seal* between the neck skin of the patient and the surface of the neck vibrator. The vibrator head must be firmly buried against the neck, or the sound source will escape freefield and not be directed into the oral cavity. This optimum site of contact, such as just above the site of the laryngeal excision in the midline, is found best by trial and error. The patient should say the same monosyllabic word repeatedly as he or she searches for the site of contact where the intraoral speech or voice sounds best. Much time should be given to achieving this optimum contact of vibrator and neck, because a great deal of early disillusionment with the artificial larynx can come from improper positioning of the instrument. Patients with extensive scarring, such as those who have had radical neck dissections or radiation, may experience real difficulties at first in finding the optimum site of contact. No practice in using the instrument should begin, however, until this critical contact point has been found. Also, once a good sound has been established, the patient will require some practice in working the on-off switch to match his or her articulations. Most patients can learn to do this rather quickly. For the oral instrument, care must be exercised to have the patient place the tube optimally within the mouth and ensure that it not interfere with tongue movement. We

first use the phrase "How are you?" because it can be made with relatively little tongue interference. Following this phrase, we generally use number counting as the practice words to find the optimal oral placement of the tube. Trial and error can usually locate the best place to introduce the tube (again, we find that toward the side of the mouth with the tube angled high toward the palate and about halfway back in the mouth seems to provide the best placement).

5.   The patient should then practice saying single monosyllabic words in a series, and after that go on to phrases and short sentences. At this point, remind the patient that he or she is now practicing speech. The sharper and clearer one can articulate, the more intelligible the speech will be. The patient should be instructed to discard his or writing pad and begin talking to everyone. The tremendous advantage afforded by the artificial larynx is that it permits the patient to talk shortly after the operation, which provides valuable articulation practice. The more one talks using the artificial larynx, the better his or her speech will usually become. Point out to the patient that the artificial larynx is providing him or her with a voice source while he or she practices improving articulation. After a few days of practice using the instrument, the patient will start learning how to supply his or her own voice by using some form of esophageal voice. Make it very clear to the patient that the artificial larynx and esophageal speech are not competitive forms of voice, but compatible methods that help achieve good functional speech *whenever there is a need to talk.*

We had one laryngectomee patient, a retired marine first sergeant, who learned esophageal speech quite well but also used a Western Electric device. He actually talked with the esophageal air charge but then, when it was expended, he clicked on the electrolarynx, which he held at the neck to provide pressure on the P-E or pharyngo-esophageal segment for increased loudness during esophageal speech. He finished the phrase with the electrolarynx and smoothly alternated back and forth between the two sound sources continually during connected speech. He was a prolific, incessant talker who was rated as a successfully fluent speaker by his listeners.

Teaching Esophageal Speech

Two methods of teaching esophageal speech may be employed: injection and inhalation. We usually begin with the injection method, which is the easiest to teach and is quite compatible with the articulation practice the patient may have used with the artificial larynx.

Both methods, however, employ the same basic principle of compressing air within the oropharynx and injecting this denser air into the more rarefied (less dense) space of the esophagus. Denser air within a body moves in the direction of the less dense body of air whenever the two bodies are coupled together. Some of the compressed air within the oral cavity undoubtedly escapes through the lips, some through the nasopharyngeal port, and some (particularly if the opening of the esophagus is open) into the esophagus. Both methods for esophageal voice bring compressed air into the esophagus; once the air is in the esophagus, external forces compress the air within it and expel it. Hopefully, the esophageal expulsion sets up a vibration of the P-E segment and the patient experiences an eructation or "voice." We consider separately the procedures for teaching the injection method (we try this one first) and the inhalation method (sometimes we combine it with injection).

The Injection Method   Certain consonants appear to have a facilitating effect in producing good esophageal voice. Individual patients may have their own favorite facilitating sounds, but more often than not these are plosive consonants (/p/, /b/, /t/, /d/, /k/, and /g/) or affricatives containing plosives (/tʃ/ or /dʒ/). Stetson (1937) reported many years ago that /p/, /t/, and /k/ were the easiest sounds for the new laryngectomee to use; Moolenaar-Bijl (1953) reported that the same phonemes produced esophageal speech faster in most patients than the traditional swallow method of teaching. Diedrich and Youngstrom (1966) recommended the voiceless /p/, /t/, /k/, /s/, /ʃ/, and /tʃ/ phonemes as good sounds to employ in the injection method of air intake. The injection of air is best accomplished by using speech that employs some of the consonants just identified. As the patient whispers monosyllabic words with a facilitating consonant before and after the vowel, he or she will sometimes spontaneously inject air into the esophagus and produce an "unplanned" esophageal voice. The production of the consonant facilitates the transfer of air into the esophagus (Shanks, 1986). The injection method is preferred for teaching esophageal voice. Specific steps for teaching injection might include the following:

1. Discuss with the patient the dynamics of air flow, explaining that compressed, dense air will always flow in the direction of less dense, rarefied air. Explain also how the movements of the tongue in the injection method increase the density of the air within the mouth, enabling the air to move into the esophagus. Then demonstrate how the whispered articulation of a phoneme, such as a /t/ or a /k/, is the kind of tongue movement that produces the injection of air into the esophagus. After producing the whispered /t/, demonstrate for the patient an esophageal voice for the word "tot" or "talk."

2. Now ask the patient to produce the phoneme /p/ by intraoral whisper. Care must be taken that the sound is made by good firm compression of the lips, with no need for stoma noise. Make sure that the patient avoids pushing out the pulmonary exhalation or using tongue and palatal-pharyngeal contact as the noise source. The intraoral whisper can be effectively taught by having the patient hold his or her breath and then attempt to "bite-off" a /p/ by compressing the air caught between his or her abruptly closed lips. The patient should continue practicing this until true intraoral articulation is clearly grasped. This is demonstrated when he or she is consistently able to produce a precise /p/. Once the patient can do this, he or she should move to the next voiceless plosive, /t/. Here, the tongue tip against the upper central alveolar process is the site of contact, and practice should be continued until the patient can produce a precise, clear /t/. The same procedure should be repeated for /k/, again first demonstrating for the patient the different site of contact.

3. When good intraoral voiceless plosives have been produced, the patient is ready to add the vowel /a/ to each plosive. With /p/, for instance,

he or she makes the plosive, and then immediately attempts to produce an esophageal phonation of /a/, producing in effect the word
"pa." If this is successful, the patient may combine the /p/ with a few
other vowel combinations before going on to the /t/ and /k/. If the patient fails to produce the esophageal voice at this point, he or she
should go back and work for even crisper articulation of the plosive
sounds. If the patient is still unsuccessful after increased practice in
articulation, he or she should attempt the inhalation method as the
primary means of air intake.

4. The average laryngectomee experiences some success with the injection method when using the /p/, /t/, and /k/ phonemes. Therefore, he
   or she might be provided with about five monosyllabic words for each
   of the phonemes—for example, for /p/, the words "pat," "pip," "pack,"
   "pot," and "pop." The task is now to say each word, one at a time,
   renewing the esophageal air supply *as he or she speaks,* which is an obvious advantage of using the injection method. It is through the mere
   process of articulation that the patient takes in air. After the patient
   has demonstrated success with these phonemes, introduce their voiced
   cognates, /b/, /d/, and /g/. The same procedure should be repeated, ending with about five practice words for each new phoneme.

5. Additional phonemes, such as /s/, /z/, /ʃ/, /tʃ/, /ʒ/, and /dʒ/, may be introduced for practice. As the patient gains phonatory skill with each new
   consonant, he or she must spend extra time learning to improve both
   the quickness and the quality of production. Too many patients err
   in trying to develop functional conversation too early. Considerable
   practice should be spent at the monosyllabic word level, practicing
   one word at a time and making constant efforts to produce sharp articulation and good-sounding voice.

6. Practice with some basic control techniques is essential for developing
   successful and fluent esophageal speech. Therefore, we have the patient practice several skills directly in each speech session. These skills
   are:

   a. Rapid production (½ second or less) of esophageal phona-
      tion on command from the clinician with 100 percent success
      in response. If we call for ten productions of the /a/ vowel, the
      patient must respond with ten.
   b. Ability to sustain a tone for two and a half to three seconds
      or longer.
   c. Ability to interrupt the tone into three or four segments.
   d. Ability to stress the first or second syllable on command (such
      as in the word "upper" for first syllable stress, and "above"
      for second syllable stress).
   e. Ability to make a soft or loud tone on command.

Each of these skills is practiced for a part of each speech session, much
as a serious golfer practices on the putting green and driving range as
well as playing in a real game. Patients who are too anxious to achieve
connected speech and ignore practice may carry bad habits into
speech that will detract from their developing good esophageal
speech, and that are difficult to correct at a later date.

7. At this point, if the patient has been successful, the inhalation method
   can be introduced to further improve air intake and esophageal phonation. The patient should produce a normal inhalation and, at the

initial moment of exhalation, produce the consonant and say the word. Beyond the single words alone, we often couple the words together in phrases, such as "bake a cake, stop at church, park the black cart," and so on. Once plosive-laden phrases are mastered, we then use the oral reading materials from voice and diction books, including, when possible, the facilitative consonants we have been using.

The Inhalation Method   The flow of air in normal respiration is achieved by the transfer of air from one source to another because of the relative disparity of air pressure between the two sources. For example, when the thorax enlarges because of muscle movement, the air reservoir within the lung increases in size, rarefying (decreasing) the air pressure within the lung. Because the outside atmospheric air pressure is now greater, the air rushes in until the pressure within equals the outside pressure. The flow of air is always from the more dense to the less dense air body, and the flow continues until the two bodies are equal in pressure. By this same air-flow mechanism the esophagus inflates in the inhalation method of air intake. The patient experiences a thoracic enlargement during pulmonary inhalation, which reduces the compression on all thoracic structures, including the esophagus. If the cricopharyngeus opening into the esophagus is slightly open at the time of the slight increase in the size of the esophagus, air from the hypopharynx will flow into the esophagus. During the exhalation phase of pulmonary respiration, when there is a general compression of thoracic structures, the esophagus also experiences some compression, which aids in the expulsion of the entrapped air. As this air passes through the approximated structures of the lower pharynx-upper esophagus (P-E or pharyngo-esophageal segment), a vibration is set up, producing esophageal phonation. The advantage of the inhalation method of esophageal air intake is that it follows the patient's natural inclination of pulmonary inhalation followed by exhalation-phonation. Simply to take a breath and then talk is the most natural way of speaking, and for this reason the inhalation method offers the patient learning esophageal speech some early advantages.

In proceeding to the following steps for teaching the inhalation method, remember that the approach is best used in combination with the injection method.

1. Explain and demonstrate to the patient some aspects of normal respiration. Many normal speakers, for example, have never thought much about normal respiration, and many do not know that their voicing has always been an exhalation event. Explain to the patient that when the chest is enlarged by muscle action, the air flows into the lungs, and that, in the laryngectomee's case, the air comes through the stoma opening in the trachea and down into the lungs. Point out that the chest enlarges by muscle action, not by air inflation; thus, the air comes in as the chest enlarges. When the laryngectomee's chest enlarges, a concomitant enlargement of the esophagus usually takes place; when the esophagus is enlarged, there is a greater chance for air to come into it. When the chest becomes smaller, the pulmonary air is forced out, and the air within the esophagus is also more likely

to be forced out. If possible, demonstrate esophageal voice using this method.

2. Before attempting to produce voice, the patient should practice conscious relaxation and correct breathing methods. He or she should become aware of thoracic expansion and abdominal distention on inhalation and of thoracic contraction on exhalation. Respiration practice should only be long enough to permit the patient to develop this kind of breathing awareness, because patients do not seem to benefit much from extended breathing exercises per se.

3. Now the patient should attempt to add air into the esophagus during his or her pulmonary inhalation. Diedrich and Youngstrom (1966) recommended that "the patient be told to close his mouth, imagine that he is sniffing through his nose, and to do so in a fairly rapid manner" (p. 112). Even though the sniff is basically a constricted inhalation, it is frequently accompanied by esophageal dilation (the normal person often swallows what he or she sniffs). As an extension of the sniff, the patient should be asked to take a fairly large pulmonary breath (through the stoma, of course). When his or her lungs appear to be about half inflated, the patient should say "up" on exhalation. This procedure can be repeated until the patient experiences some phonatory success.

4. For the patient who does not experience success in step 3, the following variation of the inhalation method sometimes produces good esophageal air: Ask the patient to take a deep breath, and, as he or she begins the inhalation, to cover the stoma. While the muscular enlargement of the thorax continues (despite the patient's lack of continuing inhalation), there will be a corresponding enlargement of the esophagus, perhaps permitting air to flow into the esophagus. For the patient who can get air into the esophagus but cannot produce the air escape necessary for phonation, the same mechanism applies in reverse. Here, the patient takes a deep inhalation and, as he or she begins to exhale, occludes the stoma; as the thorax begins to decrease in size, there will be increased pressure on the esophagus, which might well result in expulsion of esophageal air (and phonation).

5. If esophageal phonation is achieved by either of the last two steps, the patient should proceed from his or her "up" response to single monosyllabic words beginning and ending with /p/, /b/, /t/, /d/, /k/, and /g/. Considerable time should be spent practicing at this single-word level, until the technique is mastered in terms of loudness, quality of sound, and articulation. The patient who masters the basic techniques of air intake and phonation at the single-word level may well become the best esophageal speaker.

6. At this level, use steps 4 to 7 from the injection method.

Trouble Shooting

We find that, with these patients who have trouble getting air in and air out, extra work with a stethoscope can help. The stethoscope is held to the neck of the clinician or another esophageal speaker so the patient can hear the "clunk" sound of injection when the air charge is injected. The same technique is helpful to hear the "click" sound of inhalation. Also, turning the head slightly to one side or the other may help the patient get air into the esophagus. Digital manipulation, whereby we gently squeeze the neck, in the area of the P-E segment, between the thumb and first finger has helped some patients get their first air charge into the esophagus. In some cases, when all else has failed to get air in the esophagus, we have instructed the patient to attempt a half-swallow. We have, however, eliminated the swallowing method as a useful technique for teaching esophageal speech because it has major drawbacks and limitations. Once swallowing is initiated, it is not controllable and air often passes on into the stomach. Also, swallowing is too slow to be an effective method for developing fluent speech. In addition, several good artificial devices and surgical options are now available. The use of artificial devices and esophageal speech training in voice therapy provides these patients from the beginning with a method of effective communication.

One female patient worked for two full months without producing a single sound esophageally. By this time, we wanted to give up further instruction and let the patient depend on the electrolarynx, which she used proficiently. However, the patient had as her target goal the achievement of esophageal speech, and she asked us to continue instruction. Using the head-turning and digital-pressure techniques mentioned earlier, the patient was finally able to produce a weak, short esophageal /a/. The patient was nearly overcome with joy, as we were. From this point, she moved quickly and became a superior esophageal speaker. We must add, however, that had she wanted to use the artificial larynx, this would have been a very acceptable choice for us as well.

VOICE THERAPY FOR THE PATIENT WITH A TOTAL LARYNGECTOMY AND SOME SURGICAL MODIFICATION

It has long been the hope of surgeons and speech pathologists that the patient with a total laryngectomy would one day be able to have a surgically created pseudoglottis that would provide a good and useful voice. Such a pseudoglottis would enable a patient to speak after total laryngectomy with very little speech training and with a minimum of problems (Shedd and Weinberg, 1980). Although many surgical attempts have been successful in creating a mechanism that can produce voice, many serious problems have been associated with such attempts, the most common of which has been aspiration. The patient can produce voice on expiration with very little difficulty, but during swallowing, liquids sometimes enter the airway. Often the procedures that seem to encourage the best communication between the airway and the esophagus, and that produce the best voice, are the ones that have a greater propensity for aspiration (Sisson, McConnell, and Logemann, 1974). The most comprehensive reference text on historical and new surgical and prosthetic approaches for voice rehabilitation is *Surgical and Prosthetic Approaches to Speech Rehabilitation* (Shedd and Weinberg, 1980).

One of the earliest successful prosthetic devices for the production of esophageal voice after laryngectomy was developed by Taub (1975). An external, tube-like apparatus was attached to the chest for conducting pulmonary expiration directly into the esophagus (Taub and Bergner, 1973). The patient was able to have esophageal voice with no training. Another prosthetic approach by Sisson, McConnell, and Logemann (1974) enabled the patient to have voice using a flapper valve placed at the base of the hypopharynx that vibrated on expiration without hand activation. The authors felt this prosthesis was particularly effective for those laryngectomy patients who had extensive radiation therapy; because of the edema and tenderness associated with the radiation, the patients had been unable to tolerate using either the electrolarynx or esophageal speech.

A surgically innovative approach was developed by Asai (1972), who attached a dermal tube superior to the trachea to conduct pulmonary expiration (when the open stoma was occluded by the patient's finger) into the hypopharynx. The end of the tube in the hypopharynx vibrated, thus producing voice. Although some patients experienced good success with the Asai method, many complained of severe aspiration, continued hair growth within the skin tube, and other problems related to maintenance of the open tube.

Recent approaches have been developed that take pulmonary air from the trachea and introduce it by way of a shunt directly into the esophagus. This tracheal-esophageal shunt approach (Saito, et al. 1977) requires that the patient occlude the stoma opening with a finger so that the outgoing tracheal air can be diverted through the shunt into the esophagus; once the air is in the esophagus, it produces vibration of the pharyngo-esophageal segment similar to the normal mechanism of esophageal voice. Recently, too, Singer and Blom (1980) reported experience with a valved prosthesis that is placed after total laryngectomy in a tracheal-esophageal shunt. The insertion of the small prosthesis (about 3 cm long), which is called the "duckbill," into the shunt prevents aspiration while swallowing and eliminates any stenosis of the surgically created tissue shunt. Fifty-four of sixty of Singer and Blom's patients experienced "fluent voices" after only minimal speech therapy postoperatively. This prosthesis also is available in a low-pressure model that requires less air pressure to overcome the valve resistance. When skin irritation and neck configuration are not problems, some patients may wear a valve cover, which allows them to use the Blom-Singer prosthesis without having to occlude the device with the finger. Although patients who can use this method are very successful, the approach, like all others, does not work for everyone. In our experience, the best candidates for the Blom-Singer prosthesis are also the best candidates for learning esophageal speech by traditional methods.

In general, the individual patient can make one procedure look good and another one look poor. Individual differences among patients have much to do with patients' successful intelligibility after laryngectomy, using either esophageal speech (conventional or by way of shunt) or artificial larynx speech (Kalb and Carpenter, 1981). Speech-language pathologists who work with laryngectomy patients must keep abreast of new surgical approaches with and without the use of prostheses. Methods for introducing tracheal air via a shunt into the esophagus are going to have continued use with laryngectomees, and only minimal training should be required for these patients. Let us review a few management steps.

1. The speech-language pathologist should review for himself or herself the procedures the patient has had. The Shedd and Weinberg (1980) book is helpful here because it summarizes most of the surgical procedures available at the time the book was edited.

2. A review of how normal voice is produced is helpful for the patient who may never have realized, for example, that all speech is produced on pulmonary expiration.

3. Practice should be given producing precise articulation. The patient should be encouraged to practice intraoral whispers so that the words are distinct and clearly understandable to listeners.

4. The patient is asked to take in a normal breath, occlude his or her stoma with a thumb or a finger, and say a monosyllabic word on expiration. It is important that the patient be counseled to use the thumb or finger only as a diverting body to the air stream. Sending the air through the shunt (or the appliance in the shunt) does not require heavy finger pressure. Only very light touch is required to divert the air from the stoma on expiration. If voice is achieved on the single word, the patient can go to the next step. If not, the patient should practice the timing of inspiration (open stoma) and expiration (closed stoma) in synchrony with saying one word. Trial-and-error repetitions may be needed here. Most patients can produce an effortless esophageal voice with very little difficulty. It has been our observation that patients who cannot successfully divert tracheal air through the shunt are pushing too hard with their fingers. Only light touch on the stoma opening is needed.

5. Go from single words to phrases as soon as the patient can do so. It is important to keep the inspiratory breath a normal one. The patient needs no more breathing effort than he or she ever did. It takes some practice to time the inspiratory-expiratory phonation to match the words or phrases one is attempting to say.

6. Once the patient can say phrases, it has been our observation that, by using natural articulation, he or she begins injecting air into the esophagus from above and using the pulmonary air passing out through the esophagus. Therefore, some patients can speak some words and phrases without occluding their stomas, obviously renewing the air reservoir within the esophagus by injection. Extended daily practice of several hours for a week or two is required before a patient with a tracheal-esophageal shunt is able to use his or her new esophageal voice conversationally.

7. Review with the patient that the best voice seems to be produced with the least amount of effort—that is, a normal speaking breath, light finger touch, and so on.

PROBLEMS IN TEACHING ESOPHAGEAL SPEECH

Regardless of the method of getting air into the esophagus (injection, inhalation, tracheal-esophageal shunt), many esophageal speakers develop poor speaking habits that diminish their overall speech effectiveness. These faulty forms of behavior need to be identified early, before they become habituated. Some of the more common problems include:

1. *Unnecessary stoma noise.* It is not necessary for laryngectomees to force out air from their tracheal stoma when attempting to speak. Some laryngectomees do this, particularly those who use the inhalation method of air intake. A few make the stoma noise on inhalation, but most do it primarily on exhalation, usually as part of normal pulmonary exhalation. Such a patient is often trying to speak too loudly, and thus uses too much force. Often, identifying the problem is enough to make the patient eliminate stoma noise. However, an occasional patient will have to practice holding his or her breath while attempting to speak, or practice fixing the thorax, which slows down the rapidity of exhalation. Either breath holding or thorax fixing will eliminate the problem, particularly when it has been identified early and has not yet become a habitual response.

2. *Excessive swallowing of air.* Some laryngectomees swallow too much air in their attempt to inflate the esophagus. Many patients thus become bloated, experiencing a great deal of stomach and intestinal gas, with the typical discomforts of abdominal-chest fullness, pain, and heartburn. One of the best methods to reduce excessive swallowing of air is to place more focus on producing precise articulation, which facilitates better air injection.

3. *Distracting noises.* Gurgling esophageal noises are occasionally related to poor sphincteric action at the distal (bottom) end of the esophagus and are difficult to control. A few such patients will profit from using antacids to reduce the esophageal gurgle. A more common noise is the clunking sound that characterizes too rapid an air intake. The pharyngeal noise must be extinguished immediately by the clinician, because it can quickly become habitual. The best method of eliminating it is to have the patient practice taking in air in an easier manner, producing single words free of the "clunk." Clunking is often the result of too much effort, particularly if the patient is attempting to increase the loudness of his or her voice. The patient must be asked what it feels like to speak with the clunk as opposed to speaking without it; the typical patient can feel the difference, and from that point on can monitor himself or herself so that the clunk will not be produced. Once the clunk has been established for several months, it is very difficult to eliminate.

4. *Facial grimacing.* Some laryngectomees begin early in their training programs to do some unnecessary things to get air into the esophagus. For instance, they may purse their lips, make exaggerated facial movements, double pump with their lips, or clench their teeth. Such extraneous behavior must be quickly pointed out and eliminated. Many laryngectomees get started with some facial posture, thinking that this helps them speak, and from that point on they assume the posture as a habit whenever they proceed to speak. A frank, frontal assault should be made by the clinician to eliminate such undesirable facial behavior. Like any other undesirable behavior, it is much easier to eliminate during its formative stages than after it has become habitual.

SUMMARY

Most patients survive cancer of the larynx, even though they often require radiation therapy and surgery, a partial or a total laryngectomy. We have reviewed the importance of the preoperative and the postoperative visits by the speech-language pathologist. Voice training after partial removal of the larynx usually requires searching with the patient for the best voice he or she can produce using various facilitating approaches. After total laryngectomy, the patient may use an artificial larynx or esophageal speech produced by injection, inhalation, or introducing air into the esophagus through a tracheal-esophageal shunt.

REFERENCES

AHLSTROM, R. H. (1984). Speech pathology: Views from medicine and dentistry, in S. C. McFarlane, *Coping with Communicative Handicaps.* San Diego: College Hill Press, Chapter 7 Appendix.

AINSWORTH, S. (1980). Disorders of voice, in *Otolaryngology,* ed. G. M. English. Philadelphia: Harper & Row, Volume 4, Chapter 13.

American Cancer Society (1980). *Cancer Facts and Figures, 1980.* New York: American Cancer Society.

American Cancer Society (1986). *First Aid for Laryngectomees.* New York: American Cancer Society.

AMINOFF, M. J., DEDO, H. H., & IZDEBSKI, L. (1978). Clinical aspects of spasmodic dysphonia. *J. Neurology, Neurosurgery and Psychiatry, 41:* 361–365.

ANDREWS, M. (1986). *Voice Therapy for Children.* New York: Longman.

ARNDT, W. B., SHELTON, R. L., & BRADFORD, L. J. (1965). Articulation, voice, and obturation in persons with acquired and congenital palate defects. *Cleft Palate J., 2:* 377–383.

ARONSON, A. E. (1980). *Clinical Voice Disorders.* New York: Brian C. Decker Division, Thieme-Stratton, Inc.

ARONSON, A. E. (1985). *Clinical Voice Disorders,* 2nd ed. New York: Thieme-Stratton, Inc.

ARONSON, A. E., & DeSANTO, L. W. (1983). Adductor spastic dysphonia: Three years after recurrent laryngeal nerve resection. *Annals of Otol. Rhinol. Laryngol., 93:* 1–8.

ARONSON. A. E., PETERSON, H. W., & LITIN, E. M. (1966). Psychiatric symptomatology in hypernasality in cleft palate children. *Cleft Palate J., 1:* 329–335.

Artik. Arion Products, 1022 Nicollet Avenue, Minneapolis, Minnesota 55403.

ASAI, R. (1972). Laryngoplasty after total laryngectomy. *Arch. Otolaryngol., 75:* 114–119.

B & K Real-Time Frequency Analyzer (1987). Naerum, Denmark: Bruel & Kjaer.

B & K Sound Level Meter Type 2225 (1987). Naerum, Denmark: Bruel & Kjaer.

BATSAKIS, J. G. (1979). *Tumors of the Head and Neck.* Baltimore: Williams and Wilkins.

BEERY, Q. C. (1986). *The Resnick tone emitter for alaryngeal speech.* Video presentation at American Speech-Language-Hearing Association Convention, Detroit, Michigan.

BENNETT, S., & WEINBERG, B. (1973). Acceptability ratings of normal, esophageal, and artificial larynx speech. *J. Speech Hearing Research, 16:* 608–615.

BLESS, D. (1984). *Transcripts of the Eleventh Symposium: Care of the Professional Voice,* ed. V. L. Lawrence, New York: The Voice Foundation.

BLESS, D., & MILLER, J. (1972). *Influence of mechanical and linguistic factors on lung volume events during speech.* American Speech and Hearing Association Convention paper.

BLESS, D., & SAXMAN, J. H. (1970). *Maximum phonation time, flow rate, and volume change during phonation: Normative information on third-grade children.* American Speech and Hearing Convention paper.

BOONE, D. R. (1966a). Modification of the voices of deaf children. *Volta Review, 68:* 686–692.

BOONE, D. R. (1966b). Treatment of functional aphonia in a child and an adult. *J. of Speech and Hearing Disorders, 31:* 69–74.

BOONE, D. R. (1973). Voice therapy for children. *J. Human Communication, 1:* 30–43.

BOONE, D. R. (1974). Dismissal criteria in voice therapy. *J. Speech Hearing Disorders, 39:* 133–139.

BOONE, D. R. (1977). Voice disorders: Communicative disorders. *An Audio Journal for Continuing Education.* New York: Grune and Stratton.

BOONE, D. R. (1980a). *The Boone Voice Program for Children.* Austin, Texas: PRO-ED.

BOONE, D. R. (1980b). The optimal use of the larynx. *J. Research in Singing, 4:* 35–43.

BOONE, D. R. (1980c). Voice disorders, in *Introduction to Communication Disorders,* ed. T. Hixon, L. Shriberg, & J. Saxman. Englewood Cliffs, New Jersey: Prentice-Hall.

BOONE. D. R. (1982). *The Boone Voice Program for Adults.* Austin, Texas: PRO-ED.

BOONE. D. R. (1983). *The Voice and Voice Therapy,* 3rd ed. Englewood Cliffs, New Jersey: Prentice-Hall.

BOONE, D. R. (1987). *Human Communication and Its Disorders.* Englewood Cliffs, New Jersey: Prentice-Hall.

BOUHUYS, A., PROCTOR, D. F., & MEAD, T. (1966). Kinetic aspects of singing. *Applied Physiology, 21:* 483–496.

BOWMAN, S. A., & SHANKS, J. C. (1978). Velopharyngeal relationships of /i/ and /s/ as seen cephalometrically. *J. Speech Hearing Disorders, 43:* 185–191.

BRADFORD, L. J., BROOKS, A. R., & SHELTON, R. L. (1964). Clinical judgment of hypernasality in cleft palate children. *Cleft Palate J., 1:* 329–335.

BROAD, D. J. (1973). Phonation, in *Normal Aspects of Speech, Hearing, and Language,* eds. F. D. Minifie, T. J. Hixon, & F. Williams. Englewood Cliffs, New Jersey: Prentice-Hall.

BRODNITZ, F. S. (1971). *Vocal Rehabilitation.* Rochester, Minnesota: Whiting Press.

BULL, T., & COOK, J. (1976). *Speech Therapy and ENT Surgery.* Oxford: Blackwell Scientific Publications.

BULLER, A. (1942). Nasality: Cause and remedy of our American blight. *Quarterly J. of Speech, 28:* 83–84.

BZOCH, K. R. (1964). The effects of a specific pharyngeal flap operation upon the speech of forty cleft-palate persons. *J. Speech Hearing Disorders, 29:* 111–120.

CASE, J. L. (1984). *Clinical Management of Voice Disorders.* Rockville, Maryland: Aspen Systems Corporation.

CASPER, J., COLTON, R., & BREWER, D. (1986). Selected therapy techniques and laryngeal physiological changes in patients with vocal fold immobility. *Folia Phoniatricia, 38*(5–6): 288–289.

CHARLIP, W. S. (1968). *The Aging Female Voice: Selected Fundamental Frequency Characteristics and Listener Judgments.* Unpublished doctoral dissertation, Purdue University, West Lafayette, Indiana.

CHERRY, J., & MARGULIES, S. (1968). Contact ulcer of the larynx. *Laryngoscope, 78:* 1937–1940.

COFFIN, B. (1981). *Overtones of Bel Canto.* New Jersey: The Scarecrow Press.

COLTON, R. H., & ESTILL, J. A. (1981). Elements of voice quality: Perceptual, acoustic, and physiologic aspects. *Speech and Language: Advances in Basic Research and Practice,* Volume 5. New York: Academic Press.

COMROE, J. H. (1956). *The Lung.* Chicago: The Year Book Publishers.

COOPER, M. (1973). *Modern Techniques of Vocal Rehabilitation.* Springfield, Illinois: Charles C. Thomas.

COOPER, M. (1977). Direct vocal rehabilitation, in *Approaches to Vocal Rehabilitation,* ed. M. Cooper & M. H. Cooper. Springfield, Illinois: Charles C. Thomas.

COULTHARD, S. W. (1987). Personal Communication. Tucson: University of Arizona College of Medicine.

CRUMLEY, R. L., & IZDEBSKI, K. (1986). Voice quality following laryngeal reinnervation by ansa hypoglossi transfer. *Laryngoscope, 96*(6): 611–616.

CURRY, E. T. (1949). Hoarseness and voice change in male adolescents. *J. Speech Hearing Disorders, 16:* 23–24.

DANILOFF, R. G. (1973). Normal articulation process, in *Normal Aspects of Speech, Hearing, and Language*, ed. F. D. Minifie, T. J. Hixon, & F. Williams. Englewood Cliffs, New Jersey: Prentice-Hall.

DARLEY, F. L. (1965). *Diagnosis and Appraisal of Communication Disorders*. Englewood Cliffs, New Jersey: Prentice-Hall.

DARLEY, F. L., ARONSON, A. E., & BROWN, J. R. (1969). Differential diagnostic patterns of dysarthria. *J. Speech Hearing Research, 12:* 246-269.

DARLEY, F. L., ARONSON, A. E., & BROWN, J. R. (1975). *Motor Speech Disorders*. Philadelphia: W. B. Saunders.

DAVIS, D. S., & BOONE, D. R. (1967). Pitch discrimination and tonal memory abilities in adult voice patients. *J. Speech Hearing Research, 10:* 811-815.

DAVIS P., BOONE, D. R., CARROLL, R. L., DARVENIZA, P., & HARRISON, G. A. (1987). Adductor spastic dysphonia: Heterogeneity of physiological and phonatory characteristics. *Archives of Otolaryngology, 97.*

DEDO, D. D., & DEDO, H. H. (1980). Vocal cord paralysis. *Otolaryngology, Volume 3: Head and Neck*. Philadelphia: W. B. Saunders.

DEDO, H. H., & IZDEBSKI, K. (1983a). Intermediate results of 306 recurrent laryngeal nerve sections for spastic dysphonia. *Laryngoscope, 93:* 9-16.

DEDO, H. H., & IZDEBSKI, K. (1983b). Problems with surgical (RLN section) treatment of spastic dysphonia. *Laryngoscope, 93:* 268-271.

DEDO, H. H., & JACKLER, R. K. (1982). Laryngeal papilloma: Results of treatment with the CO_2 laser and podophyllum. *Annals of Otology, Rhinology, and Laryngology, 91:* 425-430.

DELAHUNTY, J., & CHERRY, J. (1968). Experimentally produced vocal cord granulomas. *Laryngoscope, 78:* 1941-1947.

DICKSON, D., & MAUE-DICKSON, W. (1982). *Anatomical and Physiological Bases of Speech*. Boston: Little, Brown and Co.

DICKSON, D. R. (1962). Acoustic study of nasality. *J. Speech Hearing Research, 5:* 103-111.

DICKSON, S., & JANN, G. R. (1974). Diagnostic principles and procedures, in *Communication Disorders, Remedial Principles, and Practices*, ed. S. Dickson. Glenview, Illinois: Scott, Foresman & Co.

DIEDRICH, W. M., & YOUNGSTROM, K. A. (1966). *Alaryngeal Speech*. Springfield, Illinois: Charles C. Thomas.

DUGUAY, M. J. (1986). Using speech aid(e)s, in *Current Strategies of Rehabilitation of the Laryngectomized Patient*, ed. J. C. Shanks. New York: Thieme Inc.

Echorder and Echordette (1980). RIL Electronics, Inc., Street Road and Second Street Pike, Southhampton, Pennsylvania, 18966.

ECKEL, F. C., & BOONE, D. R. (1981). The s/z ratio as an indicator of laryngeal pathology. *J. Speech Hearing Disorders, 46:* 147-150.

ELLIS, P. D. M., & BENNETT, J. (1977). Laryngeal trauma after prolonged endotracheal intubation. *J. Laryngol., 91:* 69-76.

EYSENCK, H. (ed.) (1961). *Handbook of Abnormal Psychology*. New York: Basic Books, Inc.

FAIRBANKS, G. (1960). *Voice and Articulation Drillbook*. New York: Harper and Brothers.

FANT, G. (1960). *Acoustic Theory of Speech Production*. The Hague: Mouton.

FILTER, M. D. (1982). *Phonatory Voice Disorders in Children*. Springfield, Illinois: Charles C. Thomas.

FILTER, M. D., & URIOSTE, K. (1981). Pitch imitation abilities of college women with normal voices. *J. Speech Hearing Assoc., Virginia, 22:* 20-26.

FISHER, H. B. (1975). *Improving Voice and Articulation*, 2nd ed. New York: Houghton-Mifflin.

FLETCHER, S. G. (1972). Contingencies for bioelectronic modification of nasality. *J. Speech Hearing Disorders, 37:* 329-346.

FLETCHER, S. G., & DALY, D. A. (1976). Nasalance in utterances of hearing impaired speakers. *J. Communication Disorders, 9:* 63-73.

FORNER, L., & HIXON, T. J. (1977). Respiratory kinematics in profoundly hearing-impaired speakers. *J. Speech Hearing Res., 20:* 373-408.

FRABLE, M. S. (1972). Hoarseness, a symptom of pre-menstrual tension. *Arch. Otolaryngol., 75:* 66-67.

FROESCHELS, E. (1943). Hygiene of the voice. *Arch. Otolaryngol., 37:* 122-130.

FROESCHELS, E. (1952). Chewing method as therapy. *Arch. Otolaryngol., 56:* 427-434.

FROESCHELS, E., KASTEIN, S., & WEISS, D. A. (1955). A method of therapy for paralytic conditions of the mechanisms of phonation, respiration, and glutination. *J. Speech Hearing Disorders, 20:* 365–370.

GARDNER, W. H. (1961). Problems of laryngectomees. *Rehabilitation Record,* 15–18.

GORDON, M. T., MORTON, F. M., & SIMPSON, I. C. (1978). Airflow measurements in diagnosis assessment and treatment of mechanical dysphonia. *Folia Phoniatrica, 30:* 372–379.

GOULD, W. J. (1975). Quantitative assessment of voice function in microlaryngology. *Folia Phoniatrica, 27:* 190–200.

GRACE, S. G. (1984). Speech pathology: Views from medicine and dentistry, in S. C. McFarlane, *Coping With Communicative Handicaps.* San Diego: College Hill Press, Chapter 7 Appendix.

GRAY, B. B., ENGLAND, G., & MAHONEY, J. L. (1965). Treatment of benign vocal nodules by reciprocal inhibition. *J. Behavioral Research Therapy, 3:* 187–193.

GREENE, M. C. L. (1980). *The Voice and Its Disorders,* 4th ed. Philadelphia: J. B. Lippincott Company.

HIXON, T. J. (ed.) (1987). *Respiratory Function in Speakers and Singers.* Boston: College Hill Division, Little-Brown.

HIXON, T. J., & ABBS, J. H. (1980). Normal speech production, in *Introduction to Communication Disorders,* ed. T. J. Hixon, L.D. Shriberg, & J. H. Saxman. Englewood Cliffs, New Jersey: Prentice-Hall.

HIXON, T. J., GOLDMAN, M. D., & MEAD, J. (1973). Kinematics of the chest wall during speech production: Volume displacements of the rib cage, abdomen, and lung. *J. Speech Hearing Research, 16:* 78–115.

HIXON, T. J., KLATT, D., & MEAD, J. (1970). *Separate volume changes of the rib cage and abdomen during speech.* Paper presented at the Annual Convention of the American Speech and Hearing Association, New York.

HIXON, T. J., MEAD, J., & GOLDMAN, M. D. (1976). Dynamics of the chest wall during speech production: Function of the thorax, rib cage, diaphragm, and abdomen. *J. Speech Hearing Research, 19:* 297–356.

HIXON, T. J., SAXMAN, J. H., & MCQUEEN, H. D. (1967). The respirometric technique for evaluating velopharyngeal competence during speech. *Folia Phoniatrica, 19:* 203–219.

HIXON, T. J., WATSON, P. J., & MAHER, M. Z. (1987). Respiratory kinematics in classical (Shakespearean) actors, in *Respiratory Function in Speakers and Singers,* ed. T. J. Hixon. Boston: College Hill Division, Little-Brown.

HOLLIEN, H. (1960). Vocal pitch variation related to changes in vocal fold length. *J. Speech Hearing Research, 3:* 150–156.

HOLLIEN, H. (1962). Vocal fold thickness and fundamental frequency of phonation. *J. Speech Hearing Research, 5:* 237–243.

HOLLIEN, H., & SHIPP, T. (1972). Speaking fundamental frequency and chronologic age in males. *J. Speech Hearing Research, 15:* 155–159.

HONJO, I., & ISSHIKI, N. (1980). Laryngoscopic and voice characteristics of aged persons. *Arch. Otolaryngol., 106:* 149–150.

HORN, D. (1962). Laryngectomees: Survey report. *International Assoc. Laryngectomees News,* 7.

HOSHIKO, M. S. (1962). Electromyographic investigation of the intercostal muscles during speech. *Archives Physical Medicine & Rehabilitation, 43:* 115–119.

HULL, F. M., MIELKE, P. W., WILLEFORD, J. A., & TIMMONS, R. J. (1976). *National Speech Hearing Survey,* Final Report, Project 50978, Bureau of Education for the Handicapped, United States Office of Education.

ISSHIKI, N., TANADE, M. & SAWADE, M. (1978). Arytenoid adduction for unilateral vocal cord paralysis. *Arch. Otolaryngol., 104:* 555–558.

ISSHIKI, N., & VON LEDEN, H. (1964). Hoarseness: Aerodynamic studies. *Arch. Otolaryngol., 80:* 206–213.

JACOBSON, E. (1957). *You Must Relax.* New York: McGraw-Hill Book Co.

JOHNSON, J. T., NEWMAN, R. K., & OLSON, J. E. (1980). Persistent hoarseness: An aggressive approach for early detection of laryngeal cancer. *Postgrad Med., 67:* 122–126.

JUDSON, L. S., & WEAVER, A. T. (1965). *Voice Science.* New York: Appleton-Century-Crofts.

KAHANE, J. C. (1983). Postnatal development and aging of the human larynx. *Seminars in Speech and Language, 4:* 189–204.

KALB, M. B., & CARPENTER, M. A. (1981). Individual speaker influence on relative intelligibility of esophageal speech and artificial larynx speech. *J. Speech Hearing Disorders, 46:* 77–80.

KALFUSS, H. A. (1969). Counseling the laryngectomee. *Ninth Annual International Association of Laryngectomees (IAL) Institute.* Pittsburgh: University of Pittsburgh.

KALLEN, L. A. (1934). Vicarious vocal mechanisms. *Arch. Otolaryngol., 20:* 460–503.

KANTNER, C. E. (1947). The rationale of blowing exercises for patients with repaired cleft palates. *J. Speech Disorders, 12:* 281–286.

KLEINSASSER, O. (1979). *Microlaryngoscopy and Endolaryngeal Microsurgery: Technique and Typical Findings.* Baltimore: University Park Press.

KOUFMAN, T. A. (1986). Laryngoplasty for vocal cord medialization: An alternative to Teflon. *Laryngoscope, 96(7):* 726–731.

Language Master (1979). Bell and Howell Co., 7100 N. McCormick Road, Chicago, Illinois.

LAVER, J. (1980). *The Phonetic Description of Voice Quality. Cambridge Studies in Linguistics: 31.* Cambridge, England: Cambridge University Press.

LAVORATO, A. S., & McFARLANE, S. C. (1983). Treatment of the professional voice, in *Current Therapy of Communication Disorders: Voice Disorders,* ed. W. H. Perkins, New York: Thieme-Stratton, Inc.

LAWRENCE, V. L. (1983). Vocal problems of the professional user of voice, in *Seminars in Speech and Language, 4:* 233–244.

LEEPER, H. A. (1976). Voice initiation characteristics of normal children and children with vocal nodules: A preliminary investigation. *J. Commun. Disorders, 9:* 83–94.

LEHMANN, Q. H. (1965). Reverse phonation: A new maneuver for examining the larynx. *Radiology, 84:* 215–222.

LIM, R. Y. (1985). Laser arytenoidectomy. *Arch. Otolaryngol., 111(4):* 262–263.

LING, D. (1976). *Speech and the Hearing Impaired Child: Theory and Practice.* Washington, D.C.: Alexander Graham Bell Association for the Deaf.

LUCHSINGER, R., & ARNOLD, G. E. (1965). *Voice-Speech-Language Clinical Communicology: Its Physiology and Pathology.* Belmont, California: Wadsworth.

LUNDQUIST, P. G., HAGLUND, S., CARLSON, B., STRANDER, H., & LUNDGREN, E. (1984). Interferon therapy in juvenile laryngeal papillomatosis. *Otol. Head Neck Surgery, 92(4):* 386–391.

MARTENSSON, A. (1968). The functional organization of the intrinsic laryngeal muscles, in *Sound Production in Man,* ed. M. Krauss. New York: New York Academy of Sciences, pp. 91–97.

MASON, R. M., & WARREN, D. W. (1980). Adenoid involution and developing hypernasality in cleft palate. *J. Speech Hearing Disorders, 45:* 469–480.

MAZAHERI, M. (1979). Prosthodontic care, in *Cleft Palate and Cleft Lip: A Team Approach,* eds. Cooper, Harding, Krogman, Mazaheri, & Millard. Philadelphia: W. B. Saunders.

McCLOSKY, D. B. (1977). General techniques and specific procedures for certain voice problems, in *Approaches to Vocal Rehabilitation,* ed. M. Cooper and M. H. Cooper. Springfield, Illinois: Charles C. Thomas.

McDOWELL, F. H., & LEE, J. E. (1973). Extrapyramidal diseases, in *Clinical Neurology,* 4th ed., ed. A. B. Baker & L. H. Baker. Hagerstown, Maryland: Harper & Row, Chapter 26.

McFARLANE, S. C., FUJIKI, M., & BRINTON, B. (1984). *Coping With Communicative Handicaps: Resources for the Practicing Clinician.* San Diego: College Hill Press.

McFARLANE, S. C., HOLT, T. L., & LAVORATO, A. S. (1985). Unilateral cord paralysis: Vocal characteristics following three methods of treatment. *ASHA, 27:* 114.

McFARLANE, S. C., & LAVORATO, A. S. (1983). Treatment of Psychogenic hyperfunctional voice disorders, in *Current Therapy of Communication Disorders: Voice Disorders,* ed. W. H. Perkins, New York: Thieme-Stratton, Inc.

McFARLANE, S. C., & LAVORATO, A. S. (1984). The use of video endoscopy in the evaluation and treatment of dysphonia. *Communicative Disorders, 9:* 117–126.

McGLONE, R. E., & HOLLIEN, H. (1963). Vocal pitch characteristics of aged women. *J. Speech Hearing Research, 6:* 164–170.

McGUIRT, W. F., & BLALOCK, D. (1980). The otolaryngologist's role in the diagnosis and treatment of amyotrophic lateral sclerosis. *Laryngoscope, 90:* 1496–1501.

McWILLIAMS, B. J., LAVORATO, A. S., & BLUESTONE, C. D. (1973). Vocal cord abnormalities in children with velopharyngeal valving problems. *Laryngoscope, 83:* 1745–1753.

MICHEL, J. F., & WENDAHL, R. (1971). Correlatives of voice production, in *Handbook of Speech Pathology and Audiology,* ed. L. E. Travis. Englewood Cliffs, New Jersey: Prentice-Hall.

MILISEN, R. (1957). Methods of evaluation and diagnosis of speech disorders, in *Handbook of Speech Pathology,* ed. L. E. Travis. New York: Appleton-Century-Crofts.

MINIFIE, F. D. (1973). Speech acoustics, in *Normal Aspects of Speech, Hearing, and Language,* ed. F. D. Minifie, T. J. Hixon, and F. Williams. Englewood Cliffs, New Jersey: Prentice-Hall.

MINIFIE, F. D. (1984). *Transcripts of the Eleventh Symposium: Care of the Professional Voice,* ed. V. L. Lawrence. New York: The Voice Foundation.

MIYAZAKI, T., MATSUYA, T., & YAMAOKA, M. (1975). Fiberscopic methods for assessment of velopharyngeal closure during various activities. *Cleft Palate J., 12:* 107–114.

MODISETT, N. F., & LUTER, J. G. (1984). *Speaking Clearly: The Basics of Voice and Articulation,* 2nd ed. Minneapolis: Burgess Publishing Company.

MOLL, K. L. (1968). Speech characteristics of individuals with cleft lip and palate, in *Cleft Palate and Communication,* ed. D. C. Spriestersbach and D. Sherman. New York: Academic Press.

MONCUR, J. P., & BRACKETT, I. P. (1974). *Modifying Vocal Behavior.* New York: Harper & Row.

MONSEN, R. B. (1976). Second formant transitions in the speech of deaf and normal-hearing children. *J. Speech Hearing Research, 19:* 279–289.

MONSEN, R. B., ENGEBRETSON, A. M., & VERNULA, N. R. (1979). Some effects of degrees on the generation of voice. *J. Acoust. Soc. Amer., 66:* 1680–1690.

MOOLENAAR-BIJL, A. (1953). The importance of certain consonants in esophageal voice after laryngectomy. *Annals Otol., Rhin, and Laryngo., 62:* 979–989.

MOORE, G. P., & VON LEDEN, H. (1958). Dynamic variations of the vibratory pattern in the normal larynx. *Folia Phoniatrica, 10:* 205–238.

MORRIS, H. L., & SMITH, J. K. (1962). A multiple approach for evaluating velopharyngeal competency. *J. Speech Hearing Disorders, 27:* 218–226.

MOSES, P. J. (1954). *Voice of Neurosis.* New York: Grune and Stratton, Inc.

MURPHY, A. T. (1964). *Functional Voice Disorders.* Englewood Cliffs, New Jersey: Prentice-Hall.

MURRY, T., & DOHERTY, E. T. (1980). Selected acoustic characteristics of pathologic and normal speakers. *J. Speech Hearing Research, 23:* 361–369.

MYSAK, E. D. (1959). Pitch and duration characteristics of older males. *J. Speech Hearing Research, 2:* 46–54.

Nasometer (1987). Pinebrook, New Jersey: Kay Elemetrics Corp.

NATION, J. E., & ARAM, D. M. (1977). *Diagnosis of Speech and Language Disorders.* St. Louis: C. V. Mosby.

NEGUS, V. E. (1957). The mechanism of the larynx. *Laryngoscope, 67:* 961–986.

NETSELL, R. (1973). Speech physiology, in *Normal Aspects of Speech, Hearing, and Language,* ed. F. D. Minifie, T. J. Hixon, & F. Williams. Englewood Cliffs, New Jersey: Prentice-Hall.

NETSELL, R., & HIXON, T. J. (1978). A noninvasive method for clinically estimating subglottal air pressure. *J. Speech Hearing Disorders, 43:* 326–330.

NEWBY, H. A. (1972). *Audiology.* New York: Appleton-Century-Crofts.

NEWCOMBE, P. J. (1986). *Voice and Diction.* Raleigh, North Carolina: Contemporary Publishing Company.

OFFER, D. (1980). Normal adolescent development, in *Comprehensive Textbook of Psychiatry,* 3rd ed., ed. H. I. Kaplan, A. M. Freedman, & B. J. Sadock. Baltimore: The Williams & Williams Co.

OGURA, J. H., & BILLER, H. F. (1969). Glottal reconstruction following extended frontolateral hemilaryngectomy. *Laryngoscope, 74:* 2181–2184.

OLSEN, B. D. (1972). *Comparisons of Sequential Interaction Patterns in Therapy of Experienced and Inexperienced Clinicians in the Parameters of Articulation, Delayed Language, Prosody, and Voice Disorders.* Unpublished doctoral dissertation, University of Denver.

OTIS, A. B., & CLARK, R. G. (1968). Ventilatory implications of phonation and phonatory implications of ventilation, in *Sound Production in Man,* ed. M. Krauss. New York: New York Academy of Sciences, pp. 122–238.

PEARL, N. B., & McCALL, G. N. (1986). Laryngeal function during two types of whisper: A fiberoptic study. Detroit: 1986 ASHA Convention.

PERKINS, W. H. (1971). Vocal function: Assessment and therapy, in *Handbook of Speech Pathology and Audiology,* ed. L. E. Travis. Englewood Cliffs, New Jersey: Prentice-Hall, pp. 505–534.

PERKINS, W. H. (1977a). Behavioral management of vocal abuse: A case of contact ulcer, in *Approaches to Vocal Rehabilitation,* ed. M. Cooper and M. H. Cooper. Springfield, Illinois: Charles C. Thomas.

PERKINS, W. H. (1977b). *Speech Pathology, an Applied Behavioral Science,* 2nd ed. St. Louis: C. V. Mosby.

PERKINS, W. H. (1981). *Preventing Functional Dysphonia.* Los Angeles: Center for the Study of Communication Disorders (ASHA Convention Scientific Exhibit).

PERKINS, W. H. (1983). Optimal use of voice: Prevention of chronic vocal abuse, in *Seminars in Speech and Language, 4:* 273–286.

PERSHALL, K. E., & BOONE, D. R. (1986). A video-endoscopic and computerized tomographic study of hypopharyngeal and supraglottic activity during assorted vocal tasks. *Transcripts of the Fourteenth Symposium: Care of the Professional Voice.* New York: The Voice Foundation.

PETERSON, G. E., & BARNEY, H. L. (1952). Control methods used in a study of the vowels. *J. Acoustical Society, 24:* 175–184.

Phonatory Function Analyzer, PS-77 (1987). Nagashima Medical Instruments. Richmond, Virginia: Kelleher Medical Instruments.

Phonic Ear Vois (1987). H. C. Electronics, Inc., 250 Camino Alto, Mill Valley, California 94941.

PM 100 Pitch Analyzer. (1987). Pine Brook, New Jersey: Kay Elemetrics Corp.

PRASAD, U. (1985). CO_2 surgical laser in the management of bilateral vocal cord paralysis. *J. Laryngology and Otology, 99(9):* 891–894.

PTACEK, P. H., & SANDER, E. K. (1963). Maximum duration of phonation. *J. Speech Hearing Disorders, 28:* 171–182.

RAMIG, L. A., & RINGEL, R. L. (1983). Effects of physiological aging on selected acoustic characteristics of voice. *J. Speech Hearing Research, 26:* 22–30.

REICH, A. R., & LERMAN, J. W. (1978). Teflon larynogoplasty: An acoustical and perceptual study. *J. Speech Hearing Disorders, 43:* 496–505.

RUBIN, H. J., & HIRT, C. C. (1960). The falsetto, a high speed cinematographic study. *Laryngoscope, 70:* 1305–1324.

SAITO, H., MATSUI, T., TACHIBANA, M., NISHIMURA, H., & MIZUKOSHI, O. (1977). Experiences with the tracheo-esophageal shunt method for vocal rehabilitation after total laryngectomy. *Arch. Otolaryngol., 28:* 135–142.

SANSONE, F. E., & EMANUEL, F. W. (1970). Spectral noise levels and roughness severity ratings for normal and simulated rough vowels produced by adult males. *J. Speech Hearing Research, 13:* 489–502.

SATALOFF, R. T. (1981). Professional singers: The science and art of clinical care. *Amer. J. Otolaryngology, 2:* 251–266.

SEASHORE, C. E., LEWIS, E., & SAETVIET, J. G. (1980). *Manual of Instructions and Interpretations for the Seashore Measures of Musical Talent.* New York: The Psychological Corp.

SENTURIA, B. H., & WILSON, F. B. (1968). Otorhinolaryngic findings in children with voice deviations. *Annals Oto-Rhino-Laryngo., 72:* 1027–1042.

SEVER, J. C. (1982). An introduction to objective acoustic analyses of the voice, in *Phonatory Voice Disorders in Children,* ed. M. D. Filter. Springfield, Illinois: Charles C. Thomas.

SHANKS, J. C. (1986). Evoking esophageal voice, in *Current Strategies of Rehabilitation of the Laryngectomized Patient,* ed. J. C. Shanks. New York: Thieme, Inc.

SHEDD, D. P., & WEINBERG, B. (1980). *Surgical and Prosthetic Approaches to Speech Rehabilitation.* Boston: G. K. Hall.

SHELTON, R. L., BEAUMONT, K., TRIER, W. C., & FURR, M. L. (1978). Videoendoscopic feedback in training velopharyngeal closure. *Cleft Palate J., 15:* 6–14.

SHELTON, R. L., HAHN, E., & MORRIS, H. L. (1968). Diagnosis and therapy, in *Cleft Palate and Communication,* ed. D. C. Spriestersbach & D. Sherman. New York: Academic Press.

SHELTON, R. L., PAESANI, A., McCLELLAND, K. D., & BRADFIELD, S. S. (1975). Panendoscopic feedback in the study of voluntary velopharyngeal movements. *J. Speech Hearing Disorders, 40:* 232–243.

SHELTON, R. L., & TRIER, W. C. (1976). Issues involved in the evaluation of velopharyngeal closure. *Cleft Palate J., 13:* 127–137.

SHERMAN, D. (1954). The merits of backward playing of connected speech in the scaling of voice quality disorders. *J. Speech Hearing Disorders, 19:* 312–321.

SHIPP, T., IZDEBSKI, K., REED, C., & MORRISSEY, P. (1985). Intrinsic laryngeal muscle activity in a spastic dysphonic patient. *J. Speech Hearing Disorders, 50:* 54–59.

SHIPP, T., MUELLER, P., & ZWITMAN, D. (1980). Letter: Intermittent abductory dysphonia. *J. Speech Hearing Disorders, 45:* 283.

SINGER, M. I., & BLOM, E. D. (1980). An endoscopic technique for restoring voice after laryngectomy. *Annals Oto-Rhino-Laryngo., 89:* 529–533.

SISSON, G. A., McCONNELL, F. M., & LOGEMANN, J. A. (1974). Rehabilitation after laryngectomy with a hypopharyngeal voice prosthesis, in *Century Conference on Laryngeal Cancer,* ed. P. Alberti & D. Bryce. New York: Appleton-Century-Crofts.

SKOLNICK, M. L., GLASER, E. R., & McWILLIAMS, B. J. (1980). The use and limitations of the barium pharyngogram in the detection of velopharyngeal insufficiency. *Radiology, 135:* 301–304.

SLOANE, H. N., & MACAULAY, B. D. (1968). *Operant Procedures in Remedial Speech and Language Training.* Boston: Houghton Mifflin.

SOM, M. L., & ARNOLD, L. M. (1960). Hemilaryngectomy, in *Otolaryngology, Volume 5,* ed. D. Schenck and M. Miller. Hagerstown, Maryland: W. F. Prior, pp. 31–38.

SONNINEN, A. (1968). The external frame function in the control of pitch in the human voice. *Sound production in Man,* ed. M. Krauss. New York: New York Academy of Sciences.

SPRIESTERSBACH, D. C. (1955). Assessing nasal quality in cleft palate speech of children. *J. Speech Hearing Disorders, 20:* 266–270.

STAATS, A. (1968). *Learning, Language, and Cognition.* New York: Holt, Rinehart & Winston.

STETSON, R. H. (1937). Can all laryngectomized patients be taught esophageal speech? *Transactions of American Laryngological Assoc., 59:* 59–71.

STEVENS, H. (1968). Conversion hysteria: A neurologic emergency. *Mayo Clinic Proceedings, 43:* 54–64.

STONE, R. E. (1982). Management of childhood dysphonias of organic bases, in *Phonatory Voice Disorders in Children,* ed. M. D. Filter. Springfield, Illinois: Charles C. Thomas.

STROEBEL, C. (1983). *Quieting Reflex Training for Adults.* New York: BMA Audio Cassettes.

STROME, M. (1982). Common laryngeal disorders in children, in *Phonatory Voice Disorders in Children,* ed. M. D. Filter. Springfield, Illinois: Charles C. Thomas.

TAIT, N. A., MICHEL, J. F., & CARPENTER, M. A. (1980). Maximum duration of sustained /s/ and /z/ in children. *J. Speech Hearing Disorders, 45:* 239–246.

TAKAHASHI, H., & KOIKE, Y. (1975). Some perceptual dimensions and acoustical correlates of pathologic voices. *Acta Oto-Laryngologica, 338:* 1–24.

TAUB, S. (1975). Air bypass voice prosthesis for vocal rehabilitation of laryngectomees. *Annals Oto-Rhino-Laryngo., 84:* 45–48.

TAUB, S., & BERGNER, L. H. (1973). Air bypass voice prosthesis for vocal rehabilitation of laryngectomees. *Amer. J. Surgery, 125:* 748–752.

TEMPLIN, M. C., & DARLEY, F. L. (1980). *The Templin-Darley Tests of Articulation.* Iowa City: Bureau of Educational Research and Service.

THOMPSON, A. E. (1978). *Nasal Air Flow during Normal Speech Production.* Unpublished Master's Thesis, University of Arizona, Tucson.

THURMAN, W. L. (1958). Intensity relationships and optimum pitch level. *J. Speech Hearing Research, 1:* 117–123.

THURMAN, W. L. (1977). Restructuring voice concepts and production, in *Approaches to Vocal Rehabilitation,* ed. M. Cooper & M. H. Cooper. Springfield, Illinois: Charles C. Thomas, pp. 230–255.

TOOHILL, R. J. (1975). The psychosomatic aspects of children with vocal nodules. *Arch. Otolaryngol., 101:* 591–595.

TUCKER, H. M. (1977). Reinnervation of the unilaterally paralyzed larynx. *Annals Oto-Rhino-Laryngo., 86:* 789–794.

TUCKER, H. M. (1980). Vocal cord paralysis—1979: Etiology and management. *Laryngoscope, 90:* 585–590.

TUCKER, H. M., WOOD, B. G., LEVINE, H., & KATZ, R. (1979). Glottic reconstruction after near total laryngectomy. *Laryngoscope, 89:* 609–618.

Tunemaster III (1975). Berkshire Instruments, Inc., 170 Chestnut Street, Ridgewood, New Jersey 07450.

VAN DEN BERG, J. W. (1958). Myo-elastic-aerodynamic theory of voice production. *J. Speech Hearing Research, 1:* 227–244.

VAN DEN BERG, J. W. (1968). Register problems, in *Sound Production in Man,* ed. M. Krauss. New York: New York Academy of Sciences, pp. 129–134.

Visi-Pitch Model 6087 (1987). Pinebrook, New Jersey: Kay Elemetrics Corp.

Vocaid, Texas Instruments (1986). Communication Skill Builders, P.O. Box 42030, Tucson, Arizona 85733.

Vocal Loudness Indicator (1980). LinguiSystems, Suite 806, 1630 Fifth Avenue, Moline, Illinois 61265.

Voice Monitor (1977). Communications Research Unit. Hollins, Virginia: Hollins College.

WARREN, D. W. (1979). PERCI: A method for rating palatal efficiency. *Cleft Palate J., 16:* 279–285.

WATSON, P. J., & HIXON, T. J. (1985). Respiratory kinematics in classical (opera) singers. *J. Speech Hearing Research, 28:* 104–122.

WEBER, R. S., NEUMAYER, L., ALFORD, B. R., & WEBER, S. C. (1984). Clinical restoration of voice function after loss of the vagus nerve. *Head and Neck Surgery, 7:* 448–457.

WEINBERG, B., & RIEKENA, A. (1973). Speech produced with the Tokyo artificial larynx. *J. Speech Hearing Disorders, 38:* 383–389.

WEISS, D., & BEEBE, H. (1951). *The Chewing Approach in Speech and Voice Therapy.* Basel, Switzerland: S. Karger.

WETMORE, S. J., KEY, J. M., & SUEN, J. Y. (1985). Complications of laser surgery for laryngeal papillomatosis. *Laryngoscope, 95(7):* 798–801.

WHITED, R. E. (1979). Laryngeal dysfunction following prolonged intubation. *Annals. Oto-Rhino-Laryngo., 88:* 474–478.

WHITLER, L. E. (1961). One of a million. *Brotherhood of Locomotive Firemen and Enginemen's Magazine,* 1–6.

WILCOX, K. A., & HORII, Y. (1980). Age and changes in vocal jitter. *J. Gerontol., 35:* 194–198.

WILLIAMS, R. T., FARQUHARSON, I. M., & ANTHONY, J. (1975). Fiberoptic laryngoscopy in the assessment of laryngeal disorder. *J. Laryngo., 89:* 299–306.

WILLIAMSON, A. B. (1945). Diagnosis and treatment of seventy-two cases of hoarse voice. *Quarterly J. Speech, 31:* 189–202.

WILSON, D. K. (1979). *Voice Problems of Children,* 2nd ed. Baltimore: Williams and Wilkins Co.

WILSON, D. K. (1987). *Voice Problems of Children,* 3rd ed. Baltimore: Williams and Wilkins Co.

WILSON, F. B., OLDRING, D. J., & MUELLER, J. (1980). Recurrent laryngeal nerve dissection: A case report involving return of spastic dysphonia after initial surgery. *J. Speech Hearing Disorders, 45:* 112–118.

WILSON, F. B., & RICE, M. (1977). *A Programmed Approach to Voice Therapy.* Austin, Texas: Learning Concepts.

WILSON, F. B., & STARR, C. D. (1985). Use of the phonation analyzer as a clinical tool. *J. Speech Hearing Disorders, 50:* 351–356.

WOLPE, J. (1973). *The Practice of Behavior Therapy,* 2nd ed. New York: Pergamon Press.

WOLPE, J. (1987). *Essential Principles and Practices of Behavior Therapy.* Phoenix: The Milton H. Erickson Foundation.

WOODSON, G. E., & MILLER, R. H. (1981). The timing of surgical intervention of vocal cord paralysis. *Otolaryngology Head and Neck Surgery, 89:* 264–267.

YAMAGUCHI, H., YOTSUKURA, Y., KONDO, R., HANYUU, Y., HORIGUCHI, S., IMAIZUMI, S., & HIROSE, H. (1986). Nonsurgical therapy for vocal nodules. *Folia Phoniatrica, 38(5–6):* 372–373.

YANAGIHARA, N. Y., & VON LEDEN, H. (1967). Respiration and phonation. *Folia Phoniatrica, 19:* 153–166.

YATES, A., & DEDO, H. H. (1984). Carbon dioxide laser enucleation of polypoid vocal cords. *Laryngoscope, 94(6):* 731–736.

ZEMLIN, W. R. (1981). *Speech and Hearing Science,* 2nd ed. Englewood Cliffs, New Jersey: Prentice-Hall.

ZWITMAN, D. H., GYEPES, M. T., & WARD, P. H. (1976). Assessment of velar and lateral wall movement by oral telescope and radiographic examination in patients with velopharyngeal inadequacy and in normal subjects. *J. Speech Hearing Disorders, 41:* 381–389.

ZWITMAN, D. H., KNORR, S. G., & SONDERMAN, J. (1978). Development and testing of an intraoral electrolarynx for laryngectomy patients. *J. Speech Hearing Disorders, 43:* 263–269.

ZWITMAN, D. H., SONDERMAN, J. C., & WARD, P. H. (1974). Variations in velopharyngeal closure assessed by endoscopy. *J. Speech Hearing Disorders, 39:* 366–372.

INDEX

Quality of voice. *See* Voice, quality of.